STUDENT STUDY
AND
REVIEW GUIDE

TO ACCOMPANY

Psychology in Action

Ninth Edition

Prepared by

Karen Huffman
Palomar College

Richard Hosey
Palomar College

John Wiley & Sons, Inc.

Cover Photo (left):   Mike Powell
Cover Photo (right):   Photodisc/Getty Images
Back Cover Photo: Blend Images/Getty Images

To order books or for customer service, please call 1-800-CALL-WILEY (225-5945).

ISBN-13 978- 0-470-42425-4

Printed in the United States of America

10 9 8 7 6 5 4 3 2 1

Printed and bound by Bind-Rite, Inc.

CONTENTS

TIPS FOR USING THIS STUDENT STUDY AND REVIEW GUIDE

Congratulations! Your decision to buy and use this study guide is an important step toward student success. It is carefully designed to help you master the most important material in *Psychology in Action* (9e) in the shortest possible time. It also will significantly improve your performance on quizzes and exams, and ultimately to help you achieve the highest grade possible in your first introduction to psychology course.

This study guide is coordinated with your text, *Psychology in Action (9e)*, and is divided into seven major sections: *Chapter Outlines, Learning Objectives, Key Terms, Active Learning Exercises, Chapter Overview, Self-Tests,* and *Answers*. These seven sections are explained and identified throughout each chapter with the following boxes and icons:

OUTLINE SQ4R (Survey, Question, Read, Recite, Review, & wRite)

This outline section incorporates all six steps in the well-researched SQ4R method of learning. Begin by surveying the list of chapter topics in the left column. This "big picture" will help focus and guide your attention while you read. As you read through the chapter, briefly summarize each section in your own words in the space to the right. Also write down any *questions* that come to mind. Surveying, Questioning, Reading, Reciting, Reviewing, and wRiting are the foundation of the SQ4R method and an invaluable form of active learning. They also make your reading time more enjoyable and efficient! One thorough, focused SQ4R reading of a chapter is far better than several passive readings.

LEARNING OBJECTIVES (Read, Recite, Review, & wRite)

In addition to the work you did in the Outline above, you can significantly improve your performance on exams by focusing on the following learning objectives. While reading the chapter or reviewing for exams, check your understanding by stopping periodically to *recite* (or repeat in your own words) and *writing* down your answers on a separate sheet. [Page numbers correspond to Chapter 1 in *Psychology in Action* (9e).]

KEY TERMS (Review & wRite)

Like other survey courses, introductory psychology is filled with a "wealth" of new and unfamiliar terminology. To do well on exams, you must master this new language! Writing a brief definition of each term in the space provided and carefully reviewing them before exams will significantly improve your course grade.

ACTIVE LEARNING EXERCISES

True mastery of information requires you to be an ACTIVE learner. Completing the following active learning exercises will improve your understanding of the chapter material and greatly improve your performance on exams. Answers to some exercises appear in Appendix A at the end of this study guide.

CHAPTER OVERVIEW (Review)

The following chapter overview provides a narrative overview of the main topics covered in the chapter. Like the *Visual Summary* found at the end of each chapter in the text, this narrative summary provides a final opportunity to *review* chapter material.

SELF-TESTS (Review & wRite)

Completing the following self-tests will provide immediate feedback on how well you have mastered the material. In the labeling exercises, *crossword puzzle,* and *fill-in exercises,* write the appropriate word or words in the blank spaces. The *matching exercise* requires you to match the terms in one column to their correct definitions in the other. For the *multiple-choice questions* in Practice Tests I and II, circle or underline the correct answer. If you are unsure of any answer, mark the item, and then go back to the text for further review. Correct answers are provided in Appendix A at the end of this study guide.

Did you notice that most of these sections have six repeated terms in parentheses (Survey, Question, Read, Recite, Review, & wRite)? This is because both your study guide and text, *Psychology in Action*, are designed around the best-known studying technique—the SQ4R method. The symbols "S,Q, R, R, R, R" stand for:

Survey

The SURVEY step provides a map or big picture of the chapter contents. If you were new to the United States and planning a car trip from California to New York, you would not jump in your car and simply start driving. However, most students do jump into their texts and start reading the first page with no idea of what road signs to look for or what lies ahead. To make the most of your car trip to New York, you would begin with a large map of the entire United States and try to plan the most efficient route. Similarly, since you are new to the country of psychology, you need to begin with a large overall road map--the *survey* step of the SQ4R method.

Before you start reading each chapter of the text, you should skim through the pages. Note the title, major headings and subheadings, and figure captions. Then read the interim summaries that come before each set of review questions sprinkled throughout the chapter. Finally, carefully examine the visual summary at the end of the chapter. This overall *survey* of the chapter helps organize the material into a larger unit that will help focus your attention during later careful reading and studying.

Question

As you are surveying the material, ask yourself QUESTIONS about what you are going to read. What did your instructor say about this topic when it was assigned? What questions do the headings and subheadings suggest? What will I learn in this chapter? How can I use this information in my everyday life? Questions aid retention because they require active participation on your part and increase personal relevance of the material.

Read

The survey and question procedure provides a natural lead-in to careful READING. While reading the chapter, attempt to answer the questions you generated, as well as paying close attention to all figures, tables, and **boldfaced** terms. Read in small units from one major heading to the next. In Chapter 7 of your textbook, you will discover why cramming (or massed practice) is not a good method for studying, retention, or retrieval of information. Space your studying throughout the time allocated by your instructor for the assigned chapters. This type of *distributed versus massed practice* has been scientifically proven to be more effective than cramming because you retain more information and will remember it longer.

Recite

Have you ever found yourself having to reread sections of a text because your mind wandered off as you were studying? Do you find that you can spend hours studying and yet remember little of what you have read? This is because you are not RECITING. Recite means to go over what you just read by orally summarizing, making notes, and/or completing the review questions in the text (and the active learning exercises in this study guide). A well-known principle of education states that learning is much more effective when people are *actively* responding to the material than when they are *passive* recipients. By orally summarizing, taking notes, completing the review questions and active learning exercises, you will be taking an active role in your studying—and your grades will improve!

Review

REVIEWING is a combination of all parts of the SQ4R formula. Briefly repeat the survey and questioning you did before you began the chapter, reread all your notes (from the text, your class lecture notes, and notes in this study guide). You also should check your memory by completing the review questions sprinkled throughout the text and the various self-tests in this study and review guide.

w<u>R</u>ite

WRITING is the final element in the SQ4R method, and it is perhaps the most important element in true mastery and full comprehension of material. By writing a response and taking notes while reading or listening to lectures, you will retain more than simply listening to a lecture or silently reading a text. This study guide is carefully designed in a unique workbook format that allows space for writing responses to the learning objectives, your definitions for the key terms, your responses to the activities, and your answers to the sample self-tests. Taking this study and review guide with you to class will be an important aid in organizing your lecture notes.

The SQ4R method can be used with any textbook. However, *Psychology in Action (9e)* and this study and review guide have been carefully designed to maximize this technique. We hope you will try this method and *actively* use this study and review guide. Research finds those students who purchase and USE study guides almost always do better on exams and overall course performance. Your text has numerous built-in *tools for student success*, your instructor is available to assist and inspire you, and this study and review guide is here to guide and support your studying efforts. The next step is yours. Best wishes for an exciting journey in the new country called Psychology.

Karen Huffman/Palomar College
Richard Hosey/Palomar College

1

Introduction to Psychology & Its Research Methods

OUTLINE SQ4R (Survey, Question, Read, Recite, Review, & wRite)

This outline section incorporates all six steps in the well-researched SQ4R method of learning. Begin by surveying the list of chapter topics in the left column. This "big picture" will help focus and guide your attention while you read. As you read through the chapter, briefly summarize each section in your own words in the space to the right. Also write down any *questions* that come to mind. Surveying, Questioning, Reading, Reciting, Reviewing, and wRiting are the foundation of the SQ4R method and an invaluable form of active learning. They also make your reading time more enjoyable and efficient! One thorough, focused SQ4R reading of a chapter is far better than several passive readings.

TOPIC	NOTES

I. INTRODUCING PSYCHOLOGY

A. What Is Psychology?

B. Psychology's Goals

Psychology at Work: Careers in the Field

II. ORIGINS OF PSYCHOLOGY

A. Early Psychological Science

B. Modern Perspectives

III. THE SCIENCE OF PSYCHOLOGY

A. The Scientific Method

B. Ethical Guidelines

IV. RESEARCH METHODS

A. Experimental Research

Research Highlight: Love at First Fright?

Critical Thinking/Active Learning: Applying Critical Thinking to Psychological Science

B. Descriptive Research

Case Study/Personal Story: A Life Without Fear?

C. Correlational Research

D. Biological Research

Psychology at Work: Becoming a Better Consumer of Scientific Research

Gender & Cultural Diversity: Are There Cultural Universals?

V. TOOLS FOR STUDENT SUCCESS

A. Active Reading

B. Time Management

C. Strategies for Grade Improvement

D. Additional Resources

E. A Final Word

LEARNING OBJECTIVES (Read, Recite, Review, & wRite)

In addition to the work you did in the Outline above, you can significantly improve your performance on exams by focusing on the following learning objectives. While reading the chapter or reviewing for exams, check your understanding by stopping periodically to *recite* (or repeat in your own words) and *writing* down your answers on a separate sheet. [Page numbers correspond to Chapter 1 in *Psychology in Action* (9e).]

1.1 Define psychology. (p. 4)
1.2 What are psychology's four main goals? (p. 6)
1.3 Summarize psychology's major career specialties. (pp. 7-8)
1.4 Contrast structuralism versus functionalism, and list the seven major perspectives that guide modern psychology. (pp. 9-14)
1.5 Describe the biopsychosocial model. (p. 14)
1.6 What is the difference between basic and applied research, and what are the six basic steps of the scientific method? (p. 16)
1.7 What are the key ethical issues in psychological research and therapy? (p. 18)
1.8 Explain how experiments help researchers determine cause and effect. (p. 21)
1.9 Compare and contrast experimental versus control groups and independent versus dependent variables. (pp. 22-24)
1.10 How do researchers guard against experimenter bias and ethnocentrism? (pp. 22, 25)
1.11 How do researchers safeguard against sample bias and participant bias? (pp. 25-26)
1.12 Why do we sometimes mislabel our emotions? (p. 27)
1.13 Explain descriptive research and its three key methods—naturalistic observation, surveys, and case studies. (pp. 28-30)
1.14 Compare correlational research and correlation coefficients. (pp. 31-33)
1.15 Describe biological research and its major tools for discovery. (p. 33)

1.16 Are there cultural universals? (p. 38)
1.17 How can I use psychology to study and learn psychology? (p. 39)

KEY TERMS (Review & wRite)

Like other survey courses, introductory psychology is filled with a "wealth" of new and unfamiliar terminology. To do well on exams, you must master this new language! Writing a brief definition of each term in the space provided and carefully reviewing them before exams will significantly improve your course grade.

Applied Research: _____

_____

Basic Research: _____

_____

Behavioral Perspective: _____

_____

Biological Research: _____

_____

Biopsychosocial Model: _____

_____

Case Study: _____

_____

Cognitive Perspective: _____

_____

Control Group: _____

_____

Correlation Coefficient: _____

_____

Correlational Research: _____

_____

Critical Thinking: _____

_____

Debriefing: _____

_____

Dependent Variable (DV): _____

_____

Descriptive Research: _____

_____

Double-Blind Study: _____

_____

Ethnocentrism: _____

_____

Evolutionary Perspective: _____

_____

Experiment: _____

_____

Experimental Group: _____

_____

Experimenter Bias: _____

_____

Humanistic Perspective: _____

_____

Hypothesis: _____

_____

Independent Variable (IV): _____

_____

Informed Consent: ✓ _____

_____

Misattribution of Arousal: _____

_____

Meta-Analysis: _____

_____

Naturalistic Observation: _____

_____

Nature-Nurture Controversy: ✓ _____

_____

Neuroscience / Biopsychology Perspective: _____

_____

Operational Definition: _____

_____

Participant Bias: ✓ _____

_____

Placebo: ✓ _____

_____

Positive Psychology: _____ _____

_____

Psychoanalytic / Psychodynamic Perspective: _____

_____

Psychology: ✓ _____

_____

Random Assignment: ✓ _____

_____

Sample Bias: ✓ _____

_____

Sociocultural Perspective: ✓ _____

_____

Survey: ✓ _____

_____

Theory: ✓ _____

_____

ACTIVE LEARNING EXERCISES

True mastery of information requires you to be an ACTIVE learner. Completing the following active learning exercises will improve your understanding of the chapter material and greatly improve your performance on exams. Answers to some exercises appear in Appendix A at the end of this study guide.

ACTIVE LEARNING EXERCISE I *For each of the three studies:*
- Decide whether the study is correlational or experimental.
- If the study is correlational, briefly describe how the variables are related and whether the correlation is positive, negative, or zero.
- If the study is experimental, identify the independent variable (IV) and dependent variable (DV).

Study 1 A Princeton study found that lifetime earnings for women who graduate from college were approximately the same as those of men who graduate from high school.

Study II A Canadian study investigated whether large doses of vitamin C reduce the number or severity of cold symptoms, as previously reported. The researcher first informed participants she was studying the effectiveness of a new treatment for colds. She then offered them a month's supply of tablets containing either vitamin C or a placebo. She found no significant difference in the number or severity of cold symptoms between the vitamin C and the placebo groups.

Study III *USA Today* featured a major university study that found couples who live together before marriage are more likely to divorce than couples who don't live together.

ACTIVE LEARNING EXERCISE II *To help you understand and appreciate the complexity of the experimental method, think of a specific problem or topic that you are interested in studying. For example, "Does caffeine increase studying effectiveness?" Using your own problem or topic, answer the following:*

1. What would be your hypothesis?
2. What would be the independent and dependent variable(s)?

3. List possible experimental controls for the experiment.
4. Could your hypothesis also be tested with nonexperimental methods? If so, describe them.

ACTIVE LEARNING EXERCISE III *In Chapter 1 of Psychology in Action (9e), you learned important key terms and research methods that can be useful in evaluating everyday reports from politicians, advertisers, teachers, the news media, and even close friends. Read each of the following reports, and decide what is the primary problem or research limitation. Then, in the space provided, make one of the following marks:*

CC = Report is misleading because correlational data are used to suggest causation.
CG = Research is inconclusive because there was no control group.
EB = Results may have been unfairly influenced by experimenter bias.
SB = Results may be in question due to possible sample bias.

_CG_ 1. A shoe company owner is concerned with slumping sales and decides to conduct a survey in one of his factories to determine how employees feel about shoes produced in Italy.
_CC_ 2. A group of hospital physicians claim that cycles of the moon have an effect on behavior because accidents and injuries show a sharp increase during a full moon.
_CC_ 3. At a major league baseball park, researchers found that beer and soft-drink sales are highest when color advertising is used on all billboards.
_SB_ 4. After failing an important exam in his psychology class, Alex decides to personally interview fellow classmates regarding their study strategies and tips for success.

CHAPTER OVERVIEW (Review)

The following chapter overview provides a narrative overview of the main topics covered in the chapter. Like the *Visual Summary* found at the end of each chapter in the text, this narrative summary provides a final opportunity to *review* chapter material.

I. INTRODUCING PSYCHOLOGY
1.1: Define Psychology. (p. 4)
Psychology is the scientific study of behavior and mental processes. It emphasizes the empirical approach and the value of **critical thinking**. Psychology is not the same as common sense, "pop psychology," or pseudopsychology.

1.2: What are psychology's four main goals? (pp. 6-7)
The goals of psychology are to describe, explain, predict, and change behavior and mental processes.

1.3: Summarize psychology's major career specialties. (pp. 7-9)
Many avenues exist for those who want to pursue a career in psychology. These include biopsychology or neuroscience, experimental, cognitive, developmental, clinical, counseling, industrial/organizational, educational/school psychology, social, health, and so on.

II. ORIGINS OF PSYCHOLOGY
1.4: Contrast structuralism versus functionalism, and list the seven major perspectives that guide modern psychology. (pp. 9-14)

Among the early contributors to psychology, the *structuralists* sought to identify elements of consciousness and how those elements formed the structure of the mind. They relied primarily on the method of introspection. *Functionalists* studied how mental processes help the individual adapt to the environment. Seven major perspectives guide modern psychology: **psychoanalytic/psychodynamic, behavior, humanist, cognitive, neuroscience/ biopsychology, evolutionary, and sociocultural**.

1.5: Describe the biopsychosocial model. (pp. 14-15)
The **biopsychosocial model** draws from all seven modern perspectives and also incorporates biological, psychological, and social processes.

III. THE SCIENCE OF PSYCHOLOGY
1.6: What is the difference between basic and applied research, and what are the six basic steps of the scientific method? (pp. 16-18)
Basic research studies theoretical issues. **Applied research** seeks to solve specific problems. The scientific method consists of six carefully planned steps: (1) identifying questions of interest and reviewing the literature, (2) formulating a testable **hypothesis**, (3) choosing a research method and collecting the data, (4) analyzing the data and accepting or rejecting the hypothesis, (5) publishing followed by replication and scientific review, and (6) building further **theory**. The steps are arranged in a circle to show the circular, cumulative nature of science.

1.7: What are the key ethical issues in psychological research and therapy? (pp. 18-20)
Psychologists must maintain high standards in their relations with human and nonhuman research participants, as well as in therapeutic relationships with clients. The APA has published specific guidelines detailing these ethical standards.

IV. EXPERIMENTAL RESEARCH
1.8: Explain how experiments help researchers determine cause and effect. (pp. 21-22)
By manipulating and carefully controlling variables, an **experiment** is the only research method that can be used to identify *cause-and-effect* relationships.

1.9: Compare and contrast experimental versus control groups and independent versus dependent variables. (pp. 22-24)
Experimental groups receive treatment, whereas **control groups** receive no treatment. **Independent variables (IVs)** are the factors the experimenter manipulates, and **dependent variables (DVs)** are measurable behaviors of the participants. Experimental controls include having one control group and one or more experimental groups, and holding extraneous variables constant.

1.10: How do researchers guard against experimenter bias and ethnocentrism? (pp. 22, 25)
To safeguard against the researcher problem of **experimenter bias**, researchers employ blind observers, single- and **double-blind studies**, and **placebos**. To control for **ethnocentrism**, they use cross-cultural sampling.

1.11: How do researchers safeguard against sample bias and participant bias? (pp. 25-26)
To offset participant problems with **sample bias**, researchers use random/representative sampling and **random assignment**. To control for **participant bias**, they rely on many of the same controls in place to prevent experimenter bias, such as double-blind studies. They also attempt to ensure anonymity and confidentiality and sometimes use deception.

V. DESCRIPTIVE, CORRELATIONAL, AND BIOLOGICAL RESEARCH

1.12: *Why do we sometimes mislabel our emotions?* (p. 27)

According to the **misattribution of arousal** model, different emotions produce similar feelings of arousal, which leads to mistaken inferences about these emotions and the source of their arousal.

1.13: *Explain descriptive research and its three key methods—naturalistic observation, surveys, and case studies.* (pp. 28-30)

Unlike experiments, **descriptive research** cannot determine the causes of behavior. But it can describe specifics. **Naturalistic observation** is used to study and describe behavior in its natural habitat without altering it. **Surveys** use interviews or questionnaires to obtain information on a sample of participants. Individual **case studies** are in-depth studies of a participant.

1.14: *Compare correlational research and correlation coefficients.* (pp. 31-33)

Correlational research examines how one naturally occurring trait or behavior accompanies another, and how well one variable predicts the other. **Correlation coefficients** are numerical values from correlational research that indicate the degree and direction of the relationship between two variables. Correlation coefficients range from 0 to +1.00 or 0 to -1.00, and the plus or minus signs indicate whether the relationships are positively or negatively correlated. Both correlational studies and correlation coefficients provide important research findings and valuable predictions. However, it is also important to remember that *correlation does not imply causation.*

1.15: *Describe biological research and its major tools for discovery.* (pp. 33-36)

Biological research studies the brain and other parts of the nervous system through dissection of brains of cadavers, ablation/lesion techniques, observation or case studies, electrical recordings, and electrical stimulation of the brain (ESB). (Electrical recording techniques involve attaching electrodes to the skin or scalp to study the brain's electrical activity, whereas electrical stimulation involves a probe inserted in the brain.) Computed tomography (CT), positron emission tomography (PET), magnetic resonance imaging (MRI), functional magnetic resonance imaging (fMRI) scans, and transcranial magnetic stimulation (TMS) are noninvasive techniques that provide visual images of intact, living brains.

VI. CULTURAL UNIVERSALS AND TOOLS FOR STUDENT SUCCESS

1.16: *Are there cultural universals?* (pp. 38-39)

Some cultural psychologists do believe certain aspects of human behavior and mental processes are true and universal for all cultures, and they suggest that emotions and facial recognition are prime examples. Critics say that Western psychologists have no experience with culturally specific emotions, and that if cultural universals exist they are innate and biological. The answer appears to be that certain behaviors are both biological and culturally universal.

1.17: *How can I use psychology to study and learn psychology?* (pp. 39-47)

There are several important psychological techniques that will help you study and learn psychology. They fall into the general categories of active reading, time management, strategies for grade improvement, and additional resources.

SELF-TESTS (<u>R</u>eview & w<u>R</u>ite)

Completing the following self-tests will provide immediate feedback on how well you have mastered the material. In the labeling exercises, *crossword puzzle*, and *fill-in exercises*, write the appropriate word or words in the blank spaces. The *matching exercise* requires you to match the terms in one column to their correct definitions in the other. For the *multiple-choice questions* in Practice Tests I and II, circle or underline the correct answer. If you are unsure of any answer, mark the item, and then go back to the text for further review. Correct answers are provided in Appendix A at the end of this study guide.

Crossword Puzzle for Chapter 1

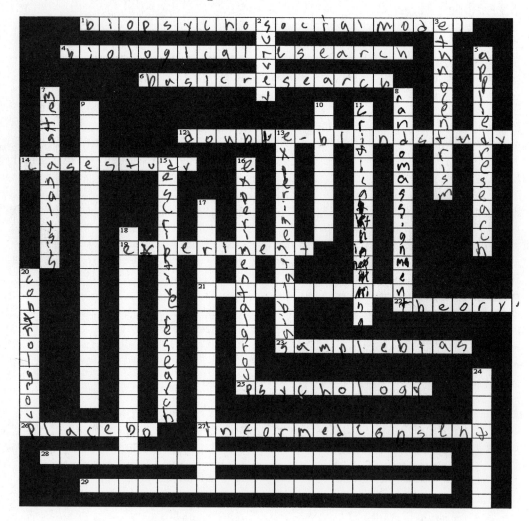

ACROSS

1 A unifying theme of modern psychology, which considers biological, psychological, and social processes.

4 Scientific studies of the brain and other parts of the nervous system.

6 Research conducted to advance scientific knowledge rather than practical application.

12 A procedure in which both the researcher and the participants are unaware (blind) of who is in the experimental or control group.

14 An in-depth study of a single research participant.

19 Carefully controlled scientific procedure that determines whether variables manipulated by the experimenter have a causal effect on other variables.

21 A process whereby multiple factors mutually influence one another and the outcome.

22 An interrelated set of concepts, which explains a body of data.

23 Occurs when research participants are not representative of the larger population.

25 The scientific study of behavior and mental processes.

26 An inactive substance or fake treatment used as a control technique, usually in drug research, or given by a medical practitioner to a patient.

27 Participant's agreement to take part in a study after being told what to expect.

28 Any scientific study in which the researcher observes or measures (without directly manipulating) two or more variables to find relationships between them.

29 Variable that is manipulated to determine its causal effect on the dependent variable.

DOWN

2 Research technique that assesses behaviors and attitudes of a sample or population.

3 Believing that one's culture is typical of all cultures; also, viewing one's own ethnic group (or culture) as central and correct and then judging the rest of the world according to this standard.

5 Research designed to solve practical problems.

7 A statistical procedure for combining and analyzing data from many studies.

8 Participants are assigned to experimental conditions based on chance, thus minimizing the possibility of biases or preexisting differences in the groups

9 A number that indicates the degree and direction of the relationship between the two variables.

10 Informing participants after the research about the purpose of the study, the nature of the anticipated results, and any deceptions used.

11 The process of objectively evaluating, comparing, analyzing, and synthesizing information.

13 Occurs when researcher influences research results in the expected direction.

15 Research methods that observe and record behavior without producing causal explanations.

16 Group that receives a treatment in an experiment.

17 A precise description of how the variables in a study will be observed and measured.

18 Variable that is measured.

20 Group that receives no treatment in an experiment.

24 A specific prediction about how one variable is related to another.

FILL-IN EXERCISES

1. Psychology as a science began in ~~1879~~ when the first psychological laboratory was established (p.9).

2. Explaining behavior in terms of unconscious processes and unresolved past conflicts is key to the ~~psychoanalytic~~ perspective (pp. 10-11).

3. The _humanistic_ perspective emphasizes the importance of the inner, subjective self and stresses the positive side of human nature (pp. 11-12).

4. Basic research is conducted to _learn_, whereas applied research is designed to _solve_ (p. 16).

5. When researchers _debrief_ their research participants, they explain the reasons for conducting the research and clear up any misconceptions or concerns (p. 19).

6. The causes of behavior can be determined by using the _experimental_ method of research (p. 21).

7. A(n) _independent_ is a factor that is selected and manipulated by the experimenter and is totally independent of anything the research participant does (pp. 23-24).

8. A(n) _case study_ is an in-depth examination of a single research participant. (p. 30)

9. _correlation_ research observes or measures two or more variables to find relationships between them (pp. 31-32).

10. The six steps in the SQ4R method for active reading are _____, _____, _____, _____, _____, and _____ (pp. 41-42).

MATCHING EXERCISES

Column A

- ⓐ. Father of Psychology
- ⓑ. Evolutionary Perspective
- ⓒ. Sociocultural Perspective
- ⓓ. Cognitive Perspective
- ⓔ. Functionalism
- ⓕ. Biopsychosocial Model
- ⓖ. Humanistic Perspective
- ⓗ. Biopsychology
- ⓘ. Psychoanalytic Theory
- ⓙ. B. F. Skinner

Column B

1. _e_ Studied how mental processes help adaptation
2. _i_ Emphasizes influence of the unconscious mind
3. _d_ Focuses on mental processing of information
4. _a_ Wilhelm Wundt
5. _h_ Studies the biology of behavior
6. _g_ Emphasizes inner, subjective self and positive nature
7. _b_ Based on theory of evolution and natural selection
8. _c_ Studies the influence of culture and ethnicity
9. _e_ Focuses on objective or observable behaviors
10. _f_ Biological, psychological, and social processes

PRACTICE TEST I

1. In your text, psychology is defined as the _____.
   a. scientific study of the mind
   b. empirical study of conscious and unconscious forces
   c. study of mind and behavior
   d. scientific study of behavior and mental processes

2. Dr. Lucille offers quick, on-the-spot advice to problems presented by her call-in radio listeners, using mostly her own common sense beliefs and values rather than scientific research. This practice is more like _____ than _____.
   a. critical thinking; psychology
   b. social psychology; clinical psychology
   c. pseudopsychology; psychology
   d. none of these options

3. Which of the following are the goals of psychology?
   a. describe, manipulate, control, and examine behavior
   b. describe, explain, predict, and change behavior
   c. predict, control, examine, and change behavior
   d. manipulate, control, explain, and change behavior

4. _____ is acknowledged as the "father of psychology."
   a. Freud
   b. Skinner
   c. Wundt
   d. Maslow

5. Who developed psychoanalytic theory?
   a. Freud
   b. James
   c. Wundt
   d. Watson

6. _____ emphasized objective, observable behaviors.
   a. Functionalism
   b. Gestalt psychology
   c. Freud
   d. Behavior perspective

7. The _____ views biological processes, psychological factors, and social forces as interrelated influences, and it is one of the most widely accepted themes of modern psychology.
   a. eclectic perspective
   b. nature-nurture model
   c. interactionist position
   d. biopsychosocial model

8. Applied research is conducted to study _____.
   a. how people apply knowledge in an educational setting
   b. theoretical questions that may or may not have real-world applications
   c. the goals of psychology
   d. real-world, practical problems

9. Research conducted to advance scientific knowledge rather than practical application is _____.
   a. applied
   b. descriptive
   c. basic
   d. correlation

10. Most scientific investigations begin with _____ and sometimes end with _____.
    a. a testable hypothesis; replication
    b. designing a study; collecting data
    c. identifying questions of interest; building a theory
    d. reviewing the literature; theory

11. A precise description of how the variables in a study will be observed and measured is known as _____.
    a. a hypothesis
    b. an operational definition
    c. a theory
    d. the scientific method

12. What are the four major types of psychological research?
    a. correlation, case study, naturalistic observation, survey
    b. experiment, nonexperiment, pseudopsychology, correlational
    c. structuralism, functionalism, behaviorism, psychoanalytic
    d. experimental, descriptive, correlational, biological

13. Only the experiment allows researchers to determine _____.
    a. relationships
    b. correlations
    c. cause and effect
    d. the goals of psychology

14. An experimenter wishes to see if there is a difference between two types of memory techniques. She teaches one group of participants Technique A and another group Technique B. Then she gives each group a list of words to memorize. Two weeks later she tests the participants to measure how many words they have remembered. What is the dependent variable in this experiment?
    a. number of words in the list
    b. memory techniques
    c. sex of the experimenter
    d. number of words remembered

15. What is the independent variable in the experiment described in the previous question?
    a. number of words in the list
    b. memory Technique A or B
    c. sex of the experimenter
    d. number of words remembered

16. When participants are not exposed to any amount or level of the independent variable, they are members of the _____.
    a. control condition
    b. experimental condition
    c. observation group
    d. none of these options

17. The tendency of experimenters to influence the results of their experiment in an expected direction is called _____.
    a. experimenter bias
    b. control bias
    c. observational bias
    d. experimental bias

18. When both the researcher and the participants are unaware of who is in the experimental or control group, the research design can be called _____.
    a. reliable
    b. a double-blind
    c. valid
    d. deceptive

19. A number that indicates the degree and direction of the relationship between two variables is known as _____.
    a. statistics
    b. a correlation coefficient
    c. statistical significance
    d. none of these options

20. The _____ indicates which areas of the brain are active or inactive during ordinary activities or responses.
    a. computed tomography (CT)
    b. positron emission tomography (PET)
    c. functional magnetic resonance imaging (fMRI)
    d. magnetic resonance imaging (MRI)

PRACTICE TEST II

1. When you objectively evaluate, compare, analyze, and synthesize information about a ballot proposition or political candidate, you are using _____.
    a. psychological processing
    b. critical thinking
    c. behaviorism
    d. the scientific method

2. One of the most enduring debates in science is the _____ controversy, which asks whether we're controlled by biological and genetic factors or by the environment and learning.
    a. mind-body
    b. nature-nurture
    c. biopsychosocial
    d. none of these options

3. Hsao-Wei was sent to the school psychologist to be tested, and based on her IQ score, she was placed in a program for gifted children. This illustrates psychology's goal of _____ behavior.
    a. describing
    b. explaining
    c. predicting
    d. changing

4. The goal of _____ is to tell "what" occurred, whereas the goal of _____ is to tell "why."
   a. health psychologists; biological psychologists
   b. description; explanation
   c. psychologists; psychiatrists
   d. pseudopsychologists; clinical psychologists

5. Observable behaviors are the primary focus in which of the following approaches to psychology?
   a. humanistic
   b. psychodynamic
   c. behaviorism
   d. cognitive

6. Which of the following terms are properly matched?
   a. psychoanalysis and free-will
   b. humanist and self-actualization
   c. functionalism and unconscious conflict
   d. biopsychology and introspection

7. Someone who believes that behavior is the result of complex chemical and biological events within the brain is known as a(n) _____.
   a. information processor
   b. ecological psychologist
   c. evolutionary psychologist
   d. neuroscientist/biopsychologist

8. _____ was the first woman president of the American Psychological Association, and _____ was the first African American to earn a Ph.D. in psychology.
   a. Calkins, Washburn
   b. Skinner, Watson
   c. Titchener, Wundt
   d. Calkins, Sumner

9. _____ research is conducted to explore new theories and advance scientific knowledge. _____ research attempts to solve real-world, practical problems.
   a. Experimental; Nonexperimental
   b. Correlational; Survey
   c. Basic; Applied
   d. Theoretical; Hypothetical

10. Describing drug abuse as "the number of missed work days due to excessive use of an addictive substance" is an example of _____.
    a. a theory
    b. a hypothesis
    c. an operational definition
    d. meta-analysis

11. Sometimes _____ is used in order to create a realistic situation with genuine reactions from participants.
    a. trickery
    b. deception
    c. a nonmonetary incentive
    d. case observation

12. The explanation a researcher provides to participants about the research process when it is over is called a(n) _____.
    a. case conference
    b. study's footnote
    c. debriefing
    d. exit interview

13. _____ research is NOT one of the four major research methods in psychology?
    a. Experimental
    b. Participant observation
    c. Descriptive
    d. Correlational

14. In an experiment, the researcher _____.
    a. isolates one or more variables and examines their effects on a behavior
    b. controls the dependent variable and measures the independent variable
    c. tests subjects, manipulates variables, and establishes correlations
    d. observes one behavior to the exclusion of all other variables

15. In the statement, "This causes that," *this* is the _____.
    a. constant
    b. independent variable
    c. dependent variable
    d. hypothesis

16. Participants in the _____ are treated the same as participants in the _____, except they are not exposed to the independent variable.
    a. experiment; nonexperiment
    b. survey; case study
    c. selection group; placebo group
    d. control group; experimental group

17. An inactive substance or fake treatment used as a control technique in experiments is known as a _____.
    a. double-blind
    b. single-blind
    c. independent variable
    d. placebo

18. Jane Goodall's study of chimpanzees in the jungle was an example of a _____.
    a. survey
    b. naturalistic observation
    c. case study
    d. single-blind study

19. The relationship between the color of your shoes and your teacher's mood today would be called a _____.
    a. mood correlation
    b. zero correlation
    c. random sampling
    d. negative correlation

20. Four types of brain scans are the _____.
    a. BRW, LEF, SSRS, MGI
    b. CAT, PET, DOG
    c. CT, PET, MRI, fMRI
    d. GRE, SAT, GPA, USA

Process Diagram 1.1
The Scientific Method

Study Tip

This ongoing, circular nature of theory building often frustrates students. In most chapters you will encounter numerous and sometimes conflicting hypotheses and theories. You will be tempted to ask, "Which theory is right?" But remember that theories are never absolute. Like most aspects of behavior, the "correct" answer is usually an interaction. In most cases, multiple theories contribute to the full understanding of complex concepts.

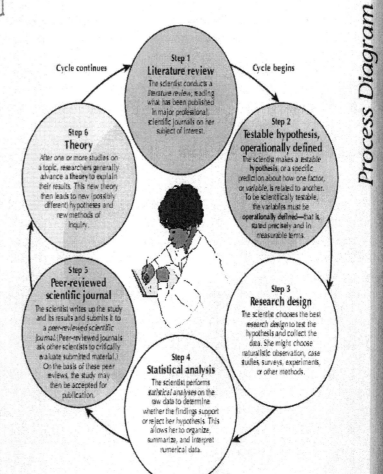

Cycle continues

Step 1
Literature review
The scientist conducts a *literature review*, reading what has been published in major professional, scientific journals on her subject of interest.

Cycle begins

Step 6
Theory
After one or more studies on a topic, researchers generally advance a theory to explain their results. This new theory then leads to new (possibly different) hypotheses and new methods of inquiry.

Step 2
Testable hypothesis, operationally defined
The scientist makes a *testable hypothesis*, or a specific prediction about how one factor, or variable, is related to another. To be scientifically testable, the variables must be operationally defined—that is, stated precisely and in measurable terms.

Step 5
Peer-reviewed scientific journal
The scientist writes up the study and its results and submits it to a *peer-reviewed scientific journal.* (Peer-reviewed journals ask other scientists to critically evaluate submitted material.) On the basis of these peer reviews, the study may then be accepted for publication.

Step 3
Research design
The scientist chooses the best *research design* to test the hypothesis and collect the data. She might choose naturalistic observation, case studies, surveys, experiments, or other methods.

Step 4
Statistical analysis
The scientist performs *statistical analyses* on the raw data to determine whether the findings support or reject her hypothesis. This allows her to organize, summarize, and interpret numerical data.

Study Tip

Statistics play a vital role in the scientific method. If you are interested in learning more about statistical analysis, see Appendix A at the back of this book.

Hypothesis *Specific, testable prediction about how one factor, or variable, is related to another*

Operational Definition *Precise description of how the variables in a study will be observed and measured (For example, drug abuse might be operationally defined as "the number of missed work days due to excessive use of an addictive substance.")*

Theory *Interrelated set of concepts that explain a body of data*

Process Diagram 1.2

Key Features of an Experiment

Imagine yourself as a psychologist interested in determining how watching violence on television affects aggressiveness in viewers. After reviewing the literature and developing your hypothesis (Steps 1 and 2 of the scientific method), you decide to use an experiment for your research design (Step 3). (See Process Diagram 1.1 for a full review of the scientific method.)

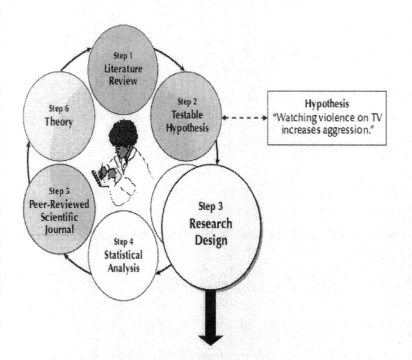

Hypothesis
"Watching violence on TV increases aggression."

Experimental Versus Control Groups

Using a very simple experiment, you begin by *randomly* assigning research participants to one of two groups: the **experimental group**, who watch a prearranged number of violent television programs, and the **control group**, who watch the same amount of television, except the programs they watch are nonviolent. (Having at least two groups allows the performance of one group to be compared with that of another.)

Independent and Dependent Variables

Now you arrange which factors, or variables, you will control, and those you will measure and examine for possible changes. The factor that is *manipulated*, or controlled, by the experimenter is called the **independent variable (IV)**. In contrast, the factor that is *measured* by the experimenter is called the **dependent variable (DV)**. [Note: The goal of any experiment is to learn how the dependent variable is affected by (depends on) the independent variable.]

Continuing the example of research on the effects of violence on TV and aggression, the experimenter (you) could decide to randomly assign children to watch either violent or nonviolent TV programs—the *independent variable (IV)*. More specifically, your *experimental group* would watch three violent television programs, while your *control group* would watch three nonviolent TV programs for the same amount of time. [Note: For both experimental and control groups, experimenters must ensure that all *extraneous variables* (those that are not being directly manipulated or measured) are held constant (the same). For example, time of day, heating, and lighting would need to be kept constant for all participants so that they do not affect participants' responses.]

Measuring the Dependent Variable

After all children watched either violent or nonviolent programs, you could put a large plastic, "Bobo," doll in front of each child and record for one hour the number of times the child hits, kicks, or punches the plastic doll—the *dependent variable* (DV).

[Note: Experiments can also have different *levels* of an independent variable (IV). In the TV violence example, two experimental groups could be created, with one group watching three hours of violent programming and the other watching six hours. The control group would watch only nonviolent programming. Then a researcher could relate differences in aggressive behavior (DV) to the amount (or level) of violent programming viewed (IV).]

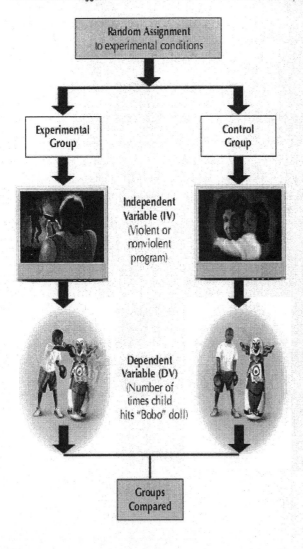

Experimental Group *Group that receives a treatment in an experiment*

Control Group *Group that receives no treatment in an experiment*

Independent Variable (IV) *Variable that is manipulated to determine its causal effect on the dependent variable*

Dependent Variable (DV) *Variable that is measured; it is affected by (or dependent on) the independent variable*

Study Tip

Because the IV is independent and freely selected and varied by the experimenter, it is called independent. *The DV is called* dependent *because the behavior (or outcome) exhibited by the participants is assumed to depend, at least in part, on manipulations of the IV.*

Concept Diagram 1.1

Understanding Correlations

Correlational research is very important because it reveals naturally occurring relationships and assesses how well one variable predicts another. How would we study nicotine use and possible fetal damage? After randomly selecting a group of pregnant women volunteers and obtaining their *informed consent*, researchers might survey or interview the women about the amount and timing of any cigarette smoking during their pregnancies.

After the data are collected, the researchers can analyze their results using a statistical formula that results in a **correlation coefficient**, a numerical value that indicates the degree and direction of the relationship between the two variables. (Note: *Correlational research* is a methodology researchers use to identify relationships between variables, whereas *correlation coefficients* are statistical measures used in correlational research, as well as with surveys and other research designs.)

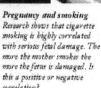

Pregnancy and smoking
Research shows that cigarette smoking is highly correlated with serious fetal damage. The more the mother smokes the more the fetus is damaged. Is this a positive or negative correlation?

Key Features in Correlations

1. Correlation coefficients are calculated by a formula (described in Appendix A) that produces a number ranging from +1.00 to −1.00. The number indicates the strength of the relationship. Both +1.00 and −1.00 indicate the strongest possible relationship. As the number decreases and gets closer to 0.00, the relationship weakens. Note that the sign (+ or −) in front of the number indicates the direction of the correlation, positive (+) or negative (−).

2. A *positive correlation* (−) indicates that two variables move (or vary) in the same direction—they increase or decrease in a similar way. For example, when studying increases, exam scores generally increase. Conversely, when studying decreases, exam scores decrease. Both are positive correlations. The factors vary in the same direction—upward or downward.

3. A *negative correlation* occurs when two variables vary in opposite directions—as one factor increases, the other factor decreases. Have you noticed that the more hours you work (or party) outside of college, the lower your exam scores? This is an example of a negative correlation—working and partying vary in opposite directions to exam scores.

4. A *zero correlation* indicates no relationship between two variables. For example, there is no relation (zero correlation) between your birthday and your exam scores. And, despite popular belief, repeated scientific investigations of astrology have found no relationship between personality and the position of the stars when you were born (a zero correlation).

5. Positive, negative, and zero correlations are sometimes shown on graphs (called *scatterplots*), with each dot representing an individual participant's score on the two variables. In scatterplot (a), each dot corresponds to one person's salary and years of education. Because salary and education are strongly correlated, the dots are closely aligned around the dark line, which points in an upward direction—a positive correlation. Scatterplots (b) and (c) show a negative and zero correlation.

6. In sum: A "correlation coefficient" is delineated by the letter "r," and it would be expressed something like this, r +.62. The sign in front of the number (+ or −) indicates the *direction* of the relationship, and the number (.62) indicates the *strength*. The closer the number is to 1.00, either positive or negative, the stronger the correlation between the variables. A correlation of +.92 or −.92 would represent a high (or strong) correlation, whereas a correlation of +.15 or −.15 would indicate a low (or weak) correlation.

(a) (b)   (a) (b)

(a) (b)   (a) (b)

(a) (b) ?

(a) Positive Correlation

(b) Negative Correlation

(c) Zero, or no Correlation

Sample Correlation Coefficient

r = (+) (62)

| Indicates the direction of the correlation (positive or negative) | Indicates the strength of a correlation (0 to +1.00 or 0 to −1.00) |

Correlation Coefficient *Number indicating strength and direction of the relationship between two variables*

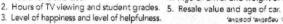

Try This Yourself

Can you spot the positive, negative, and zero correlations?

1. Health and exercise.
2. Hours of TV viewing and student grades.
3. Level of happiness and level of helpfulness.
4. Age of driver and weight of car.
5. Resale value and age of car.

(Answers: positive, negative, positive, zero, negative)

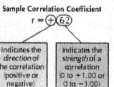

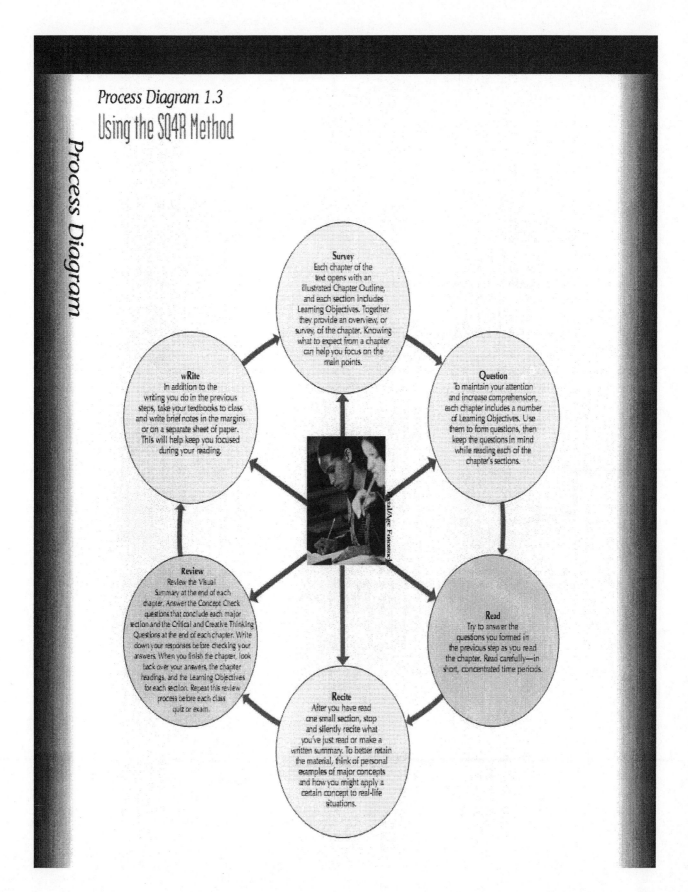

Process Diagram 1.3

Using the SQ4R Method

Survey
Each chapter of the text opens with an illustrated Chapter Outline, and each section includes Learning Objectives. Together they provide an overview, or survey, of the chapter. Knowing what to expect from a chapter can help you focus on the main points.

Question
To maintain your attention and increase comprehension, each chapter includes a number of Learning Objectives. Use them to form questions, then keep the questions in mind while reading each of the chapter's sections.

Read
Try to answer the questions you formed in the previous step as you read the chapter. Read carefully—in short, concentrated time periods.

Recite
After you have read one small section, stop and silently recite what you've just read or make a written summary. To better retain the material, think of personal examples of major concepts and how you might apply a certain concept to real-life situations.

Review
Review the Visual Summary at the end of each chapter. Answer the Concept Check questions that conclude each major section and the Critical and Creative Thinking Questions at the end of each chapter. Write down your responses before checking your answers. When you finish the chapter, look back over your answers, the chapter headings, and the Learning Objectives for each section. Repeat this review process before each class quiz or exam.

wRite
In addition to the writing you do in the previous steps, take your textbooks to class and write brief notes in the margins or on a separate sheet of paper. This will help keep you focused during your reading.

Process Diagram

Chapter 1 Visual Summary

Introducing Psychology

What Is Psychology?

Scientific study of behavior and mental processes that values empirical evidence and **critical thinking**.

Psychology's Goals

Describe, explain, predict, and change behavior and mental processes.

Careers in the Field

Occupational examples include experimental, biopsychology, cognitive, developmental, clinical, and counseling.

Gary D. Landsman/©Corbis

Origins of Psychology

* *Structuralism:* Focused on consciousness and the structure of the mind using introspection.

* *Functionalism:* Emphasized function of mental processes in adapting to the environment and practical applications of psychology.

Modern Perspectives

1. Psychoanalytic/Psychodynamic: Emphasizes unconscious processes and unresolved past conflicts.

2. Behavioral: Studies objective, observable, environmental influences on overt behavior.

3. Humanistic: Focuses on free will, self-actualization, and human nature as positive and growth seeking.

4. Cognitive: Emphasizes thinking, perception, problem solving, memory, language and information processing.

5. Neuroscience/Biopsychology: Studies genetics and biological processes in the brain and other parts of the nervous system.

6. Evolutionary: Studies natural selection, adaptation, and evolution of behavior and mental processes.

7. Sociocultural: Focuses on social interaction and cultural determinants of behavior and mental processes.

■ Women and Minorities: Sumner, Clark, Calkins, and Washburn made important contributions.

The Science of Psychology

Ethical Guidelines

Human research participants have rights, including **informed consent**, voluntary participation, limited and careful use of deception, **debriefing**, and **confidentiality**. Psychologists are expected to maintain high ethical standards in their relations with human and nonhuman animal research participants, as well as with clients in therapy. The APA has published guidelines detailing these ethical standards.

Research Methods

Four Major Research Methods

1. Experimental Research

Distinguishing feature: Establishes cause and effect *Components:*

* **Independent variables** (what the experimenter manipulates)
* **Dependent variables** (what the experimenter measures)
* *Experimental controls* (including **control group**, **experimental group**, extraneous variables)

2. Descriptive Research

Distinguishing feature: Unlike experiments, cannot determine causes of behavior but can describe specifics. *Types of descriptive research:*

* **Naturalistic observation** describes behavior in its natural habitat without altering it.
* **Surveys** use interviews or questionnaires on a sample of participants.
* **Case studies** are in-depth investigations.

3. Correlational Research

Distinguishing feature: Provides important research findings and predictions by examining how strongly two variables are related, and if the relationship is positively, negatively, or not at all (zero) correlated.

4. Biological Research

Methods include brain dissection, lesioning, direct observation, case studies, electrical recording (EEG), and brain imaging (such as CT, PET, MRI, fMRI).

Experimental Safeguards

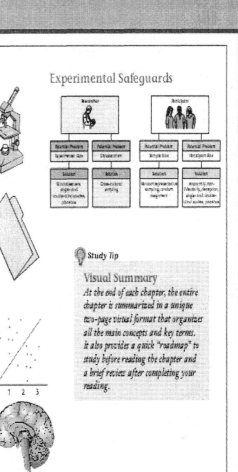

💡 **Study Tip**

Visual Summary
At the end of each chapter, the entire chapter is summarized in a unique two-page visual format that organizes all the main concepts and key terms. It also provides a quick "roadmap" to study before reading the chapter and a brief review after completing your reading.

Tools for Student Success

1. Use Active Reading to Study this Text
   * Familiarize yourself with the general text
   * Use SQ4R to read each chapter: Survey/Question/Read/Recite/ Review/wRite

2. Use Time Management to Succeed in College
   * Establish a baseline, set up a realistic activity schedule, reward yourself for good behavior, maximize your time

3. Strategies for Grade Improvement
   * Focus on note taking, distributed study time, complete learning, understanding your instructor, and general test-taking skills

4. Additional Resources
   * Instructors, typing and speed-reading courses, friends and family, roommates, classmates, and study groups

2
Neuroscience & Biological Foundations

OUTLINE SQ4R (Survey, Question, Read, Recite, Review, & wRite)

This outline section incorporates all six steps in the well-researched SQ4R method of learning. Begin by surveying the list of chapter topics in the left column. This "big picture" will help focus and guide your attention while you read. As you read through the chapter, briefly summarize each section in your own words in the space to the right. Also write down any *questions* that come to mind. Surveying, Questioning, Reading, Reciting, Reviewing, and wRiting are the foundation of the SQ4R method and an invaluable form of active learning. They also make your reading time more enjoyable and efficient! One thorough, focused SQ4R reading of a chapter is far better than several passive readings.

TOPIC   **NOTES**

I. NEURAL BASES OF BEHAVIOR

    A. What Is a Neuron?

       transmitter

    B. How Do Neurons Communicate?

    Psychology at Work: How Neurotransmitters and Hormones Affect Us

II. NERVOUS SYSTEM ORGANIZATION

    A. Central Nervous System (CNS)

    B. Peripheral Nervous System (PNS)

III. A TOUR THROUGH THE BRAIN

A. Lower-Level Brain Structures

B. Cerebral Cortex

Case Study/Personal Story: Phineas Gage

C. Two Brains in One?

Critical Thinking/Active Learning:
Biology of Critical Thinking

Psychology at Work: Working with Traumatic Brain
Injuries (TBIs)

IV. OUR GENETIC INHERITANCE

A. Behavioral Genetics

Psychology at Work: Overcoming Genetic Misconceptions

B. Evolutionary Psychology

Gender & Cultural Diversity:
The Evolution of Sex Differences

LEARNING OBJECTIVES (Read, Recite, Review, & wRite)

In addition to the work you did in the Outline above, you can significantly improve your performance on exams by focusing on the following learning objectives. While reading the chapter or reviewing for exams, check your understanding by stopping periodically to *recite* (or repeat in your own words) and *writing* down your answers on a separate sheet. [Page numbers correspond to Chapter 2 in *Psychology in Action* (9e).]

2.1 What are the key parts and functions of the neuron? (p. 52)
2.2 Describe how communication occurs within the neuron (the action potential) and between neurons. (p. 54)
2.3 How do neurotransmitters and hormones relate to our everyday life? (p. 54)
2.4 Describe the nervous system's two major divisions, and explain their respective functions. (p. 60)
2.5 Discuss neuroplasticity, neurogenesis, and stem cells. (p. 61)
2.6 What are the major functions of the spinal cord? (p. 61)
2.7 What are the subdivisions of the peripheral nervous system, and what are their functions? (p. 63)
2.8 Identify the three major sections of the brain. (p. 67)
2.9 What are the three key components of the hindbrain, and what are their functions? (p. 68)
2.10 Describe the functions of the midbrain and the reticular formation. (p. 68)
2.11 Identify the major structures of the forebrain, and describe their functions. (p. 68)
2.12 What is the cerebral cortex, and what is its major function? (p. 71)
2.13 Describe the major functions of the lobes of the cerebral cortex? (p. 72)
2.14 Why is the case study of Phineas Gage important? (p. 72)
2.15 Explain why the corpus callosum and split-brain research are important? (p. 75)
2.16 Describe traumatic brain injury (TBI). (p. 79)
2.17 What is behavioral genetics? (p. 81)
2.18 Describe the four methods of behavioral genetics research. (p. 82)
2.19 Identify three key genetic misconceptions. (p. 82)
2.20 What is evolutionary psychology? (p. 84)
2.21 How does evolutionary theory explain current sex differences? (p. 85)

KEY TERMS (Review & wRite)

Like other survey courses, introductory psychology is filled with a "wealth" of new and unfamiliar terminology. To do well on exams, you must master this new language! Writing a brief definition of each term in the space provided and carefully reviewing them before exams will significantly improve your course grade.

Action Potential: _____

_____

Amygdala: _____

_____

Association Areas: _____

_____

Autonomic Nervous System (ANS): _____

_____

Axon: _____

_____

Behavioral Genetics: _____

_____

Brainstem: _____

_____

Cell Body: _____

_____

Central Nervous System (CNS): _____

_____

Cerebellum: _____

_____

Cerebral Cortex: _____

_____

Chromosomes: _____

_____

Corpus Callosum: _____

_____

Dendrites: _____

_____

Endocrine System: _____

_____

Endorphins: _____

_____

Evolutionary Psychology: _____

_____

Forebrain: _____

_____

Frontal Lobes: _____

_____

Genes: _____

_____

Glial Cells: _____

_____

Heritability: _____

_____

Hindbrain: _____

_____

Hippocampus: _____

_____

Hormones: _____

_____

Hypothalamus: _____

_____

Limbic System: _____

_____

Medulla: _____

_____

Midbrain: _____

_____

Myelin Sheath: _____

_____

Natural Selection: _____

_____

Neurogenesis: _____

_____

Neuron: _____

_____

Neuroplasticity: _____

_____

Neurotransmitters: _____

_____

Occipital Lobes: _____

_____

Parasympathetic Nervous System: _____

_____

Parietal Lobes: _____

_____

Peripheral Nervous System (PNS): _____

_____

Pons: _____

_____

Reflexes: _____

_____

Reticular Formation (RF): _____

_____

Somatic Nervous System (SNS): _____

_____

Split-Brain Surgery:_____

_____

Stem Cell: _____

_____

Sympathetic Nervous System: _____

_____

Synapse: _____

_____

Temporal Lobes: _____

_____

Thalamus: _____

_____

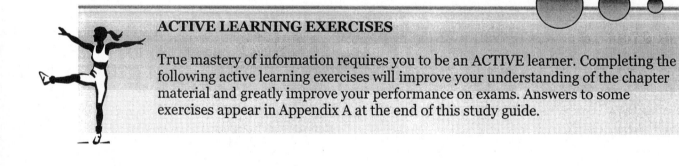

ACTIVE LEARNING EXERCISES

True mastery of information requires you to be an ACTIVE learner. Completing the following active learning exercises will improve your understanding of the chapter material and greatly improve your performance on exams. Answers to some exercises appear in Appendix A at the end of this study guide.

ACTIVE LEARNING EXERCISE I *For each of the following behaviors, identify which cerebral lobes would be the primary receiving areas for incoming neural messages (frontal, parietal, occipital, or temporal).*

1. Watching television   _____
2. Feeling a rough texture with your right hand   _____
3. Listening to music   _____
4. Catching a baseball with your left hand   _____
5. Reading silently   _____

ACTIVE LEARNING EXERCISE II *Using information from Chapter 2, fill in the appropriate label or term in the space next to the corresponding number or letter.*

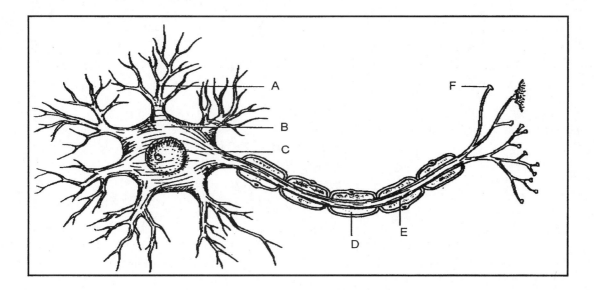

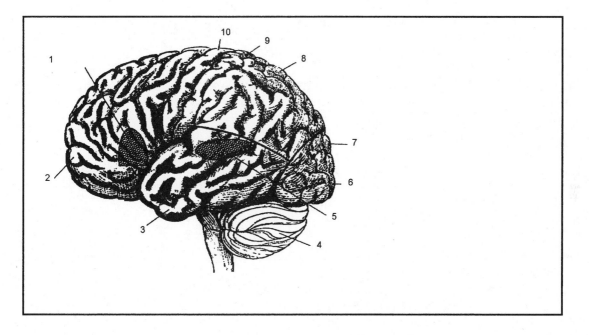

ACTIVE LEARNING EXERCISE III *A critical thinker understands that simply defining a term is not evidence of true understanding. We must be able to extend basic definitions to more complex applications. The following exercise will help clarify your understanding of brain terminology and function, while also improving your quiz and exam performance.*

The Setting You are a famous neurosurgeon who specializes in brain damage. Can you diagnose each of the following patients? (Despite being a famous neurosurgeon, you may need to review information from Chapter 2).

Case 1: A 56-year-old man recently suffered a brain stroke and was admitted to the hospital. During your interview with him, you note that he comprehends verbal and written instructions perfectly and can even write them down, but cannot repeat them verbally. You diagnose the problem as probable damage in the _____ of his brain.

Case 2: A 12-year-old boy has serious difficulties controlling his emotions. At age 3, he was riding in the front seat of an automobile when a serious car accident occurred and he his car seat toppled forward. His forehead hit the dashboard of the car causing a serious head concussion and long-term moderate brain damage. His mother points out that he is very intelligent and she cannot understand why he cannot control his wild moods and stick to any task. You explain that his difficulties may be due to problems with his _____.

Case 3: At age 5, a young girl's corpus callosum was cut to reduce the severity of her epileptic seizures. She is now 11 years of age and reads at the lowest level despite having tested very high on overall intelligence. Her reading problems are most likely a result of _____.

Case 4: An intelligent businessperson comes to you and explains rather agitatedly that she awoke yesterday morning to find she could no longer read. Your tests show:
1. She is completely blind in the right visual field.
2. She speaks fluently and comprehends speech.
3. She can write with her right hand but cannot read what she has written.
4. She can copy written words but only with her left hand.

You turn to your puzzled assistant and remark that this is indeed a tough one, but you are willing to bet you will find brain damage in at least two areas--the _____ and _____.

CHAPTER OVERVIEW (Review)

The following chapter overview provides a narrative overview of the main topics covered in the chapter. Like the *Visual Summary* found at the end of each chapter in the text, this narrative summary provides a final opportunity to *review* chapter material.

I. NEURAL BASES OF BEHAVIOR
2.1 What are the key parts and functions of the neuron? (p. 52)
Neurons are cells that transmit information throughout the body. They have three main parts: **dendrites,** which receive information from other neurons; the **cell body,** which provides nourishment and "decides" whether the axon should fire; and the **axon,** which sends along the neural information. **Glial cells** support and provide nutrients for neurons in the central nervous system (CNS).

2.2 Describe how communication occurs within the neuron (the action potential) and between neurons.
   (p. 54)

The process of neural communication begins within the neuron when the dendrites and cell body receive information and transmit it to the axon. The axon is specialized for transmitting neural impulses, or **action potentials.** During times when no action potential is moving down the axon, the axon is at rest. The neuron is activated, and an action potential occurs when positively charged ions move in and out through channels in the axon's membrane. Action potentials travel more quickly down myelinated axons because the **myelin sheath** serves as insulation.

Information is transferred from one neuron to another at **synapses** by chemicals called **neurotransmitters.** Neurotransmitters bind to receptor sites much as a key fits into a lock, and their effects can be excitatory or inhibitory.

2.3 How do neurotransmitters and hormones relate to our everyday life? (p. 54)

Neurotransmitters regulate glands and muscles, sleep, alertness, learning, memory, motivation, emotion, psychological disorders, etc. **Hormones** are released from glands in the **endocrine system** directly into the bloodstream. They act at a distance on other glands, on muscles, and in the brain. The major functions of the endocrine system, including the hypothalamus, pituitary gland, thyroid gland, adrenals, and pancreas, are to help with the regulation of long-term bodily processes (such as growth and sex characteristics), maintain ongoing bodily processes, and assist in regulating the emergency response to crisis.

II. NERVOUS SYSTEM ORGANIZATION

2.4 Describe the nervous system's two major divisions, and explain their respective functions. (p. 60)

The nervous system is divided into two major divisions: the **central nervous system (CNS),** composed of the brain and the spinal cord, and the **peripheral nervous system (PNS),** including all nerves connecting the CNS to the rest of the body. The CNS processes and organizes information, whereas the PNS carries information to and from the CNS.

2.5 Discuss neuroplasticity, neurogenesis, and stem cells. (p. 61)

Neuroplasticity is the brain's ability to reorganize and change its structure and function throughout the life span. **Neurogenesis** is the process by which new neurons are generated. **Stem cells** are immature (uncommitted) cells that have the potential to develop into almost any type of cell depending on the chemical signals they receive.

2.6 What are the major functions of the spinal cord? (p. 61)

The *spinal cord* is the communication link between the brain and the rest of the body, and it is involved in all voluntary and **reflex** responses.

2.7 What are the subdivisions of the peripheral nervous system (PNS), and what are their functions? (p. 63)

The two major subdivisions of the PNS are the **somatic nervous system** and **the autonomic nervous system**. The **somatic nervous system** includes all nerves carrying incoming sensory information and outgoing motor information to and from the sense organs and skeletal muscles. The **autonomic nervous system** includes the nerves outside the brain and spinal cord that maintain normal functioning of glands, heart muscle, and the smooth muscle of blood vessels and internal organs.

The autonomic nervous system is further divided into two branches, the *parasympathetic* and the *sympathetic*, which tend to work in opposition to one another. The **parasympathetic nervous system** normally dominates when a person is relaxed. The **sympathetic nervous system** dominates when a person is under physical or mental stress. It mobilizes the body for fight or flight by increasing heart rate and blood pressure and slowing digestive processes.

III. LOWER-LEVEL BRAIN STRUCTURES

2.8 Identify the three major sections of the brain. (p. 67)
The brain is generally divided into three major sections: the *hindbrain, midbrain,* and *forebrain.*

2.9 What are the three key components of the hindbrain, and what are their functions? (p. 68)
Parts of the **hindbrain**, the **pons and medulla,** are involved in sleeping, waking, dreaming, and control of automatic bodily functions; another part, the **cerebellum,** coordinates fine muscle movement, balance, and some aspects of perception and cognition.

2.10 Describe the functions of the midbrain and the reticular formation. (p. 68)
The **midbrain** helps coordinate movement patterns, sleep, and arousal. The **reticular formation** runs through the midbrain, hindbrain, and **brainstem**, and is responsible for screening incoming information and arousing the cortex.

2.11 Identify the major structures of the forebrain, and describe their functions. (p. 68)
The **forebrain** includes several structures, including the *thalamus, hypothalamus, limbic system,* and *cerebral cortex.* The **thalamus** relays sensory messages to the cerebral cortex. The **hypothalamus** is involved in hormones and drives associated with survival, such as regulation of thirst, hunger, sex, and aggression. The **limbic system** is a group of forebrain structures (including the **hippocampus** and **amygdala**) involved with emotions and memory. Because the cerebral cortex controls most complex mental activities it is discussed in the next section.

IV. THE CEREBRAL CORTEX AND TWO BRAINS IN ONE?

2.12 What is the cerebral cortex, and what is its major function? (p. 71)
The **cerebral cortex**, the thin surface layer on the cerebral hemispheres, regulates most complex behaviors and higher mental processes.

2.13 Describe the major functions of the lobes of the cerebral cortex? (p. 72)
The left and right cerebral hemispheres make up most of the weight of the brain, and each hemisphere is divided into four lobes. The two **frontal lobes** control movement, speech, and higher functions. The two **parietal lobes** are the receiving area for sensory information. The two **temporal lobes** are concerned with hearing, language, memory, and some emotional control. The two **occipital lobes** are dedicated to vision and visual information processing.

2.14 Why is the case study of Phineas Gage important? (p. 72)
Phineas Gage experienced a horrific blow to his frontal lobes when a metal rod pierced his face and brain. Historical records of changes in his behavior and mental processes following the accident provides invaluable clues to the important role of the frontal lobes in motivation, emotion, and other cognitive activities.

2.15 Explain why the corpus callosum and split-brain research are important? (p. 75)
The two hemispheres are linked by the **corpus callosum,** through which they communicate and coordinate. **Split-brain** research shows that each hemisphere performs somewhat separate functions. In most people, the left hemisphere is dominant in verbal skills, such as speaking and writing, and also for analytical tasks. The right hemisphere appears to excel at nonverbal tasks, such as spatio-manipulative skills, art and music, and visual recognition.

2.16 Describe traumatic brain injury (TBI). (p. 79)
Traumatic brain injury (TBI) is any injury to the brain caused by significant trauma. Two of the most common TBIs are *concussions* (blows to the head) and *contusions* (bruises in the brain).

V. OUR GENETIC INHERITANCE

2.17 What is behavioral genetics? (p. 81)

Behavioral genetics studies the relative effects of heredity and the environment on behavior and mental processes. Two important keys to heredity are genes and chromosomes. **Genes** hold the code for certain traits that are passed on from parent to child, and they can be dominant or recessive. Each of the 46 human **chromosomes** contains many genes, which ae found in DNA molecules.

2.18 Describe the four methods of behavioral genetics research. (p. 82)

Behavioral geneticists use twin studies, family studies, adoption studies, and genetic abnormalities to explore genetic contributions to behavior and make estimates of **heritability.**

2.19 Identify three key genetic misconceptions. (p. 82)

The three key misconceptions are: Genetic traits are not fixed or inflexible, hereditary estimates do not apply to individuals, and genes and the environment are inseparable.

2.20 What is evolutionary psychology? (p. 84)

Evolutionary psychology is the branch of psychology that looks at evolutionary changes related to behavior and mental processes. Several different processes, including **natural selection,** mutations, and social and cultural factors can affect evolution.

2.21 How does evolutionary theory explain current sex differences? (p. 85)

According to evolutionary theory, modern sex differences (like the male's superior spatial and motor skills and the female's superior verbal fluency and fine motor coordination) are the product of gradual genetic adaptations. They helped our ancestors adapt and survive in their environment.

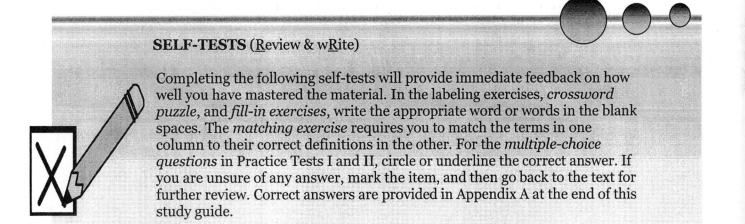

SELF-TESTS (Review & wRite)

Completing the following self-tests will provide immediate feedback on how well you have mastered the material. In the labeling exercises, *crossword puzzle*, and *fill-in exercises*, write the appropriate word or words in the blank spaces. The *matching exercise* requires you to match the terms in one column to their correct definitions in the other. For the *multiple-choice questions* in Practice Tests I and II, circle or underline the correct answer. If you are unsure of any answer, mark the item, and then go back to the text for further review. Correct answers are provided in Appendix A at the end of this study guide.

Crossword Puzzle for Chapter 2

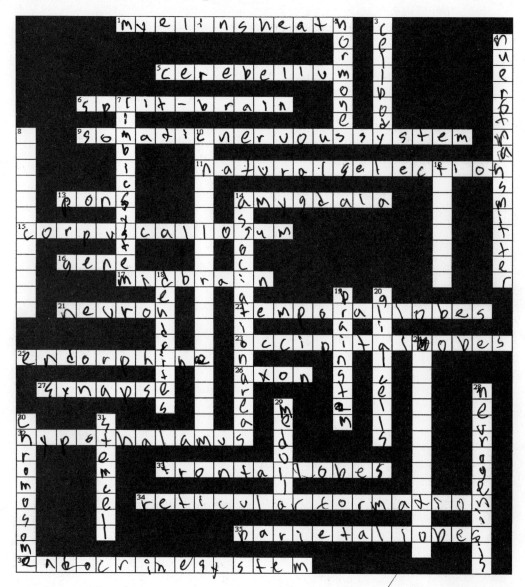

ACROSS

1 A layer of fatty insulation wrapped around the axon of some neurons that increases the rate at which nerve impulses travel along the axon.

5 Structure at the base of the brain responsible for maintaining smooth movement, balance, and some aspects of perception and cognition.

6 A surgical separation of the brain's two hemispheres used medically to treat severe epilepsy.

9 A subdivision of the peripheral nervous system (PNS) that connects to sensory receptors and controls skeletal muscles.

11 The driving mechanism behind evolution, which allows individuals with genetically influenced traits that are adaptive in a particular environment to stay alive and produce offspring.

13 Structure at the top of the brain stem involved in respiration, movement, waking, sleep, and dreaming.

14 An almond-shaped lower-level brain structure that is part of the limbic system and involved in emotion.

15 Bundle of nerve fibers connecting the brain's left and right hemispheres.

16 A segment of DNA occupying a specific place on a particular chromosome that carries the code for hereditary transmission.

17 Neural centers located near the top of the brainstem involved in coordinating movement patterns, sleep, and arousal.

21 Individual nerve cell responsible for processing, storing, and transmitting information throughout the body.

22 Cortical lobes above the ears involved in auditory (hearing), language comprehension, memory, and some emotional control.

23 Cortical lobes at the back of the brain responsible for vision and visual perception.

25 Chemical substances in the nervous system similar in structure and action to opiates.

26 A long, tube-like structure that conveys impulses away from the neuron's cell body toward other neurons or to muscles or glands.

27 Junction between the axon tip of the sending neuron and the dendrite or cell body of the receiving neuron.

32 A small brain structure beneath the thalamus that maintains the body's internal environment and regulates emotions and drives, such as hunger, thirst, sex, and aggression.

33 Cortical lobes responsible for motor control, speech production, and higher functions, such as thinking, personality, emotion, and memory.

34 Diffuse set of neurons in the core of the brainstem that screens incoming information and arouses the cortex.

35 Cortical lobes at the top of the brain where bodily sensations are interpreted.

36 A collection of glands located throughout the body that manufacture and secrete hormones into the bloodstream.

DOWN

2 Chemicals manufactured by endocrine glands and circulated in the bloodstream to produce bodily changes or maintain normal bodily functions.

3 Part of the neuron containing the cell nucleus, as well as other structures, which helps the neuron carry out its functions.

4 Chemicals manufactured and released by neurons that alter activity in other neurons.

7 An interconnected group of lower-level brain structures involved with the arousal and regulation of emotion, motivation, memory, and many other aspects of behavior and mental processes.

8 An interdisciplinary field studying how biological processes relate to behavior and mental processes.

10 System located centrally in the body that includes the brain and spinal cord.

12 Relays sensory messages to the cerebral cortex.

14 So-called quiet areas in the cerebral cortex involved in interpreting, integrating and acting on information processed by other parts of the brain.

18 Branching neuron structures receiving neural impulses from other neurons and conveying impulses toward the cell body.

19 Area at the base of the brain responsible for automatic, survival functions.

20 Cells that provide structural, nutritional, and other support for the neuron, as well as communication within the nervous system.

24 Specialization of the left and right hemispheres of the brain for particular operations.

28 The division of non-neuronal cells to produce neurons.

29 Structure at the base of the brainstem responsible for automatic body functions such as breathing and heart rate.

30 Threadlike strands of DNA (deoxyribonucleic acid) molecules that carry genetic information.

31 Precursor (immature) cells that give birth to new specialized cells.

FILL-IN EXERCISES

1. A neuron contains three key parts, the _axon_ , _cell body_ and _dendrites_ (p.53).

2. _Myelin_ is a type of fatty insulation on some axons helping insulate and speed neural messages (p. 53).

3. Neurons transmit information to each other, muscles, and glands via _neuro transmitter_ released into the bloodstream (p. 58).

4. Two major divisions of the nervous system are the _____, consisting of the brain and spinal cord, and the _____, which includes all nerves and neurons connecting the CNS to the rest of the body (p. 60).

5. The _____ is involved in reflexes and relaying neural information to and from the brain (pp. 61-62).

6. The _____ part of the autonomic nervous system is dominant during normal, relaxed times. In contrast, the _____ is dominant during times of mental or physical stress (p. 63).

7. The _cerebellum_ is responsible for maintaining smooth movement, balance, and some aspects of perception and cognition (pp. 67-68).

8. The _____ maintains the body's internal environment and regulates drives, such as hunger, thirst, sex, and aggression (pp. 67, 69).

9. The _occipital_ _____ lobes are responsible for vision and visual perception (pp. 71, 73).

10. Specialization of the hemispheres of the brain was first discovered as a result of _____ (p. 75).

MATCHING EXERCISE

Column A

a. Hippocampus
b. Temporal Lobes
c. Myelin Sheath
d. Parietal Lobes
e. Cell Body
f. Limbic System
g. Cerebral Cortex
h. Action Potential
i. Corpus Callosum
j. Dendrite

Column B

1. _j_ Receives information from other neurons
2. _e_ Integrates incoming information from dendrites
3. _i_ Transmits messages from one hemisphere to the other
4. _h_ Electrochemical impulse that travels down the axon
5. _d_ Interprets bodily sensations
6. _f_ Involved in emotions and drives
7. _g_ Thin surface layer on the cerebral hemispheres
8. _a_ Involved in forming and retrieving memories
9. _c_ Fatty insulation that speeds up action potential
10. _b_ Involved in audition and language comprehension

PRACTICE TEST I

1. _____ studies how biological processes in the nervous system relate to behavior and mental processes.
   a. Evolutionary psychology
   b. Neuroscience
   c. Biofunctionalism
   d. None of these options

2. _____ are basic cells of the nervous system responsible for receiving and transmitting electrochemical information.
   a. Dendrites
   b. Neurons
   c. Axons
   d. Nucleotides

3. The three major parts of a neuron are the _____.
   a. glia, dendrites, and myelin
   b. myelin, dendrites, and axon
   c. dendrites, axon, and cell body
   d. axon, glia, and myelin

4. Juan has been diagnosed with multiple sclerosis and has trouble walking because of his poor muscle coordination. His coordination problem is primarily due to the progressive deterioration of his _____.
   a. axons
   b. myelin sheath
   c. action potential
   d. glial cells

5. The _____ explains how an axon either fires or does not fire an action potential _____
   a. sodium-potassium
   b. axon terminal
   c. shotgun
   d. all-or-nothing law

6. _____ are chemical messengers secreted into the synapse.
   a. ions
   b. neurotransmitters
   c. nucleotides
   d. neurocommunicators

7. The synapse is the point where _____.
   a. the soma attaches to the dendrite
   b. neurotransmitters are manufactured
   c. information transfers from neuron to neuron
   d. the action potential begins

8. _____ is a neurotransmitter and suspected factor in Parkinson's disease (PD) and schizophrenia.
   a. Acetylcholine
   b. Dopamine
   c. Serotonin
   d. all of these options

9. Chemicals manufactured by endocrine glands and circulated in the bloodstream to produce bodily changes or maintain normal bodily functions are called _____.
   a. endorphins
   b. neurotransmitters
   c. endoseals
   d. hormones

10. Neurotransmission at the synapse is similar to making an individual phone call. In contrast, messages from the __C__ system resemble a very large group email message.
    a. lympathic
    b. hormonal
    c. endocrine
    d. reticular activating

11. The major divisions of the central nervous system (CNS) are the _____.
    a. sympathetic and parasympathetic
    b. somatic and autonomic
    c. gray matter and white matter
    d. brain and spinal cord

12. The __√__ carries messages between the CNS and the periphery of your body.
    a. parasympathetic nervous system
    b. spinal cord
    c. peripheral nervous system (PNS)
    d. none of these options

13. _____ *C* is the brain's ability to reorganize and change its structure and function throughout the life span.
    a.   Neurogenesis
    b.   Stem cells
    c.   Neuroplasticity
    d.   All of these options

14. The parasympathetic nervous system is dominant when a person is _____.
    a.   stressed
    b.   relaxed
    c.   frightened
    d.   angry

15. Damage to the medulla can lead to loss of _____.
    a.   vision
    b.   respiration
    c.   hearing
    d.   smell

16. The _____ *d* is a hindbrain structure involved in respiration, movement, waking, sleep, and dreaming.
    a.   medulla
    b.   thalamus
    c.   reticular formation (RF)
    d.   pons

17. The frontal, parietal, occipital, and temporal lobes make up the _____.
    a.   brain
    b.   left and right hemispheres
    c.   subcortex
    d.   brain stem

18. If you are accidentally hit on the head and you see flashes of light, most likely the blow activated cells in the _____.
    a.   frontal lobes
    b.   temporal lobes
    c.   occipital lobes
    d.   parietal lobes

19. Your left brain doesn't know what your right brain is doing. It is MOST likely that your _____ has been severed.
    a.   amygdala
    b.   frontal lobe
    c.   association cortex
    d.   corpus callosum

20. Split-brain research has indicated that, in most people, the left hemisphere is largely responsible for _____ abilities.
    a.   musical
    b.   spatial
    c.   artistic
    d.   language

PRACTICE TEST II

1. _____ *C* are branching neuron structures that receive neural impulses from neurons and convey impulses toward the cell body.
    a.   Axons
    b.   Cell bodies
    c.   Dendrites
    d.   none of these options

2. The _____ is a part of the neuron that integrates incoming information, absorbs nutrients, and produces proteins necessary for the functioning of the neuron.
    a.   axon hillock
    b.   myelin sheath
    c.   synaptic gap
    d.   cell body

3. A(n) _____ is an electrochemical impulse that travels through a neuron.
    a.   ganglial message
    b.   muscular potentiation
    c.   action potential
    d.   neuroelectrical message

4. According to the all-or-nothing law, the _____.
    a.   neuron cannot fire again during the refractory period
    b.   neurotransmitter either attaches to a receptor site or is destroyed in the synapse
    c.   neuron either fires completely or not at all
    d.   none of these options

5. Neurotransmitters are _____.
   a. charged ions that carry action potentials down the axon
   b. hormones that pass electrical energy from the dendrite into the soma
   c. chemical messengers that are released from an axon and stimulate dendrites on another neuron
   d. lubricants and nutrients needed by the soma to keep the neuron alive

6. Growth, reproduction, moods, and our responses to stress are all influenced by our _____.
   a. vasopressors
   b. hormones
   c. steroids
   d. gonadotropins

7. The sensory and motor nerves that go to and from the central nervous system, body organs, and skeletal muscles make up the _____ nervous system.
   a. somatic
   b. fight or flight
   c. autonomic
   d. peripheral

8. A reflex arc occurs in the _____.
   a. skeletal muscles
   b. brain
   c. spinal cord
   d. reticular activating system

9. The _____ system prepares your body to respond to stress.
   a. central nervous
   b. sympathetic
   c. peripheral
   d. somatic

10. The brainstem is involved with your _____.
   a. ability to move and maintain posture
   b. sense of touch and pain
   c. basic survival functions
   d. emotional behavior

11. An interconnected group of forebrain structures particularly responsible for emotions, drives, and memory is known as the _____.
   a. subcortical center
   b. homeostatic controller
   c. limbic system
   d. master endocrine gland

12. The _____ lobes govern motor control, speech production, and higher functions, such as thinking, personality, emotion, and memory.
   a. parietal
   b. master
   c. frontal
   d. temporal

13. A stroke that damages Broca's area would affect a person's ability to _____.
   a. make speech sounds
   b. read and write
   c. understand language
   d. read, write, and understand language

14. If Hannibal Lecter removed and ate the _____ of your brain, you would no longer understand language.
   a. corpus callosum
   b. association areas
   c. Wernicke's area
   d. parietal lobes

15. The occipital lobes are primarily responsible for _____.
   a. vision
   b. hearing
   c. smell and taste
   d. touch and pain

16. Specialization of the left and right hemispheres of the brain for particular operations is technically referred to as _____.
   a. centralization
   b. asymmetrical processing
   c. localization of function
   d. lateralization

17. The corpus callosum _____.
    a.   maintains your balance
    b.   keeps you breathing
    c.   connects your right and left
         cerebral hemispheres
    d.   all of these options

18. Split-brain patients _____.
    a.   do not exist
    b.   have split personalities
    c.   cannot name an object if they hold
         it in their left hand without looking
         at it
    d.   deteriorate gradually at first and
         usually die within a year

19. Threadlike strands of DNA that carry
    genetic information are called _____.
    a.   stem cells
    b.   genes
    c.   neurons
    d.   chromosomes

20. The proportion of observed variance in a
    particular trait (such as intelligence) that
    can be attributed to inherited genetic
    factors in contrast to environmental ones
    is known as _____.
    a.   behavioral genetics
    b.   genetic determinism
    c.   heritability
    d.   Mendelian factors

Process Diagram 2.1

How Neurons Communicate

Communication WITHIN the Neuron (Part A)

The process of neural communication begins within the neuron itself when the dendrites and cell body receive information and conduct it toward the axon. From there, the information travels down the entire length of the axon via a brief traveling electrical charge called an ***action potential****, which can be described in three steps:*

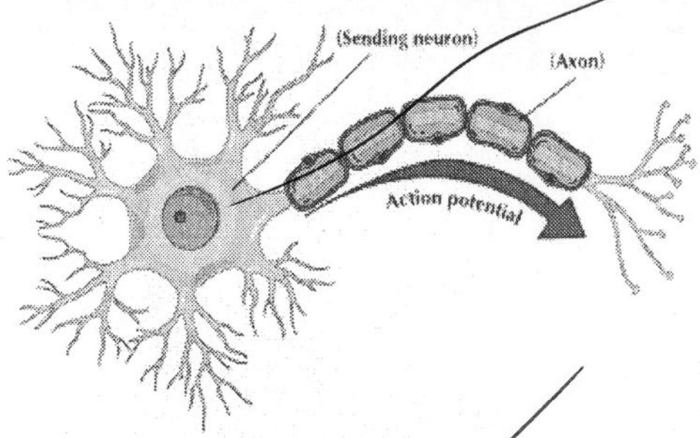

Process Diagram

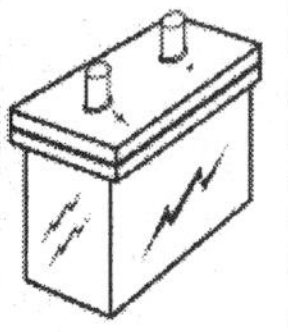

Step 1: Resting Potential When an axon is not stimulated, it is in a polarized state, called the *resting potential*. "At rest," the fluid inside the axon has more negatively charged ions than the fluid outside. This results from the selective permeability of the axon membrane and a series of mechanisms, called *sodium-potassium pumps*, which pull potassium ions in and pump sodium ions out of the axon. The inside of the axon has a charge of about -70 millivolts relative to the outside.

[Note that neurons, like a standard battery, generate electrical potential from chemical processes, and batteries have positive and negative poles that are similarly "polarized."]

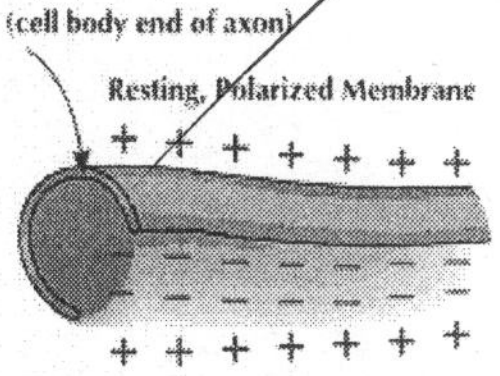

Masterfile

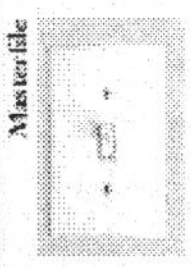

Step 2: Action Potential Initiation When an "at rest" axon membrane is stimulated by a sufficiently strong signal, it produces an *action potential* (or depolarization). This action potential begins when the first part of the axon opens its "gates" and positively charged sodium ions rush through. The additional sodium ions change the previously negative charge inside the axon to a positive charge—thus depolarizing the axon.

[Note that an action potential is either "on" or "off"—the so-called *all-or-nothing law*. Like a standard light switch (without a dimmer), if the axon receives a stimulus above a certain threshold, the action potential "turns on." Increasing the stimulation (like flipping the switch harder) will not affect the intensity of the light or the speed or intensity of the neural message.]

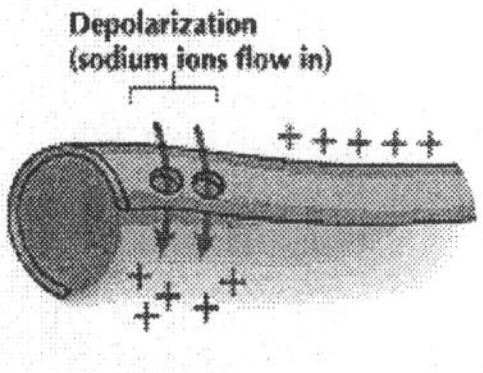

Step 3: Spreading of Action Potential and Repolarization *The initial depolarization (or action potential) of Step 2 produces a subsequent imbalance of ions in the adjacent axon membrane. This imbalance thus causes the action potential to spread to the next section. Meanwhile, "gates" in the axon membrane of the initially depolarized section open and potassium ions flow out, thus allowing the first section to repolarize and return to its resting potential.*

Overall Summary: As you can see in the figure to the right, this sequential process of depolarization, followed by repolarization, transmits the action potential along the entire length of the axon from the cell body to the terminal buttons. This is similar to an audience at an athletic event doing "the wave." One section of fans initially stands up for a brief time (action potential). This section then sits down (resting potential), and the "wave" then spreads to adjacent sections.

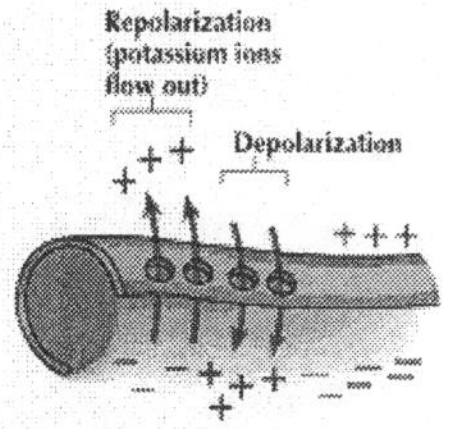

Lori Adamski Peek/Getty Images

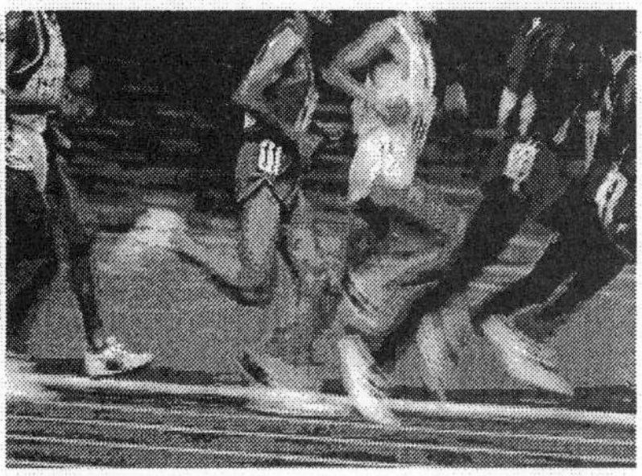

[Note: This three-step description of the action potential applies to a "bare" axon. As you saw in Figure 2.1, many axons are covered with a fatty insulation, the *myelin sheath*, which blankets the axon with the exception of periodic nodes (points at which the myelin is very thin or absent). These nodes allow the neural message to travel about 10 times faster than in a bare axon because the action potential jumps from node to node rather than traveling along the entire axon.]

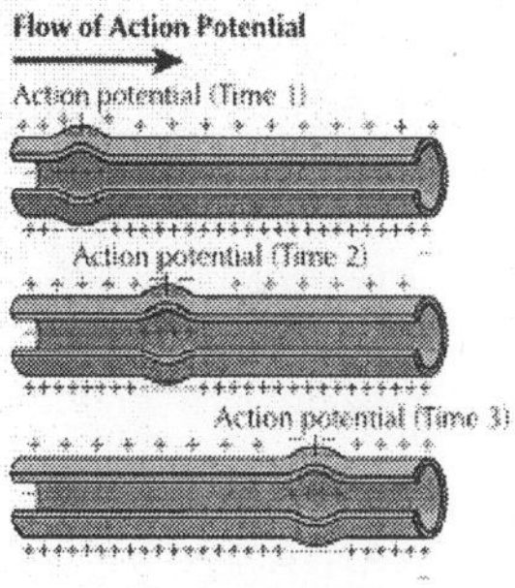

Action Potential *Neural impulse, or brief electrical charge, that carries information along the axon of a neuron. The action potential is generated when positively charged ions move in and out through channels in the axon's membrane*

Process Diagram

Communication BETWEEN Neurons (Part B)

Communication within the neuron (Part A) is not the same as communication between neurons (Part B): Within the neuron, messages travel electrically. Between neurons, messages are transmitted chemically. Steps 4, 5, and 6 summarize this chemical transmission:

Step 4: Sending a Chemical Signal When the action potential reaches the branching axon terminals, the previous *electrical impulse* is converted to a *chemical signal*. The action potential triggers the terminal buttons at the axon's end to release special chemicals, called **neurotransmitters**. These chemicals then flow across a small gap, called the **synapse**, to potentially attach to receptors in nearby neurons.

Step 5: Receiving a Chemical Signal Like a lock and key, the nearby neurons will only accept and receive the chemical message if the neurotransmitter molecules are of the appropriate shape. The successfully shaped "keys" will then either *excite* or *inhibit* a new action potential in the post-synaptic neuron.

(Sending neuron)

(Receiving neuron)

It's important also to know that each receiving neuron gets multiple neuro transmitter messages. As you can see in this close-up photo to the right, the axon terminals from thousands of other nearby neurons almost completely cover the cell body of the receiving neuron.

Courtesy E.R. Lewis, Berkeley

Sending neuron

Action potential

Vesicle containing neurotransmitters

Axon terminal button

Synapse

Receptor sites on receiving neuron

Neurotransmitter

Step 6: Dealing with Left-overs What happens to excess neurotransmitters or to those that do not "fit" into the adjacent receptor sites? The sending neuron normally reabsorbs the excess (called "reuptake") or they are broken down by special enzymes.

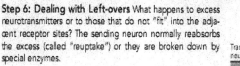
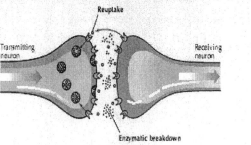

Reuptake

Transmitting neuron

Receiving neuron

Enzymatic breakdown

Neurotransmitters *Chemicals released by neurons that travel across the synaptic gap*

Synapse [SIN-aps] *Junction between the axon tip of the sending neuron and the dendrite or cell body of the receiving neuron. During an action potential, chemicals called neurotransmitters are released and flow across the synaptic gap*

Concept Diagram 2.1

Visualizing Your Motor Cortex and Somatosensory Cortex

This drawing represents a vertical cross section taken from the left hemisphere's *motor cortex* and right hemisphere's *somatosensory cortex*. If a surgeon applied electrical current to your motor cortex in your frontal lobes, you might move your arm, hand, or fingers—depending on the precise area that the surgeon stimulated.

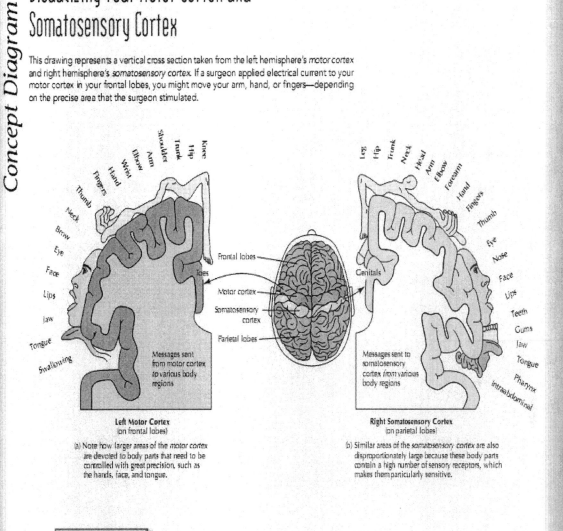

Left Motor Cortex
(on frontal lobes)

(a) Note how larger areas of the *motor cortex* are devoted to body parts that need to be controlled with great precision, such as the hands, face, and tongue.

Right Somatosensory Cortex
(on parietal lobes)

(b) Similar areas of the *somatosensory cortex* are also disproportionately large because these body parts contain a high number of sensory receptors, which makes them particularly sensitive.

Try This Yourself

Would you like a quick way to understand your motor cortex and somatosensory cortex?

1. **Motor cortex.** Try wiggling each of your fingers one at a time. Now try wiggling each of your toes. Note on this figure how the area of your motor cortex is much larger for your fingers than for your toes, thus explaining your greater control in your fingers.

2. **Somatosensory cortex.** Ask a friend to close his or her eyes. Using a random number of fingers (one to four), press down on the skin of your friend's back for one or two seconds. Then ask, "How many fingers am I using?"

    Repeat the same procedure on the palm or back of his or her hand. You will find much more accuracy when you are pressing on the hand than on the back. Again, note how the area of the somatosensory cortex is much larger for the hands than for the back, which explains the greater sensitivity in our hands versus our backs.

Concept Diagram 2.2
Explaining Split-Brain Research

Experiments on split-brain patients often present visual information to only the patient's left or right hemisphere, which leads to some intriguing results. For example,

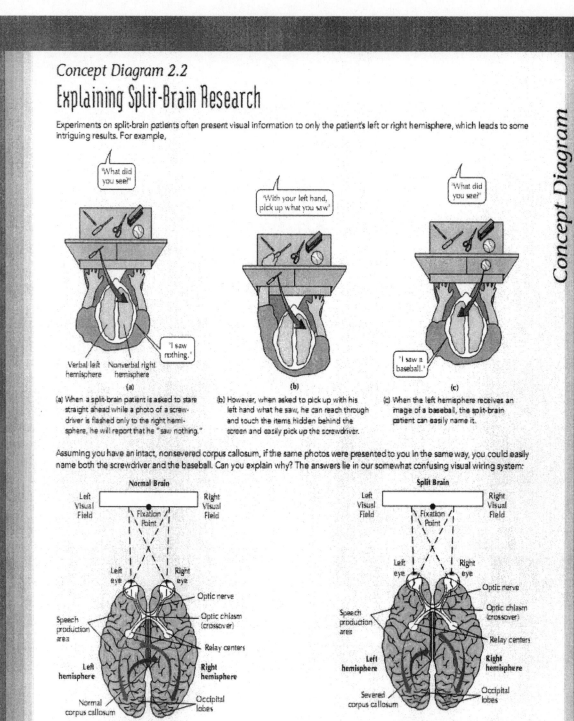

Verbal left   Nonverbal right
hemisphere   hemisphere
                (a)

(a) When a split-brain patient is asked to stare straight ahead while a photo of a screwdriver is flashed only to the right hemisphere, he will report that he "saw nothing."

(b)

(b) However, when asked to pick up with his left hand what he saw, he can reach through and touch the items hidden behind the screen and easily pick up the screwdriver.

(c)

(c) When the left hemisphere receives an image of a baseball, the split-brain patient can easily name it.

Assuming you have an intact, nonsevered corpus callosum, if the same photos were presented to you in the same way, you could easily name both the screwdriver and the baseball. Can you explain why? The answers lie in our somewhat confusing visual wiring system:

Normal Brain

Left Visual Field — Fixation Point — Right Visual Field

Left eye — Right eye

Optic nerve

Speech production area

Optic chiasm (crossover)

Relay centers

Left hemisphere   Right hemisphere

Normal corpus callosum   Occipital lobes

(d) Corpus callosum intact

Split Brain

Left Visual Field — Fixation Point — Right Visual Field

Left eye — Right eye

Optic nerve

Speech production area

Optic chiasm (crossover)

Relay centers

Left hemisphere   **Right hemisphere**

Severed corpus callosum   Occipital lobes

(e) Corpus callosum severed

As you can see in (d), our eyes connect to our brains in such a way that, when we look straight ahead, information from the left visual field (the blue line) travels to our right hemisphere, and information from the right visual field (the red line) travels to our left hemisphere. The messages received by either hemisphere are then quickly sent to the other across the corpus callosum. In this testing situation, you can easily name the objects because your right hemisphere sent the message to your left hemisphere, which controls speech in most adults. In contrast, when the corpus callosum is severed (e), and information is presented only to the right hemisphere, a split-brain patient cannot verbalize what he sees because the information cannot travel to the opposite (verbal) hemisphere.

Concept Diagram

Concept Diagram 2.3

Four Methods of Behavioral Genetics Research

1. **Twin Studies** Psychologists study twins because they have a uniquely high proportion of shared genes. Identical (monozygotic—one egg) twins share 100 percent of the same genes, whereas fraternal (dizygotic—two egg) twins share, on average, 50 percent of their genes, just like any other pair of siblings. As you can see in the figure to the right, identical twins develop from a single egg fertilized by a single sperm. They share the same placenta and have the same sex and same genetic makeup. Fraternal twins are formed when two separate sperm

Brad Wilson/Stone/Getty Images

SW Production/Age Fotostock America, Inc.

Identical twins

Same sex only

Fraternal twins

Same or opposite sex

fertilize two separate eggs. They are genetically no more alike than brothers and sisters born at different times. Fraternal twins are simply nine-month "womb mates."

Because both identical and fraternal twins share the same parents and develop in relatively the same environment, they provide a valuable type of "natural experiment." If heredity influences a trait or behavior to some degree, identical twins should be more alike than fraternal twins. As you'll see in Chapter 8, pp. 306–307, scientists use an even more stringent twin study method when they compare identical and fraternal twins who were separated very early in life and raised in different environments. If researchers find that identical twins who were reared apart are more like their biological families than their adoptive families, can you see how this provides even stronger evidence for a genetic influence?

2. **Family Studies** Why study families? If a specific trait is inherited, blood relatives should show increased trait similarity, compared with unrelated people. Also, closer relatives, like siblings, should be more similar than distant relatives. Family studies have shown that many traits and mental disorders, such as intelligence, sociability, and depression, do indeed run in families.

3. **Adoption Studies** Another "natural experiment," adoption, also provides valuable information for researchers. If adopted children are more like their biological family in some trait, then genetic factors probably had the greater influence. Conversely, if adopted children resemble their adopted family, even though they do not share similar genes, then environmental factors may predominate.

4. **Genetic Abnormalities** Research in behavioral genetics also explores disorders and diseases that result when genes malfunction. For example, an extra twenty-first chromosome fragment almost always causes a condition called *Down syndrome*. Abnormalities in several genes or chromosomes also are suspected factors in *Alzheimer's disease*, which involves serious brain deterioration and memory loss, and *schizophrenia*, a severe mental disorder characterized by loss of contact with reality.

Shared Genes

Shared Environment

Biological Parents

Adopted Child

Adoptive Parents

Concept Diagram

Chapter 2 Visual Summary

Neural Bases of Behavior

What Is a Neuron?

Neurons: Transmit information throughout the body.
Glial cells: Provide structural, nutritional, and other support for neurons, as well as some information transfer.

Key features of a neuron
* **Dendrites:** Receive information and send impulses to cell body.
* **Cell body:** Integrates incoming information.
* **Axon:** Carries information from cell body to other neurons. (**Myelin Sheath:** Fatty insulation around some axons that speeds up action potential.)

How Do Neurons Communicate?

* Communication *within the neuron* is through the **action potential**, a neural impulse that carries information along the axon.
* Communication *between neurons* occurs when an action potential reaches the axon terminal and stimulates the release of **neurotransmitters** into the **synapse**, and the chemical message is picked up by receiving neurons.

How Do Neurotransmitters and Hormones Affect Us?

Two key chemical messengers:
1. **Neurotransmitters:** Chemicals manufactured and released by neurons that alter activity in other neurons, which thereby affects behavior and mental processes.
2. **Hormones:** Chemicals released from the **endocrine system** into the bloodstream to produce bodily changes or to maintain normal bodily functions.

Nervous System Organization

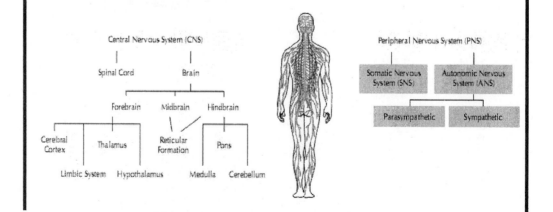

A Tour Through the Brain

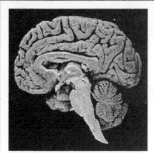

Science Pictures Limited/Photo Researchers

Three Major Sections of the Brain

* **Hindbrain:** Lower-level functions and structures (medulla, cerebellum, and pons)
* **Midbrain:** Middle of the brain (reticular formation (RF))
* **Forebrain:** Higher-level functions and structures (thalamus, hypothalamus, limbic system, and cerebral cortex)

The Cerebral Cortex

The **cerebral cortex** is responsible for all higher mental processes and is divided into four sections

Frontal Lobes

Coordinates messages from other lobes and regulates motor control, speech production, and higher functions (thinking, personality, emotion, and memory).

Parietal Lobes

Sensory processing (pressure, pain, touch, and temperature).

Temporal Lobes

Hearing, language comprehension, memory, and some emotional control.

Occipital Lobes

Vision and visual perception.

Two Brains in One

Splitting the **corpus callosum**, which normally transfers neural impulses between the brain's left and right hemispheres, is a treatment for some forms of epilepsy. **Split-brain** research on these patients shows some specialization of functions in each hemisphere.

Our Genetic Inheritance

Behavioral Genetics

Each of the 46 human **chromosomes** contains many **genes**, which are found in DNA molecules.

Genetics studies are done with twins, adopted children, families, and genetic abnormalities. Such studies allow estimates of **heritability**.

Evolutionary Psychology

Studies evolutionary principles, like **natural selection** and genetic mutations, which affect adaptation to the environment and help explain commonalities in behavior.

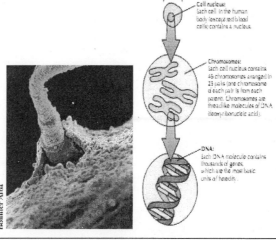

Bonnier Alba

3
Stress & Health Psychology

OUTLINE SQ4R (Survey, Question, Read, Recite, Review, & wRite)

This outline section incorporates all six steps in the well-researched SQ4R method of learning. Begin by surveying the list of chapter topics in the left column. This "big picture" will help focus and guide your attention while you read. As you read through the chapter, briefly summarize each section in your own words in the space to the right. Also write down any *questions* that come to mind. Surveying, Questioning, Reading, Reciting, Reviewing, and wRiting are the foundation of the SQ4R method and an invaluable form of active learning. They also make your reading time more enjoyable and efficient! One thorough, focused SQ4R reading of a chapter is far better than several passive readings.

TOPIC   **NOTES**

I. UNDERSTANDING STRESS

    A. Sources of Stress

        Research Highlight: Hurricane Katrina and Local College Students

        Gender & Cultural Diversity: "Karoshi"-- Can Job Stress be Fatal?

    B. Effects of Stress

        Psychology at Work: Is My Job Too Stressful?

II. STRESS AND ILLNESS

A. Cancer

B. Cardiovascular Disorders

C. Posttraumatic Stress Disorder (PTSD)

Case Study/Personal Story:
"Surviving" 9/11

Research Highlight:
Does Stress Cause Gastric Ulcers?

III. HEALTH PSYCHOLOGY IN ACTION

Psychology at Work: Would You Like to be
a Health Psychologist?

A. Tobacco

B. Alcohol

C. Chronic Pain

IV. HEALTH AND STRESS MANAGEMENT

A. Cognitive Appraisal and Coping

Psychology at Work: Why You Shouldn't Procrastinate

B. Resources for Healthy Living

Psychology at Work: Coping with TechnoStress

Critical Thinking/Active Learning:
    Reducing Stress Though Critical Thinking

LEARNING OBJECTIVES (Read, Recite, Review, & wRite)

In addition to the work you did in the Outline above, you can significantly improve your performance on exams by focusing on the following learning objectives. While reading the chapter or reviewing for exams, check your understanding by stopping periodically to *recite* (or repeat in your own words) and *writing* down your answers on a separate sheet. [Page numbers correspond to Chapter 3 in *Psychology in Action* (9e).]

3.1 Define stress, eustress, and distress. (p. 92)
3.2 What are the major sources of stress? (p. 93)
3.3 Describe the effects of Katrina on local New Orleans' college students. (p. 96)
3.4 Discuss how Karoshi is related to stress. (p. 99)
3.5 Describe the SAM system and the HPA axis. (p. 100)
3.6 How does stress affect cognitive functioning? (p. 102)
3.7 What is the generalized adaptation syndrome (GAS)? (p. 102)
3.8 How does stress affect our immune system? (p. 102)
3.9 Identify four factors important to job satisfaction. (p. 104)
3.10 How is stress related to cancer? (p. 105)
3.11 Describe the links between stress and heart disease. (p. 106)
3.12 How is stress connected to PTSD and ulcers? (p. 109)
3.13 What is health psychology? (p. 111)
3.14 Why do people start smoking, how do we prevent it, and what are the best ways to quit? (p. 112)
3.15 Describe the personal and social risks associated with alcohol. (p. 113)
3.16 What is chronic pain and how do psychologists treat it? (p. 115)
3.17 How do we cognitively appraise and cope with stress? (p. 116)
3.18 What are the best resources for stress management? (p. 318)

KEY TERMS (<u>R</u>eview & w<u>R</u>ite)

Like other survey courses, introductory psychology is filled with a "wealth" of new and unfamiliar terminology. To do well on exams, you must master this new language! Writing a brief definition of each term in the space provided and carefully reviewing them before exams will significantly improve your course grade.

Approach-Approach Conflict: _____

_____

Approach-Avoidance Conflict: _____

_____

Avoidance-Avoidance Conflict: _____

_____

Binge Drinking: _____

_____

Burnout: _____

_____

Chronic Pain: _____

_____

Chronic Stress: _____

_____

Conflict: _____

_____

Distress: _____

_____

Emotion-Focused Forms of Coping: _____

_____

Eustress: _____

_____

External Locus of Control: _____

_____

Frustration: _____

_____

General Adaptation Syndrome (GAS): _____

_____

Hardiness: _____

_____

Hassles: _____

_____

Health Psychology: _____

_____

Homeostasis: _____

_____

HPA Axis: _____

_____

Internal Locus of Control: _____

_____

Job Stress: _____

_____

Posttraumatic Stress Disorder (PTSD): _____

_____

Primary Appraisal: _____

Problem-Focused Forms of Coping: _____

_____

Psychoneuroimmunology: _____

_____

Role Conflict: _____

_____

SAM System: _____

_____

Secondary Appraisal: _____

_____

Stress: _____

_____

Type A Personality: _____

_____

Type B Personality: _____

ACTIVE LEARNING EXERCISES

True mastery of information requires you to be an ACTIVE learner. Completing the following active learning exercises will improve your understanding of the chapter material and greatly improve your performance on exams. Answers to some exercises appear in Appendix A at the end of this study guide.

ACTIVE LEARNING EXERCISE I *Create an emotion-focused and a problem-focused coping strategy for each of the following situations:*
1. It is the first day of class and you suddenly discover that your tuition check has bounced.
2. Your significant other informs you that he/she is in love with someone else.
3. Your car breaks down on a deserted country road.
4. Your car insurance has just been canceled because of a mistake on your driving record.
5. Your employer unexpectedly schedules you for work on the same day as your college class's no "make-up" final exam.

ACTIVE LEARNING EXERCISE II *Critical thinkers recognize decisions are often stressful but cannot be avoided. Avoiding a decision is, in fact, making one without the benefit of a careful analysis of the problem. To improve your decision-making skills, complete the following chart with these instructions:*
1. At the top of the chart, identify an ongoing personal conflict as approach-approach, avoidance-avoidance, or approach-avoidance.
2. On the lines in the left-hand column, list all possible alternatives or possible courses of action. Although wording like "approach-approach conflict" may imply only two choices, most conflicts involve several options or alternatives. Identifying all your options will require hard work. Research your problem and consult others.
3. List the logical outcome or consequence of each alternative. Then assess both the probability and significance of each outcome using a 0 to 5 rating scale (0 = won't occur and 5 = certain to occur). Using a similar 0 to 5 rating scale, assess the importance you place on each consequence (0 = no significance and 5 = high significance).
4. Now review the chart. In some cases, you may find it helpful to multiply your probability and significance ratings and then compare your results for the various alternatives. In other cases, you will find it difficult to assign numerical values to complex issues and feelings. Even in the most difficult decisions, however, the thinking and evaluation elicited by this chart may provide useful insights to your conflict. Also, note the feelings you associate with each alternative. Careful decision-making tries to integrate both thoughts and feelings.
5. After reviewing each alternative, ask yourself which choice is most in line with your overall goals and values. Some alternatives may look more or less appealing when weighed against long-term relationship plans, career goals, and personal belief systems. You may want to discuss your chart with a trusted friend before you make a final decision.
6. Once you make your decision, fully commit yourself. Throw away your expectations. Many decisions do not turn out the way we imagine, and if we focus on the way it is "supposed to be," we miss enjoying the way it is. On the other hand, if the decision is wrong, do not be afraid to change or correct your course. ("When you're in a hole, stop digging!")

TYPE OF CONFLICT: _____

    Alternatives   Logical Outcome   Probability   Significance

1.

2.

3.

CHAPTER OVERVIEW (Review)

The following chapter overview provides a narrative overview of the main topics covered in the chapter. Like the *Visual Summary* found at the end of each chapter in the text, this narrative summary provides a final opportunity to *review* chapter material.

I. SOURCES OF STRESS

3.1 Define stress, eustress, and distress. (p. 92)

Stress is a nonspecific response of the body to any demand made on it. The definition also includes the body's arousal, both physical and mental, to situations or events that we perceive as threatening or challenging. A situation or event that is perceived as pleasant or desirable is called **eustress**, whereas unpleasant, threatening stress is known as **distress**.

3.2 What are the major sources of stress? (p. 93)

The seven major sources of stress are life changes, chronic stressors, job stress, hassles, frustration, conflict, and cataclysmic events. Life changes require adjustment in our behaviors, which cause stress. **Chronic stress** is a state of ongoing physiological arousal, in which our parasympathetic system cannot activate the relaxation response. **Job stress** is work-related stress that includes **role conflict** and **burnout**. **Hassles** are little everyday life problems that pile up to cause major stress. **Frustration** has to do with blocked goals. **Conflict** involves two or more competing goals. Conflicts can be classified as **approach-approach, avoidance-avoidance**, or **approach-avoidance.** Cataclysmic events are stressors that occur suddenly and affect many people simultaneously.

3.3 Describe the effects of Katrina on local New Orleans' college students. (p. 96)

Researchers found that the hurricane led to both temporary and lasting ill-effects, which also exposed resiliency, strengths, and various coping mechanisms.

3.4 Discuss how Karoshi is related to stress. (p. 99)

Job stress and overwork can greatly increase your risk of dying from heart disease and stroke, and the Japanese have a specific word, "Karoshi," which means "death from overwork."

II. EFFECTS OF STRESS

3.5 Describe the SAM system and the HPA axis. (p. 100)

When stressed, the body undergoes significant biological changes due primarily to the SAM system and the HPA axis. The **SAM system** (short for Sympatho-Adreno-Medullary) provides an initial, rapid-acting stress response due to an interaction between the sympathetic nervous system and the adrenal medulla. The **HPA axis** (short fot the Hypothalamic-Pituitary-Adrenocortical) allows for a delayed stress response, involving the *hypothalamus, pituitary gland,* and *adrenal cortex.* One of the main stress hormones released by the HPA axis, cortisol, helps combat inflammation and mobilize energy resources. It also sends feedback messages to the brain and pituitary to regain **homeostasis**.

3.6 How does stress affect cognitive functioning? (p. 102)

During acute stress, cortisol can prevent the retrieval of existing memories, as well as the laying down of new memories and general information processing. Under prolonged stress, cortisol can permanently damage the hippocampus, a key part of the brain involved in memory.

3.7 What is the generalized adaptation syndrome (GAS)? (p. 102)

Hans Selye described a generalized physiological reaction to severe stressors, which he called the **general adaptation syndrome (GAS)**. It has three phases: the *alarm reaction,* the *resistance phase,* and the *exhaustion phase.*

3.8 How does stress affect our immune system? (p. 102)

Prolonged stress suppresses the immune system, which increases the risk for many diseases (e.g., colds, colitis, cancer). The new field of **psychneuroimmunology** studies the effects of stress and other factors on the immune system.

3.9 Identify four factors important to job satisfaction. (p. 104)

Supportive colleagues, supportive working conditions, mentally-challenging work, and equitable rewards are all very important to our job satisfaction.

III. STRESS AND ILLNESS

3.10 How is stress related to cancer? (p. 105)

Cancer appears to result from an interaction of heredity, environmental insults (such as smoking), and immune system deficiency. Stress may be an important cause of decreased immunity. During times of stress, the body may be less able to check cancer cell multiplication because the immune system is suppressed.

3.11 Describe the links between stress and heart disease. (p. 106)

The leading cause of death in the United States is heart disease. Risk factors include smoking, stress, obesity, a high-fat diet, lack of exercise, and **Type A personality** (if it includes cynical hostility). The two main approaches to modifying Type A behavior are the *shotgun approach* and the *target behavior approach.* People with psychological **hardiness** are less vulnerable to stress because of three distinctive personality characteristics—*commitment, control,* and *challenge.*

3.12 How is stress connected to PTSD and ulcers? (p. 109)

Exposure to extraordinary stress (like war or rape) may lead to **posttraumatic stress disorder (PTSD).** Contrary to current opinion that gastric ulcers are caused only by the *H. pylori* bacterium, psychological research shows that stress increases vulnerability to the bacterium.

IV. HEALTH PSYCHOLOGY IN ACTION

3.13 What is health psychology? (p. 111)

Health psychology, the study of how biological, psychological, and social factors affect health and illness, is a growing field in psychology with a wide variety of career opportunites.

3.14 Why do people start smoking, how do we prevent it, and what are the best ways to quit? (p. 112)

Almost everyone knows that it's dangerous to smoke, but they first begin out of curiosity, peer pressure, imitation of role models, and other motives. Once started, the addictive nature of nicotine creates a biological need to continue. Smokers also develop pleasant associations with smoking and negative associations with withdrawal.

Because smoking is the single most preventable cause of death and disease in the United States, prevention and cessation of smoking are of primary importance to all health practitioners, including health psychologists. Smoking prevention programs focus on educating the public about short- and long-term consequences of smoking, trying to make smoking less socially acceptable, and helping nonsmokers resist social pressures to smoke. For teens, the emphasis is on immediate dangers.

Most approaches to help people quit smoking include cognitive and behavioral techniques to aid smokers in their withdrawal from nicotine, along with nicotine replacement therapy (using patches, gum, and pills).

3.15 Describe the personal and social risks associated with alcohol. (p. 113)
Alcohol is one of our most serious health problems. In addition to health risks to the individual, alcohol also plays a major role in social issues, such as murder, suicide, spousal abuse, and accidental death. **Binge drinking** also is a serious problem that occurs when a man has five or more drinks in a row and a woman has four or more drinks at one time, in about two hours.

3.16 What is chronic pain and how do psychologists treat it? (p. 115)
Chronic pain is continuous or recurrent pain that persists over a period of six months or more. Although psychological factors rarely are the source of chronic pain, they can encourage and intensify it. Increased activity, exercise, and dietary changes help to reduce chronic pain. Health psychologists also use behavior modification, biofeedback, and relaxation techniques to treat chronic pain.

V. HEALTH AND STRESS MANAGEMENT
3.17 How do we cognitively appraise and cope with stress? (p. 116)
When facing a stressor, we first evaluate it in two steps: **primary appraisal** (deciding if a situation is harmful, threatening, or challenging) and **secondary appraisal** (assessing our resources and choosing a coping method). We then tend to choose either **emotion-focused coping** (attempting to manage our emotional reactions) or **problem-focused coping** (dealing directly with the situation or the factor causing the stress so as to decrease or eliminate it).

3.18 What are the best resources for stress management? (p. 318)
The ability to cope with a stressor also depends on the resources available to a person, and researchers have identified at least eight important resources: health and exercise, positive beliefs, social skills, social support, material resources, control, relaxation, and sense of humor.

SELF-TESTS (Review & wRite)

Completing the following self-tests will provide immediate feedback on how well you have mastered the material. In the labeling exercises, *crossword puzzle*, and *fill-in exercises*, write the appropriate word or words in the blank spaces. The *matching exercise* requires you to match the terms in one column to their correct definitions in the other. For the *multiple-choice questions* in Practice Tests I and II, circle or underline the correct answer. If you are unsure of any answer, mark the item, and then go back to the text for further review. Correct answers are provided in Appendix A at the end of this study guide.

Crossword Puzzle for Chapter 3

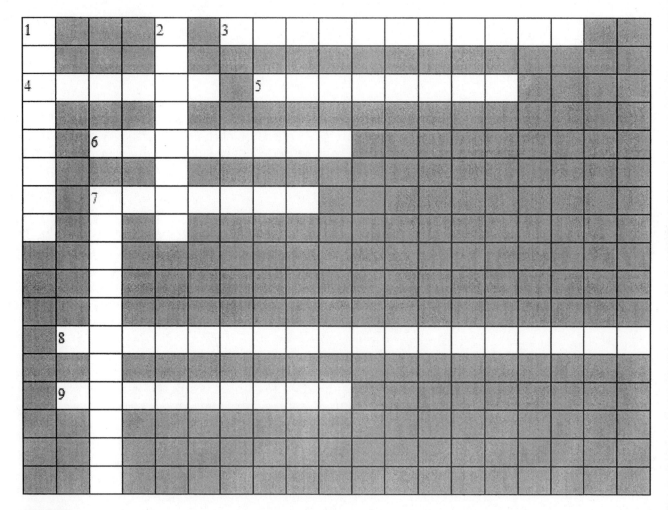

ACROSS
3. Unpleasant tension, anxiety, and heightened sympathetic activity resulting from a blocked goal
4. Nonspecific response of the body to any demand made on it; the arousal, both physical and mental, to situations or events that we perceive as threatening or challenging
5. Forced choice between two or more incompatible goals or impulses

6. State of psychological and physical exhaustion resulting from chronic exposure to high levels of stress and little personal control
7. Small problems of daily living that accumulate and sometimes become a major source of stress
8. Interdisciplinary field that studies the effects of psychological and other factors on the immune system
9. Resilient personality that includes a strong commitment to personal goals, control over life, and viewing change as a challenge rather than a threat

DOWN

1. Pleasant, desirable stress
2. Unpleasant, objectionable stress
7. Body's tendency to maintain a relatively balanced and stable internal state

FILL-IN EXERCISES

1. Unpleasant or threatening stress is called _____ (p. 92).

2. _____ are defined as small problems of daily living that accumulate and sometimes become a major source of stress (p. 94).

3. A(n) _____ conflict involves having to choose between two alternatives that will both lead to undesirable results (p. 95).

4. The three-phase bodily response to chronic stress (Selye's general adaptation syndrome) includes the _____, the _____, and the _____ (pp. 102-103).

5. Being hard driving, competitive, ambitious, impatient, and hostile is characteristic of the _____ personality. Having a laid-back, calm, relaxed attitude toward life is typical of the _____ personality (pp. 106-108).

6. The study of how biological, psychological, and social factors interact in health and illness is known as _____ (p. 111).

7. _____ occurs when a man consumes five or more drinks or a woman consumes four or more drinks in two hours (p. 114).

8. An increase in activity and exercise levels can be beneficial to pain patients because exercise increases the release of _____ (p. 115).

9. If you decide to confront a coworker to tell him/her that they are not doing their share of the work, you are using a _____ coping strategy (pp. 117-118).

10. People with a(n) _____ believe they are in charge of their own destiny (p. 120).

MATCHING EXERCISES

Column A   *Column B*

a. SAM system   1.____ Small everyday problems
b. Type A personality   2.____ Ambitious, competitive, hard driving
c. Hassles   3.____ Exhaustion from emotionally demanding situations
d. Frustration   4.____ Unpleasant state from two or more competing goals
e. Burnout   5.____ Conflict with both desirable and undesirable results
f. Hardiness   6.____ Provides an initial, rapid-acting stress response
g. Psychoneuroimmunology   7.____ Resilient personality
h. Approach-Avoidance   8.____ Alarm reaction, resistance, and exhaustion phase
i. Hans Selye   9.____ Unpleasant state resulting from a blocked goal
j. Conflict   10.____ Studies effect of psychological function on immune system

PRACTICE TEST I

1. According to your text, stress is _____.
    a. a nonspecific response of the body to any demand made on it
    b. the arousal to situations or events we perceive as threatening or challenging
    c. both of these options
    d. none of these options

2. Life changes may affect health because they _____.
    a. require adjustments in behavior and lifestyle
    b. cause us to reassess our lifestyle
    c. are always the result of something bad happening
    d. are known to increase the level of cortisol above normal

3. A bad marriage, poor working conditions, and an intolerable political climate are all examples of possible _____.
    a. life changes
    b. avoidance-avoidance conflicts
    c. chronic stressors
    d. hassles

4. An example of a(n) _____ conflict would be trying to decide which of two equally good concerts to attend on a Friday night.
    a. approach-avoidance conflict
    b. avoidance-avoidance conflict
    c. approach-approach conflict
    d. transitory positive conflict

5. Research has shown that _____ can permanently damage the hippocampus, a key part of the brain involved in memory.
    a. prolonged stress
    b. cortisol
    c. corticoamnestics
    d. all but one of these options

6. Which is **NOT** a factor known to contribute to the onset of cancer?
    a. heredity
    b. essential hypertension
    c. environment
    d. immune system changes

7. A heart attack is _____.
    a. a disorder of the lining of the heart
    b. death of heart muscle tissue
    c. elevated blood pressure that leads to death
    d. elevated blood pressure because of kidney failure

8. A laid back, calm, relaxed attitude toward life are characteristic of _____.
    a. brain disease
    b. Type A personalities
    c. Type B personalities
    d. Alzheimer's disease

9. Hardy people see change as _____.
   a. obstacles to self-actualization
   b. a challenge rather than a threat
   c. a chance for purposeful activity and problem solving
   d. opportunities for enlisting social support

10. People who survive a horrific attack or personal tragedy may develop _____.
    a. an approach-approach conflict
    b. posttraumatic stress disorder (PTSD)
    c. a problem-focused form of coping with stress
    d. a Type A personality

11. _____ studies how biological, psychological, and social factors interact in health and illness.
    a. Environmental psychology
    b. Gestalt psychology
    c. Humanistic psychology
    d. Health psychology

12. Why do young people start smoking?
    a. peer pressure
    b. imitation of role models
    c. simple curiosity
    d. all of the above

13. If you wanted to help teenagers stop smoking, you should emphasize the _____.
    a. link between nicotine and lung cancer
    b. link between nicotine and emphysema
    c. link between smoking and bad breath
    d. all of the above

14. The American Medical Association considers _____ to be the most dangerous and damaging of all drugs.
    a. cocaine
    b. methamphetamine
    c. alcohol
    d. none of these options.

15. Which of the following statements is true?
    a. Chronic pain should never last longer than a few days.
    b. Exercise is an effective way to treat chronic pain.
    c. Chronic pain is the leading cause of drug addiction in the 45- to 60-year-old age group.
    d. All of these options.

16. Naturally produced brain chemicals that reduce pain perception are called _____.
    a. opiates
    b. adrenaline
    c. endorphins
    d. epinephrine

17. During _____, we assess our resources and choose a coping method.
    a. health psychology intervention
    b. biofeedback
    c. secondary appraisal
    d. complaint-catharsis therapy

18. _____ deals directly with a stressor to decrease or eliminate it.
    a. Problem-focused coping
    b. Emotion-focused coping
    c. both of these options
    d. none of these options

19. Which of the following is a good resource for effectively coping with stress?
    a. sense of humor
    b. health and energy
    c. social skills
    d. all of these options

20. _____ refers to a person's belief that life's circumstances are under his or her internal, personal control or outside, external factors.
    a. Positive beliefs
    b. Locus of control
    c. Self-efficacy
    d. none of these options

PRACTICE TEST II

1. An unpleasant state of tension resulting from a blocked goal is called _____.
   a. conflict
   b. burnout
   c. heart disease
   d. frustration

2. _____ is a forced choice between two or more incompatible goals.
   a. Frustration
   b. Burnout
   c. Distress
   d. Conflict

3. Approach-avoidance conflicts are caused by _____.
   a. increasing life demands, hassles, and chronic stressors
   b. an exaggerated response to a real or perceived threat
   c. forced choice between two or more alternatives, both of which have desirable and undesirable results
   d. a blocked goal

4. The SAM system _____.
   a. is activated by the hypothalamus during stress
   b. increases heart rate
   c. releases hormones such as epinephrine and norepinephrine
   d. all of these options

5. Hans Selye described a generalized physiological reaction to severe stressors that he called the _____.
   a. HPA axis
   b. posttraumatic stress disorder (PTSD)
   c. general adaptation syndrome (GAS)
   d. internal locus of control (ILOC)

6. _____ is an interdisciplinary field that studies the effects of psychological factors on the immune system.
   a. Health psychology
   b. Psychiatry
   c. Psychoneuroimmunology
   d. None of the above

7. Chest pain due to an insufficient blood supply to the heart is called _____.
   a. angina
   b. heart disease
   c. atherosclerosis
   d. a heart attack

8. Having a Type A personality is associated with _____.
   a. chronic pain
   b. cancer
   c. smoking cigarettes
   d. heart disease

9. Hardiness is _____.
   a. a high level of phenylalanine
   b. a resilient personality characteristic
   c. aerobic stamina
   d. none of the above

10. An increase in acetylcholine and norepinephrine is associated with _____.
    a. nicotine
    b. any alcohol consumption
    c. binge drinking
    d. stress

11. Once you begin smoking, you continue because _____.
    a. nicotine is addictive
    b. it increases alertness
    c. it stimulates the release of dopamine
    d. all of these options

12. Chronic pain from tension headaches and lower back pain has been effectively treated by _____.
    a. EMG biofeedback
    b. EEG biofeedback
    c. psychopharmacology
    d. emotion-focused forms of coping

13. Chronic pain is frequently _____.
    a. increased by psychological factors
    b. treated with behavior modification
    c. helped by regular exercise
    d. all of these options

14. Deciding if a situation is harmful, threatening, or challenging is known as _____.
    a. problem-focused forms of coping
    b. emotional approaches
    c. primary appraisal
    d. secondary appraisal

15. When you manage your emotional reaction to stress, you are using _____.
    a. an emotion-focused form of coping
    b. a problem-solving set
    c. a problem-focused form of coping
    d. a practical defense mechanism

16. Taking this practice test is a(n) _____ form of coping.
    a. primary appraisal
    b. overachiever's
    c. problem-focused
    d. resource enlisted coping style (RECS)

17. Compared to nonprocrastinators, students who procrastinate on class assignments _____.
    a. get higher grades because they work better under pressure
    b. drop out of college in greater numbers
    c. have fewer illnesses because they are less stressed
    d. receive lower grades on term papers

18. A(n) _____ locus of control is associated with better coping skills.
    a. extrinsic
    b. internal
    c. heightened
    d. relaxed

19. John has been diagnosed with hypertension and is making no attempts to follow his doctor's advice because he thinks he has little or no power over his health. John is likely to have a(n) _____.
    a. Type-A personality
    b. hardy personality
    c. posttraumatic stress disorder (PTSD)
    d. external locus of control

20. _____ helps people recognize the difference between tense and relaxed muscles.
    a. Biomuscular training
    b. Progressive relaxation
    c. Posttraumatic stress retraining (PTSR)
    d. none of these options

Process Diagram 3.1

The Biology of Stress

Under stress, the sympathetic nervous system prepares us for immediate action—to "fight or flee." Parts of the brain and endocrine system then kick in to maintain our arousal. How does this happen? See steps 1 and 2 to the right.

1. The **SAM system** (short for *Sympatho-Adreno-Medullary*) provides an initial, rapid-acting stress response thanks to cooperation between the sympathetic nervous system and the adrenal medulla.

2. The **HPA Axis** (short for the Hypothalamic-Pituitary Adrenocortical system) responds more slowly but lasts longer. It also helps restore the body to its baseline state, *homeostasis*.

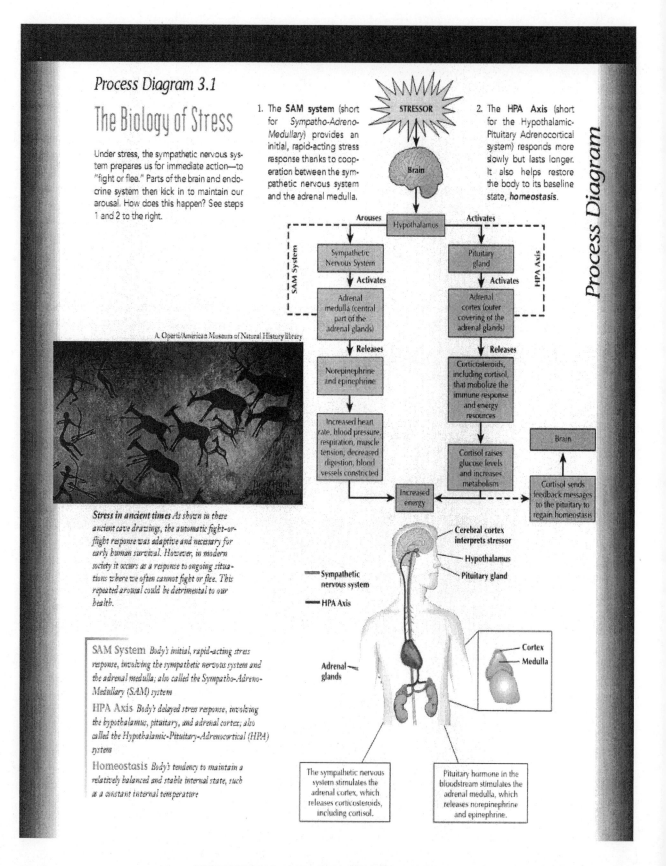

A. Operti/American Museum of Natural History Library

Stress in ancient times *As shown in these ancient cave drawings, the automatic fight-or-flight response was adaptive and necessary for early human survival. However, in modern society it occurs as a response to ongoing situations where we often cannot fight or flee. This repeated arousal could be detrimental to our health.*

SAM System *Body's initial, rapid-acting stress response, involving the sympathetic nervous system and the adrenal medulla; also called the Sympatho-Adreno-Medullary (SAM) system*

HPA Axis *Body's delayed stress response, involving the hypothalamus, pituitary, and adrenal cortex; also called the Hypothalamic-Pituitary-Adrenocortical (HPA) system*

Homeostasis *Body's tendency to maintain a relatively balanced and stable internal state, such as a constant internal temperature*

Process Diagram 3.2

The General Adaptation Syndrome (GAS)

Note how the three stages of this syndrome (*alarm, resistance,* and *exhaustion*) focus on the biological response to stress—particularly the "wear and tear" on the body with prolonged stress. As a critical thinker, can you see how the "alarm stage" corresponds to the SAM system in Process Diagram 3.1, whereas the "resistance" and "exhaustion" stages are part of the HPA axis?

(1) Alarm Reaction
In the initial *alarm reaction,* your body experiences a temporary state of shock and your resistance to illness and stress falls below normal limits.

(2) Stage of Resistance
If the stressor remains, your body attempts to endure the stressor, and enters the *resistance phase.* Physiological arousal remains higher than normal, and there is a sudden outpouring of hormones. Selye maintained that one outcome of this stage for some people is the development of *diseases of adaption,* including asthma, ulcers, and high blood pressure.

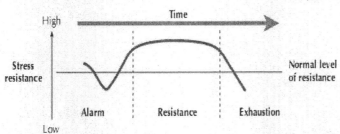

(3) Stage of Exhaustion
Long-term exposure to the stressor eventually depletes your body's reserves, and you enter the *exhaustion phase.* In this phase, you become more susceptible to serious illnesses, and possibly irreversible damage to your body. Unless a way of relieving stress is found, the result may be complete collapse and death.

Age Fotostock America, Inc.

Process Diagram

Process Diagram 3.3
Cognitive Appraisal and Coping

Research suggests that our emotional response to an event depends largely on how we interpret the event.

Brain's Interpretation

Step 1:
Primary Appraisal
Is the situation...
harmful?
threatening?
challenging?

Step 2:
Secondary Appraisal
...assess resources
...choose a coping method

Emotion-Focused Coping
Manage emotional reaction to the stressor

Problem-Focused Coping
Deal directly with a stressor to decrease or eliminate it

People often combine *emotion-focused* and *problem-focused* coping strategies to resolve complex stressors or to respond to a stressful situation that is in flux. In some situations, an emotion-focused strategy can allow people to step back from an especially overwhelming problem. Then they can reappraise the situation and use the problem-solving approach to look for solutions. Can you see how each form of coping is represented in these two photos?

©AP/Wide World Photos

©AP/Wide World Photos

Process Diagram

Chapter 3 Visual Summary

Understanding Stress

Sources of Stress

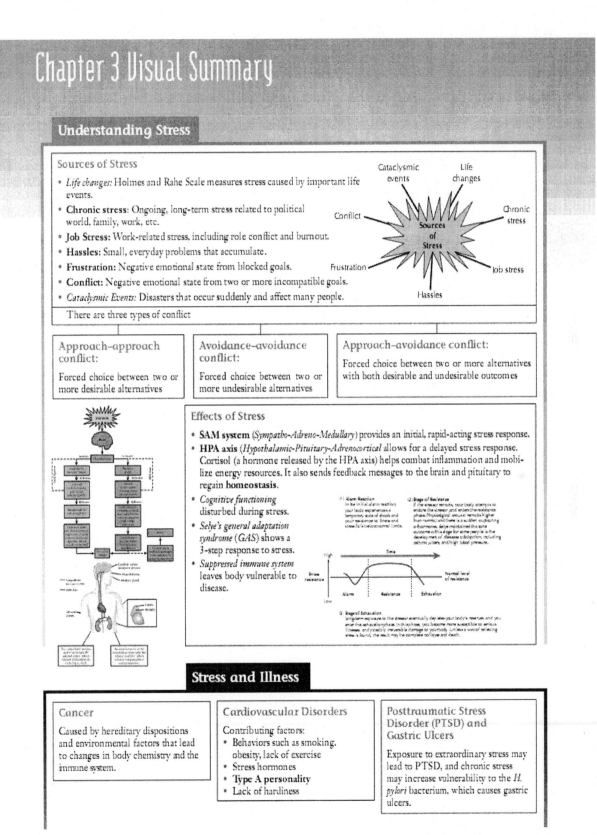

- *Life changes:* Holmes and Rahe Scale measures stress caused by important life events.
- **Chronic stress:** Ongoing, long-term stress related to political world, family, work, etc.
- **Job Stress:** Work-related stress, including role conflict and burnout.
- **Hassles:** Small, everyday problems that accumulate.
- **Frustration:** Negative emotional state from blocked goals.
- **Conflict:** Negative emotional state from two or more incompatible goals.
- *Cataclysmic Events:* Disasters that occur suddenly and affect many people.

There are three types of conflict

Approach–approach conflict:

Forced choice between two or more desirable alternatives

Avoidance–avoidance conflict:

Forced choice between two or more undesirable alternatives

Approach–avoidance conflict:

Forced choice between two or more alternatives with both desirable and undesirable outcomes

Effects of Stress

- **SAM system** (*Sympatho-Adreno-Medullary*) provides an initial, rapid-acting stress response.
- **HPA axis** (*Hypothalamic-Pituitary-Adrenocortical*) allows for a delayed stress response. Cortisol (a hormone released by the HPA axis) helps combat inflammation and mobilize energy resources. It also sends feedback messages to the brain and pituitary to regain **homeostasis**.
- *Cognitive functioning* disturbed during stress.
- *Selye's general adaptation syndrome (GAS)* shows a 3-step response to stress.
- *Suppressed immune system* leaves body vulnerable to disease.

Stress and Illness

Cancer

Caused by hereditary dispositions and environmental factors that lead to changes in body chemistry and the immune system.

Cardiovascular Disorders

Contributing factors:
- Behaviors such as smoking, obesity, lack of exercise
- Stress hormones
- **Type A personality**
- Lack of hardiness

Posttraumatic Stress Disorder (PTSD) and Gastric Ulcers

Exposure to extraordinary stress may lead to PTSD, and chronic stress may increase vulnerability to the *H. pylori* bacterium, which causes gastric ulcers.

Health Psychology in Action

Tobacco

* *Why do people smoke?* Curiosity, peer pressure, role models, addictive properties of nicotine, pleasant associations with smoking, and negative (withdrawal) experiences when not smoking.

* *Prevention?* Educate about short- and long-term consequences, help nonsmokers resist social pressures, and make smoking less convenient and socially acceptable, while emphasizing the financial costs.

* *Stopping?* Use cognitive and behavioral techniques to deal with withdrawal; supplement with nicotine replacement therapy (patches, gum, and pills).

Alcohol

Alcohol is one of our most serious health problems.
Binge drinking: When a man consumes 5 or more drinks, or a woman consumes 4 or more in about 2 hours.

Chronic Pain

Chronic pain: Pain lasting 6 months or longer.
How to reduce?

* Increase activity and exercise.

* Use behavior modification strategies to reinforce changes.

* Employ *biofeedback* with *electromyograph (EMG)* to reduce muscle tension.

* Use relaxation techniques.

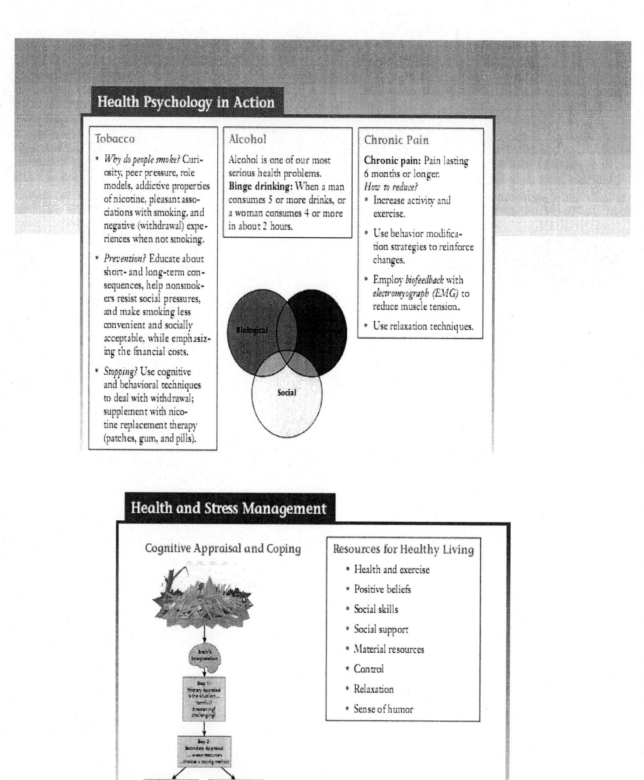

Health and Stress Management

Cognitive Appraisal and Coping

Resources for Healthy Living

* Health and exercise
* Positive beliefs
* Social skills
* Social support
* Material resources
* Control
* Relaxation
* Sense of humor

4
Sensation & Perception

OUTLINE SQ4R (Survey, Question, Read, Recite, Review, & wRite)

This outline section incorporates all six steps in the well-researched SQ4R method of learning. Begin by surveying the list of chapter topics in the left column. This "big picture" will help focus and guide your attention while you read. As you read through the chapter, briefly summarize each section in your own words in the space to the right. Also write down any *questions* that come to mind. Surveying, Questioning, Reading, Reciting, Reviewing, and wRiting are the foundation of the SQ4R method and an invaluable form of active learning. They also make your reading time more enjoyable and efficient! One thorough, focused SQ4R reading of a chapter is far better than several passive readings.

TOPIC	NOTES

I. UNDERSTANDING SENSATION

   A. Processing

   B. Thresholds

   Psychology at Work: Do Subliminal
     Messages Improve Sales?

   C. Adaptation

   Case Study/Personal Story:
     Helen Keller's Triumph and Advice

II. HOW WE SEE AND HEAR

   A. Vision

   B. Hearing

Research Highlight: Perfect
        Yet (Imperfect) Pitch

III. OUR OTHER SENSES

A. Smell and Taste

B. The Body Senses

IV. UNDERSTANDING PERCEPTION

A. Selection

B. Organization

Gender & Cultural Diversity:
        Are the Gestalt Laws Universally True?

C. Interpretation

Research Highlight: Is There Scientific
        Evidence for Extrasensory Perception (ESP)?

Critical Thinking/Active Learning: Problems
        with Believing in Extrasensory Perception (ESP)

LEARNING OBJECTIVES (Read, Recite, Review, & wRite)

In addition to the work you did in the Outline above, you can significantly improve your performance on exams by focusing on the following learning objectives. While reading the chapter or reviewing for exams, check your understanding by stopping periodically to *recite* (or repeat in your own words) and *writing* down your answers on a separate sheet. [Page numbers correspond to Chapter 4 in *Psychology in Action* (9e).]

4.1 Contrast sensation and perception, and compare bottom-up processing with top-down processing. (p. 128)
4.2 Explain how transduction, coding, and sensory reduction turn raw sensory data into signals the brain can understand. (p. 129)
4.3 Define psychophysics, and differentiate between absolute and difference thresholds. (p. 131)

4.4 What are the effects of subliminal stimuli? (p. 132)

4.5 Define sensory adaptation and explain why it is helpful. (p. 133)

4.6 Explain the gate-control theory of pain perception. (p. 133)

4.7 What can Helen Keller teach us about sensation and perception? (p. 134)

4.8 What is light? (p. 136)

4.9 Identify the key structures and functions of the eye. (p. 136)

4.10 Identify common problems with vision. (p. 138)

4.11 Contrast the trichromatic, opponent-process, and dual-process theories of color vision. (p. 139)

4.12 Define audition and identify the three key parts of the ear. (p. 141)

4.13 Briefly explain the physical properties of sound waves. (p. 141)

4.14 Describe the place and frequency theories related to hearing. (p. 143)

4.15 Differentiate between conduction and nerve deafness. (p. 143)

4.16 Define and discuss the research on "perfect pitch." (p. 144)

4.17 Briefly explain the processes of olfaction and gestation. (p. 146)

4.18 What are the body senses, and how do they work? (p. 148)

4.19 What are illusions and why are they important? (p. 150)

4.20 Describe the selection process and its three key factors—selective attention, feature detectors, and habituation. (p. 150)

4.21 Describe the Gestalt laws of perceptual organization. (p. 153)

4.22 Do the Gestalt laws apply cross-culturally? (p. 155)

4.23 What are perceptual constancies, and why are they important? (p. 156)

4.24 How do we perceive depth, and why are binocular and monocular cues important? (p. 156)

4.25 What factors influence how we interpret sensations? (p. 158)

4.26 What is ESP, and why is it so controversial? (p. 161)

4.27 Identify four forms of faulty reasoning behind ESP. (p. 162)

KEY TERMS (Review & wRite)

Like other survey courses, introductory psychology is filled with a "wealth" of new and unfamiliar terminology. To do well on exams, you must master this new language! Writing a brief definition of each term in the space provided and carefully reviewing them before exams will significantly improve your course grade.

Absolute Threshold: _____

_____

Accommodation: _____

_____

Amplitude: _____

_____

Audition: _____

_____

Binocular Cues: _____

_____

Blind Spot: _____

_____

Bottom-Up Processing: _____

_____

Cochlea: _____

_____

Coding: _____

_____

Conduction Deafness: _____

_____

Cones: _____

_____

Convergence: _____

_____

Depth Perception: _____

_____

Difference Threshold: _____

_____

Extrasensory Perception (ESP): _____

_____

Farsightedness (hyperopia): _____

_____

Feature Detectors: _____

_____

Fovea: _____

_____

Frequency: _____

_____

Frequency Theory: _____

_____

Gate-Control Theory of Pain: _____

_____

Gustation: _____

_____

Habituation: _____

_____

Illusion: _____

_____

Inner Ear: _____

_____

Kinesthesia: _____

_____

Middle Ear: _____

_____

Monocular Cues: _____

_____

Nearsightedness (myopia): _____

_____

Nerve Deafness: _____

_____

Olfaction: _____

_____

Opponent-Process Theory: _____

_____

Outer Ear: _____

_____

Perception: _____

_____

Perceptual Constancy: _____

_____

Perceptual Set: _____

_____

Pheromones: _____

_____

Place Theory: _____

_____

Psychophysics: _____

_____

Retina: _____

_____

Retinal Disparity: _____

_____

Rods: _____

_____

Selective Attention: _____

_____

Sensation: _____

_____

Sensory Adaptation: _____

_____

Sensory Reduction: _____

_____

Subliminal: _____

_____

Synesthesia: _____

_____

Top-Down Processing: _____

_____

Transduction: _____

_____

Trichromatic Theory: _____

_____

Wavelength: _____

_____

ACTIVE LEARNING EXERCISES

True mastery of information requires you to be an ACTIVE learner. Completing the following active learning exercises will improve your understanding of the chapter material and greatly improve your performance on exams. Answers to some exercises appear in Appendix A at the end of this study guide.

ACTIVE LEARNING EXERCISE I

Auditory Perception

Have you noticed that music often sounds better when it is played loudly, but not to the point that it hurts your ears? This is primarily because very high and very low frequencies are not perceived as well at a low volume. The music sounds "flat."

To try this yourself, find a stereo system with separate bass and treble controls and a "loudness" button. Set the bass and treble controls to their middle position, while making sure the "loudness" button is off.

Now choose your favorite music, turn on the stereo, and then increase the volume until the music sounds best to you. (Be careful not to overdo the volume. As you discovered in the text, loud noises can permanently damage your hearing.) Try decreasing the volume. The music should begin to seem "flat" or not as pleasing as before. Experiment with increasing only the low or high bass and treble. Turn on the "loudness" button and note how the music automatically sounds better. This button is specifically designed to amplify the highs and lows.

This exercise may help you enjoy your music more without excessive volume (and potential hearing loss). Just make sure that you can perceive all frequencies, not just those in the middle range.

ACTIVE LEARNING EXERCISE II

Empathizing (An Affective Skill)

In Chapter 4, you read about Helen Keller, an extraordinary woman who was blind from infancy. The following exercise will improve your ability to empathize a bit with her and other visually handicapped people you might know. As you have read in the text, noncritical thinkers view everything and everyone else in relationship to themselves. They fail to understand or appreciate another's thoughts, feelings, or behaviors, as critical thinkers do.

Find a partner to take you on a "blind walk" for at least 20 to 30 minutes. Have the person first blindfold you and then lead you on a walk filled with varied sensory experiences. Go up a hill, over a gravel driveway, across a dirt field full of potholes, through the college cafeteria, next to a rough wall, past an open freezer door, through a quiet library, etc. Try to identify each of these varied sensory experiences. Now exchange roles and lead your partner on a similar "blind walk."

What happened when you or your partner were without your sense of sight? Did you adapt? How did you compensate for your lack of sight?

ACTIVE LEARNING EXERCISE III

Are Psychics for Real?
(Contributed by Thomas Frangicetto)

Imagine you are watching the local TV news and the commentator says: "We're going to take a look at a real life medium, Valerie Morrison. Tonight we really put her to the test. Can she help the Fairmount Police Department solve some cold case murders?" Morrison is escorted by a police captain into Room 800 where evidence from 60,000 cases is stored. The medium performs quick readings of several sealed, brown envelopes and then focuses on a pair of running shoes inside a clear plastic bag. She begins speaking from the supposed point-of-view of the victim:

> **Morrison**: *My legs are numb...I see a child, more like a child in-between...a person grown up, yet a child... feel a woman...raped...blood, lots of blood...there's something going wrong with my body...I feel pain (grabs neck)... I can't breathe...I feel trapped...man...woman...*
> **Police Captain**: *Can you give me a description of the man?*
> **Morrison**: *The man that did it...the man that did it...he's 6, no, 5 (feet) 10, 5 (feet) 11...dark-skinned features...*
> **Commentator**: *It sounds like Morrison is describing the unsolved case of the Fairmount Park rapist and his first victim, Rebecca Park, who was raped and* strangled last year.
> **Police Captain**: *We need to stop! I've got enough information.*
> **Commentator** (turning to the camera): *As you can see, the medium's information has clearly impressed the Captain! He's so convinced that he's referred the case on to the homicide unit. He's also asked that we not divulge other information she provided, including a street name, house description, and an area of the city where the killer might live. Rest assured, we'll keep tabs on this case and let you know how it turns out.*

Critical Thinking Exercise: What do you think? Are you a true believer in the validity of psychic ability? Or are you a skeptic, one of the ardent disbelievers? This exercise will help clarify your critical thinking skills on this highly controversial topic. It also provides a brief review of several important key terms found in Chapter 4.

Step 1. Briefly explain how each of the following key terms might be applied to this situation. *Top-Down Processing, Selective Attention, Habituation, Perceptual Set, Extrasensory Perception*

Step 2. Two critical thinking components (CTCs) from the Prologue of your text are particularly helpful in evaluating claims of psychic abilities.
   * Recognizing personal biases
   * Analyzing data for value and content
Write a brief explanation of how these CTCs could be used to explain Morrison's supposed psychic abilities. **Check your answers to this exercise in Appendix A at the end of this Study Guide.**

CHAPTER OVERVIEW (Review)

The following chapter overview provides a narrative overview of the main topics covered in the chapter. Like the *Visual Summary* found at the end of each chapter in the text, this narrative summary provides a final opportunity to *review* chapter material.

I. UNDERSTANDING SENSATION

Objective 4.1: Contrast sensation and perception, and compare bottom-up processing with top-down processing. (pp. 128-129)

Sensation refers to the process of receiving, converting, and transmitting raw sensory data to the brain. **Perception** is the process of selecting, organizing, and interpreting sensory information into useful mental representations of the world. **Bottom-up processing** refers to information processing that begins "at the bottom" with raw sensory data that are sent "up" to the brain for higher-level analysis. **Top-down processing** starts "at the top," with higher-level cognitive processes (such as, expectations and knowledge), and then works down.

Objective 4.2: Explain how transduction, coding, and sensory reduction turn raw sensory data into signals the brain can understand. (pp. 129-130)

Sensory processing includes *transduction, reduction,* and *coding.* **Transduction** converts receptor energy into neural impulses that are sent to the brain, and **coding** converts these sensory inputs into different sensations (e.g., sight versus sound). Through **sensory reduction** we eliminate excessive and unnecessary sensory stimuli.

Objective 4.3: Define psychophysics, and differentiate between absolute and difference thresholds. (p. 131)

Psychophysics studies the link between the physical characteristics of stimuli and our sensory experience of them. The **absolute threshold** is the smallest magnitude of a stimulus we can detect. The **difference threshold** is the smallest change in a stimulus that we can detect.

Objective 4.4: What are the effects of subliminal stimuli? (pp. 132-133)

Research shows that we can perceive **subliminal** stimuli that are presented below our conscious awareness. However, they are weak stimuli that have little or no effect.

Objective 4.5: Define sensory adaptation and explain why it is helpful. (p. 133)

Sensory adaptation is a decrease in sensory sensitivity as a result of repeated or constant stimulation. It offers important survival benefits because can't afford to waste time paying attention to unchanging stimuli.

Objective 4.6: Explain the gate-control theory of pain perception. (pp. 133-134)

According to the **gate-control theory** of pain perception, our experience of pain depends in part on a "gate" in the spinal cord that either blocks or allows pain signals to pass on to the brain.

Objective 4.7: What can Helen Keller teach us about sensation and perception? (p. 134)

Helen Keller was blind and deaf from an early age, but she learned to use her remaining senses to achieve greatness, and she reminds us to fully appreciate all our senses.

II. HOW WE SEE
Objective 4. 8: What is light? (p. 136)
Light is a form of energy that is part of the electromagnetic spectrum. The **wavelength** of a light determines its *hue*, or color; how often a light or sound wave cycles is known as the **frequency**; and the **amplitude**, or height of a light wave, determines its *intensity* or brightness.

Objective 4. 9: Identify the key structures and functions of the eye. (pp. 136-138)
The function of the eye is to capture light and focus it on visual receptors that convert light energy into neural impulses. Light enters through the pupil and lens to the retina, and then travels along the optic nerve to the brain. Cells in the **retina** called **rods** are specialized for night vision. **Cones** are specialized for color and fine detail.

Objective 4. 10: Identify common problems with vision. (pp. 138-140)
Nearsightedness (myopia) and *farsightedness* (hyperopia) result from problems with the lens and cornea focusing the image in front or behind the retina. *Presbyopia* occurs when the lens becomes less flexible. *Light adaptation* and *dark adaptation* result from visual peculiarities related to the rods and cones. *Dichromats* and *monochromats* are terms related to problems with color perception.

Objective 4. 11: Contrast the trichromatic, opponent-process, and dual-process theories of color vision. (pp. 139-140)
The **trichromatic theory** proposes three color systems in the retina, each of which is maximally sensitive to blue, green, or red. The **opponent-process theory** also proposes three color systems, but holds that each responds in an "either-or" fashion—blue or yellow, red or green, and black or white. According to the modern dual-process theory, both previous theories are correct. The trichromatic theory operates at the level of the retina, whereas the opponent-process theory occurs in the brain.

III. HOW WE HEAR
Objective 4.12: Define audition and identify the three key parts of the ear. (pp. 141-142)
The sense of hearing is known as **audition**. The **outer ear** conducts sound waves to the **middle ear**, which in turn conducts vibrations to the **inner ear**. Hair cells in the inner ear are bent by a traveling wave in the fluid of the **cochlea** and transduced into neural impulses. The neural impulse is then carried along the auditory nerve to the brain.

Objective 4.13: Briefly explain the physical properties of sound waves. (pp. 141-143)
We hear sound via sound waves, which result from rapid changes in air pressure caused by vibrating objects. The wavelength of these sound waves is sensed as the *pitch* of the sound. The amplitude of the waves is perceived as *loudness*. And the range of sound waves is sensed as *timbre*, the purity or complexity of the tone.

Objective 4.14: Describe the place and frequency theories related to hearing. (p. 143)
Place theory proposes that pitch perception corresponds to the particular spot (or place) on the cochlea's basilar membrane that is most stimulated. **Frequency theory** suggests that pitch perception occurs when nerve impulses sent to the brain match the frequency of the sound waves. Both place and frequency theories are correct, but place theory best explains how we hear high-pitched sounds, whereas frequency theory best explains how we hear low-pitched sounds.

Objective 4.15: Differentiate between conduction and nerve deafness. (pp. 143-144)
Conduction deafness results from problems with transferring sound waves to the cochlea, whereas nerve deafness involves damage to the inner ear or auditory nerve.

Objective 4.16: Define and discuss the research on "perfect pitch." (p. 144-145)
Perfect pitch is the ability to recognize individual sound frequencies without any external reference, which results from a rare genetic trait and learning. The fact that these people still make a few consistent mistakes may help researchers better understand neuroplasticity, or how the brain changes with experience.

IV. OUR OTHER SENSES
Objective 4.17: Briefly explain the processes of olfaction and gestation. (pp. 146-148)
The sense of smell **(olfaction)** and the sense of taste **(gustation)** are called the chemical senses and are closely interrelated. The receptors for olfaction are at the top of the nasal cavity. The receptors for gustation are located primarily on the tongue and are sensitive to five basic tastes: salty, sweet, sour, bitter, and umami.

Objective 4.18: What are the body senses, and how do they work? (pp. 148-149).
The body senses are the skin senses, the vestibular sense, and the **kinesthesia**. The skin senses detect touch or pressure, temperature, and pain. The vestibular apparatus is located in the inner ear and supplies balance information. The kinesthetic sense provides the brain with information about body posture and orientation, as well as body movement. The kinesthetic receptors are spread throughout the body in muscles, joints, and tendons.

V. SELECTION
Objective 4.19: What are illusions and why are they important? (p. 150)
Illusions are false or misleading perceptions that can be produced by actual physical distortions, as in desert mirages, or by errors in perception. These errors allow psychologists insight into normal perceptual processes.

Objective 4.20: Describe the selection process and its three key factors—selective attention, feature detectors, and habituation. (pp. 150-153)
The selection process allows us to choose which of the billions of separate sensory messages will eventually be processed. **Selective attention** allows us to direct our attention to the most important aspect of the environment at any one time. **Feature detectors** are specialized cells in the brain that distinguish between different sensory inputs. The selection process is very sensitive to changes in the environment. We **habituate** to unchanging stimuli and pay attention when stimuli change in intensity, novelty, location, and so on.

VI. ORGANIZATION—FORM AND CONSTANCIES
Objective 4.21: Describe the Gestalt laws of perceptual organization. (pp. 153-155)
The Gestalt psychologists set forth laws explaining how people perceive form. The most fundamental principle is the distinction between *figure and ground*. Other principles include *proximity, continuity, closure,* and *similarity*.

Objective 4.22: Do the Gestalt laws apply cross-culturally? (pp. 155-156)
Some believe that these laws only apply to cultures formally educated in geometrical concepts, while others say the laws reflect experience with two-dimensional figures portraying three-dimensional forms.

Objective 4.23: What are perceptual constancies, and why are they important? (pp. 156-157)
Through the **perceptual constancies** of *size, shape, color,* and *brightness,* we are able to perceive a stable environment, even though the actual sensory information we receive may be constantly changing. These constancies are based on our prior experiences and learning.

VII. DEPTH PERCEPTION, INTERPRETATION, AND ESP
Objective 4.24: How do we perceive depth, and why are binocular and monocular cues important? (pp. 156-160)
Depth perception allows us to accurately estimate the distance of perceived objects and thereby perceive the world in three dimensions. But how do we perceive a three-dimensional world with two-dimensional receptors called eyes? There are two major types of cues: **binocular cues,** which require two eyes, and **monocular cues,** which require only one eye. The binocular cues are **retinal disparity** and **convergence.** Monocular cues include *linear perspective, aerial perspective, texture gradients, interposition, light and shadow, relative size, accommodation,* and *motion parallax.*

Objective 4.25: What factors influence how we interpret sensations? (pp. 158-161)
Interpretation, the final stage of perception, can be influenced by *perceptual adaptation,* **perceptual set,** and frame of reference.

Objective 4.26: What is ESP, and why is it so controversial? (pp. 161-162)
Extrasensory perception (ESP) is the supposed ability to perceive things outside the normal senses. ESP research has produced "fragile" results, and critics condemn its lack of experimental control and replicability.

Objective 4.27: Identify four forms of faulty reasoning behind ESP. (p. 162).
Belief in ESP may reflect the *fallacy of positive instances, innumeracy, willingness to suspend disbelief,* and the *"vividness"* problem.

SELF-TESTS (<u>R</u>eview & w<u>R</u>ite)

Completing the following self-tests will provide immediate feedback on how well you have mastered the material. In the labeling exercises, *crossword puzzle*, and *fill-in exercises*, write the appropriate word or words in the blank spaces. The *matching exercise* requires you to match the terms in one column to their correct definitions in the other. For the *multiple-choice questions* in Practice Tests I and II, circle or underline the correct answer. If you are unsure of any answer, mark the item, and then go back to the text for further review. Correct answers are provided in Appendix A at the end of this study guide.

LABELING EXERCISES

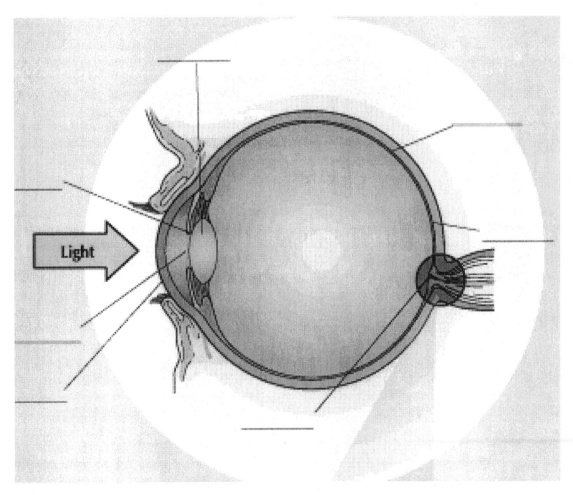

Enter the correct label on each line and then compare your answers with Process Diagram 4.1 p. 137

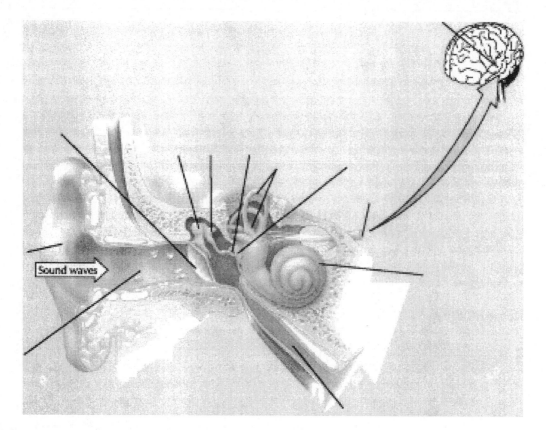

Enter the correct label on each line and then compare your answers with Process Diagram 4.2 p. 142

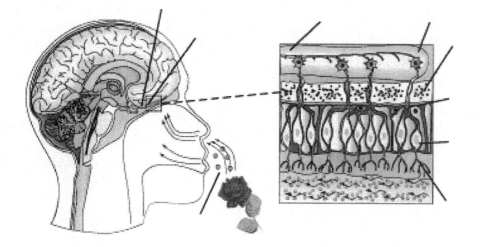

Enter the correct label on each line and then compare your answers with Process Diagram 4.3 p. 147

CROSSWORD PUZZLE FOR CHAPTER 4

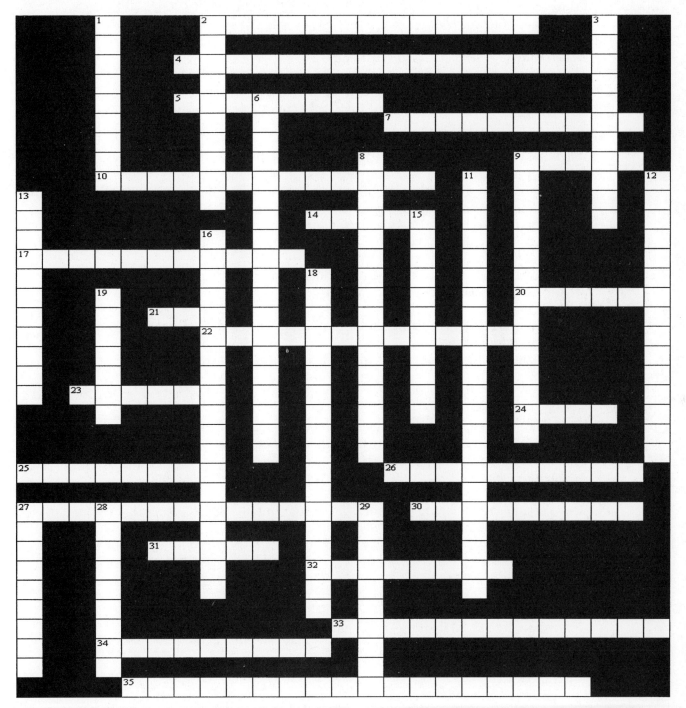

ACROSS

2 Study of the relation between attributes of the physical world and our psychological experience of them.

4 Repeated or constant stimulation decreases the number of sensory messages sent to the brain, which causes decreased sensation.

5 Intensity of sound determined by the amplitude of sound waves.

7 Distances between the crests (or peaks) of light or sound waves.

9 A tiny pit in the center of the retina filled with cones and responsible for sharp vision.

10 Inner-ear deafness resulting from damage to the cochlear hair cells or auditory nerve.

14 Tone or sound determined by the frequency of vibration of the sound waves.

17 Binocular depth cue in which the closer the object, the more the eyes converge, or turn inward.

20 Process that converts a particular sensory input into a specific sensation.

21 Visual dimension seen as a particular color; determined by the length of a light wave.

22 Readiness to perceive in a particular manner, based on expectations.

23 Light-sensitive inner surface of the back of the eye, which contains the receptor cells for vision.

24 Receptor cells in the retina that detect shades of gray, are responsible for peripheral vision, and are most sensitive in dim light.

25 Sense of hearing.

26 Process of selecting, organizing, and interpreting sensory data into useful mental representations of the world.

27 Visual acuity problem that results when the cornea and lens focus an image behind the retina.

30 Height of a light or sound wave; pertaining to light, it refers to brightness, and for sound, it refers to loudness.

31 Visual receptors concentrated near the center of the retina that are responsible for color vision and fine detail; most sensitive in brightly lit conditions.

32 False impression of the environment.

33 Visual input from two eyes that allows perception of depth or distance.

34 Sense of smell.

35 Three arching structures in the inner ear, which contain hair receptors that respond to head movements in order to provide information on balance.

DOWN

1 Sense of taste.

2 Airborne chemicals that affect behavior, including recognition of family members, aggression, territorial marking, and sexual mating.

3 Sensory system for body posture and orientation.

6 Minimal difference needed to notice a stimulus change; also called the just noticeable difference (JND).

8 Specialized neurons that respond only to certain sensory information.

9 Theory explaining how we hear lower-pitched sounds.

11 Perceptual, or "psychic," abilities that supposedly go beyond the known senses, including telepathy, clairvoyance, precognition, and psychokinesis.

12 Visual acuity problem that occurs when the cornea and lens focus an image in front of the retina.

13 Theory explaining how we hear higher-pitched sounds.

15 Tendency of the brain to ignore environmental factors that remain constant.

16 Tendency for the environment to be perceived as remaining the same even with changes in sensory input.

18 Filtering out and attending only to important sensory messages.

19 Three-chambered, snail-shaped structure in the inner ear that contains the receptors for hearing.

27 How often a light or sound wave cycles.

28 Process of receiving, translating, and transmitting raw sensory data from the external and internal environments to the brain.

29 Pertaining to any stimulus presented below the threshold of conscious awareness.

FILL-IN EXERCISES

1. _____ is a type of data driven processing that moves from the parts to the whole, whereas _____ is conceptually driven and moves from the whole to the parts (p. 129).

2. _____ is the branch of psychology that studies the relation between the physical characteristics of stimuli and our sensory experience of them _____ (p. 131).

3. In light waves, the wavelength determines the _____, whereas the amplitude determines _____ (p. 136).

4. Light waves first enter the eye through a rough transparent shield called the _____. They then pass through a small opening called the _____, and are then focused by the muscularly-controlled _____ onto the _____ at the back of the eye (pp. 136-138).

5. The process of _____ allows our eyes to gradually adjust to dim or dark light (p. 139).

6. _____ results from damage to the cochlea, hair cells, or auditory nerve, which may be caused by exposure to loud noise (p. 143).

7. False impressions of the physical world produced by physical distortions (such as desert mirages) are known as _____ (p. 150).

8. A decrease in response of a sensory system to continuous stimulation is known as_____, whereas _____ involves the tendency of the brain to ignore environmental factors that remain constant (p. 152)

9. _____ are depth cues requiring one eye, whereas _____ are depth cues involving both eyes (pp. 158-160).

10. The supposed "psychic" ability to read others' minds is called _____ (p. 161).

MATCHING EXERCISES

Column A

a. Olfaction
b. Transduction
c. Sensory Adaptation
d. Cones
e. Audition
f. ESP
g. Blind Spot
h. Accommodation
i. Electromagnetic Spectrum
j. Depth Perception

Column B

1. _____ Part of the retina lacking visual receptors.
2. _____ Band of radiant energy from the sun.
3. _____ Bulging and flattening of the lens for focusing.
4. _____ Supposed "psychic" abilities.
5. _____ Decrease in response from constant stimulation.
6. _____ Receptors that respond to color and fine detail.
7. _____ Sense of hearing.
8. _____ Sense of smell.
9. _____ Ability to perceive distance and 3-D.
10. _____ Receptors convert stimuli into neural impulse.

PRACTICE TEST I

1. _____ starts at the "bottom" with raw sensory data that are sent "up" to the brain for higher level analysis
   a. Perception
   b. Bottom-up processing
   c. Sensation
   d. Integration

2. Converting a receptor's energy into a neural impulse is called _____.
   a. reduction
   b. conduction
   c. transduction
   d. neural stimulation

3. The _____ is the lowest or quietest sound people can hear.
   a. threshold of excitation
   b. absolute threshold
   c. difference threshold
   d. low point

4. The _____ of light determines its hue, whereas the _____ determines its brightness.
   a. wavelength, amplitude
   b. pitch, wavelength
   c. timbre, amplitude
   d. wavelength, frequency

5. _____ are involved with color vision, whereas _____ are responsible for dim or night vision.
   a. Rods, cones
   b. Hair cells, cilia
   c. Lens, cornea
   d. Cones, rods

6. _____ results when the cornea and lens focus an image in front of the retina.
   a. Presbyopia
   b. Hyperopia
   c. Myopia
   d. None of these options

7. The _____ amplifies sound and sends it along to the cochlea's oval window.
   a. pinna
   b. middle ear
   c. inner ear
   d. outer ear

8. Airborne chemicals released from one individual that affect another individual's behavior are known as _____.
   a. olfactory attractants
   b. sexual odorificants
   c. pheromones
   d. olfactory hormones

9. The skin senses include pressure, pain, and _____.
   a. posture
   b. movement
   c. balance
   d. temperature

10. The _____ sense is located in the inner ear and is responsible for our sense of balance.
    a. auditory
    b. gustatory
    c. kinesthetic
    d. vestibular

11. Filtering out and attending only to important sensory messages is the definition of _____.
    a. love-at-first sight
    b. selective attention
    c. transduction
    d. habituation

12. Which of the following is the most fundamental Gestalt principle of organization?
    a. roundness
    b. isolation
    c. symmetry
    d. figure and ground

13. Monocular and binocular are two cues for _____.
    a. depth perception
    b. size adaptations
    c. perceptual constancies
    d. visual corrections

14. The neuromuscular cue to distance caused by both eyes turning in or out to focus on an object is called _____.
    a. binocular rivalry
    b. retinal disparity
    c. convergence
    d. accommodation

15. When an observer moves, near objects seem to pass quickly, intermediate objects seem to pass rather slowly, and far objects seem to stand almost still. The name of this monocular cue is _____.
    a. linear perspective
    b. accommodation
    c. relative size
    d. motion parallax

16. The readiness to perceive in a particular manner based on expectations is called _____.
    a. perceptual bias
    b. selective attention
    c. the self-fulfilling prophecy
    d. perceptual set

17. Thanks to _____, an elephant is perceived as much larger when it is standing next to a mouse than it is when it stands next to a giraffe.
    a. telekinesis
    b. hallucinations
    c. illusions
    d. frame of reference

18. The supposed "psychic" ability to predict the future is called _____.
    a. telekinesis
    b. telepathy
    c. precognition
    d. None of these options

19. Scientists sometimes find that one person will demonstrate ESP in one laboratory but not in another. This suggests that _____.
    a. replication of studies is useless
    b. the studies were probably not valid
    c. the researcher or the participant was biased against ESP
    d. ESP is not a reliable phenomenon

20. Concerning ESP (extrasensory perception), research suggests that people should be _____.
    a. believers
    b. doing more research to support ESP
    c. very skeptical of ESP claims
    d. developing their own ESP

PRACTICE TEST II

1. _____ involves a mixing of sensory experiences.
    a. sensation
    b. perception
    c. transduction
    d. synesthesia

2. Subliminal messages, those messages presented below conscious awareness, can affect behavior in which of the following ways?
   a. They can help you learn while asleep.
   b. They can cause you to change your behavior to comply with the message.
   c. They can improve your memory for things that you learn while awake.
   d. None of these options

3. Sensory adaptation occurs when _____.
   a. one sensory system takes over for another that has been damaged
   b. information from several sensory systems are organized together in the brain
   c. a sensory system becomes less responsive to continuous stimulation
   d. a stroke or other brain damage prevents full sensory capability

4. Light travels through the cornea on to the _____.
   a. pupil, lens, and retina
   b. lens, pupil, and retina
   c. vitreous humor, aqueous humor, and retina
   d. retina on the back of the lens

5. The _____ theory of color vision states that there are three systems of color opposites (blue-yellow, red-green, and black-white).
   a. trichromatic
   b. opponent-process
   c. tri-receptor
   d. lock-and-key

6. _____ are people who perceive only two colors.
   a. Monochromats
   b. Dual-processors
   c. Dichromats
   d. Trio-processors

7. Which of the following is an example of pitch?
   a. You switch the lever on your telephone from soft to loud.
   b. Your mother raises the volume of her voice when you ignore her.
   c. You can barely hear your television because of the traffic noise outside.
   d. Your neighbor's car alarm alternates between high and low tones.

8. Rock concerts, blaring radios, and raucous pep rallies are _____.
   a. adolescent rites of passage
   b. signs of a good time
   c. damaging to auditory receptor cells
   d. the reason parents lose their sanity by age 50

9. Smell and taste can be adversely affected by the _____.
   a. trichromatic theory
   b. common cold
   c. opponent-process theory
   d. all of these options

10. _____ results from stimulation of receptor cells in the nose.
    a. Audition
    b. Pheromones
    c. Olfaction
    d. Gustation

11. Children are picky about food because _____.
    a. their taste buds are replaced quickly
    b. of childhood experiences and cultural influences
    c. of evolutionary preference
    d. all of these options

12. Light stimulation of both pressure and pain receptors results in the sensation of _____.
    a. itching
    b. tickling
    c. vibration
    d. all of these options

13. The _____ provide the brain with balance information, particularly information about the rotation of the head.
    a. hairs in the nasal cavity
    b. myelinated fibers in the olfactory system
    c. semicircular canals
    d. none of these options

14. _____ are false impressions of the environment. _____ are sensory perceptions that occur without external stimulus.
    a. Hallucinations; Delusions
    b. Delusions; Illusions
    c. Illusions; Delusions
    d. Illusions; Hallucinations

15. Specialized cells in the brain that respond only to certain sensory information are known as _____.
    a. visual constancies
    b. retinal disparity
    c. convergence
    d feature detectors

16. The tendency for the environment to be perceived as remaining the same even with changes in sensory input is known as _____.
    a. habituation
    b. sensory adaptation
    c. perceptual constancy
    d. sensory sensitivity

17. When you look at a chair from the back or front, it looks like a rectangle. However, when you see it from the side, it has an "h" shape, but you still recognize it as a chair because of _____.
    a. sensory adaptation
    b. shape constancy
    c. size constancy
    d. sensory habituation

18. The _____ is an apparatus used by scientists to study depth perception.
    a. trichromatic blender
    b. opponent-process dicer
    c. visual cliff
    d. Ames Room

19. Which of the following is responsible for depth perception?
    a. thalamus
    b. binocular cues
    c. retinal disparity
    d. all but one of these options

20. _____ is a monocular depth cue that occurs when parallel lines converge in the distance.
    a. Aerial perspective
    b. Relative size
    c. Linear perspective
    d. Interposition

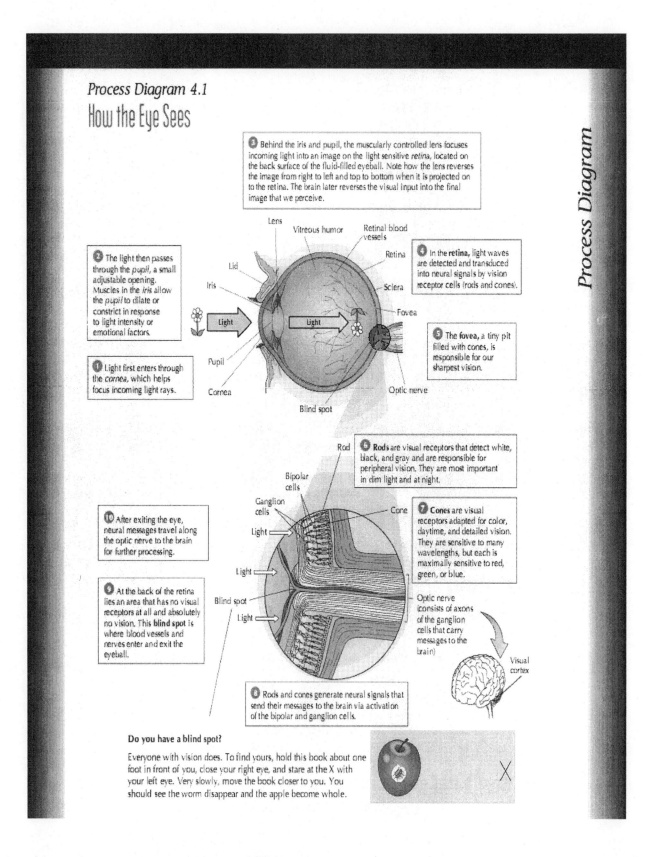

Process Diagram 4.1
How the Eye Sees

3 Behind the iris and pupil, the muscularly controlled lens focuses incoming light into an image on the light sensitive *retina*, located on the back surface of the fluid-filled eyeball. Note how the lens reverses the image from right to left and top to bottom when it is projected on to the retina. The brain later reverses the visual input into the final image that we perceive.

2 The light then passes through the *pupil*, a small adjustable opening. Muscles in the *iris* allow the *pupil* to dilate or constrict in response to light intensity or emotional factors.

1 Light first enters through the *cornea*, which helps focus incoming light rays.

4 In the **retina**, light waves are detected and transduced into neural signals by vision receptor cells (rods and cones).

5 The **fovea**, a tiny pit filled with cones, is responsible for our sharpest vision.

6 **Rods** are visual receptors that detect white, black, and gray and are responsible for peripheral vision. They are most important in dim light and at night.

10 After exiting the eye, neural messages travel along the optic nerve to the brain for further processing.

7 **Cones** are visual receptors adapted for color, daytime, and detailed vision. They are sensitive to many wavelengths, but each is maximally sensitive to red, green, or blue.

9 At the back of the retina lies an area that has no visual receptors at all and absolutely no vision. This **blind spot** is where blood vessels and nerves enter and exit the eyeball.

8 Rods and cones generate neural signals that send their messages to the brain via activation of the bipolar and ganglion cells.

Do you have a blind spot?

Everyone with vision does. To find yours, hold this book about one foot in front of you, close your right eye, and stare at the X with your left eye. Very slowly, move the book closer to you. You should see the worm disappear and the apple become whole.

Process Diagram

Process Diagram 4.2

How the Ear Hears

Process Diagram

The **outer ear** (pinna, auditory canal, and eardrum) funnels sound waves to the middle ear. In turn, the three tiny bones of the **middle ear** (hammer, anvil, and stirrup) amplify and send along the eardrum's vibrations to the cochlea's oval window, which is part of the **inner ear** (cochlea, semicircular canals and vestibular sacs). Vibrations from the oval window cause ripples in the fluid-filled **cochlea**, which then cause bending of the hair cells in the cochlea's basilar membrane. The bending hair cells then trigger neural messages that are sent to the brain via the auditory nerve. Finally, when the brain's temporal lobe receives and interprets the neural messages, we hear!

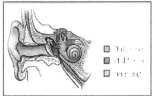

2 Sound waves collected by the outer ear cause the eardrum, or tympanic membrane, to vibrate.

3 Vibrations from the eardrum are then passed along to the middle ear, which contains three tiny bones called the *malleus* (hammer), *incus* (anvil), and *stapes* (stirrup).

4 Next, the stapes presses on a membrane, known as the *oval window*, and causes it to vibrate.

Temporal lobe's auditory cortex

Eardrum

Malleus (hammer) Incus (anvil) Stapes (stirrup) Semicircular canals Oval window (membrane)

Vestibular sacs

Auditory nerve

5 Movement of the oval window creates waves in the fluid that fills the cochlea, a snail-shaped structure that contains the *basilar membrane*, which holds the hair cell receptors for hearing.

Pinna

Sound waves

1 The outer ear, or *pinna*, channels the sound waves into the tube-like *auditory canal*, which focuses the sound.

Cochlea

Auditory canal

6 As the waves travel through the *cochlear fluid*, the hair cells on the basilar membrane bend from side to side. This movement stimulates the cells to transduce the mechanical energy of the sound waves into electrochemical impulses that are carried by the auditory nerve to the brain.

Eustachian tube

Outer Ear *Pinna, auditory canal, and eardrum, which funnel sound waves to the middle ear*

Middle Ear *Hammer, anvil, and stirrup, which concentrate eardrum vibrations onto the cochlea's oval window*

Inner Ear *Cochlea, semicircular canals and vestibular sacs, which generate neural signals sent to the brain*

Cochlea [KOK-lee-uh] *Three-chambered, snail-shaped structure in the inner ear containing the receptors for hearing*

Process Diagram 4.3

How The Nose Smells

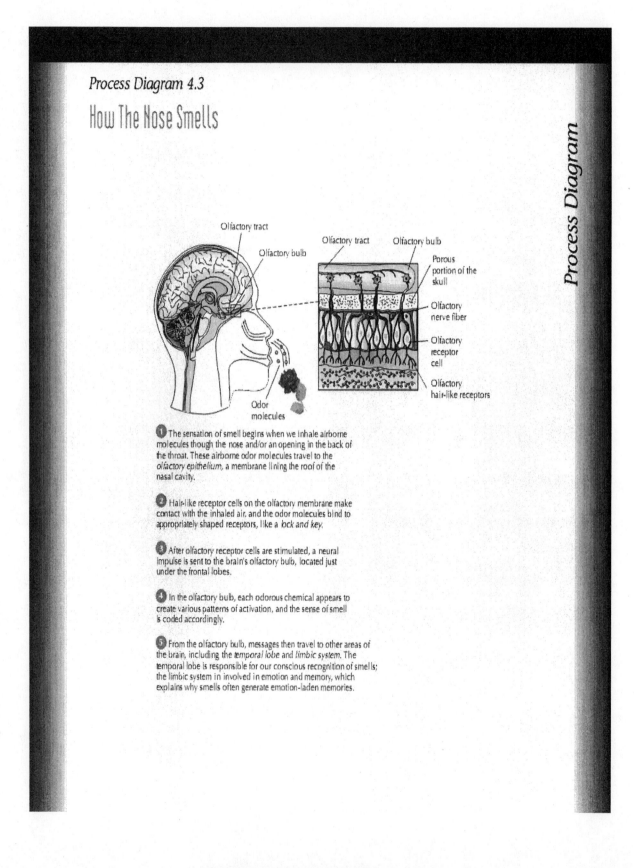

1 The sensation of smell begins when we inhale airborne molecules though the nose and/or an opening in the back of the throat. These airborne odor molecules travel to the *olfactory epithelium*, a membrane lining the roof of the nasal cavity.

2 Hair-like receptor cells on the olfactory membrane make contact with the inhaled air, and the odor molecules bind to appropriately shaped receptors, like a *lock and key*.

3 After olfactory receptor cells are stimulated, a neural impulse is sent to the brain's olfactory bulb, located just under the frontal lobes.

4 In the olfactory bulb, each odorous chemical appears to create various patterns of activation, and the sense of smell is coded accordingly.

5 From the olfactory bulb, messages then travel to other areas of the brain, including the *temporal lobe* and *limbic system*. The temporal lobe is responsible for our conscious recognition of smells; the limbic system in involved in emotion and memory, which explains why smells often generate emotion-laden memories.

Process Diagram

Concept Diagram 4.2
Four Perceptual Constancies

Courtesy Wayne Townsend-Merino

1. **Size Constancy** Our retinal image of the couple in the foreground is much larger than the trees and mountains behind them. Thanks to size constancy, however, we readily perceive them as people of normal size. Interestingly, size constancy, like all constancies, appears to develop from learning and experience. Studies of people who have been blind since birth, and then have their sight restored, find they have little or no size constancy (Sacks, 1995).

2. **Shape Constancy** As the coin is rotated, it changes shape, but we still perceive it as the same coin because of shape constancy.

An American ophthalmologist, Adelbert Ames, demonstrated the power of shape and size constancies by creating a distorted room, which is known as the *Ames room illusion.* In this photo, the young boy on the right appears to be much larger than the woman on the left. The illusion is so strong that when a person walks from the left corner to the right, the observer perceives the person to be "growing," even though that is not possible. How can this be?

The illusion is based on the unusual construction of the room, and our perceptual constancies have falsely filled in the wrong details. To the viewer, peering through the peephole, the room appears to be a normal cubic-shaped room. But the true shape is trapezoidal: the walls are slanted and the floor and ceiling are at an incline. Because our brains mistakenly assume the two people are the same distance away, we compensate for the apparent size difference by making the person on the left appear much smaller.

Several Ames room sets were used in *The Lord of the Rings* film series to make the heights of the hobbits appear correct when standing next to Gandalf.

Barron Wolman/Woodfin Camp

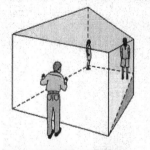

Mark Raycroft/Minden Pictures/Getty Images

New Line/Saul Zaentz/Wing Nut/The Kobal Collection, Ltd.

3. **Color Constancy** and 4. **Brightness Constancy** We perceive the dog's fur in this photo as having a relatively constant hue (or color) and brightness despite the fact that the wavelength of light reaching our retinas may vary as the light changes.

Concept Diagram

Concept Diagram 4.3

Binocular Depth Cues

One of the most important cues for depth perception comes from **retinal disparity**. Because our eyes are about 2½ inches apart, the retina of each eye receives a slightly different view of the world. Such *stereoscopic vision* provides important cues to depth. You can demonstrate this for yourself by trying the following exercise:

(a) Stare at your two index fingers a few inches in front of your eyes with their tips half an inch apart. Do you see the "floating finger"? Move it farther away and the "finger" will shrink. Move it closer and it will enlarge. (b) Because of retinal disparity, objects at different distances (such as the "floating finger") project their images on different parts of the retina. Far objects project on the retinal area near the nose, whereas near objects project farther out, closer to the ears.

(a)

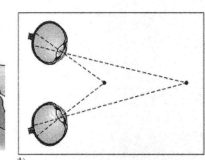

(b)

As we move closer and closer to an object, a second binocular (and neuromuscular) cue, **convergence**, helps us judge depth (c) and (d). The closer the object, the more our eyes are turned inward toward our noses. Hold your index finger at arm's length in front of you and watch it as you bring it closer and closer until it is right in front of your nose. The amount of strain in your eye muscles created by the convergence, or turning inward of the eyes, is used as a cue by your brain to interpret distance.

(c)

Why are coaches always reminding players to "keep their eyes on the ball"? Convergence and depth perception are better when you are looking directly at an object, rather than out of the corner of your eye. Thus, if you turn your body or your head so that you look straight at your tennis opponent or the pitcher, you will more accurately judge the distance of the ball and thereby be more likely to swing at the right time.

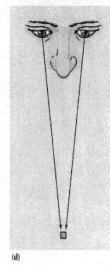

(d)

Retinal Disparity *Binocular cue to distance in which the separation of the eyes causes different images to fall on each retina*

Convergence *Binocular depth cue in which the closer the object, the more the eyes converge, or turn inward*

Andy Sacks/Riser/Getty Images

Concept Diagram

Concept Diagram 4.4

Monocular Depth Cues

The binocular (two eyes) cues of retinal disparity and convergence are inadequate in judging distances longer than the length of a football field. Luckily, we have several monocular (one eye) cues available separately to each eye. Imagine yourself as an artist and see if you can identify each of these cues in this photo of the Taj Mahal in India.

Ed George/NG Image Collection

Monocular Depth Cues

Linear perspective *parallel lines converge, or angle toward one another, as they recede into the distance.*

Interposition *objects that obscure or overlap other objects are perceived as closer.*

Relative size *close objects cast a larger retinal image than distant objects.*

Texture gradient *nearby objects have a coarser and more distinct texture than distant ones.*

Aerial perspective *distant objects appear hazy and blurred compared to close objects because of intervening atmospheric dust or haze.*

Light and shadow *brighter objects are perceived as being closer than distant objects.*

Relative height *objects positioned higher in our field of vision are perceived as farther away.*

Two additional monocular cues for depth perception, accommodation of the lens of the eye and motion parallax, cannot be used by artists. In accommodation, muscles that adjust the shape of the lens as it focuses on an object send neural messages to the brain, which interprets the signal to perceive distance. For near objects, the lens bulges; for far objects, it flattens.

Motion parallax (also known as relative motion) refers to the fact that when we are moving, close objects appear to whiz by, whereas farther objects seem to move more slowly or remain stationary. This effect can easily be seen when traveling by car or train.

Jimmy Cohrssen/Getty Images

Chapter 4 Visual Summary

Understanding Sensation

General Definitions

* **Sensation:** Detecting, converting, and transmitting raw sensory data to the brain.
* **Perception:** Selecting, organizing, and interpreting sensory information.
* **Bottom-up processing:** Data driven processing moving from parts to the whole.
* **Top-down processing:** Conceptually driven processing moving from the whole to the parts.

Processing

* *Receptors:* Body cells that detect and respond to stimulus energy.
* **Transduction:** Converting receptor energy into neural impulses that are sent to the brain.
* **Coding:** Converting sensory input into specific sensations (sight, sound, touch, etc.).
* **Sensory reduction:** Filtering and analyzing of sensations before messages are sent to the cortex.

Measuring the Senses

* **Psychophysics:** Studies link between physical characteristics of stimuli and our sensory experience of them.

Thresholds

* **Absolute threshold:** Smallest *magnitude* of a stimulus we can detect.
* **Difference threshold:** Smallest *change* in a stimulus we can detect.

Adaptation

* **Sensory adaptation:** Decreased sensory response to continuous stimulation.
* **Gate-control theory:** "Gate" in spinal cord blocks or allows pain signals to pass on to brain.

How We See and Hear

Vision: Light is a form of energy and part of the *electromagnetic spectrum*.

Eye Anatomy and Function

* *Cornea:* Clear bulge at front of eye, where light enters.
* *Pupil:* Hole through which light passes into eye.
* *Iris:* Colored muscles that surround pupil.
* *Lens:* Elastic structure that bulges and flattens to focus an image on retina (a process called **accommodation**).
* **Retina:** Contains visual receptor cells, called **rods** (for night vision) and **cones** (for color vision and fine detail).
* **Fovea:** Pit in the retina responsible for sharp vision.
* **Blind Spot:** Point where optic nerve leaves the eye which has no visual receptors.

The eye's function is to capture light waves and focus them on receptors in the retina, which convert light energy to neural impulses that travel to the brain.

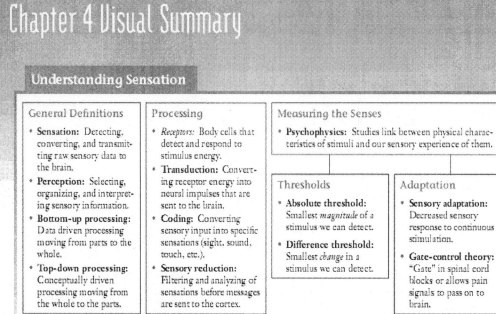

Hearing: **Audition** (or hearing) occurs via *sound waves*, which result from rapid changes in air pressure caused by vibrating objects.

Ear Anatomy and Function

* **Outer ear:** Pinna, auditory canal, and eardrum.
* **Middle ear:** Hammer, anvil, and stirrup.
* **Inner ear:** Oval window, cochlea, and basilar membrane.

The ear's function is to capture sound waves and focus them on receptors in the cochlea, which convert sound energy to neural impulses that travel to the brain.

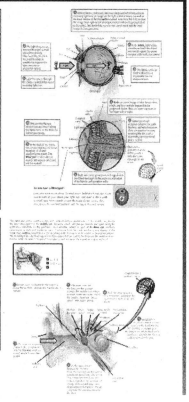

Our Other Senses

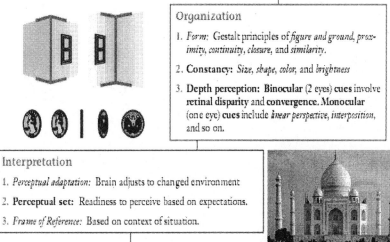

Smell and Taste

Olfaction (sense of smell) Receptors located at the top of the nasal cavity.

Gustation (sense of taste) Five basic tastes: salty, sweet, sour, bitter, and umami

The Body Senses

* *Skin sense*s detect touch (pressure), temperature, and pain.
* *Vestibular sense* (or sense of balance) results from receptors in inner ear.
* **Kinesthesia** (body posture, orientation, and body movement) results from receptors in muscles, joints, and tendons.

A taste bud

Understanding Perception

Selection

1. **Selective attention:** Filtering out and attending only to important sensory messages.

2. **Feature detectors:** Specialized brain cells that respond only to specific sensory information.

3. **Habituation:** Brain's tendency to ignore environmental factors that remain constant.

Organization

1. *Form:* Gestalt principles of *figure and ground, proximity, continuity, closure,* and *similarity.*

2. **Constancy:** *Size, shape, color,* and *brightness*

3. **Depth perception: Binocular** (2 eyes) **cues** involve **retinal disparity** and **convergence.** Monocular (one eye) **cues** include *linear perspective, interposition,* and so on.

Interpretation

1. *Perceptual adaptation:* Brain adjusts to changed environment

2. **Perceptual set:** Readiness to perceive based on expectations.

3. *Frame of Reference:* Based on context of situation.

Extrasensory Perception

Extrasensory perception (ESP) is the supposed ability to perceive things through unknown and unproven "extra" senses.

5
States of Consciousness

<u>O</u>UTLINE SQ4R (<u>S</u>urvey, <u>Q</u>uestion, <u>R</u>ead, <u>R</u>ecite, <u>R</u>eview, & w<u>R</u>ite)

This outline section incorporates all six steps in the well-researched SQ4R method of learning. Begin by surveying the list of chapter topics in the left column. This "big picture" will help focus and guide your attention while you read. As you read through the chapter, briefly summarize each section in your own words in the space to the right. Also write down any *questions* that come to mind. Surveying, Questioning, Reading, Reciting, Reviewing, and wRiting are the foundation of the SQ4R method and an invaluable form of active learning. They also make your reading time more enjoyable and efficient! One thorough, focused SQ4R reading of a chapter is far better than several passive readings.

TOPIC	NOTES

I. UNDERSTANDING CONSCIOUSNESS

II. SLEEP AND DREAMS

   A. The Power of Circadian Rhythms

   Psychology at Work: Dangers of
     Sleeping on the Job

   B. Stages of Sleep

   C. Why Do We Sleep and Dream?

   Gender & Cultural Diversity:
     Dream Variations and Similarities

Critical Thinking/Active Learning:
Interpreting Your Dreams

D. Sleep Disorders

Psychology at Work: Self-Help for
Sleep Problems

III. PSYCHOACTIVE DRUGS

A. Understanding Psychoactive Drugs

Research Highlight: Addictive Drugs as
the Brain's "Evil Tutor"

B. Four Major Categories of Psychoactive Drugs

Psychology at Work: Club Drug Alert!

IV. HEALTHIER WAYS TO ALTER CONSCIOUSNESS

A. Getting "High" on Meditation

B. The Mystery of Hypnosis

LEARNING OBJECTIVES (Read, Recite, Review, & wRite)

In addition to the work you did in the Outline above, you can significantly improve your performance on exams by focusing on the following learning objectives. While reading the chapter or reviewing for exams, check your understanding by stopping periodically to *recite* (or repeat in your own words) and *writing* down your answers on a separate sheet. [Page numbers correspond to Chapter 5 in *Psychology in Action* (9e).]

5.1 Define and describe consciousness and alternate states of consciousness (ASCs). (p. 168)
5.2 Contrast controlled versus automatic processing. (p. 168)
5.3 List six common myths about sleep. (p. 171)
5.4 What are circadian rhythms and how do they affect our lives? (p. 171)
5.5 List the stages of sleep and describe a typical night's sleep. (p. 174)
5.6 Why do we sleep? (p. 178)
5.7 Why do we dream? (p. 179)
5.8 How do gender and culture affect dreams? (p. 180)
5.9 Describe the major sleep disorders. (p. 182)
5.10 Define psychoactive drugs and explain how they work. (p. 185)
5.11 Clarify the major misconceptions and confusing terminology related to psychoactive drugs. (p. 186)
5.12 Why do addicts abuse drugs? (p. 188)
5.13 List the four main categories of psychoactive drugs and explain how they work. (p. 189)
5.14 Discuss issues and concerns related to "club drugs." (p. 194)
5.15 Define meditation and discuss its effects. (p. 195)
5.16 Define hypnosis, and describe its myths and potential benefits. (p. 196)

KEY TERMS (Review & wRite)

Like other survey courses, introductory psychology is filled with a "wealth" of new and unfamiliar terminology. To do well on exams, you must master this new language! Writing a brief definition of each term in the space provided and carefully reviewing them before exams will significantly improve your course grade.

Activation-Synthesis Hypothesis: _____

_____

Addiction: _____

_____

Agonist drug: _____

_____

Alternate States of Consciousness (ASCs): _____

_____

Antagonist drug: _____

_____

Automatic Processes: _____

_____

Circadian Rhythms: _____

_____

Consciousness: _____

_____

Controlled Processes: _____

_____

Depressants: _____

_____

Drug Abuse: _____

_____

Evolutionary/Circadian Theory: _____

_____

Hallucinogens: _____

_____

Hypnosis: _____

_____

Insomnia: _____

_____

Latent Content: _____

_____

Manifest Content: _____

_____

Meditation: _____

_____

Narcolepsy: _____

_____

Night Terrors: _____

_____

Nightmares: _____

_____

Non-Rapid-Eye-Movement (NREM) Sleep: _____

_____

Opiates: _____

_____

Physical Dependence: _____

_____

Psychoactive Drugs: _____

_____

Psychological Dependence: _____

_____

Rapid Eye Movement (REM) Sleep: _____

_____

Repair/Restoration Theory: _____

_____

Sleep Apnea: _____

_____

Stimulants: _____

_____

Tolerance: _____

_____

Withdrawal: _____

_____

ACTIVE LEARNING EXERCISES

True mastery of information requires you to be an ACTIVE learner. Completing the following active learning exercises will improve your understanding of the chapter material and greatly improve your performance on exams. Answers to some exercises appear in Appendix A at the end of this study guide.

ACTIVE LEARNING EXERCISE I (Contributed by Thomas Frangicetto) *Would you like to use critical thinking to analyze your own dreams? Write down as much detail as possible about your most recent, most vivid, and most troubling or interesting dream. Now briefly review the Critical Thinking Components in the Prologue, which appears in the beginning pages of your text and can help you analyze your dream content. For example:*

1. **Employing metacognition.** Dreaming is another way of thinking. As you review and analyze your dreams you are *employing metacognition.*

Sample student dream: *I am looking for my husband...Feeling lonely, I notice that I am being followed by a strange man. At first I'm afraid, but then I'm excited. He gets closer. As he's about to touch me I hear my husband in the distance. What surprises me is that I don't want him to find me. This dream made me very sad.*

To *employ metacognition* this dreamer might ask questions such as: "Is there a problem the dream is trying to help me face or solve? Is there some problem in my marriage that I have been avoiding? Intelligent and honest metacognition might help this dreamer find solutions for a real life dilemma.

2. **Tolerating ambiguity.** This is a prerequisite for doing "dream work." Keeping a dream log of all your dreams for a given time period is essential. The meaning of an ambiguous dream you record today might become more obvious when linked to a seemingly unrelated dream you record a month later.

3. **Welcoming divergent views.** Occasionally, *one* single theory can adequately explain a dream. But it is generally better to apply several theories for maximum understanding. Although dream theorists are divided about the specific *meanings* of dreams, they all agree that dreams have the potential to increase self-awareness and provide insight into our emotional lives.

4. **Synthesizing.** Freud's theory of dreaming remains highly controversial. But some dreamers find that examining their own unique dream symbols helps them understand their "real world." They look for symbols, patterns, and themes that reappear in different dreams. They then frame their dreams as a metaphor--assuming that surface events (*manifest content*) reflect meanings that are hidden from view (*latent content*).

Sample student dream: *In my dream a week before my grandfather died, I was sitting in a room...There was a grandfather clock ticking that chimed and then stopped ticking completely.*

Can you see how a ticking grandfather clock in one person's dream might reflect a simple concern for the passing of time? In this dream the clock is an obvious metaphor/symbol that stands for the dreamer's grandfather. The stopped ticking of the clock dramatically reflects the dreamer's fear of losing him. Rather than feeling guilty when the death occurs, the dream could inspire the awakened dreamer to make a long-overdue visit to an ailing grandfather.

ACTIVE LEARNING EXERCISE II *Using the following list of common dream themes, place a check mark next to each theme you remember from your own dreams.*

_____1. Snakes
_____2. Seeing yourself as dead
__✓__3. Being nude in public
_____4. School, teachers, studying
__✓__5. Sexual experiences
_____6. Arriving too late
_____7. Eating
__✓__8. Being frozen with fright
__✓__9. Death of a loved person
_____10. Being locked up
_____11. Finding money
_____12. Swimming
_____13. Falling
_____14. Being dressed inappropriately
_____15. Being smothered
__✓__16. Trying repeatedly to do something
_____17. Fire
_____18. Failing an examination
_____19. Flying
__✓__20. Being attacked or pursued

Now compare your responses to those of 250 other college students:
1. 49%; 2. 33%; 3. 43%; 4. 71%; 5. 66%; 6. 64%; 7. 62%; 8. 58%; 9. 57%; 10. 56%; 11. 56%; 12. 52 %; 13. 83%; 14. 46%; 15. 44%; 16. 71%; 17. 41%; 18. 39%; 19. 34%; 20. 77%.

How did you compare? Do you think your responses might differ from others due to your age, gender, culture, or other variables? How? If you would like to read more about the "universality of dreams," check out the following reference: Griffith, R. M., Miyago, O., & Tago, A. (1958). The universality of typical dreams: Japanese vs. Americans. American Anthropologist, 60, 1173-1179.

ACTIVE LEARNING EXERCISE III *The topic of drugs often generates heated debate between people with different perspectives. When discussing controversial issues, it is helpful to make a distinction between statements of fact and statements of opinion. (A fact is a statement* *that can be proven true. An opinion is a statement that expresses how a person feels about an issue or what someone thinks is true.) Although it is also important to determine whether the facts are true or false, in this exercise simply mark "O" for opinion and "F" for fact to test your ability to distinguish between the two.*

_____1. Marijuana is now one of America's principal cash crops.

_____2. Friends do not let friends drive drunk.

_____3. People who use drugs are not hurting anyone but themselves.

_____4. Legalizing drugs such as cocaine, marijuana, and heroin would make them as big a problem as alcohol and tobacco.

_____5. The number of cocaine addicts is small compared with the number of alcoholics.

_____6. The American Medical Association considers alcohol to be the most dangerous of all psychoactive drugs.

_____7. Random drug tests are justified for personnel involved with public safety (e.g., air traffic controllers, police officers, etc.).

_____8. If parents use drugs, their children are more likely to use drugs.

_____9. Mothers who deliver cocaine-addicted babies are guilty of child abuse.

_____10. Alcohol abuse by pregnant mothers is one of the most important factors in mental retardation.

ANSWERS: We recommend discussing your responses with classmates and friends. Listening to the reasons others give for their answers often provides valuable insights and helps in distinguishing between fact and opinion. (Adapted from Bach, 1988.)

CHAPTER OVERVIEW (Review)

The following chapter overview provides a narrative overview of the main topics covered in the chapter. Like the *Visual Summary* found at the end of each chapter in the text, this narrative summary provides a final opportunity to *review* chapter material.

I. UNDERSTANDING CONSCIOUSNESS

5.1 Define and describe consciousness and alternate states of consciousness (ASCs). (p. 168)

Most of our lives are spent in normal, waking **consciousness,** an organism's awareness of its own self and surroundings. However, we also spend considerable time in various **alternate states of consciousness (ASCs),** such as sleep and dreaming, daydreams, and states induced by psychoactive drugs, hypnosis, and meditation. Consciousness has always been difficult to study and define. William James described it as a "flowing stream." Modern researchers emphasize that consciousness exists along a continuum.

5.2 Contrast controlled versus automatic processing. (p. 168)

Controlled processes, which require focused attention, are at the highest level of awareness. **Automatic processes,** which require minimal attention, are found in the middle of the continuum. Unconsciousness and coma are at the lowest level of awareness.

II. CIRCADIAN RHYTHMS AND STAGES OF SLEEP

5.3 List six common myths about sleep. (p. 171)

Six of the most common myths include: Everyone needs 8 hours of sleep. It's easy to learn complicated things while asleep. Some people never dream. Dreams only last a few seconds. Genital arousal means the sleeper is having a sexual dream. And, dreaming of dying can be fatal.

5.4 What are circadian rhythms and how do they affect our lives? (p. 171)
Circadian rhythms are biological changes that occur on a 24-hour cycle. Our sleep and waking cycles, alertness, moods, learning, blood pressure, and the like all follow circadian rhythms. Disruptions due to shift work, jet lag, and sleep deprivation can cause accidents and other serious problems.

5.5 List the stages of sleep and describe a typical night's sleep. (p. 174)
A typical night's sleep consists of four to five 90-minute cycles. The cycle begins in Stage 1 and then moves through Stages 2, 3, and 4. After reaching the deepest level of sleep, the cycle reverses up to the **REM (rapid-eye-movement) sleep**, in which the person often is dreaming. Sleep stages 1, 2, 3, and 4 are called **NREM (non-rapid-eye-movement) sleep**.

III. THEORIES OF SLEEP AND DREAMING
5.6 Why do we sleep? (p. 178)
The exact function of sleep is not known. But according to the **evolutionary/circadian theory,** sleep evolved to conserve energy and protect us from predators. According to the **repair/ restoration theory**, sleep is thought to be necessary for its restorative value, both physically and psychologically.

5.7 Why do we dream? (p. 179)
Three major theories attempt to explain why we dream: According to the *psychoanalytic/ psychodynamic view*, dreams are disguised symbols of repressed desires, conflicts, and anxieties. The *biological perspective* **(activation–synthesis hypothesis)** proposes that dreams are simple by-products of random stimulation of brain cells. The *cognitive view* suggests that dreams are an important part of information processing of everyday experiences.

5.8 How do gender and culture affect dreams? (p. 180)
Researchers have found many similarities and differences between genders and across cultures. How people interpret and value their dreams also varies across cultures.

IV. SLEEP DISORDERS
5.9 Describe the major sleep disorders. (p. 182)
Many people suffer from various sleep problems. These problems fall into two major diagnostic categories—*dyssomnias* (including insomnia, sleep apnea, and narcolepsy) and *parasomnias* (such as nightmares and night terrors). People who have repeated difficulty falling or staying asleep, or awakening too early experience **insomnia**. A person with **sleep apnea** temporarily stops breathing during sleep, causing loud snoring, or poor quality sleep. **Narcolepsy** is excessive daytime sleepiness characterized by sudden sleep attacks. **Nightmares** are bad dreams that occur during REM sleep. **Night terrors** are abrupt awakenings with feelings of panic that occur during NREM sleep.

V. PSYCHOACTIVE DRUGS
5.10 Define psychoactive drugs and explain how they work. (p. 185)
Psychoactive drugs change conscious awareness, mood, and/or perception. These drugs work primarily by changing the amount and effect of neurotransmitters in the synapse. Some drugs act as *agonists*, which mimic neurotransmitters. *Antagonists* oppose or block normal neurotransmitter functioning.

5.11 Clarify the major misconceptions and confusing terminology related to psychoactive drugs. (p. 186)
Drug abuse refers to drug taking that causes emotional or physical harm to the individual or others. **Addiction** is a broad term referring to a person's feeling of compulsion to use a specific drug or to engage in certain activities. Psychoactive drug use can lead to psychological dependence

or physical dependence or both. **Psychological dependence** is a desire or craving to achieve the effects produced by a drug. **Physical dependence** is a change in bodily processes resulting from continued drug use that results in **withdrawal** symptoms when the drug is withheld. **Tolerance** is a decreased sensitivity to a drug brought about by its continuous use.

5.12 Why do addicts abuse drugs? (p. 188)
Research shows that their brains "learn" to be addicted. Neurotransmitters, like dopamine and glutamate, activate the brain's reward system and create lasting cravings and memories of the drug use.

5.13 List the four main categories of psychoactive drugs and explain how they work. (p. 189)
The major categories of psychoactive drugs are **depressants, stimulants, opiates,** and **hallucinogens**. Depressant drugs slow the central nervous system, whereas stimulants increase or activate it. Opiates numb the senses and relieve pain, whereas hallucinogens produce sensory or perceptual distortions called *hallucinations*.

5.14 Discuss issues and concerns related to "club drugs." (p. 194)
Club drugs can produce desirable effects, but they also can cause serious health problems. Impaired decision making is also a dangerous side effect of club drugs.

VI. HEALTHIER WAYS TO ALTER CONSCIOUSNESS
5.15 Define meditation and discuss its effects. (p. 195)
Meditation is a group of techniques designed to focus attention, block out all distractions, and produce an alternate state of consciousness. Meditation can produce dramatic changes in physiological processes, including brain changes, heart rate, and respiration.

5.16 Define hypnosis, and describe its myths and potential benefits. (p. 196)
Hypnosis is an alternate state of heightened suggestibility characterized by deep relaxation and intense focus. Hypnosis is the subject of many myths, such as "forced hypnosis." But it also has been used successfully to reduce pain, to increase concentration, and as an adjunct to psychotherapy.

SELF-TESTS (Review & wRite)

Completing the following self-tests will provide immediate feedback on how well you have mastered the material. In the labeling exercises, *crossword puzzle*, and *fill-in exercises*, write the appropriate word or words in the blank spaces. The *matching exercise* requires you to match the terms in one column to their correct definitions in the other. For the *multiple-choice questions* in Practice Tests I and II, circle or underline the correct answer. If you are unsure of any answer, mark the item, and then go back to the text for further review. Correct answers are provided in Appendix A at the end of this study guide.

Crossword Puzzle for Chapter 5

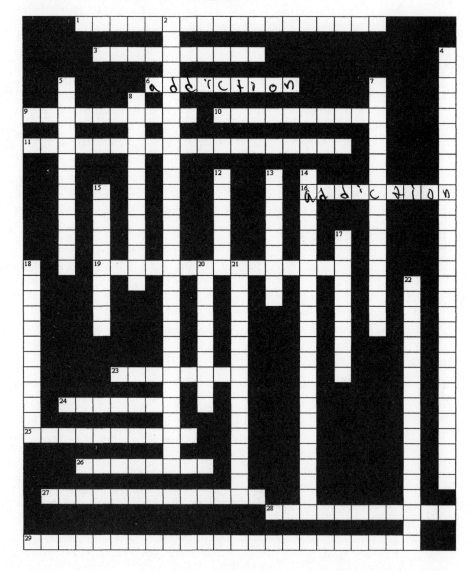

ACROSS

1 Mental activities requiring minimal attention and having little impact on other activities.

3 A group of techniques designed to refocus attention, block out all distractions, and produce an alternate state of consciousness.

6 Drug taking that causes emotional or physical harm to the drug user or others.

9 Discomfort and distress, including physical pain and intense cravings, experienced after stopping the use of addictive drugs.

10 Sudden and irresistible onsets of sleep during normal waking hours.

11 Mental activities requiring focused attention that generally interfere with other ongoing activities.

16 Broad term describing a compulsion to use a specific drug or engage in a certain activity.

19 According to Freud, the surface content of a dream, which contains dream symbols that distort and disguise the dream's true meaning.

23 Persistent problems in falling asleep, staying asleep, or awakening too early.

24 Drugs that function as an analgesic or pain reliever.

25 Repeated interruption of breathing during sleep because air passages to the lungs are physically blocked.

26 A trancelike state of heightened suggestibility, deep relaxation, and intense focus.

27 An organism's awareness of its own self and surroundings.

28 Psychoactive drugs that act on the central nervous system to suppress or slow bodily processes and reduce overall responsiveness.

29 Desire or craving to achieve the effects produced by a drug.

DOWN

2 A mental state other than ordinary waking consciousness, found during sleep, dreaming, psychoactive drug use, hypnosis, and so on.

4 Hobson's theory that dreams are by-products of random stimulation of brain cells.

5 The true, unconscious meaning of a dream, according to Freudian dream theory.

7 Chemicals that change conscious awareness, mood, or perception.

8 Drugs that produce sensory or perceptual distortions.

12 Chemical (or drug) that mimics the action of a specific neurotransmitter.

13 Decreased sensitivity to a drug brought about by its continuous use.

14 A stage of sleep marked by high-frequency brain waves, paralysis of large muscles, and dreaming.

15 Anxiety-arousing dreams generally occurring near the end of the sleep cycle, during REM sleep.

17 Chemical (or drug) that opposes or blocks the action of a neurotransmitter.

18 Abrupt awakenings from NREM sleep accompanied by intense physiological arousal and feelings of panic.

20 Drugs that act on the brain and nervous system, to increase their overall activity and general responsiveness.

21 Biological changes that occur in a 24-hour cycle.

22 Bodily processes have been so modified by repeated use of a drug that continued use is required to prevent withdrawal symptoms.

FILL-IN EXERCISES

1. _____ are defined as mental states other than ordinary waking consciousness, such as sleep, dreaming, or hypnosis (p. 166).

2. _____ are mental activities that require focused attention, while generally interfering with other ongoing activities (pp. 169-170).

3. _____ is also called paradoxical sleep because the brain is aroused and active, yet the sleeper's muscles are deeply relaxed and unresponsive (p. 176).

4. In the _____ theory, sleep serves an important recuperative function, whereas the _____ theory suggests that sleep is a part of circadian rhythms and evolved as a means to conserve energy and protect individuals from predators (p. 178).

5. According to Freud, the true, unconscious meaning of a dream is called the _____ (p. 179).

6. The major sleep disorders include _____ (difficulty falling and staying asleep or awakening too early), _____ (temporary cessation of breathing during sleep), _____ (sudden and irresistible onsets of sleep during normal waking hours), _____ (anxiety-arousing dreams that generally occur during REM sleep), and _____ (abrupt awakenings from non-REM sleep with feelings of panic) (pp. 182-184).

7. Drugs that affect the nervous system and cause a change in conscious awareness, mood, and/or perception are called _____ (p. 185).

8. _____ refers to the mental desire or craving to achieve the effects produced by a drug; whereas _____ involves modifications of bodily processes requiring use of the drug for minimal functioning (p. 186).

9. _____ are drugs that act on the brain and nervous system to increase overall activity and responsiveness; whereas _____ are drugs that suppress or slow down bodily processes (p. 189).

10. _____ is an alternate state of heightened suggestibility characterized by deep relaxation and intense focus (p. 196).

MATCHING EXERCISES

Column A

a. Sleep Apnea
b. ASC
c. Drug Abuse
d. Circadian Rhythm
e. Automatic Processes
f. Cognitive View
g. REM Sleep
h. Cocaine
i. Manifest Content
j. Agonist Drug

Column B

1. ____ Mental activities requiring minimal attention
2. ____ Stage of sleep marked by rapid eye movements
3. ____ Surface content of a dream
4. ____ Temporary cessation of breathing during sleep
5. ____ Mental state other than ordinary waking consciousness
6. ____ Causes emotional or physical harm to drug user or others
7. ____ Dangerous stimulant
8. ____ Information processing theory of dreams
9. ____ Biological changes that occur on a 24-hour cycle
10. ____ Mimic or enhance a neurotransmitter's action

PRACTICE TEST I

1. An organism's awareness of its own self and surroundings is known as _____.
   a. awareness
   b. consciousness
   c. alertness
   d. central processing

2. Mental activities that require minimal attention, without affecting other activities are called _____ processes.
   a. controlled
   b. peripheral
   c. conscious
   d. automatic

3. _____ are biological rhythms that occur on a 24-hour cycle.
   a. Circadian rhythms
   b. Synchronisms
   c. Diurnal circuits
   d. Nocturnal transmissions

4. _____ waves are associated with drowsy relaxation.
   a. Alpha
   b. Beta
   c. Theta
   d. Delta

5. With regard to sleep, research suggests that _____ is nature's first need.
   a. REM sleep
   b. non-REM sleep
   c. dreaming
   d. hypnagogic sleep

6. _____ theory says that sleep allows us to replenish what was depleted during daytime activities.
   a. Repair/restoration
   b. Evolutionary/circadian
   c. Supply-demand
   d. Conservation of energy

7. _____ suggests dreams are a coherent synthesis of random, spontaneous neuron activity.
   a. Freud
   b. Hobson and McCarley
   c. Watson and Skinner
   d. Maslow

8. According to your text, insomnia occurs when you persistently _____.
   a. have difficulty staying awake
   b. go to sleep too early
   c. awaken too early
   d. all of these options

9. A disease marked by sudden and irresistible onsets of sleep during normal waking hours is known as _____.
   a. dyssomnia
   b. parasomnia
   c. narcolepsy
   d. sleep apnea

10. _____ are chemicals that affect the nervous system and change conscious awareness, mood, and/or perception.
    a. Endocrinologists
    b. Psychoactive drugs
    c. Alternators
    d. Bio-neural drugs

11. A mental desire or craving to achieve the effects produced by a drug is called _____.
    a. withdrawal effects
    b. dependency
    c. psychological dependence
    d. physical dependence

12. Requiring larger and more frequent doses of a drug to produce a desired effect is characteristic of _____.
    a. withdrawal
    b. tolerance
    c. psychoactive dependence
    d. all of these options

13. _____ is a stimulant at low doses and a depressant at higher doses.
    a. Cocaine
    b. Valium
    c. Amphetamine
    d. Alcohol

14. Why is it so dangerous to drink alcohol and take barbiturates at the same time?
    a. They both cause addiction.
    b. They're both depressants and may stop respiration.
    c. They both interrupt blood flow to the extremities.
    d. All of these options

15. Which of the following drugs is a central nervous system stimulant?
    a. amphetamine
    b. morphine
    c. heroin
    d. barbiturates

16. Which of the following is **NOT** classified as a hallucinogen?
    a. mescaline
    b. psilocybin
    c. amphetamines
    d. LSD

17. Marijuana is classified in your text as a _____.
    a. narcotic
    b. hallucinogen
    c. barbiturate
    d. LSD derivative

18. High doses of _____ can cause dangerous increases in body temperature and blood pressure that may lead to seizures, heart attacks, and strokes.
    a. barbiturates
    b. LSD
    c. MDMA
    d. none of these options

19. Research on the effects of meditation has found a(n) _____.

    a. increase in blood pressure
    b. reduction in stress
    c. lack of evidence for changes in any physiological functions
    d. increase in appetite

20. Which of the following is a common myth regarding hypnosis?
    a. People can be hypnotized against their will.
    b. Hypnosis participants can perform acts of superhuman strength.
    c. Under hypnosis, people can recall things they otherwise could not.
    d. all of these options

PRACTICE TEST II

1. A common myth is that everyone needs _____ of sleep a night to maintain sound mental and physical health.
    a. 11 hours
    b. 8 hours
    c. ½ hour
    d. varying amounts

2. A relaxed period characterized by feelings of floating, visual images, or swift jerky movements is a_____.
    a. dream state
    b. NREM state
    c. hypnagogic state
    d. paradoxical state

3. Your breathing is regular, your heart rate and blood pressure are slowing, and you can be awakened easily. It is most likely that you are in _____.
    a. REM sleep
    b. a daydreaming state
    c. Stage 1 sleep
    d. Stage 2 sleep

4. During sleep, an _____ is often used to detect and record brain waves.
    a. electrical emissions graph
    b. electroencephalograph
    c. electro-energy grams
    d. even elephants get grumpy

5. Which of the following is **NOT** characteristic of REM sleep?
   a. irregular breathing
   b. eyes moving back and forth
   c. dreaming
   d. low-frequency brain waves

6. The activation-synthesis hypothesis theory is a _____ view of dreams.
   a. psychoanalytic
   b. psychodynamic
   c. biological
   d. cognitive

7. A prominent example of dyssomnia is/are _____.
   a. night terrors
   b. sleep walking
   c. sleep apnea
   d. all of the above

8. Narcolepsy is characterized by sudden episodes of _____.
   a. nightmares in Stage 1 sleep
   b. sudden onset of sleep in the middle of wakeful periods
   c. epileptic seizures during Stage 4 sleep
   d. not being able to breathe during any stage of sleep

9. Which of the following occurs during REM sleep?
   a. narcolepsy
   b. nightmares
   c. night terrors
   d. parental insomnia

10. This is **NOT** a characteristic of night terrors.
   a. occurrence during non-REM sleep
   b. panicky feelings
   c. embedded within a pleasant dream
   d. intense physiological arousal

11. _____ drugs enhance or mimic a neurotransmitter's effect.
   a. Antagonist
   b. Psychoactive
   c. Agonist
   d. None of these options

12. _____ act on the brain and nervous system to increase overall activity and responsiveness.
   a. Stimulants
   b. Opiates
   c. Depressants
   d. Hallucinogens

13. Drugs that are derived from the Greek word meaning "juice" and function as an analgesic are called _____.
   a. parasomnias
   b. insulin
   c. opiates
   d. nicotine

14. Jake uses this drug to relax and achieve a state of euphoria. Jaime uses the same drug as an analgesic. Jeremiah uses the drug to feel more content and to make his experience of reality more pleasant. All three may experience life-threatening side effects with this drug.
   a. cocaine
   b. heroin
   c. a sedative
   d. lithium

15. _____ drugs produce sensory distortions or perceptual illusions.
   a. Opiate
   b. Narcotic
   c. Expensive
   d. Hallucinogen

16. Marijuana is a hard drug to classify because _____.
   a. it has properties of a depressant and an opiate
   b. in low doses it produces mild euphoria
   c. in high does it may produce hallucinations, delusions, and distortions of body image
   d. All of these options

17. Which of the following is commonly known as a "Club Drug"? _____.
   a. MDMA
   b. GHB
   c. ketamine
   d. All of these options

18. ASCs can be achieved through _____.
    a.   sleep and dreaming
    b.   hypnosis and meditation
    c.   psychoactive drugs
    d.   all of these options

19. Meditation is designed to _____.
    a.   decrease attentional focus
    b.   decrease your state of awareness
    c.   decrease focus by increasing awareness
    d.   refocus attention and produce an ASC

20. This is **NOT** associated with hypnosis.
    a.   the use of imagination
    b.   broad, unfocused attention
    c.   a passive, receptive attitude
    d.   decreased pain

Process Diagram 5.1
Where Does Consciousness Reside?

One of the oldest philosophical debates is the *mind–body problem*. Is the "mind" (consciousness and other mental functions) fundamentally different from matter (the body)? How can a supposedly nonmaterial mind influence a physical body and vice versa? Most neuropsychologists today believe the mind *is* the brain and consciousness involves an activation and integration of several parts of the brain. But two aspects of consciousness, *awareness* and *arousal*, seem to rely on specific areas. Awareness generally involves the *cerebral cortex*, particularly the frontal lobes. Arousal generally results from *brain-stem activation* (Culbertson, 2008; Revonsuo, 2006; Thompson, 2007).

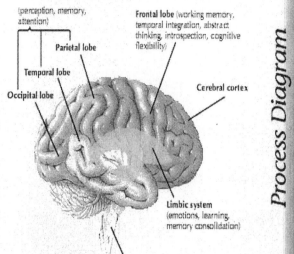

(perception, memory, attention)

Parietal lobe

Temporal lobe

Occipital lobe

Frontal lobe (working memory, temporal integration, abstract thinking, introspection, cognitive flexibility)

Cerebral cortex

Limbic system (emotions, learning, memory consolidation)

Brain stem (arousal)

Process Diagram

Levels of Awareness

High Awareness

CONTROLLED PROCESSES
Require focused, maximum attention (e.g., studying for an exam, learning to drive a car).

Middle Awareness

AUTOMATIC PROCESSES
Require minimal attention (e.g., walking to class while talking on a cell phone, listening to your boss while daydreaming).

Low Awareness

SUBCONSCIOUS
Below conscious awareness (e.g., subliminal perception, sleeping, dreaming)

NO AWARENESS
Biologically based lowest level of awareness (e.g., head injuries, anesthesia, coma); also the *unconscious mind* (a Freudian concept discussed in Chapter 13) reportedly consisting of unacceptable thoughts and feelings too painful to be admitted to consciousness)

Photodisc/Getty Images

Stockbyte Platinum/Getty Images

MM Productions/©Corbis

Getty Images

David Madison/Duomo Photography, Inc

Concept Diagram 5.1
The Scientific Study of Sleep and Dreaming

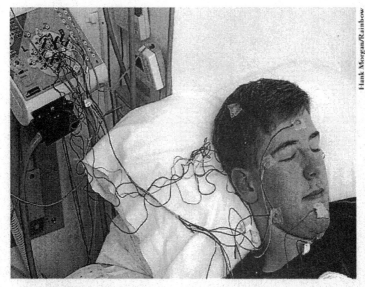

(a) Sleep research participants wear electrodes on their heads and bodies to measure brain and body responses during the sleep cycle.

Hank Morgan/Rainbow

(b) An **electroencephalograph** detects and records brain-wave changes by means of small electrodes on the scalp. Other electrodes measure muscle activity and eye movements. The stages of sleep, defined by telltale changes in brain waves, are indicated by the green stepped lines. The compact brain waves of alertness gradually lengthen as we drift into Stages 1–4. By the end of Stage 4, a change in body position generally occurs and heart rate, blood pressure, and respiratory rates all decrease. The sleeper then reverses through Stages 3 and 2 before entering the first REM period of the night. Although the brain and body are giving many signs of active arousal during REM sleep, the musculature is deeply relaxed and unresponsive. Sleepers awakened from REM sleep often report vivid, bizarre dreams, indicated in the figure by red and yellow dots. Those awakened from Stages 1–4 sleep often have more peaceful thoughts (indicated by muted dots). The heavy green line on the graph showing all four stages of sleep indicates the approximate time spent in REM sleep. Note how the length of the REM period increases as the night progresses.

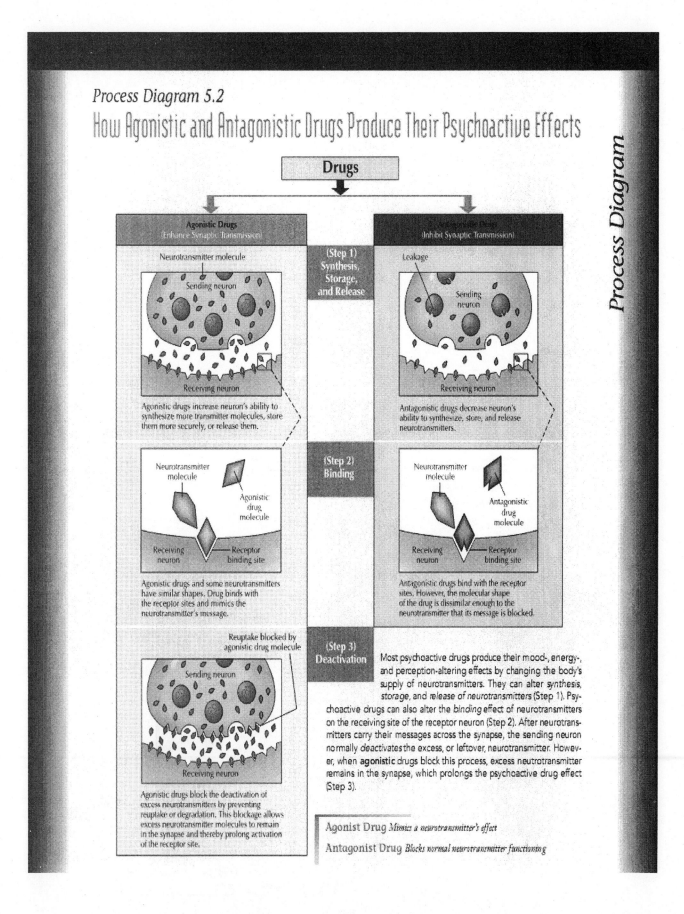

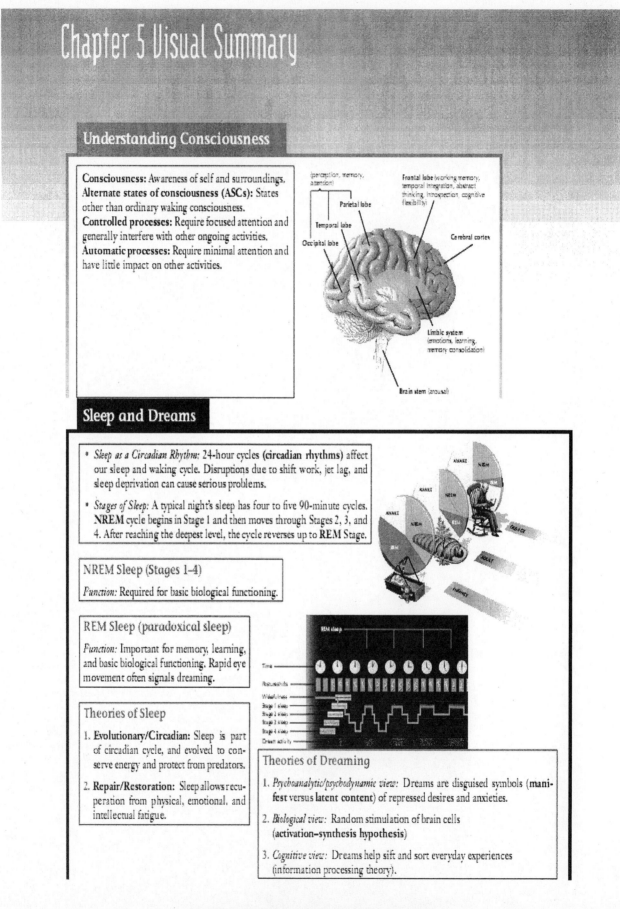

Chapter 5 Visual Summary

Understanding Consciousness

Consciousness: Awareness of self and surroundings.
Alternate states of consciousness (ASCs): States other than ordinary waking consciousness.
Controlled processes: Require focused attention and generally interfere with other ongoing activities.
Automatic processes: Require minimal attention and have little impact on other activities.

Sleep and Dreams

* *Sleep as a Circadian Rhythm:* 24-hour cycles (**circadian rhythms**) affect our sleep and waking cycle. Disruptions due to shift work, jet lag, and sleep deprivation can cause serious problems.

* *Stages of Sleep:* A typical night's sleep has four to five 90-minute cycles. **NREM** cycle begins in Stage 1 and then moves through Stages 2, 3, and 4. After reaching the deepest level, the cycle reverses up to **REM** Stage.

NREM Sleep (Stages 1-4)

Function: Required for basic biological functioning.

REM Sleep (paradoxical sleep)

Function: Important for memory, learning, and basic biological functioning. Rapid eye movement often signals dreaming.

Theories of Sleep

1. **Evolutionary/Circadian:** Sleep is part of circadian cycle, and evolved to conserve energy and protect from predators.

2. **Repair/Restoration:** Sleep allows recuperation from physical, emotional, and intellectual fatigue.

Theories of Dreaming

1. *Psychoanalytic/psychodynamic view:* Dreams are disguised symbols (**manifest** versus **latent content**) of repressed desires and anxieties.

2. *Biological view:* Random stimulation of brain cells (**activation–synthesis hypothesis**)

3. *Cognitive view:* Dreams help sift and sort everyday experiences (information processing theory).

Sleep and Dreams

Sleep Disorders

Insomnia
* Repeated difficulty falling or staying asleep or awakening too early.

Sleep Apnea
* Temporarily stopping breathing during sleep.

Narcolepsy
* Sudden and irresistible onsets of sleep during waking hours.

Nightmares
* Bad dreams generally occurring during REM sleep.

Night Terrors
* Panic, hallucinations, and abrupt awakenings during NREM sleep.

Nightmare or night terror?

Psychoactive Drugs

Important Terminology

Drug abuse: Drug taking that causes emotional or physical harm to the individual or others.
Addiction: Broad term referring to feelings of compulsion.
Psychological dependence: Desire or craving to achieve effects produced by a drug.
Physical dependence: Change in bodily processes that make a drug necessary for minimal functioning.
Withdrawal: Discomfort and distress after stopping addictive drugs.
Tolerance: Decreased sensitivity to a drug due to its continuous use.

Four Major Categories of Drugs

1) **Depressants** or "downers" (alcohol and barbiturates) slow down CNS.
2) **Stimulants** or "uppers" (caffeine, nicotine, and cocaine) activate CNS.
3) **Opiates** (heroin or morphine) numb senses and relieve pain.
4) **Hallucinogens** or psychedelics (LSD or marijuana) produce sensory or perceptual distortions.

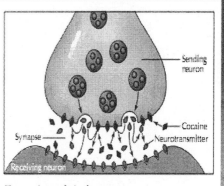

How cocaine works in the synapse.

Healthier Ways to Alter Consciousness

Meditation:

Group of techniques designed to refocus attention, and block out all distractions

Hypnosis:

Trancelike state of heightened suggestibility, deep relaxation, and intense focus.

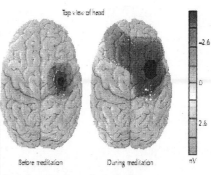

Brain scans showing meditation's effects.

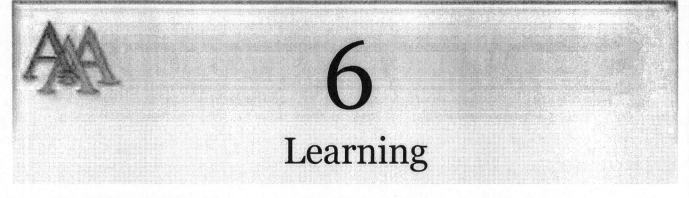

6
Learning

OUTLINE SQ4R (Survey, Question, Read, Recite, Review, & wRite)

This outline section incorporates all six steps in the well-researched SQ4R method of learning. Begin by surveying the list of chapter topics in the left column. This "big picture" will help focus and guide your attention while you read. As you read through the chapter, briefly summarize each section in your own words in the space to the right. Also write down any *questions* that come to mind. Surveying, Questioning, Reading, Reciting, Reviewing, and wRiting are the foundation of the SQ4R method and an invaluable form of active learning. They also make your reading time more enjoyable and efficient! One thorough, focused SQ4R reading of a chapter is far better than several passive readings.

TOPIC   **NOTES**

I. CLASSICAL CONDITIONING

   A. Pavlov and Watson's Contributions

   B. Basic Principles

II. OPERANT CONDITIONING

   A. Thorndike and Skinner's Contributions

   B. Basic Principles

Critical Thinking/Active Learning:
   Using Learning Principles to Succeed in College

III. COGNITIVE-SOCIAL LEARNING

A. Insight and Latent Learning

B. Observational Learning

Research Highlight: "The Theory Heard Round the World"

Gender & Cultural Diversity: Scaffolding as a Teaching Technique in Different Cultures

IV. THE BIOLOGY OF LEARNING

A. Neuroscience and Learning

B. Evolution and Learning

V. USING CONDITIONING AND LEARNING PRINCIPLES

A. *Psychology at Work: Classical Conditioning*

B. *Psychology at Work: Operant Conditioning*

C. *Psychology at Work: Cognitive-Social Learning*

LEARNING OBJECTIVES (Read, Recite, Review, & wRite)

In addition to the work you did in the Outline above, you can significantly improve your performance on exams by focusing on the following learning objectives. While reading the chapter or reviewing for exams, check your understanding by stopping periodically to *recite* (or repeat in your own words) and *writing* down your answers on a separate sheet. [Page numbers correspond to Chapter 6 in *Psychology in Action* (9e).]

6.1 Compare learning and conditioning. (p. 204)

6.2 Define classical conditioning, and describe Pavlov and Watson's contributions. (p. 204)

6.3 Describe the six principles of classical conditioning. (p. 208)

6.4 Define operant conditioning, reinforcement, and punishment. (p. 212)

6.5 Describe Thorndike and Skinner's contributions. (p. 212)

6.6 Explain how primary and secondary reinforcers and positive and negative reinforcement strengthen behavior. (p. 213)

6.7 Explain why negative reinforcement is not punishment. (p. 214)

6.8 Contrast continuous and partial (intermittent) reinforcement, and identify the four schedules of partial reinforcement. (p. 215)

6.9 Define shaping and tell why it's important. (p. 216)

6.10 Explain how positive and negative punishment weaken behavior. (p. 217)

6.11 Why is punishment "tricky," and what are its serious side effects. (p. 217)

6.12 How can we effectively use reinforcement and punishment? (p. 220)

6.13 Briefly summarize the similarities between classical and operant conditioning. (p. 221)

6.14 Define cognitive-social learning, and describe Köhler and Tolman's contributions. (p. 223)

6.15 What is observational learning and what are the four factors required for learning by observation? (p. 225)

6.16 Describe the positive cross-cultural effects of observational learning through television. (p. 227)

6.17 What is scaffolding? (p. 228)

6.18 How does learning affect the brain? (p. 229)

6.19 What role does evolution play in learning? (p. 230)

6.20 How can classical conditioning be applied to everyday life? (p. 232)

6.21 How can operant conditioning be applied to everyday life? (p. 235)

6.22 How can cognitive-social learning be applied to everyday life? (p. 237)

KEY TERMS (Review & wRite)

Like other survey courses, introductory psychology is filled with a "wealth" of new and unfamiliar terminology. To do well on exams, you must master this new language! Writing a brief definition of each term in the space provided and carefully reviewing them before exams will significantly improve your course grade.

Acquisition: _____

_____

Biofeedback: _____

_____

Biological Preparedness: _____

_____

Classical Conditioning: _____

_____

Cognitive Map: _____

_____

Cognitive-Social Theory: _____

_____

Conditioned Emotional Response (CER): _____

_____

Conditioned Response (CR): _____

_____

Conditioned Stimulus (CS): _____

_____

Conditioning: _____

_____

Continuous Reinforcement: _____

_____

Discriminative Stimulus: _____

_____

Extinction: _____

_____

Fixed Interval (FI) Schedule: _____

_____

Fixed Ratio (FR) Schedule: _____

_____

Higher-Order Conditioning: _____

_____

Insight: _____

_____

Instinctive Drift: _____

_____

Latent Learning: _____

_____

Law of Effect: _____

_____

Learning: _____

_____

Negative Punishment: _____

_____

Negative Reinforcement: _____

_____

Neutral Stimulus (NS): _____

_____

Observational Learning: _____

_____

Operant Conditioning: _____

_____

Partial (Intermittent) Reinforcement: _____

_____

Positive Punishment: _____

_____

Positive Reinforcement: _____

_____

Premack Principle: _____

_____

Primary Reinforcers: _____

_____

Punishment: _____

_____

Reinforcement: _____

_____

Secondary Reinforcers: _____

_____

Shaping: _____

_____

Spontaneous Recovery: _____

_____

Stimulus Discrimination: _____

_____

Stimulus Generalization: _____

_____

Taste Aversion: _____

_____

Unconditioned Response (UCR): _____

_____

Unconditioned Stimulus (UCS): _____

_____

Variable Interval (VI) Schedule: _____

_____

Variable Ratio (VR) Schedule: _____

_____

ACTIVE LEARNING EXERCISES

True mastery of information requires you to be an ACTIVE learner. Completing the following active learning exercises will improve your understanding of the chapter material and greatly improve your performance on exams. Answers to some exercises appear in Appendix A at the end of this study guide.

ACTIVE LEARNING EXERCISE I *Do you want to score higher on your quizzes and exams for Chapter 6, while also improving your everyday life? Correctly identifying the neutral stimulus (NS), the unconditioned stimulus (UCS), the unconditioned response (UCR), the conditioned stimulus (CS), and the conditioned response (CR) is the first step to understanding and changing problems in your own life and improving your test scores. Complete the following exercise and then compare your responses with the correct answers in Appendix A at the end of this study guide.*

1. When your teenage son leaves the house and tells you "goodbye," he always slams the door. Now you begin to flinch as soon as he says "goodbye." For your flinching behavior, identify the:

NS: _____

UCS: _____

UCR: _____

CS: _____

CR: _____

2. A researcher flashes a light and then blows a puff of air into the research participant's eye. The participant automatically blinks. After a few trials, just the flash of light will cause the participant to blink. For this light elicited blinking behavior, identify the:

NS: _____

UCS: _____

UCR: _____

CS: _____

CR: _____

ACTIVE LEARNING EXERCISE II *Read each of the following examples, and then:*
Part I. If the situation is an example of classical conditioning, label the NS, UCS, UCR, CS, and CR.
Part II. If the situation is an example of operant conditioning, label whether it is positive or negative reinforcement, or positive or negative punishment.

SITUATION 1 A very bright (mildly painful) light is turned on a rat in a cage. This rat has learned that he can turn off the light by pressing a lever on the other side of his cage. As soon as the light comes on, the rat runs across the cage and presses the lever.
A. The behavior of pressing the lever is an example of _____ conditioning.
B. If you chose classical conditioning, follow Part I of the instructions. If you chose operant conditioning, follow Part II.

SITUATION 2 When a mother strokes her infant's skin, the stroking creates pleasure responses in the baby. After this goes on for many days, the baby begins to show pleasure responses simply at the sight of the mother—even before being touched.
A. The baby's pleasure response is an example of _____ conditioning.
B. If you chose classical conditioning, follow Part I of the instructions. If you chose operant conditioning, follow Part II.

SITUATION 3 A patient in a mental hospital is very disruptive at mealtimes. She grabs food from the plates of those sitting nearby and hurriedly crams the food into her mouth. Because this behavior of stealing food is very undesirable, a plan is developed whereby every time the patient steals food from other plates, she is immediately taken to a room without food.
A. The mental health staff is attempting to change the behavior of stealing through _____ conditioning.
B. If you chose classical conditioning, follow Part I of the instructions. If you chose operant conditioning, follow Part II.

SITUATION 4 You have a friend who keeps the temperature in her home so high that whenever you visit you find yourself perspiring from the heat. The last time you went to visit, you noticed that you began perspiring as you began ringing her doorbell.
A. Your perspiring behavior can be explained as _____ conditioning.
B. If you chose classical conditioning, follow Part I of the instructions. If you chose operant conditioning, follow Part II.

CHAPTER OVERVIEW (Review)

The following chapter overview provides a narrative overview of the main topics covered in the chapter. Like the *Visual Summary* found at the end of each chapter in the text, this narrative summary provides a final opportunity to *review* chapter material.

I. PAVLOV AND WATSON'S CONTRIBUTIONS

6.1 Compare learning and conditioning. (p. 204)

Learning is a general term referring to a relatively permanent change in behavior and mental processes due to experience. **Conditioning** is a specific type of learning of associations between environmental stimuli and behavioral responses.

6.2 Define classical conditioning, and describe Pavlov and Watson's contributions. (p. 204)

In **classical conditioning,** the type of learning investigated by Pavlov and Watson, an originally **neutral stimulus (NS)** is paired with an **unconditioned stimulus (UCS)** that causes a particular reflex or **unconditioned response (UCR).** After several pairings, the neutral stimulus becomes a **conditioned stimulus (CS)** that alone will produce a **conditioned response (CR)** or **conditioned emotional response (CER)** that is similar to the original reflex response.

Pavlov's work laid a foundation for Watson's later insistence that psychology must be an objective science, studying only overt behavior without considering internal, mental activity. Watson called this position *behaviorism*. His controversial "Little Albert" study demonstrated how simple emotions, like fear, could be classically conditioned to become a **conditioned emotional response (CER).**

II. BASIC PRINCIPLES OF CLASSICAL CONDITIONING

6.3 Describe the six principles of classical conditioning. (p. 208)

Acquisition is a form of classical conditioning that occurs when a neutral stimulus (NS) is consistently paired with an unconditioned stimulus (UCS) so that the NS comes to elicit a conditioned response (CR).

The second principle, **stimulus generalization** occurs when stimuli similar to the original conditioned stimulus (CS) elicit the conditioned response (CR). **Stimulus discrimination** takes place when only the CS elicits the CR. **Extinction** occurs when the (UCS) is repeatedly withheld and the association between the CS and the UCS is weakened. **Spontaneous recovery** happens when a CR that had been extinguished reappears with no prompting. In **higher-order conditioning,** a NS becomes a CS through repeated pairings with a previously conditioned stimulus (CS).

III. OPERANT CONDITIONING

6.4 Define operant conditioning, reinforcement, and punishment. (p. 212)

In **operant conditioning,** human and nonhuman animals learn by the consequences of their voluntary responses. Whether behavior is reinforced or punished (consequences) determines whether the response will occur again. **Reinforcement** is any procedure that strengthens or increases a response, whereas **punishment** is any procedure that results in a weakening or decrease.

6.5 Describe Thorndike and Skinner's contributions. (p. 212)
Thorndike and Skinner are the two major contributors to operant conditioning. Thorndike's **law of effect** states that rewarded behavior is more likely to recur. Skinner extended Thorndike's work to more complex behaviors but emphasized only external, observable behaviors.

6.6 Explain how primary and secondary reinforcers and positive and negative reinforcement strengthen behavior. (p. 213)
To strengthen a response, we use **primary reinforcers,** which satisfy an unlearned biological need (e.g., hunger, thirst), and **secondary reinforcers,** which have learned value (e.g., money). **Positive reinforcement** (adding something) and **negative reinforcement** (taking something away) both increase the likelihood the response will occur again.

6.7 Explain why negative reinforcement is not punishment. (p. 214)
Reinforcement (either positive or negative) always strengthen a behavior, whereas punishment always weakens a behavior and makes it less likely to recur.

6.8 Contrast continuous and partial (intermittent) reinforcement, and identify the four schedules of partial reinforcement. (p. 215)
Continuous reinforcement rewards each correct response, whereas a **partial (intermittent) schedule** reinforces for some, not all, correct responses. The four partial reinforcement schedules are **variable ratio (VR), variable interval (VI), fixed ratio (FR),** and **fixed interval (FI).**

6.9 Define shaping and tell why it's important. (p. 216)
Shaping is a reinforcement that is delivered for successive approximations of the desired response. It is particularly important for new and complex behaviors that are unlikely to occur naturally.

6.10 Explain how both positive and negative punishment weaken behavior. (p. 217)
Positive punishment (adding something) and **negative punishment** (taking something away) decrease the likelihood the response will occur again.

6.11 Why is punishment "tricky," and what are its serious side effects. (p. 217)
Although some punishment is essential, it can be tricky because we often unintentionally punish the very behaviors we're trying to increase. Also, to be effective, punishment must be immediate and consistent. When it's delayed and/or inconsistent, the undesirable behavior can be unintentionally reinforced. The reinforcement then places the undesirable behavior on a partial schedule of reinforcement—thus making it even more resistant to extinction. Furthermore, punishment only teaches what not to do—not what should be done.

In addition, punishment has potentially serious side effects, including: increased aggression, passive aggressiveness, avoidance, inappropriate modeling, temporary suppression versus elimination, and learned helplessness.

6.12 How can we effectively use reinforcement and punishment? (p. 220)
To be effective, reinforcement and punishment require clear directions and feedback, appropriate timing, consistency, a correct order of presentation, and a combination of key learning principles.

6.13 Briefly summarize the similarities between classical and operant conditioning. (p. 221)
Both classical and operant conditioning share terms, such as generalization, discrimination, extinction, and spontaneous recovery. Almost all behaviors also result from a combination of both classical and operant conditioning.

IV. COGNITIVE-SOCIAL LEARNING

6.14 Define cognitive-social learning, and describe Köhler and Tolman's contributions. (p. 223)
Cognitive-social theory incorporates concepts of conditioning but emphasizes thought processes, or cognitions, and social learning. According to this perspective, people learn through insight, latent learning, observation, and modeling.

Köhler's work with chimpanzees demonstrated that learning could occur with a sudden flash of **insight.** Tolman found that **latent learning** occurs without obvious reward and remains hidden until some future time when it can be retrieved as needed. A **cognitive map** is a mental image of an area that a person or nonhuman animal has navigated.

6.15 What is observational learning and what are the four factors required for learning by observation? (p. 225)
According to Albert Bandura, **observational learning** is the process of learning how to do something by watching others and performing the same behavior in the future. It requires at least four processes--we must pay attention, remember, be able to reproduce the behavior, and be motivated by some reinforcement.

6.16 Describe the positive cross-cultural effects of observational learning through television. (p. 227)
Specially created TV "soap operas" in less-developed countries have had positive effects on social problems like illiteracy, HIV, overpopulation, and gender discrimination.

6.17 What is scaffolding? (p. 228)
Scaffolding is a type of guided practice used in many countries that provides a platform and guided assistance while the learner acquires new skills.

V. THE BIOLOGY OF LEARNING

6.18 How does learning affect the brain? (p. 229)
Learning and conditioning produce relatively permanent changes in biochemistry and in various parts of the brain.

6.19 What role does evolution play in learning? (p. 230)
At least some behavior is innate, or inborn, in the form of either reflexes or instincts, and all animals are programmed to engage in certain innate behaviors that have evolutionary survival benefits.

Through **biological preparedness** an organism is innately predisposed to form associations between certain stimuli and responses. **Taste aversions** are classically conditioned associations of food to illness that are rapidly learned, often in a single pairing, and reflect a protective survival mechanism for a species. In addition, findings on **instinctive drift** show there are biological constraints on operant conditioning.

VI. USING CONDITIONING AND LEARNING PRINCIPLES

6.20 How can classical conditioning be applied to everyday life? (p. 232)
Classical conditioning has many applications in everyday life. It explains how people market their products, how we sometimes learn negative attitudes toward groups of people (prejudice), and how we sometimes have problems with certain medical treatments and phobias.

6.21 How can operant conditioning be applied to everyday life? (p. 235)
Operant conditioning also has several practical applications. It helps explain how we learn

prejudice through positive reinforcement and stimulus generalization. **Biofeedback,** another application, is the feeding back of biological information, such as heart rate or blood pressure, which a person uses to control normally automatic functions of the body. Operant conditioning also helps explain many superstitions, which involve accidentally reinforced behaviors that are continually repeated because they are believed to cause desired effects.

6.22 How can cognitive-social learning be applied to everyday life? (p. 237)
Cognitive-social theory helps to further explain prejudice and media influences. People often learn their prejudices by imitating what they have seen modeled by friends, family, and the media. The media affect our purchasing behaviors as well as our aggressive tendencies. Video games may have a particularly strong influence.

SELF-TESTS (<u>R</u>eview & w<u>R</u>ite)

Completing the following self-tests will provide immediate feedback on how well you have mastered the material. In the labeling exercises, *crossword puzzle*, and *fill-in exercises*, write the appropriate word or words in the blank spaces. The *matching exercise* requires you to match the terms in one column to their correct definitions in the other. For the *multiple-choice questions* in Practice Tests I and II, circle or underline the correct answer. If you are unsure of any answer, mark the item, and then go back to the text for further review. Correct answers are provided in Appendix A at the end of this study guide.

CROSSWORD PUZZLE FOR CHAPTER 6

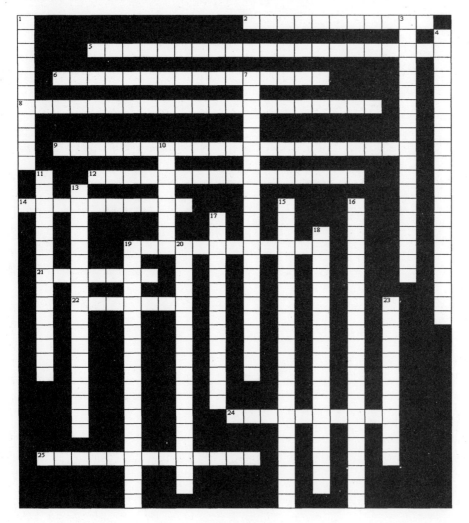

ACROSS

2 A bodily function (such as blood pressure or heart rate) is recorded and the information is fed back to an organism to increase voluntary control over that bodily function.

5 Unlearned reaction to an unconditioned stimulus (UCS) that occurs without previous conditioning.

6 Conditioned responses shift (or drift) back toward innate response patterns.

8 Reinforcement occurs after a fixed (predetermined) time has elapsed.

9 Reinforcement occurs unpredictably; the ratio (the number or amount) varies.

12 Premack's law that using a naturally occurring high-frequency response will reinforce and increase low-frequency responses.

14 Weakens a response and makes it less likely to recur.

19 Mental image of a three-dimensional space an organism has navigated.

21 Reinforcement is delivered for successive approximations of the desired response.

22 Sudden understanding of a problem that also implies the solution.

24 Gradual weakening or suppression of a previously conditioned response (CR).

25 Strengthens a response and makes it more likely to recur.

DOWN

1 According to Thorndike, the probability of an action being repeated strengthens if it is followed by a pleasant or satisfying consequence.

3 Previously neutral stimulus that through repeated pairings with an unconditioned stimulus (UCS) now causes a conditioned response (CR).

4 Taking away (or removing) a stimulus, which strengthens a response and makes it more likely to recur.

7 A cue that signals when a specific response will lead to the expected reinforcement.

10 A relatively permanent change in behavior or mental processes based on practice or experience.

11 Stimulus that before conditioning does not naturally bring about the response of interest.

13 Reinforcement occurs after a fixed (predetermined) number of responses.

15 Learned response not only to the original stimulus but also to other similar stimuli.

16 Learned response to a specific stimulus but not to other, similar stimuli.

17 Learning that occurs without an obvious reward and remains hidden until there is some incentive to demonstrate it.

18 Reappearance of a previously extinguished conditioned response (CR).

19 Learned reaction to a conditioned stimulus (CS) that occurs because of previous repeated pairings with an unconditioned stimulus (UCS).

20 Taking away (or removing) a stimulus, which weakens a response and makes it less likely to recur.

23 Learning associations between environmental stimuli and behavioral responses.

FILL-IN EXERCISES

1. _____ is a general term referring to a relatively permanent change in behavior and mental processes due to experience. _____ is a specific type of learning of associations between environmental stimuli and behavioral responses (p. 204).

2. _____ is a reflex response evoked by a stimulus without any required learning (pp. 205-206).

3. A gradual weakening or suppression of a previously conditioned response (CR) is known as _____ (pp. 209-210).

4. _____ occurs when a previously extinguished response suddenly reappears (p. 210).

5. Learning based on consequences is called _____ (p. 212).

6. _____ strengthens a response and makes it more likely to recur. In contrast, _____ weakens a response and makes it less likely to recur (p. 212).

7. A response that is _____ reinforced will be learned more rapidly. Conversely, a response that is _____ reinforced will be more resistant to extinction (p. 215).

8. _____ involves reinforcing successive approximations to the desired behavior (p. 216).

9. _____ is an innate readiness to form associations between certain stimuli and responses (p. 230).

10. Football players who only wear their "lucky" t-shirt or routinely touch their right ear three times before entering the playing field may be examples of _____ (p. 236).

MATCHING EXERCISES

Column A

a. Extinction
b. Cognitive Map
c. Positive Punishment
d. Cognitive-Social Theory
e. Reinforcement
f. Classical Conditioning
g. Latent Learning
h. Shaping
i. Instinctive Drift
j. Conditioned Stimulus (CS)

Column B

1.____ Occurs in the absence of a reward
2.____ Gradual unlearning by presenting CS without the UCS
3.____ Shifting back toward innate response patterns
4.____ Reinforcing successive approximations
5.____ Previously NS that now causes CR
6.____ Anything likely to cause an increase in response
7.____ Mental image of a three-dimensional space
8.____ Something added that causes a decrease in response
9.____ Focuses on thinking and social learning processes
10.____ Involuntary response to a stimulus

PRACTICE TEST I

1. Salivation was the _____ in Pavlov's classical conditioning experiments with dogs.
    a. unconditioned stimulus (UCS)
    b. conditioned response (CR)
    c. unconditioned response (UCR)
    d. both b and c

2. When a young child learns to fear dogs after being bitten, the unconditioned STIMULUS (UCS) is the _____.
    a. dog
    b. bite
    c. fear
    d. none of these options

3. When a young child learns to fear dogs after being bitten, the unconditioned RESPONSE (UCR) is the _____.
    a. dog
    b. bite
    c. fear
    d. crying

4. Which of the following is the normal sequence of events in classical conditioning?
    a. UCS-CS-UCR
    b. NS-UCS-CR
    c. UCR-UCS-CS
    d. UCR-CS-UCS

5. An emotional response that is evoked by a previously neutral event is called a(n) _____.
    a. conditioned emotional response (CER)
    b. gut automatic reaction (GAR)
    c. spontaneous emotional reaction (SES)
    d. elicited emotional response (EER)

6. When the CR is elicited by stimuli that are similar to the CS. This is called _____.
    a. stimulus generalization
    b. stimulus discrimination
    c. spontaneous conditioning
    d. replication of the effect

7. Extinction in classical conditioning occurs when the _____.
    a. conditioned stimulus (CS) is no longer paired with the unconditioned response (UCR)
    b. conditioned stimulus (CS) is no longer paired with the unconditioned stimulus (UCS)
    c. conditioned response (CR) is no longer paired with the unconditioned stimulus (UCS)
    d. unconditioned stimulus (UCS) is ambiguous

8. Higher order conditioning occurs when a(n) _____.
    a. previously neutral stimulus (NS) elicits a conditioned response (CR)
    b. neutral stimulus (NS) is paired with a conditioned stimulus (CS)
    c. neutral stimulus (NS) is paired with an unconditioned stimulus (UCS)
    d. unconditioned response (UCR) is paired with a conditioned stimulus (CS)

9. Anything that causes an increase in a response is a(n) _____.
    a. conditioned stimulus (CS)
    b. reinforcement
    c. punishment
    d. unconditioned stimulus (UCS)

10. Anything that causes a decrease in a response is a(n) _____.
    a. conditioned stimulus (CS)
    b. reinforcement
    c. punishment
    d. unconditioned stimulus (UCS)

11. _____ reinforcers normally satisfy an unlearned biological need.
    a. Positive
    b. Negative
    c. Primary
    d. none of these options

12. Negative reinforcement and punishment are _____.
    a. essentially the same because they both decrease behavior
    b. the best ways to learn a new behavior
    c. not the same because negative reinforcement increases behavior and punishment decreases behavior
    d. not the same, even though they both decrease behavior

13. Making yourself exercise before turning on the tv is a good application of _____.
    a. negative reinforcement
    b. positive punishment
    c. fixed ratio schedule of reinforcement
    d. the Premack principle

14. Gamblers become addicted partially because of a _____.
    a. previously generalized response discrimination
    b. previously extinguished response recovery
    c. partial (intermittent) reinforcement
    d. behavior being learned and not conditioned

15. If you receive payment for every ten boxes you pack, this is a _____.
    a. continuous schedule of reinforcement
    b. random ratio reinforcement schedule
    c. fixed interval reinforcement schedule
    d. fixed ratio reinforcement schedule

16. A _____cue signals when a particular response is likely to be followed by a certain type of consequence.
    a. primary reinforcer
    b. negative reinforcer
    c. discriminative stimulus
    d. variable ratio stimulus

17. Learning that occurs in the absence of a reward and remains hidden until some future time when it can be retrieved is called _____.
    a. latent learning
    b. insight
    c. spontaneous recovery
    d. trial-and-error learning

18. Albert Bandura's social learning theory emphasized _____.
    a. classical conditioning
    b. operant conditioning
    c. extinction
    d. modeling

19. Being innately predisposed to form associations between certain stimuli and responses is called _____.
    a. prejudice
    b. superstitious priming
    c. vicarious learning
    d. biological preparedness

20. Children may learn to be prejudiced because of _____.
    a. operant conditioning
    b. classical conditioning
    c. observational learning
    d. all of these options

PRACTICE TEST II

1. _____ is defined in your text as a relatively permanent change in behavior or mental processes resulting from practice or experience.
    a. Conditioning
    b. Learning
    c. Behavior modification
    d. Modeling

2. When your mouth waters at the sight of a broiling steak, it is an example of _____.
    a. operant conditioning
    b. social learning
    c. vicarious conditioning
    d. classical conditioning

3. John B. Watson and Rosalie Rayner demonstrated how the emotion of _____ could be classically conditioned.
   a. love
   b. anger
   c. joy
   d. fear

4. In Watson and Rayner's experiment, _____ was the neutral stimulus (NS).
   a. the sight of the experimental room
   b. a loud noise
   c. a rabbit
   d. a rat

5. In Watson and Rayner's experiment, _____ was the conditioned emotional response (CER).
   a. avoidance behavior
   b. superstitious behavior
   c. fear
   d. none of the above

6. In Watson and Rayner's experiment, _____ was the unconditioned stimulus (UCS)?
   a. the sight of the experimental room
   b. a loud noise
   c. a rabbit
   d. a rat

7. _____ is defined in your text as a learned response to a specific stimulus but not to other, similar stimuli.
   a. Extinction
   b. The Premack principle
   c. Stimulus discrimination
   d. none of these options

8. Spontaneous recovery occurs when _____ suddenly reappears.
   a. your lost wallet
   b. a previously extinguished response
   c. an extinct instinct
   d. a forgotten stimulus-response sequence

9. Thanks to _____, children often beg to stop at McDonald's after simply seeing the golden arches.
   a. instrumental conditioning
   b. higher-order conditioning
   c. operant conditioning
   d. all of these options

10. _____ meet a learned, not biological, need.
   a. Primary instincts
   b. Secondary instincts
   c. Primary reinforcers
   d. Secondary reinforcers

11. Gamblers continue play slot machines because they pay off _____.
   a. on a variable ratio
   b. at variable intervals
   c. at fixed intervals
   d. on a fixed ratio

12. Which of the following is an example of passive aggressiveness, which may be a side effect of punishment?
   a. Janeel is late to dinner every night and never does her chores on time.
   b. Enrique refuses to do anything his father asks him to do, unless strictly supervised.
   c. Gabe intentionally leaves food on dishes he puts in the dishwasher.
   d. all of these options

13. Insight is _____.
   a. based on unconscious classical conditioning
   b. divinely inspired
   c. a sudden flash of understanding
   d. an artifact of operant conditioning

14. Latent learning occurs without being rewarded and _____.
   a. remains hidden until a future time when it is needed
   b. is spontaneously recovered
   c. serves no useful purpose
   d. has been found only in nonhuman species

15. Observational learning theory suggests that we learn many behaviors by _____
   a. imitating others
   b. observing our inner processes
   c. teaching others
   d. shaping our own and others behaviors

16. "Follow my lead" could be a motto for
    _____.
    a. classical conditioning
    b. operant conditioning
    c. latent learning
    d. observational learning

17. In Albert Bandura's classic Bobo doll
    study, children acted aggressively
    because _____.
    a. they were rewarded for their
       behavior
    b. of observational learning
    c. they were positively punished
    d. all of these options

18. According to your text, a biological
    constraint where an animal's conditioned
    responses tend to shift toward innate
    response patterns is called _____.
    a. biological preparedness
    b. reflexes
    c. instinctive drift
    d. taste aversion

19. When you use biofeedback equipment to
    lower your blood pressure, this provides
    you with a sense of accomplishment and
    a more relaxed physiological state. In
    this case, biofeedback is a(n) _____.
    a. operant conditioning agent
    b. fixed interval reinforcer
    c. secondary reinforcer
    d. unconditioned stimulus (UCS)

20. Superstitious behavior often occurs
    because _____.
    a. it has been reinforced on a fixed
       ratio schedule
    b. a person or an animal thinks the
       behavior causes a reinforcer when
       in reality the behavior and the
       reinforcement are not connected
    c. it is reinforced on a random ratio
       schedule
    d. the behavior and the reinforcement
       come in close proximity to one
       another, causing the superstitious
       behavior to increase in magnitude

Process Diagram 6.1
Pavlov's Classical Conditioning

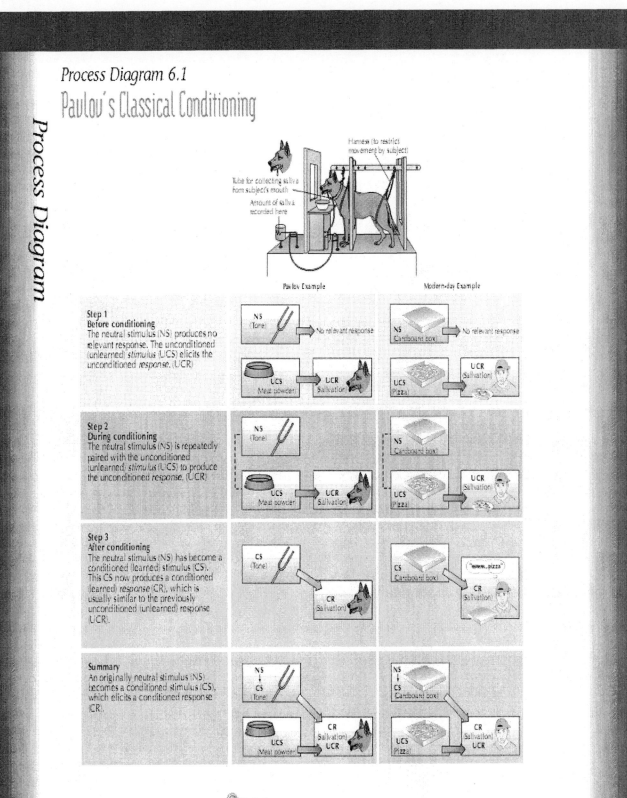

Study Tip

Use this figure to help you visualize and organize the three major stages of classical conditioning and their associated key terms. If it's confusing, first remember conditioning is essentially the same as learning. Next, when thinking of a UCS or UCR, picture how a newborn baby, with little or no previous learning, would respond. The baby's innate, unlearned response to the UCS would be the UCR.

Concept Diagram 6.1
Higher-order Conditioning

If you wanted to demonstrate higher-order conditioning in Pavlov's dogs, you would first condition the dogs to salivate in response to the sound of the tone (a). Then you would pair a flash of light with the tone (b). Eventually, the dogs would salivate in response to the flash of light alone (c). Similarly, children first learn to pair McDonald's restaurants with food and later learn that two golden arches are a symbol for McDonald's. Their salivation and begging to eat at the restaurant upon seeing the arches are classic examples of higher-order conditioning (and successful advertising).

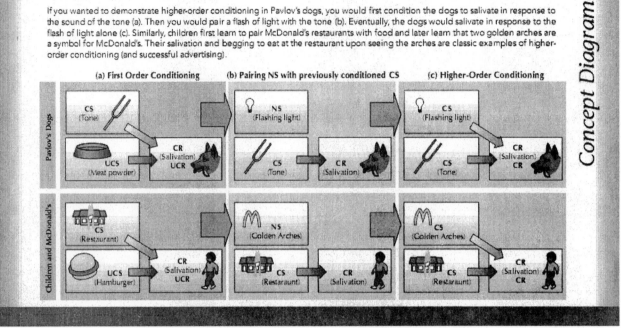

Concept Diagram

SUMMARY TABLE 6.6 COMPARING CLASSICAL AND OPERANT CONDITIONING

	Classical Conditioning	Operant Conditioning
Pioneers	Ivan Pavlov John B. Watson	Edward Thorndike B. F. Skinner
Major Terms	Neutral stimulus (NS) Unconditioned stimulus (UCS) Conditioned stimulus (CS) Unconditioned response (UCR) Conditioned response (CR) Conditioned emotional response (CER)	Reinforcers (primary and secondary) Reinforcement (positive and negative) Punishment (positive and negative) Shaping Reinforcement schedules (continuous and partial)
Example	Cringing at the sound of a dentist's drill	A baby cries and you pick it up
Shared Terms	Generalization Discrimination Extinction Spontaneous recovery	Generalization Discrimination Extinction Spontaneous recovery
Major Differences	Learning based on paired associations Involuntary (subject is passive)	Learning based on consequences Voluntary (subject is active and "operates" on the environment)
Order of Effects	NS generally comes *before* the UCS	Reinforcement or punishment come *after* the behavior

Concept Diagram

Concept Diagram 6.2
Four Key Factors in Observational Learning

1. ATTENTION

Observational learning requires attention. This is why teachers insist on having students watch their demonstrations.

2. RETENTION

To learn new behaviors, we need to carefully note and remember the model's directions and demonstrations.

3. REPRODUCTION

Observational learning cannot occur if we lack the motivation or motor skills necessary to imitate the model.

4. REINFORCEMENT

We are more likely to repeat a modeled behavior if the model is reinforced for the behavior.

Anne-Christine Poujoulat/AFP/Getty Images

Using the four factors of observational learning Does the sight of this litter upset you? Why do people help destroy their own environment? Some stores are now banning plastic bags or charging extra for their use. Is this the best way to reduce litter? Can you explain how littering (and its solution) could involve a combination of all four factors of observational learning—attention, retention, reproduction, and reinforcement?

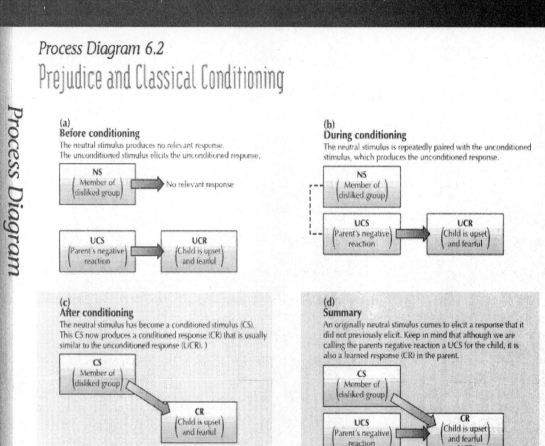

Process Diagram 6.2
Prejudice and Classical Conditioning

(a)
Before conditioning
The neutral stimulus produces no relevant response.
The unconditioned stimulus elicits the unconditioned response.

NS (Member of disliked group) → No relevant response

UCS (Parent's negative reaction) → UCR (Child is upset and fearful)

(b)
During conditioning
The neutral stimulus is repeatedly paired with the unconditioned stimulus, which produces the unconditioned response.

NS (Member of disliked group)

UCS (Parent's negative reaction) → UCR (Child is upset and fearful)

(c)
After conditioning
The neutral stimulus has become a conditioned stimulus (CS).
This CS now produces a conditioned response (CR) that is usually similar to the unconditioned response (UCR.)

CS (Member of disliked group) → CR (Child is upset and fearful)

(d)
Summary
An originally neutral stimulus comes to elicit a response that it did not previously elicit. Keep in mind that although we are calling the parents negative reaction a UCS for the child, it is also a learned response (CR) in the parent.

CS (Member of disliked group)

UCS (Parent's negative reaction) → CR (Child is upset and fearful) UCR

As described in the chapter opener, James Byrd was viciously murdered because of his skin color. How did this prejudice develop? (a) Before children are conditioned to be prejudiced, they show no response to a member of a different group. (b) Given that children are naturally upset and fearful when they see their parents upset, they can learn to be upset and fearful (UCR) if they see their parents respond negatively (UCS) to a member of a disliked group (NS). (c) After several pairings of the person from this group with their parents' negative reactions, the sight of the other person becomes a conditioned stimulus (CS). Being upset and fearful becomes the conditioned response (CR). (d) A previously unbiased child has now learned to be prejudiced.

Chapter 6 Visual Summary

Classical Conditioning

Process: Involuntary
Pavlov and Watson's Contributions

1) Before conditioning, originally **neutral stimulus (NS)** causes no relevant response, whereas **unconditioned stimulus (UCS)** causes **unconditioned response (UCR)**.

2) During conditioning, NS is paired with UCS that elicits the UCR.

3) After conditioning, previous NS becomes **conditioned stimulus (CS)**, which now causes a **conditioned response (CR)**, or **conditioned emotional response (CER)**.

Principles of Classical Conditioning

* **Acquisition:** NS is paired with an UCS, so that the NS comes to elicit the CR.

* **Stimulus generalization:** Stimuli similar to original CS elicit CR.

* **Stimulus discrimination:** Only the CS elicits the CR.

* **Extinction:** Repeatedly presenting the CS without the UCS, which gradually weakens the CR.

* **Spontaneous recovery:** Sudden reappearance of a previously extinguished CR.

* **Higher-order conditioning:** NS becomes a CS through repeated pairings with a previously conditioned stimulus (CS).

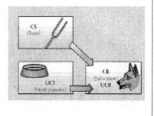

Operant Conditioning

Process: Voluntary
Organisms learn through consequences of their behavior. When responses are **reinforced**, they are strengthened and likely to increase; when **punished**, they are weakened and likely to decrease.

Thorndike and Skinner's Contributions

Thorndike emphasized the law of effect.

Skinner emphasized observable behaviors.

Principles of Operant Conditioning

* Strengthening a response occurs through:
  1) Primary and secondary reinforcers: **Primary reinforcers**, like food, satisfy a biological need. The value of **secondary reinforcers**, such as money, is learned.
  2) Positive and negative reinforcement: **Positive reinforcement** adds something that increases the likelihood of the response. **Negative reinforcement** takes away something that increases the likelihood of the response.

* Schedules of reinforcement: In a **continuous schedule of reinforcement**, every correct response is reinforced. In a **partial (or intermittent) schedule** only some response are reinforced. Partial schedules include **fixed ratio (FR)**, **variable ratio (VR)**, **fixed interval (FI)**, and **variable interval (VI)**.

* **Shaping** involves reinforcement for successive approximations of the desired response.

* Weakening a response occurs through:
  1) **Positive punishment**—adds something that decreases the likelihood of the response.
  2) **Negative punishment**—takes away something that decreases the likelihood of the response.

Cognitive–Social Learning

Insight and Latent Learning

* *Köhler:* Learning can occur with a sudden flash of understanding (**insight**).

* *Tolman:* Learning can happen without reinforcement and remain hidden until needed (**latent learning**). After navigating their environments, people and nonhuman animals create mental images called **cognitive maps**.

Observational Learning

* *Bandura:* Observational learning involves watching and imitating others. It requires *attention, retention, reproduction,* and *reinforcement*.

The Biology of Learning

Learning and conditioning produce relatively permanent changes in biochemistry and various parts of the brain. Evolutionary theorists believe some behavior is unlearned (e.g., reflexes or instincts), and that learning and conditioning are further adaptations that enable organisms to survive and prosper in a constantly changing world.

©James Balog Photography

Using Conditioning Principles

Psychology at work: Classical Conditioning in Everyday Life

* *Marketing:* Products (NS) are repeatedly paired with pleasant images (UCS) until they become a (CS).

* *Prejudice:* Negative perceptions of others may be acquired through classical conditioning processes.

* *Medical treatments:* Using nausea producing drugs, alcoholics learn to pair alcohol (CS) with nausea (CR).

* *Phobias:* Irrational fears may become a CS through association of a feared object with the UCS.

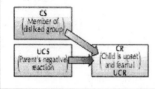

Psychology at work: Operant Conditioning in Everyday Life

* *Prejudice:* Negative perceptions of others, which may be acquired through operant conditioning.

* *Biofeedback:* "Feeding back" biological information (heart rate or blood pressure) for control of normally automatic body functions.

* *Superstitious behavior:* Develops from accidental rewarding of specific behaviors.

Psychology at work: Cognitive-Social Learning in Everyday Life

* *Prejudice:* Learned by observing, imitating, and modeling prejudices of others.

* *Media influences:* Consumerism, aggression, and other behaviors are partially learned from media models.

Joe Raedle/Getty Images News and Sport Services

7
Memory

OUTLINE SQ4R (Survey, Question, Read, Recite, Review, & wRite)

This outline section incorporates all six steps in the well-researched SQ4R method of learning. Begin by surveying the list of chapter topics in the left column. This "big picture" will help focus and guide your attention while you read. As you read through the chapter, briefly summarize each section in your own words in the space to the right. Also write down any *questions* that come to mind. Surveying, Questioning, Reading, Reciting, Reviewing, and wRiting are the foundation of the SQ4R method and an invaluable form of active learning. They also make your reading time more enjoyable and efficient! One thorough, focused SQ4R reading of a chapter is far better than several passive readings.

TOPIC	NOTES

I. THE NATURE OF MEMORY

   A. Memory Models

   B. Sensory Memory

   C. Short-Term Memory (STM)

   D. Long-Term Memory (LTM)

     Psychology at Work: Improving Long-Term Memory (LTM)

II. FORGETTING

A. How Quickly Do We Forget?

B. Why Do We Forget?

Psychology at Work: Key Factors in Forgetting

Gender & Cultural Diversity: Cultural Differences in Memory and Forgetting

III. BIOLOGICAL BASES OF MEMORY

A. How Are Memories Formed?

B. Where Are Memories Located?

C. Biological Causes of Memory Loss

Research Highlight: Memory and the Criminal Justice System

V. USING PSYCHOLOGY TO IMPROVE OUR MEMORY

A. Understanding Memory Distortions

B. Tips for Memory Improvement

Critical Thinking/Active Learning: Memory and Metacognition

LEARNING OBJECTIVES (Read, Recite, Review, & wRite)

In addition to the work you did in the Outline above, you can significantly improve your performance on exams by focusing on the following learning objectives. While reading the chapter or reviewing for exams, check your understanding by stopping periodically to *recite* (or repeat in your own words) and *writing* down your answers on a separate sheet. [Page numbers correspond to Chapter 7 in *Psychology in Action* (9e).]

7.1 Define memory, and describe the information-processing and parallel distributed processing (PDP) models of memory. (p. 244)
7.2 Summarize the three-stage memory model. (p. 247)
7.3 What is sensory memory? (p. 247)
7.4 Describe short-term memory (STM). (p. 248)
7.5 Summarize long-term memory (LTM), how it's divided into several subsystems, and how we can improve it. (p. 249)
7.6 Describe Ebbinghaus's contribution to memory research. (p. 257)
7.7 What are the five major theories of forgetting? (p. 257)
7.8 Describe four key factors that contribute to forgetting. (p. 260)
7.9 How does culture affect memory? (p. 261)
7.10 How do we form memories, and where do we store them? (p. 263)
7.11 What are the major biological causes of memory loss? (p. 264)
7.12 What's wrong with eyewitness testimony? (p. 268)
7.13 What do psychologists believe about repressed memories? (p. 268)
7.14 Why do we distort our memories? (p. 270)
7.15 How can we improve our memory? (p. 271)

KEY TERMS (Review & wRite)

Like other survey courses, introductory psychology is filled with a "wealth" of new and unfamiliar terminology. To do well on exams, you must master this new language! Writing a brief definition of each term in the space provided and carefully reviewing them before exams will significantly improve your course grade.

Alzheimer's Disease (AD): _____

_____

Anterograde Amnesia: _____

_____

Chunking: _____

_____

Constructive Processes: _____

_____

Distributed Practice: _____

_____

Elaborative Rehearsal: _____

_____

Encoding: _____

_____

Encoding Specificity Principle: _____

_____

Episodic Memory: _____

_____

Explicit (Declarative) Memory: _____

_____

Implicit (Nondeclarative) Memory: _____

_____

Levels of Processing: _____

_____

Long-Term Memory (LTM): _____

_____

Long-Term Potentiation (LTP): _____

_____

Maintenance Rehearsal: _____

_____

Massed Practice: _____

_____

Memory: _____

_____

Misinformation Effect: _____

_____

Mnemonic Device: _____

_____

Parallel Distributed Processing (PDP): _____

_____

Priming: _____

_____

Proactive Interference: _____

_____

Recall: _____

_____

Recognition: _____

_____

Relearning: _____

_____

Retrieval: _____

_____

Retrieval Cue: _____

_____

Retroactive Interference: _____

_____

Retrograde Amnesia: _____

_____

Semantic Memory: _____

_____

Sensory Memory: _____

_____

Serial Position Effect: _____

_____

Short-Term Memory (STM): _____

_____

Sleeper Effect: _____

_____

Source Amnesia: _____

_____

Storage: _____

_____

Tip-of-the-Tongue Phenomenon (TOT): _____

_____

ACTIVE LEARNING EXERCISES

True mastery of information requires you to be an ACTIVE learner. Completing the following active learning exercises will improve your understanding of the chapter material and greatly improve your performance on exams. Answers to some exercises appear in Appendix A at the end of this study guide.

ACTIVE LEARNING EXERCISE I *Collecting up-to-date, relevant information is an important component of critical thinking. To help build this skill, as well as to gain important insights into memory strategies, try the following:*

a. Interview three classmates who do well on exams and whom you believe have good memories. Ask about their study techniques and test-taking strategies. Now interview three classmates or friends who complain about their college grades and poor memories. Compare and contrast their study techniques and test-taking strategies to those who remember well.

_____

_____

b. Interview three people who have taken a reading improvement or speed-reading course. What methods were they taught that increased their reading speed and comprehension? What changes have they noticed in their college grades or exam performances after taking the course? Did they use any of the techniques or mnemonics discussed in the text?

_____

_____

ACTIVE LEARNING EXERCISE II *Now that you have discovered several mnemonic devices, you can use them to help improve your memory for names. The following exercise will help you learn how to convert a person's name into a visual image that will act as a memory retrieval cue.*

Some names, like Sandy Storm, are easily visualized. However, you can also use this system with more common names, like "Brewster." Ask yourself, "Are there any words I can visualize that sound like the name?" If not, break the name into parts and imagine substitutes for them. For example, for the name "Brewster," substitute the word "rooster" or divide it into "brew" and "stir." With "rooster," imagine a big rooster with the facial features of the person named "Brewster." For "brew" and "stir," you might visualize a large mug of beer being stirred by an oar. Each of the images you choose should be absurd, exaggerated, or as distinctive as possible. The idea is to form a *lasting* image.

For practice, use the substitute word system and create corresponding vivid images for the following names: George Washington, Albert Einstein, Martin Luther King, Julia Roberts, and Ricky Martin.

_____

_____

I. THE NATURE OF MEMORY

7.1 Define memory, and describe the information-processing and parallel distributed processing (PDP) models of memory. (p. 244)

Memory is an internal record or representation of some prior event or experience. The *information processing model* sees analogies between human memory and a computer. Like typing on a keyboard, **encoding** translates information into neural codes that match the brain's language. **Storage** retains neural coded information over time, like saving material on the computer's hard drive or a disk. **Retrieval** gets information out of long-term memory (LTM) storage and sends it to short-term memory (STM) to be used, whereas the computer retrieves information and displays it on the monitor.

According to the **parallel distributed processing (PDP),** or *connectionist*, model, the contents of our memory exist as a vast number of interconnected units distributed throughout a huge network, all operating simultaneously in parallel.

7.2 Summarize the three-stage memory model. (p. 247)

The traditional *three-stage memory model* proposes that information must pass through each of three stages before being stored: *sensory memory, short-term memory (STM),* and *long-term memory (LTM).*

7.3 What is sensory memory? (p. 247)

Sensory memory preserves a brief replica of sensory information. It has a large capacity, and information lasts from a fraction of a second to 4 seconds. Selected information is sent to short-term memory (STM).

7.4 Describe short-term memory (STM). (p. 248)

Short-term memory (STM), also called working memory, involves memory for current thoughts. STM can hold five to nine items for about 30 seconds before they are forgotten. Information can be stored longer than 30 seconds through **maintenance rehearsal,** and the capacity of STM can be increased with **chunking.**

7.5 Summarize long-term memory (LTM), how it's divided into several subsystems, and how we can improve it. (p. 249)

Long-term memory (LTM) is relatively permanent memory storage with an unlimited capacity. Storage in LTM is divided into two major systems—**explicit (declarative)** and **implicit (nondeclarative)** memory. Explicit/declarative memory can be further subdivided into two parts—**semantic** and **episodic** memory. Implicit memory is subdivided into procedural memory and classically conditioned memory. To improve LTM, we can use various concepts related to encoding, storage, and retrieval (e.g., organization, **elaborative rehearsal**, and **retrieval cues,** such as **recognition** and **recall**).

II. FORGETTING

7.6 Describe Ebbinghaus's contribution to memory research. (p. 257)

Hermann Ebbinghaus was one of the first researchers to extensively study forgetting. His famous "curve of forgetting" shows that it occurs most rapidly immediately after learning. However, Ebbinghaus also showed that **relearning** usually takes less time than original learning.

7.7 What are the five major theories of forgetting? (p. 257)

The *decay theory of forgetting* states that memory, like all biological processes, deteriorates as time passes. The *interference theory of forgetting* suggests memories are forgotten because of either proactive or retroactive interference. **Retroactive interference** occurs when new information interferes with previously learned information. **Proactive interference** occurs when old information interferes with newly learned information. The *motivated forgetting theory* states that people forget things that are painful, threatening, or embarrassing. According to *encoding failure theory*, some material is forgotten because it was never encoded from short-term memory (STM) to long-term memory (LTM). *Retrieval failure theory* suggests information stored in LTM is not forgotten but may at times be inaccessible.

7.8 Describe four key factors that contribute to forgetting. (p. 260)

To prevent problems with forgetting, you should remember: 1) the misinformation effect (distorting memory with misleading post event information); 2) **source amnesia** (forgetting the true source of a memory); 3) the **sleeper effect** (initially discounting information from an unreliable source, but later judging it as reliable because the source is forgotten); and 4) information overload (in which **distributed practice** is found to be superior to **massed practice**).

7.9 How does culture affect memory? (p. 261)

Across cultures, people remember information that matters to them, and we develop memory skills to match our differing environments.

III. BIOLOGICAL BASES OF MEMORY

7.10 How do we form memories, and where do we store them? (p. 263)

Memories are formed in at least two ways: 1) through changes in neurons [a process called **long-term potentiation (LTP)**], or 2) through elevated hormone levels. Memory storage tends to be both localized and distributed throughout the brain — not just in the cortex.

7.11 What are the major biological causes of memory loss? (p. 264)

Some memory problems are the result of injury and disease (organic pathology). Problems that result from serious brain injuries or trauma are called *amnesia*. In **retrograde amnesia**, memory for events that occurred before the accident is lost. In **anterograde amnesia**, memory for events that occur after an accident is lost. **Alzheimer's disease (AD)** is a progressive mental deterioration and severe memory loss occurring most commonly in later life.

7.12 What's wrong with eyewitness testimony? (p. 268)

Memories are not exact duplicates. We actively shape and *construct* information as it is encoded, stored, and retrieved. Eyewitness accounts are highly persuasive in the courtroom, but they are filled with potential errors.

7.13 What do psychologists believe about repressed memories? (p. 268)

Psychologists continue to debate whether recovered memories are accurate and whether they are repressed. Concern about the reliability of recovered memories has led many experts to encourage a cautious approach.

IV. USING PSYCHOLOGY TO IMPROVE OUR MEMORY
7.14 Why do we distort our memories? (p. 270)
Memory distortions tend to arise from the human need for logic and consistency, as well as because it's sometimes more efficient to do so.

7.15 How can we improve our memory? (p. 271)
This section offers eight concrete strategies for improving memory. These include paying attention and reducing interference, using rehearsal techniques (both maintenance and elaborative rehearsal), improving organization (by chunking and creating hierarchies), counteracting the serial position effect, better time management, using the encoding specificity principle, employing self-monitoring and overlearning, and using **mnemonic devices**.

SELF-TESTS (Review & wRite)

Completing the following self-tests will provide immediate feedback on how well you have mastered the material. In the labeling exercises, *crossword puzzle*, and *fill-in exercises*, write the appropriate word or words in the blank spaces. The *matching exercise* requires you to match the terms in one column to their correct definitions in the other. For the *multiple-choice questions* in Practice Tests I and II, circle or underline the correct answer. If you are unsure of any answer, mark the item, and then go back to the text for further review. Correct answers are provided in Appendix A at the end of this study guide.

Crossword Puzzle for Chapter 7

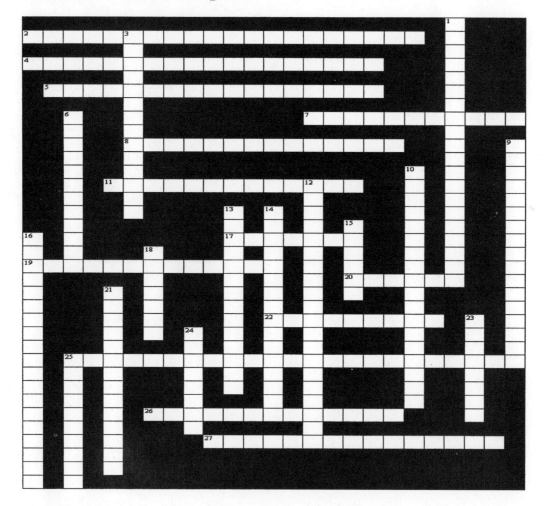

ACROSS

2 Repeating information over and over to maintain it in short-term memory (STM).
4 Progressive mental deterioration characterized by severe memory loss.
5 Loss of memory for events before an injury; backward-acting amnesia.
7 Retrieving a memory using a specific cue.

8 Memory improvement technique based on encoding items in a special way.
11 Attributing to a wrong source an event that we have experienced, heard about, read about, or imagined.
17 Retaining neurally coded information over time.
19 Delayed effectiveness of a message from an unreliable source.
20 Retrieving a memory using a general cue.
22 Recovering information from memory storage.
25 New information interferes with remembering old ("retro") information; backward-acting interference.
26 First memory stage that holds sensory information for a few seconds with relatively large capacity.
27 Third stage of memory that stores information for long periods; its capacity is virtually limitless, and its duration is relatively permanent.

DOWN

1 Linking new information to previously stored material (also known as deeper levels of processing).
3 Subpart of explicit/declarative memory that stores memories of personally experienced events.
6 A clue or prompt that helps stimulate recall and retrieval of a stored piece of information from long-term memory (LTM).
9 A retrieval failure that involves a sensation of knowing that specific information is stored in LTM, but being temporarily unable to retrieve it.
10 Inability to form new memories after an injury; forward-acting amnesia.
12 Remembering information at the beginning and the end of a list better than material in the middle.
13 Time spent learning is grouped (or massed) into long, unbroken intervals; also known as cramming.
14 Second memory stage that temporarily stores sensory information and decides whether to send it on to long-term memory (LTM).
15 An internal record or representation of some prior event or experience.
16 Practice (or study) sessions are interspersed with rest periods.
18 Prior exposure to a stimulus (or prime) facilitates or inhibits the processing of new information, even when one has no conscious memory of the initial learning.
21 A part of explicit/declarative memory that stores general knowledge.
23 Grouping separate pieces of information into a single unit (or chunk).
24 Translating information into neural codes (language).
25 Learning material a second time, which usually takes less time than original learning.

FILL-IN EXERCISES

1. The _____ sees analogies between human memory and a computer (pp. 244-246).

2. In the information-processing model, information goes through three basic operations known as _____, _____, and _____ (pp. 244-246).

3. Keeping information in STM by repeating or reviewing it is known as _____ (p. 248).

4. The capacity of STM can be improved by _____ (p. 248).

5. Factual information is stored in _____ memory, whereas memories for events are stored in _____ memory (p. 251).

6. To improve LTM, there are numerous strategies related to _____, _____, and _____ (pp. 252-256).

7. Taking a multiple-choice test requires use of the _____ retrieval strategy, whereas an essay test requires use of the _____ strategy (pp. 244, 245, 254).

8. The decay theory suggests that forgetting is largely due to _____ (pp. 258-259).

9. _____ are memory strategies based on encoding items in a special way (p. 272).

10. The _____ method creates a new code word from the first letters of items you want to remember (p. 273).

MATCHING EXERCISES

Column A   Column B

a. Priming   1.____ New information interferes with the old
b. Retroactive Interference   2.____ Also known as deeper levels of processing
c. Retrieval   3.____ Progressive mental deterioration with severe memory loss
d. Storage   4.____ Stores general knowledge and facts
e. Recognition   5.____ Retaining neurally coded information over time
f. Alzheimer's Disease   6.____ Earlier encounter with a stimulus improves later retrieval
g. Semantic Memory   7.____ Can result in errors and distortions of memory
h. Constructive Processes   8.____ Retrieving a memory using a specific cue
i. Elaborative Rehearsal   9.____ Forgetting painful or embarrassing information
j. Motivated Forgetting   10.____ Process of getting information out of LTM

PRACTICE TEST I

1. According to your text, _____ is defined as an internal record or representation of some prior event or experience.
    a. elaborative rehearsal
    b. memory
    c. encoding
    d. consolidation

2. Using the encoding, storage, and retrieval approach, memory is a process that can be compared to the workings of _____.
    a. a board of executives
    b. a flashbulb memory
    c. redintegration
    d. a computer

3. Maintenance rehearsal _____.
    a. prevents motivated forgetting
    b. prevents chunking
    c. reenters information in sensory memory
    d. reenters information in STM

4. Chunking enables a person to _____.
    a. select contents from sensory memory
    b. increase the capacity of STM
    c. overcome mnemonic overload
    d. use dual coding in sensory memory

5. Short-term memory (STM) is sometimes called _____.
   a. mental imaging
   b. present memory
   c. brief memory
   d. working memory

6. Memories for events are stored in _____.
   a. sensory memory
   b. priming memory
   c. episodic memory
   d. semantic memory

7. Which of the following is a recognition test of memory?
   a. remembering a name that goes with a face
   b. a multiple-choice test
   c. an essay test
   d. reciting the names of the state capitals

8. According to the decay theory of forgetting, we are unable to remember information when it _____.
   a. has been replaced with newer information
   b. has deteriorated with the passage of time
   c. has a negative emotional impact
   d. was learned in an emotional state different from the state we are in when trying to recall it

9. While learning French in college, you keep remembering Spanish words you learned in high school. These previously learned Spanish words are causing _____ interference with your new French language learning.
   a. retroactive
   b. proactive
   c. chunking
   d. semantic

10. You probably do not remember whose head in on a U.S. penny because of problems with _____.
   a. sensory memory
   b. STM
   c. LTM
   d. encoding failure

11. According to the _____, misleading post-event information can alter and revise our memories.
   a. anterograde amnesia effect
   b. problem of distributed practice
   c. misinformation effect
   d. sleeper effect

12. Thinking that you heard some bit of information from a friend when you actually heard it on TV is known as _____.
   a. retroactive interference
   b. Alzheimer's disease (AD)
   c. source amnesia
   d. senile dementia

13. A relatively permanent change in the strength of synaptic responsiveness believed to be a biological mechanism for learning and memory is called _____.
   a. long-term potentiation (LTP)
   b. an excitatory post-synaptic potential
   c. reverberating circuits
   d. the process of neuron transformation

14. Research on flashbulb memories has found that _____.
   a. these memories are more reliable than eyewitness testimony
   b. these stored memories are also subject to alteration
   c. inferences or assumptions are not added to information with a strong emotional impact
   d. they are extremely accurate memories, like flashbulb photos

15. Due to _____ amnesia, Alfredo was unable to remember the events occurring just before his automobile accident.
    a. anterograde
    b. retrograde
    c. proactive
    d. retroactive

16. Due to _____, patient H. M. was unable to remember information from the last few years before his operation and has difficulty forming new memories.
    a. anterograde amnesia
    b. removal of portions of his temporal lobes
    c. retrograde amnesia
    d. all of these options

17. _____ is a progressive mental deterioration characterized by severe memory loss.
    a. Source amnesia
    b. Alzheimer's disease
    c. Proactive interference
    d. all but one of these options

18. Research on eyewitness testimony has shown that it is relatively easy to create _____ memories.
    a. flashbulb
    b. false
    c. episodic
    d. none of these options

19. A(n)_____ device is a memory improvement technique based on encoding items in a special way.
    a. encoding specificity principle
    b. mnemonic device
    c. consolidation
    d. none of the above

20. The _____ mnemonic system creates a new code word from the first letters of the items you want to remember.
    a. acronym
    b. peg word
    c. method of loci
    d. none of these options

PRACTICE TEST II

1. Organizing and shaping information during processing, storage, or retrieval is known as _____.
    a. long-term potentiation (LTP)
    b. neural transformation
    c. a constructive process
    d. consolidation

2. _____ is the process of recovering information from memory storage.
    a. A flashbulb memory
    b. Motivated forgetting
    c. Elaborative rehearsal
    d. Retrieval

3. To increase the duration and capacity of your STM, you should try _____.
    a. maintenance rehearsal
    b. chunking
    c. constructive processes
    d. all but one of the above

4. Researchers believe there are three parts to working memory: visuospatial sketchpad, phonological rehearsal loop, and _____.
    a. reverberating circuits
    b. brief sensory storage
    c. a central executive
    d. short-term perceptual storage

5. A subsystem within LTM that stores facts and general knowledge is called _____.
    a. procedural memory
    b. episodic memory
    c. semantic memory
    d. none of these options

6. Actively reviewing and relating new information to material previously stored in LTM is called _____.
    a. studying
    b. elaborative rehearsal
    c. deeper levels of processing
    d. all of these options

7. A cue or prompt that helps stimulate recall and retrieval of a stored piece of information from LTM is called _____.
   a. redintegration
   b. an encoding specificity prompt
   c. a retrieval cue
   d. none of these options

8. You just finished watching a scary movie on television and find that you are more easily frightened by normal creaking sounds in your home. This is due to _____.
   a. encoding elaboration
   b. the encoding specificity principle
   c. a mnemonic device
   d. priming

9. Drinking coffee while studying or before an exam may improve your performance because of _____.
   a. the drug elaboration effect
   b. caffeine priming
   c. consolidation
   d. state-dependent memory

10. Relearning occurs when it takes _____ to regain lost information.
    a. longer
    b. less time
    c. more trials
    d. the same number of trials or amount of time

11. Forgetting that you fell off the stage during your high school graduation is an example of _____.
    a. epinephrine overexcitation
    b. adrenaline synthesis
    c. interference theory
    d. motivated forgetting theory

12. Feeling that information that is stored in LTM but you are only temporarily unable to retrieve it is called the _____.
    a. recency
    b. serial position
    c. latency
    d. tip-of-the-tongue (TOT) phenomenon

13. Hearing a movie star discuss problems with global warming and later believing you read it in your college biology text is an example of the _____.
    a. Zeigarnik effect
    b. sleeper effect
    c. source amnesia effect
    d. all but one of these options

14. Memory research suggests that, in comparison to literate cultures, preliterate cultures _____.
    a. have better short-term, but worse long-term memory abilities
    b. are better at face-recognition memory tasks
    c. demonstrate better recall for orally presented stories
    d. are not affected by the recency effect

15. _____ is a vivid image associated with surprising or emotional events, like the bombing of the World Trade Center.
    a. Long-term potentiation (LTP)
    b. A flashbulb memory
    c. Redintegration
    d. None of these options

16. Retroactive amnesia is characterized by _____.
    a. sudden memory loss
    b. progressive mental deterioration with severe memory loss
    c. loss of memory for events before a brain injury
    d. gradual memory loss for recent events

17. A hallmark of Alzheimer's disease (AD) is the extreme decrease in _____ memory.
    a. implicit/nondeclarative
    b. procedural
    c. explicit/declarative
    d. sensory

18. Research shows that we often distort our memories due to our _____.
    a. need for logic and consistency
    b. elaborative memories
    c. method of word association
    d. substitute word system

d. none of the above

19. If you want to remember the difference between "retroactive" and "proactive" interference, you break the word "retroactive" into parts and note that "retro" often means "old." Therefore, the interference is happening with the old or "retro" information. This type of memory technique is called the _____.
    a. misattribution superiority effect
    b. sleeper effect
    c. method of loci

20. Memory-improvement technique based on encoding items in a special way is known as _____.
    a. encoding elaboration
    b. the encoding specificity principle
    c. a mnemonic device
    d. priming

Information-Processing Model

Memory is *a process*, roughly analogous to a computer, where information goes through three basic processes—*encoding, storage,* and *retrieval*.

Parallel Distributed Processing Model

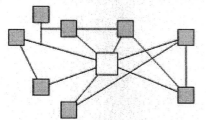

Memory is distributed across a wide network of interconnected neurons located throughout the brain. When activated, this network works simultaneously (in a *parallel* fashion) to process information.

Three-Stage Model

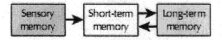

Memory requires three different storage boxes or stages to hold and process information for various lengths of time. *Sensory memory* holds information for exceedingly short intervals, *short-term memory* (STM) retains information for approximately 30 seconds or less (unless renewed), and *long-term memory* (LTM) provides relatively permanent storage.

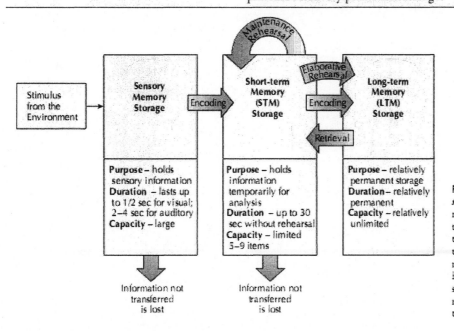

Figure 7.1 *Traditional three-stage memory model* Each "box" represents a separate memory system that differs in purpose, duration, and capacity. When information is not transferred from sensory memory or short-term memory, it is assumed to be lost. Information stored in long-term memory can be retrieved and sent back to short-term memory for use.

Process Diagram 7.1

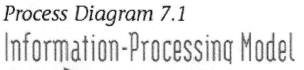

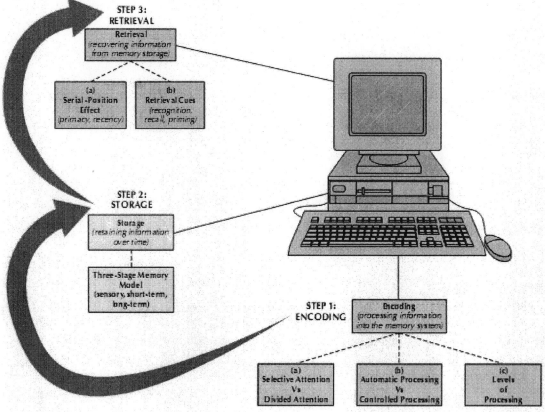

Process Diagram 7.3
Why We Forget: Five Key Theories

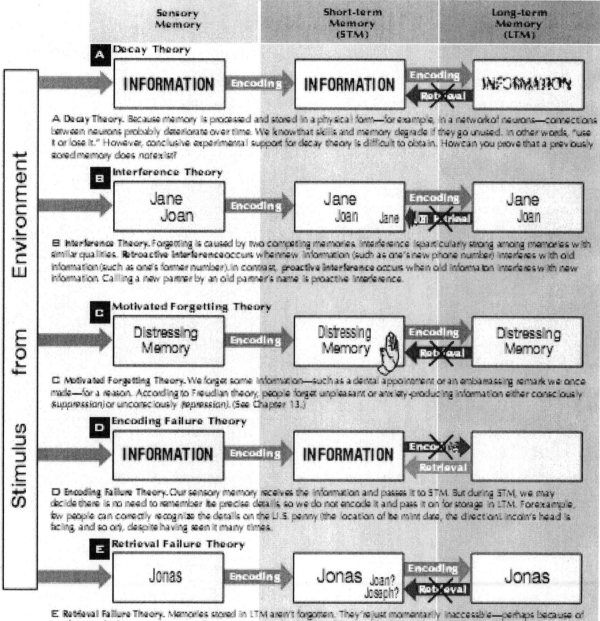

Sensory Memory | **Short-term Memory (STM)** | **Long-term Memory (LTM)**

A Decay Theory

INFORMATION → Encoding → INFORMATION ⇄ Encoding/Retrieval ⇄ INFORMATION

A Decay Theory. Because memory is processed and stored in a physical form—for example, in a network of neurons—connections between neurons probably deteriorate over time. We know that skills and memory degrade if they go unused. In other words, "use it or lose it." However, conclusive experimental support for decay theory is difficult to obtain. How can you prove that a previously stored memory does not exist?

B Interference Theory

Jane Joan → Encoding → Jane Joan Jane ⇄ Encoding/Retrieval ⇄ Jane Joan

B Interference Theory. Forgetting is caused by two competing memories. Interference is particularly strong among memories with similar qualities. Retroactive interference occurs when new information (such as one's new phone number) interferes with old information (such as one's former number). In contrast, proactive interference occurs when old information interferes with new information. Calling a new partner by an old partner's name is proactive interference.

C Motivated Forgetting Theory

Distressing Memory → Encoding → Distressing Memory ⇄ Encoding/Retrieval ⇄ Distressing Memory

C Motivated Forgetting Theory. We forget some information—such as a dental appointment or an embarrassing remark we once made—for a reason. According to Freudian theory, people forget unpleasant or anxiety-producing information either consciously (suppression) or unconsciously (repression). (See Chapter 13.)

D Encoding Failure Theory

INFORMATION → Encoding → INFORMATION ⇄ Encoding/Retrieval ⇄ [blank]

D Encoding Failure Theory. Our sensory memory receives the information and passes it to STM. But during STM, we may decide there is no need to remember the precise details, so we do not encode it and pass it on for storage in LTM. For example, few people can correctly recognize the details on the U.S. penny (the location of the mint date, the direction Lincoln's head is facing, and so on), despite having seen it many times.

E Retrieval Failure Theory

Jonas → Encoding → Jonas Joan? Joseph? ⇄ Encoding/Retrieval ⇄ Jonas

E Retrieval Failure Theory. Memories stored in LTM aren't forgotten. They're just momentarily inaccessible—perhaps because of interference, faulty cues, or emotional states. For example, the tip-of-the-tongue phenomenon—the feeling that at any second, a word or event you are trying to remember and perhaps can almost remember—will pop out from the "tip of your tongue." Although it is difficult to distinguish retrieval failure from encoding failure, most memory failures probably stem from poor encoding, not retrieval failure.

Stimulus from Environment

Decay Theory

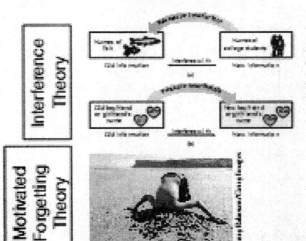

Interference Theory

Motivated Forgetting Theory

Encoding Failure Theory

Retrieval Failure Theory

💡 *Study Tip*

If ye meant to remember the five theories, think of how forgetting touches emotion that goes "dimmer." Note that the first letter of each theory has taken the same spelling—D-I-M-E-R.

Two types of interference. (a) Retroactive (backward-acting) interference occurs when new information interferes with old information. This example comes from a story about an absent-minded biology professor (a specialist) who refuses to learn the names of his college students. Asked why, he said, "Every time I learn a student's name, I forget the name of a fish." (b) Proactive (forward-acting) interference occurs when old information interferes with new information. Have you ever been in trouble because you used an old partner's name to refer to your new partner? You now have a guilt-free explanation—proactive interference.

💡 *Study Tip*

Another way to remember the difference between retroactive and proactive interference is to emphasize where the interference is occurring. In retroactive interference, forgetting occurs with old ("retro") information. During proactive interference, forgetting occurs with new information.

VISUAL QUIZ

Can you spot the real penny? If not, can you see how this may be an example of encoding failure?

Retroactive Interference *New information interferes with remembering old information; backward-acting interference*

Proactive Interference *Old information interferes with remembering new information; forward-acting interference*

Tip-of-the-Tongue (TOT) Phenomenon *Feeling that specific information is stored in long-term memory but of being temporarily unable to retrieve it*

Chapter 7 Visual Summary

The Nature of Memory

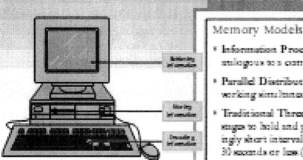

Memory Models

* **Information Processing:** Memory is a process (encoding, storage, and retrieval) analogous to a computer.

* **Parallel Distributed Processing:** Memory is distributed across a network of neurons working simultaneously (in a parallel fashion).

* **Traditional Three-Stage Memory:** Memory requires three different storage boxes or stages to hold and process information. Sensory memory holds information for exceedingly short intervals, short-term memory (STM) retains information for approximately 30 seconds or less (unless renewed), and long-term memory (LTM) provides relatively permanent storage.

Forgetting

Why Do We Forget?

* *Decay* — Memory deteriorates over time.

* *Interference* — Memory forgotten due to proactive interference (old information interferes with new) or retroactive interference (new information interferes with old).

* *Motivated Forgetting* — Painful, threatening, or embarrassing memories are forgotten.

* *Encoding Failure* — Material from STM to LTM was never successfully encoded.

* *Retrieval Failure* — Information is not forgotten, just temporarily inaccessible.

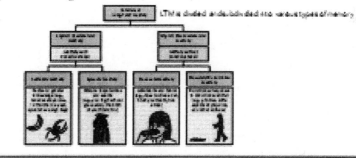

Problems with Forgetting

* *Misinformation effect:* Distorting memory with misleading post-event information

* *Source amnesia:* Forgetting the true source of a memory

* *Sleeper effect:* Delayed effectiveness of a message from an unreliable source

* *Information overload:* Distributed practice is better than massed practice

Biological Bases of Memory

Formation and Location of Memory

The biological perspective of memory focuses on changes in neurons (through long-term potentiation) and hormones, as well as on searching for the location of memory in the brain. Memory tends to be localized and distributed throughout the brain—not just in the cortex.

Biology and Memory Loss

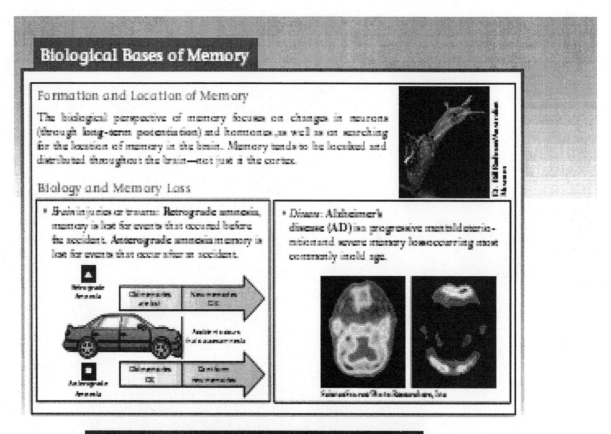

* Brain injuries or trauma: **Retrograde amnesia**, memory is lost for events that occurred before the accident. **Anterograde amnesia** memory is lost for events that occur after an accident.

* Disease: Alzheimer's disease (AD) is a progressive mental deterioration and severe memory loss occurring most commonly in old age.

Using Psychology to Improve Our Memory

Specific Tips

* Pay attention and reduce interference.

* Use rehearsal techniques (maintenance for STM and elaborative for LTM).

* Use the encoding specificity principle (including context, mood congruence, and state-dependent retrieval).

* Improve organization (chunking for STM and hierarchies for LTM).

* Counteract the serial position effect.

* Use time management (distributed versus massed practice).

* Employ self-monitoring and overlearning.

* Use mnemonic devices (method of loci, peg-word, and acronyms).

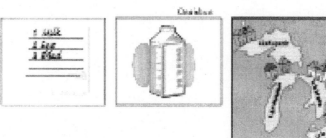

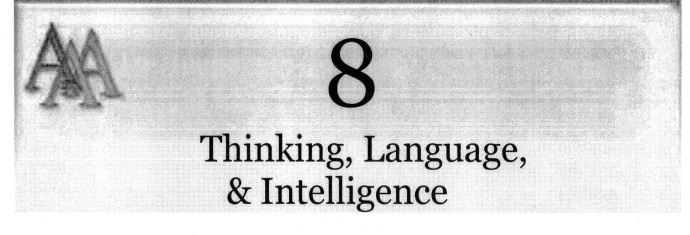

8
Thinking, Language, & Intelligence

OUTLINE SQ4R (Survey, Question, Read, Recite, Review, & wRite)

This outline section incorporates all six steps in the well-researched SQ4R method of learning. Begin by surveying the list of chapter topics in the left column. This "big picture" will help focus and guide your attention while you read. As you read through the chapter, briefly summarize each section in your own words in the space to the right. Also write down any *questions* that come to mind. Surveying, Questioning, Reading, Reciting, Reviewing, and wRiting are the foundation of the SQ4R method and an invaluable form of active learning. They also make your reading time more enjoyable and efficient! One thorough, focused SQ4R reading of a chapter is far better than several passive readings.

TOPIC	**NOTES**

I. THINKING

   A. Cognitive Building Blocks

   B. Problem Solving

    *Psychology at Work: Heuristics
     and Your Career*

    *Psychology at Work: Recognizing
     Barriers to Problem-Solving*

    *Critical Thinking/Active Learning:
     Solving Problems in College Life*

C. Creativity

II. LANGUAGE

A. Characteristics of Language

B. Language and Thought

C. Language Development

Gender & Cultural Diversity:
   Unspoken Accents

D. Animals and Language

III. INTELLIGENCE

A. What Is Intelligence?

Psychology at Work: Multiple Intelligences
   and Your Career

B. How Do We Measure Intelligence?

IV. THE INTELLIGENCE CONTROVERSY

A. Extremes in Intelligence

Research Highlight: Explaining
   Differences in IQ

Gender & Cultural Diversity:
   Are IQ Tests Culturally Biased?

LEARNING OBJECTIVES (Read, Recite, Review, & wRite)

In addition to the work you did in the Outline above, you can significantly improve your performance on exams by focusing on the following learning objectives. While reading the chapter or reviewing for exams, check your understanding by stopping periodically to *recite* (or repeat in your own words) and *writing* down your answers on a separate sheet. [Page numbers correspond to Chapter 8 in *Psychology in Action* (9e).]

8.1 Define cognition. (p. 278)
8.2 Identify the general location of thinking, and describe the roles of mental images and concepts in thinking. (p. 280)
8.3 Explain how we learn concepts. (p. 281)
8.4 Describe the three stages of problem-solving. (p. 283)
8.5 Identify five common barriers to problem solving. (p. 286)
8.6 What is creativity, and what are its three major characteristics? (p. 288)
8.7 How do we measure creativity? (p. 289)
8.8 How do creative people differ from others? (p. 289)
8.9 What is language, and what are its basic building blocks? (p. 291)
8.10 How is language related to thought? (p. 291)
8.11 Describe a child's major stages in language development. (p. 293)
8.12 Contrast the "nativist" versus the "nurturist" views of language development. (p. 293)
8.13 How does nonverbal language reveal cultural origins? (p. 293)
8.14 Describe the language research conducted with nonhuman animals. (p. 295)
8.15 What is intelligence, and is it one or many abilities? (p. 297)
8.16 Contrast Gardner's and Sternberg's theories of intelligence. (p. 298)
8.17 Describe how psychologists measure intelligence. (p. 300)
8.18 What are the three key requirements for a scientifically useful test? (p. 302)
8.19 How do studies of extremes in intelligence help validate intelligence tests? (p. 303)
8.20 Describe how research on the brain, genetics, and the environment helps explain differences in IQ. (p. 305)
8.21 How do psychologists answer the question, "Are IQ tests culturally biased"? (p. 307)

KEY TERMS (Review & wRite)

Like other survey courses, introductory psychology is filled with a "wealth" of new and unfamiliar terminology. To do well on exams, you must master this new language! Writing a brief definition of each term in the space provided and carefully reviewing them before exams will significantly improve your course grade.

Algorithm: _____

_____

Availability Heuristic: _____

_____

Babbling: _____

_____

Cognition: _____

_____

Concept: _____

_____

Confirmation Bias: _____

_____

Convergent Thinking: _____

_____

Cooing: _____

_____

Creativity: _____

_____

Crystallized Intelligence: _____

_____

Divergent Thinking: _____

_____

Fluid Intelligence: _____

_____

Functional Fixedness: _____

_____

Grammar: _____

_____

Heuristics: _____

_____

Intelligence: _____

_____

Language: _____

_____

Language Acquisition Device (LAD): _____

_____

Mental Image: _____

_____

Mental Set: _____

_____

Morpheme: _____

_____

Overextension: _____

_____

Overgeneralize: _____

_____

Phoneme: _____

_____

Prototype: _____

_____

Reliability: _____

_____

Representativeness Heuristic: _____

_____

Savant Syndrome: _____

_____

Semantics: _____

_____

Standardization: _____

_____

Stereotype Threat: _____

_____

Syntax: _____

_____

Telegraphic Speech: _____

_____

Validity: _____

_____

ACTIVE LEARNING EXERCISES

True mastery of information requires you to be an ACTIVE learner. Completing the following active learning exercises will improve your understanding of the chapter material and greatly improve your performance on exams. Answers to some exercises appear in Appendix A at the end of this study guide.

ACTIVE LEARNING EXERCISE I *The text describes two major ways to generate hypotheses during the production stage of problem solving—algorithms and heuristics.*

To improve your algorithm strategy, try the following: *There are 1025 tennis players participating in a single's elimination tournament. How many matches must be played before there is one winner and 1024 losers?*

To work on your skill in "working backwards" (a type of heuristic), try this problem: *While three security guards were guarding an orchard, a thief crept in and stole some apples. During his escape, he met the three security guards one after the other. In exchange for his freedom, he gave each one-half of the apples he had at the time, plus an extra two. After he had shared his apples with each of the three security guards, he had one left for himself. How many apples had he stolen originally?*

Answers can be found in Appendix A at the end of this study guide.

ACTIVE LEARNING EXERCISE II *Metacognition, also known as reflective or recursive thinking, involves a review and analysis of your own mental processes-- thinking about your own thinking. Try this "Tweety" problem below to test your own metacognition.*

There is a bird, Tweety, that likes to perch on the roof of Casey Jones, a locomotive that travels the 200-mile route from Cucamonga to Kalamazoo. As Casey Jones pulls out from Cucamonga, the bird takes to the air and flies to Kalamazoo, the train's destination. Because the train travels at only 50 mph whereas the bird travels at 100 mph, Tweety reaches Kalamazoo before the train and finds that it has nowhere to perch. So the bird flies back to the train and finds it still moving, whereupon Tweety flies back to Kalamazoo, then back to the train, and so on until Casey Jones finally arrives in Kalamazoo, where the bird finally rests on the locomotive's roof. How far has the bird flown?

This exercise also helps you review the three steps in problem solving discussed in the text. First identify the name of the step. Then, describe the processes you used in each step to solve this problem. Make sure you include some or all of the following terms:

algorithm	creating subgoals	evaluation
goal	heuristics	hypothesis
incubation	preparation	production

Step 1: _____ Procedure: _____

_____

_____

_____

Step 2: _____ Procedure: _____

_____

_____

_____

Step 3: _____ Procedure: _____

_____

_____

_____

CHAPTER OVERVIEW (Review)

The following chapter overview provides a narrative overview of the main topics covered in the chapter. Like the *Visual Summary* found at the end of each chapter in the text, this narrative summary provides a final opportunity to *review* chapter material.

I. COGNITIVE BUILDING BLOCKS

8.1 Define cognition. (p. 278)

Cognition, or thinking, is defined as mental activities involved in acquiring, storing, retrieving, and using knowledge.

8.2 Identify the general location of thinking, and describe the roles of mental images and concepts in thinking. (p. 280)

Thought processes are distributed throughout the brain in neural networks. However, they are also localized in the prefrontal cortex, which links to other areas of the brain, such as the limbic system. The three basic building blocks of cognition are *mental images, concepts,* and *language.* **Mental images** are mental representations of a sensory experience, including visual, auditory, olfactory, tactile, motor, and gustatory imagery. **Concepts** are mental categories that group objects, events, activities, or ideas that share similar characteristics. (Language is discussed in a later section.)

8.3 Explain how we learn concepts. (p. 281)

We develop concepts using three key strategies: (1) Artificial concepts are formed by logical, specific rules or characteristics. (2) Natural concepts are created from experiences in everyday life. When we are confronted with a new item, we compare it with the **prototype** (most typical) of that concept. (3) Concepts also are generally organized into hierarchies. We most frequently use the middle, basic-level concepts, when first learning material.

II. PROBLEM SOLVING
8.4 Describe the three stages of problem-solving. (p. 283)
Problem solving entails three stages: *preparation, production,* and *evaluation.* During the *preparation stage*, we identify given facts, separate relevant from irrelevant facts, and define the ultimate goal.

During the *production stage*, we generate possible solutions, called *hypotheses.* We typically generate hypotheses by using **algorithms** and **heuristics.** *Algorithms*, as problem-solving strategies, are guaranteed to lead to an eventual solution. But they are not practical in many situations. *Heuristics*, or simplified rules based on experience, are much faster but do not guarantee a solution. Three common heuristics are *working backward, means-end analysis,* and *creating subgoals.*

The *evaluation stage* in problem solving involves judging the hypotheses generated during the production stage against the criteria established in the preparation stage.

8.5 Identify five common barriers to problem solving. (p. 286)
Five major barriers to successful problem solving are **mental sets, functional fixedness, confirmation bias,** the **availability heuristic,** and the **representativeness heuristic.**

III. CREATIVITY
8.6 What is creativity, and what are its three major characteristics? (p. 288)
Creativity is the generation of ideas that are original, novel, and useful. Creative thinking involves *originality, fluency,* and *flexibility.*

8.7 How do we measure creativity? (p. 289)
Most tests of creativity focus on **divergent thinking**, which involves generating as many solutions as possible. In contrast, **convergent thinking**, or conventional thinking, works toward a single correct answer.

8.8 How do creative people differ from others? (p. 289)
Creative people may have a special talent or differing cognitive processes. The investment theory of creativity proposes that creative people "buy low" by pursuing promising but unpopular ideas, and "sell high" by developing the ideas until they are widely accepted. It also proposes that creativity depends on six specific resources: *intellectual ability, knowledge, thinking style, personality, motivation,* and *environment.*

IV. LANGUAGE
8.9 What is language, and what are its basic building blocks? (p. 291)
Human language is a creative form of communication consisting of symbols put together according to a set of rules. The three building blocks of language are **phonemes, morphemes,** and **grammar.** Phonemes are the basic speech sounds; they are combined to form morphemes, the smallest meaningful units of language. Phonemes, morphemes, words, and phrases are put together by rules of grammar (**syntax** and **semantics**). *Syntax* refers to the grammatical rules for ordering words in sentences; *semantics* refers to meaning in language.

8.10 How is language related to thought? (p. 291)
According to Benjamin Whorf's *linguistic relativity hypothesis*, language shapes thought. Generally, Whorf's hypothesis is not supported. However, our choice of vocabulary can influence our mental imagery and social perceptions.

8.11 Describe a child's major stages in language development. (p. 293)
Children go through two stages in their acquisition of language: prelinguistic (crying, **cooing**, and **babbling**) and linguistic (which includes single utterances, **telegraphic speech**, and the acquisition of rules of grammar).

8.12 Contrast the "nativist" versus the "nurturist" views of language development. (p. 293)
Nativists believe that language is an inborn capacity and develops primarily by maturation. Chomsky suggests that humans possess a **language acquisition device (LAD)** that needs only minimal environmental input. Nurturists emphasize the role of the environment and suggest that language development results from rewards, punishments, and imitation of models.

8.13 How does nonverbal language reveal cultural origins? (p. 293)
Nonverbal emotions are somewhat universal, but there are slight differences between cultures in how we display and perceive emotions. These subtle differences can lead to problems in communication.

8.14 Describe the language research conducted with nonhuman animals. (p. 295)
The most successful nonhuman animal language studies have been done with apes using American Sign Language and written symbols. Dolphins also have been taught to comprehend sentences that vary in syntax and meaning. Some psychologists believe that nonhuman animals can truly learn human language, but others suggest that the nonhuman animals are merely responding to rewards.

V. WHAT IS INTELLIGENCE?
8.15 What is intelligence, and is it one or many abilities? (p. 297)
Today, **intelligence** is commonly defined as the global capacity to think rationally, act purposefully, and deal effectively with the environment. Several theorists have debated whether intelligence is one or many abilities. Spearman viewed intelligence as one factor, called "g," for general intelligence. Thurstone saw it as seven distinct mental abilities. Guilford believed it was composed of 120 or more separate abilities. Cattell viewed it as two types of general intelligence (g), which he called **fluid intelligence** and **crystallized intelligence.**

8.16 Contrast Gardner's and Sternberg's theories of intelligence. (p. 298)
Both Gardner and Sternberg believe intelligence is a collection of multiple abilities. Gardner's theory of multiple intelligences that identifies eight (and possibly nine) types of intelligence. He believes that both teaching and assessing should take into account people's learning styles and cognitive strengths. Sternberg's triarchic theory of intelligence (*analytical, creative,* and *practical*) proposed that each of these components is learned rather than the result of genetics.

VI. HOW DO WE MEASURE INTELLIGENCE?
8.17 Describe how psychologists measure intelligence. (p. 300)
Although there are many tests for intelligence, the Stanford-Binet and Wechsler are the most widely used. Both tests compute an *intelligence quotient (IQ)* by comparing the deviation of a person's test score to the norms for that person's age group.

8.18 What are the three key requirements for a scientifically useful test? (p. 302)
For any test to be useful, it must be standardized, reliable, and valid. **Standardization** refers to (a) giving a test to a large number of people in order to determine norms and (b) using identical

procedures in administering a test so that everyone takes the test under exactly the same testing conditions. **Reliability** refers to the stability of test scores over time. **Validity** refers to how well the test measures what it is intended to measure.

VII. THE INTELLIGENCE CONTROVERSY

8.19 How do studies of extremes in intelligence help validate intelligence tests? (p. 303)
Intelligence testing has long been the subject of great debate. To determine whether these tests are valid, you can examine people who fall at the extremes of intelligence. People with IQs of 70 and below are identified as mentally retarded, whereas those with IQs of 135 and above are identified as gifted.

8.20 Describe how research on the brain, genetics, and the environment helps explain differences in IQ. (p. 305)
Research on intelligence has focused on three major questions: (1) Does a bigger brain mean greater intelligence? (Answer: "Not necessarily.") (2) Is a faster brain more intelligent? (Answer: "A qualified yes." And (3) Does a smart brain work harder? (Answer: "No, the smarter brain is more efficient.")

Another topic of debate is whether intelligence is inherited or due to the environment. According to the Minnesota Study of Twins Reared Apart, heredity and environment are important, inseparable factors in intellectual development. Heredity equips each of us with innate capacities, while the environment significantly influences whether an individual will reach full potential.

8.21 How do psychologists answer the question, "Are IQ tests culturally biased"? (p. 307)
Perhaps the most hotly debated topic is whether ethnic differences on IQ tests are primarily "genetic in origin." Research has shown IQ tests may be culturally biased. And environmental factors, including the Flynn effect, cultural exposure, socioeconomic differences, language, and **stereotype threat** have all been found to be contributing factors to score differences.

SELF-TESTS (Review & wRite)

Completing the following self-tests will provide immediate feedback on how well you have mastered the material. In the labeling exercises, *crossword puzzle*, and *fill-in exercises*, write the appropriate word or words in the blank spaces. The *matching exercise* requires you to match the terms in one column to their correct definitions in the other. For the *multiple-choice questions* in Practice Tests I and II, circle or underline the correct answer. If you are unsure of any answer, mark the item, and then go back to the text for further review. Correct answers are provided in Appendix A at the end of this study guide.

Crossword Puzzle for Chapter 8

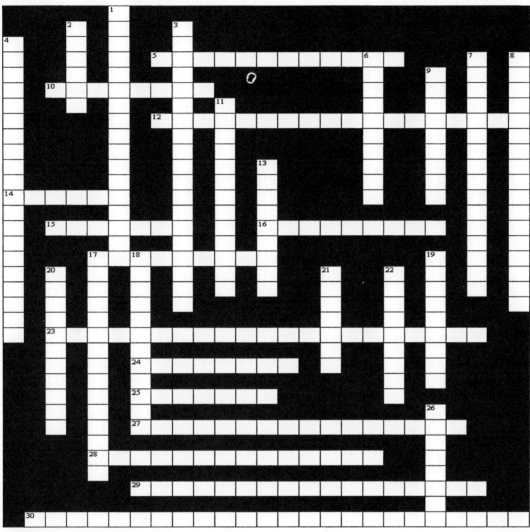

ACROSS

5 General capacity to profit from experience, acquire knowledge, and adapt to changes in the environment.

10 Ability of a test to measure what it was designed to measure.

12 Narrowing down a list of alternatives to converge on a single correct answer.

14 Vowel-like sounds infants produce beginning around 2 to 3 months of age.

15 The smallest basic unit of speech or sound.

16 A set of steps that, if followed correctly, will eventually solve the problem.

17 Meaning, or the study of meaning, derived from words and word combinations.

23 Judging the likelihood or probability of an event based on how readily available other instances of the event are in memories.

24 Smallest meaningful unit of language, formed from a combination of phonemes.

25 Rules that specify how phonemes, morphemes, words, and phrases should be combined to meaningfully express thoughts.

27 Negative stereotypes about minority groups that cause some members to doubt their abilities.

28 Applying the basic rules of grammar even to cases that are exceptions to the rule (e.g., saying "mans" instead of "men").

29 Thinking that produces many alternatives or ideas (e.g., finding as many uses as possible for a paper clip).

30 Knowledge and learning gained through experience and education.

DOWN

1 Aspects of innate intelligence that are relatively independent of education and tend to decline as people age.

2 Grammatical rules that specify how words and phrases should be arranged in a sentence to convey meaning.

3 The tendency to think of an object functioning only in its usual or customary way.

4 A subject's mental age divided by chronological age and multiplied by 100.

6 The ability to produce valued outcomes in a novel way.

7 Tendency to seek out and pay attention to information that confirms preexisting positions or beliefs, while at the same time ignoring or discounting contradictory evidence.

8 Two- or three-word sentences of young children that contain only the most necessary words.

9 Mental activities involved in acquiring, storing, retrieving, and using knowledge.

11 Overly broad use of a word to include objects that do not fit the word's meaning (e.g., calling all men "Daddy").

13 Persisting in using problem-solving strategies that have worked in the past rather than trying new ones.

17 Establishing the norms and uniform procedures for giving and scoring a test.

18 A mental representation of a previously stored sensory experience, including olfactory, tactile, motor, and gustatory imagery (e.g., visualizing a train and hearing its whistle).

19 A representation of the "best" or most typical example of a category.

20 A measure of the consistency and stability of test scores when the test is re-administered.

21 Mental representation of a group or category that shares similar characteristics.

22 Strategies, or simple rules, used in problem solving and decision making that do not guarantee a solution but offer a likely short cut to it.

26 Vowel/consonant combinations that infants begin to produce at about 4 to 6 months of age.

FILL-IN EXERCISES

1. _____ is defined as mental activities involved in acquiring, storing, retrieving, and using knowledge (p. 278).

2. An apple is a common _____ of the concept of fruits (p. 282).

3. _____, _____, and _____ are the three major steps to problem solving (pp. 283-284).

4. The five most common barriers to effective problem solving are _____, _____, _____, the _____, and the _____ (pp. 286-287).

5. Creativity is associated with _____ thinking, which is the opposite of _____ thinking (p. 289).

6. The smallest meaningful unit of language is called a _____ (p. 292).

7. _____includes vowel sounds, whereas _____ adds consonants to the vowel sounds (p. 294).

8. Wechsler defined _____ as the global capacity to think rationally, act purposefully, and deal effectively with the environment (p. 297).

9. As we age, our _____ intelligence tends to increase, whereas our _____ intelligence gradually decreases (p. 298).

10. To be scientifically acceptable, all psychological tests must fulfill three basic requirements: _____, _____ and _____ (p. 302).

MATCHING EXERCISES

Column A

a. Wechsler
b. Divergent Thinking
c. Stanford-Binet
d. Evaluation
e. Mental Images
f. Crystallized Intelligence
g. Algorithm
h. Fluid Intelligence
i. Convergent Thinking
j. Semantics

Column B

1. ____ Mental representation of a sensory experience
2. ____ Leads to many solutions
3. ____ Meaning in language
4. ____ Accumulation of knowledge over the lifespan
5. ____ Set of steps leading to a problem solution
6. ____ Speed of information processing
7. ____ Measures both verbal and nonverbal abilities
8. ____ Primarily measures verbal abilities
9. ____ Evaluating hypothesis for goal attainment
10. ____ Leads to a single solution

PRACTICE TEST I

1. Mental representations of previously stored sensory experiences are called _____.
   a. memory
   b. cognition
   c. mental images
   d. none of these options

2. We normally use _____ when building concepts.
   a. artificial concepts
   b. natural concepts
   c. hierarchies
   d. all of these options

3. Problem solving requires a movement from _____, to _____, to _____.
   a. hypothesis, implementation, solution
   b. preparation, production, evaluation
   c. algorithms, heuristics, solution
   d. hypothetical state, given state, goal state

4. What are the two major methods used in generating hypotheses for solving problems?
   a. factor analysis and analysis of variance
   b. algorithms and heuristics
   c. insight and deduction
   d. none of these options

5. Which of the following is an algorithm?
   a. a fixed ratio reinforcement schedule
   b. dream analysis
   c. 3 X 10 is 10 + 10 + 10
   d. asking the smartest person in the class

6. _____ is the failure to solve a problem because of an inability to see novel uses for a familiar object.
   a. Problem-solving set
   b. Functional fixedness
   c. Mental sets
   d. Incubation

7. When politicians accept opinion polls that support them and ignore those that do not, this is an example of _____.
   a. fluid intelligence
   b. mental set
   c. confirmation bias
   d. originality, fluency, experience

8. What are the three abilities commonly associated with creativity?
   a. fluency, vocabulary, experience
   b. fluency, flexibility, originality
   c. flexibility, heuristics, algorithms
   d. originality, fluency, experience

9. According to _____, creative people are willing to "buy low and sell high."
   a. Guilford
   b. Piaget
   c. investment theory
   d. connectionism theory

10. The smallest basic units of speech are called _____.
    a. verbalization
    b. syntax

    c. phonemes
    d. deep structure

11. Benjamin Whorf proposed that _____.
    a. language is not natural and must be learned
    b. the structure of language can influence people's thoughts

    c. American Sign Language is not a natural language
    d. All of these options

12. Knowledge and skills gained through experience and education are known as _____ intelligence.
    a. crystallized
    b. fluid
    c. general
    d. specific

13. Howard Gardner proposed a theory of _____.
    a. language development
    b. fluid and crystallized intelligence
    c. culture specificity intelligence
    d. multiple intelligences

14. Sternberg's triarchic theory of successful intelligence includes analytic intelligence, creative intelligence, and _____.
    a. fluid intelligence
    b. applying past and present knowledge to ongoing problems
    c. fluid and crystallized knowledge to problem-solving
    d. practical intelligence

15. The first IQ test to be widely used in the United States was the _____.
    a. Stanford-Binet
    b. SAT
    c. ACT
    d. AFQT

16. A ten-year-old child with a mental age of nine would have an IQ score _____.
    a. of 190
    b. that is significantly higher than expected
    c. of 90
    d. that is slightly above average

17. If a test gives you the same score each time you take it, that test would be _____.

    a. reliable
    b. valid
    c. standardized
    d. all of these options

18. Validity refers to the ability of a test to _____.
    a. return the same score on separate administrations of the test
    b. measure what it is designed to measure
    c. avoid discrimination between different cultural groups
    d. give a standard deviation of scores

19. An IQ score of _____ is the cutoff for the designation of mental retardation.
    a. 50
    b. 70
    c. 80
    d. none of the above, this term is no longer being used

20. Which of the following persons would be most likely to have similar IQ test scores?
    a. identical twins raised apart
    b. identical twins raised together
    c. fraternal twins raised apart
    d. brothers and sisters from the same parents

PRACTICE TEST II

1. According to your text, a mental image is defined as a _____.
   a. delusion based on faulty processing
   b. perception or illusion created by environmental stimuli
   c. hallucination based on information processing
   d. mental representation of a previously stored sensory experience

2. A _____ is a model or best example of items belonging to a particular category.
   a. heuristic
   b. attribute
   c. phoneme
   d. prototype

3. During the _____ step in successful problem solving, you should identify the given facts, separate relevant from irrelevant facts, and define the ultimate goal.
   a. prototype
   b. production
   c. preparation
   d. none of these options

4. The generation of possible solutions, or hypotheses, occurs during the _____ stage(s) of problem solving.
   a. preparation
   b. production
   c. preparation and production
   d. evaluation

5. _____ are simple rules, or strategies, that generally lead to a problem's solution.
   a. Heuristics
   b. Mnemonic devices
   c. Algorithms
   d. all of the above

6. If you persist in using strategies that have worked in the past rather than trying new ones, you may fall victim to barrier to problem solving called _____.
   a. implementation
   b. hypothesis bias
   c. mental sets
   d. all but one of these options

7. Statistically, it is much safer to fly in an airplane than to drive a car the same number of miles. However, people often overestimate their chances of dying in a plane crash due to _____.
   a. the confirmation bias
   b. negative mental sets
   c. functional fixedness
   d. the availability heuristic

8. George notices that the last five winning bets on a roulette wheel were on red. He therefore believes the odds are higher that red will win again on the next spin of the wheel. George is making a poor decision because of _____.
   a. the gambler's fallacy
   b. the representativeness heuristic
   c. functional fixedness
   d. the gambling confirmation bias

9. _____ is the ability to produce valued outcomes in a novel way.
   a. Fluid intelligence
   b. Multiple intelligence
   c. Creativity
   d. Insight

10. Which rule of English is violated by this sentence? <u>The girl Anne is.</u>
   a. deep structure
   b. phonemic structure
   c. semantics
   d. syntax

11. "A screaming bouquet of flowers" is an example of the improper use of _____.
   a. pragmatics
   b. schematics
   c. semantics
   d. morphemes

12. "I goed to the zoo" and "I hurt my foots" are examples of _____.
   a. prelinguistic verbalizations
   b. overexposure to adult "baby talk"
   c. overgeneralization
   d. Noam Chomsky's theory of language acquisition

13. According to Chomsky's language theory, _____.
   a. children are born "prewired" to learn language
   b. language development is primarily a result of rewards and modeling of adult speech
   c. overgeneralizations result from faulty development of the LAD
   d. none of these options

14. Reasoning abilities, memory, and speed of information are all part of _____.
   a. fluid intelligence
   b. cognition
   c. adaptation
   d. crystallized intelligence

15. Spearman believed that intelligence was composed of a general cognitive ability, which he called _____.
   a. "g"
   b. IQ
   c. GCA
   d. "I"

16. Cattell proposed that there were two types of intelligence: one that referred to new knowledge and one that referred to accumulated knowledge. He called these _____.
   a. knowledge and wisdom
   b. novel and fixed knowledge
   c. fluid and crystallized intelligence
   d. working and stored information

17. The first successful intelligence test was developed in_____ by _____.
   a. France; Terman
   b. France; Binet
   c. the United States; Terman
   d. the United States; Binet

18. _____ is (are) the term(s) used for developing specific procedures for administering and scoring a test, and establishing norms for the test scores in a given population.
   a. Reliability procedures
   b. Validity testing
   c. Specification
   d. Standardization

19. Mental retardation is related to or caused by _____.
   a. genetic abnormalities
   b. environmental factors
   c. unknown factors
   d. all of these options

20. Which of the following is true regarding the relationship between IQ scores and ethnicity.
    a. Intelligence is not a fixed trait.
    b. The bell curve applies only to Caucasian test-takers.
    c. Overall, averages for all ethnic groups fall at the same level on the IQ scale.
    d. Americans as a group consistently receive higher IQ scores than other ethnic groups.

Process Diagram 8.1

Building Blocks of Language

Phonemes

The smallest distinctive sound units that make up every language

p in pansy; *ng* in sting

Morphemes

The smallest meaningful units of language; they are created by combining phonemes. (*Function morphemes* are prefixes and suffixes. *Content morphemes* are root words.)

unthinkable = un·think·able (prefix = *un*, root word = *think*, suffix = *able*)

Grammar

A system of rules (syntax and semantics) used to generate acceptable language that enables us to communicate with and understand others.

They were in my psychology class.
versus
They was in my psychology class.

Syntax	**Semantics**
Grammatical rules for putting words in correct order	A system of rules for using words to create meaning
I am happy. versus *Happy I am.*	*I went out on a limb for you.* versus *Humans have several limbs.*

Process Diagram 8.2
Language Acquisition

Developmental Stage	Age	Language Features	Example
Prelinguistic stage	Birth to ~12 months	Crying (reflexive in newborns; soon, crying becomes more purposeful)	hunger cry anger cry pain cry
	2 to 3 months	**Cooing** (vowel-like sounds)	"ooooh" "aaaah"
	4 to 6 months	**Babbling** (consonants added)	"bahbahbah" "dahdahdah"
Linguistic stage	~12 months	Babbling begins to resemble language of the child's home. Child seems to understand that sounds relate to meaning.	
		At first, speech is limited to one-word utterances.	"Mama" "juice" "Daddy" "up"
		Expressive ability more than doubles once child begins to join words into short phrases.	"Daddy, milk" "no night-night!"
	~2 years	Child sometimes **overextends** (using words to include objects that do not fit the word's meaning).	all men = "Daddy" all furry animals = doggy
	~2 years to ~5 years	Child links several words to create short but intelligible sentences. This speech is called **telegraphic speech** because (like telegrams) it omits nonessential connecting words.	"Me want cookie" "Grandma go bye-bye?"
		Vocabulary increases at a phenomenal rate.	
		Child acquires a wide variety of rules for grammar.	adding -ed for past tense adding s to form plurals
		Child sometimes **overgeneralizes** (applying the basic rules of grammar even to cases that	"I goed to the zoo" "Two mans"

Chapter 8 Visual Summary

Thinking

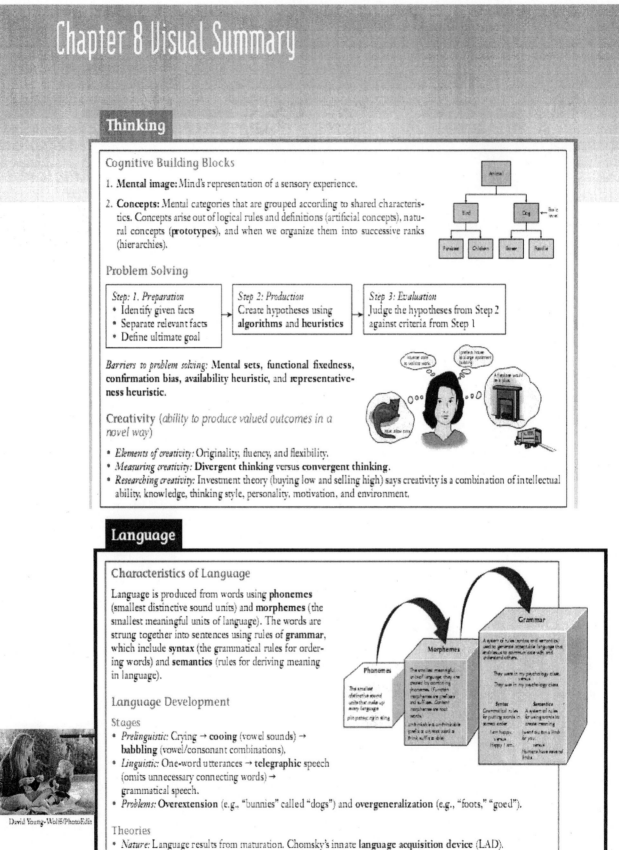

Cognitive Building Blocks

1. **Mental image:** Mind's representation of a sensory experience.

2. **Concepts:** Mental categories that are grouped according to shared characteristics. Concepts arise out of logical rules and definitions (artificial concepts), natural concepts (**prototypes**), and when we organize them into successive ranks (hierarchies).

Problem Solving

Step: 1. Preparation	*Step 2: Production*	*Step 3: Evaluation*
• Identify given facts • Separate relevant facts • Define ultimate goal	Create hypotheses using **algorithms** and **heuristics**	Judge the hypotheses from Step 2 against criteria from Step 1

Barriers to problem solving: **Mental sets, functional fixedness, confirmation bias, availability heuristic,** and **representativeness heuristic.**

Creativity (*ability to produce valued outcomes in a novel way*)

* *Elements of creativity:* Originality, fluency, and flexibility.
* *Measuring creativity:* **Divergent thinking** versus **convergent thinking.**
* *Researching creativity:* Investment theory (buying low and selling high) says creativity is a combination of intellectual ability, knowledge, thinking style, personality, motivation, and environment.

Language

Characteristics of Language

Language is produced from words using **phonemes** (smallest distinctive sound units) and **morphemes** (the smallest meaningful units of language). The words are strung together into sentences using rules of **grammar**, which include **syntax** (the grammatical rules for ordering words) and **semantics** (rules for deriving meaning in language).

Language Development

Stages

* *Prelinguistic:* Crying → cooing (vowel sounds) → **babbling** (vowel/consonant combinations).
* *Linguistic:* One-word utterances → **telegraphic** speech (omits unnecessary connecting words) → grammatical speech.
* *Problems:* **Overextension** (e.g., "bunnies" called "dogs") and **overgeneralization** (e.g., "foots," "goed").

Theories

* *Nature:* Language results from maturation. Chomsky's innate **language acquisition device (LAD).**
* *Nurture:* Environment and rewards or punishments explain language acquisition.

David Young-Wolff/PhotoEdit

Intelligence

What is Intelligence? *(Global capacity to think rationally, act purposefully, and deal effectively with the environment.)*

Competing theories and definitions.
* Spearman→Intelligence is "g," a single factor.
* Thurstone→Intelligence is seven distinct mental abilities.
* Guilford→Intelligence is composed of 120 or more separate abilities.
* Cattell→Intelligence is two types of "g" (**fluid intelligence** and **crystallized intelligence**).
* Gardner→Eight or possibly nine types of intelligence.
* Sternberg→Triarchic theory of intelligence (analytical, creative, and practical).

How Do We Measure Intelligence?

Intelligence quotient (IQ) tests are widely used in our culture.
* *Stanford-Binet* measures IQ with this formula: $IQ = (MA/CA) \times 100$.
* *Wechsler* provides an overall IQ, as well as verbal and performance IQs.

Elements of a useful test:
1. **Standardization:** Test is given to a representative sample to establish norms, and uniform administration procedures are used.
2. **Reliability:** Scores are consistent and reproducible over time.
3. **Validity:** Test measures what it is designed to measure.

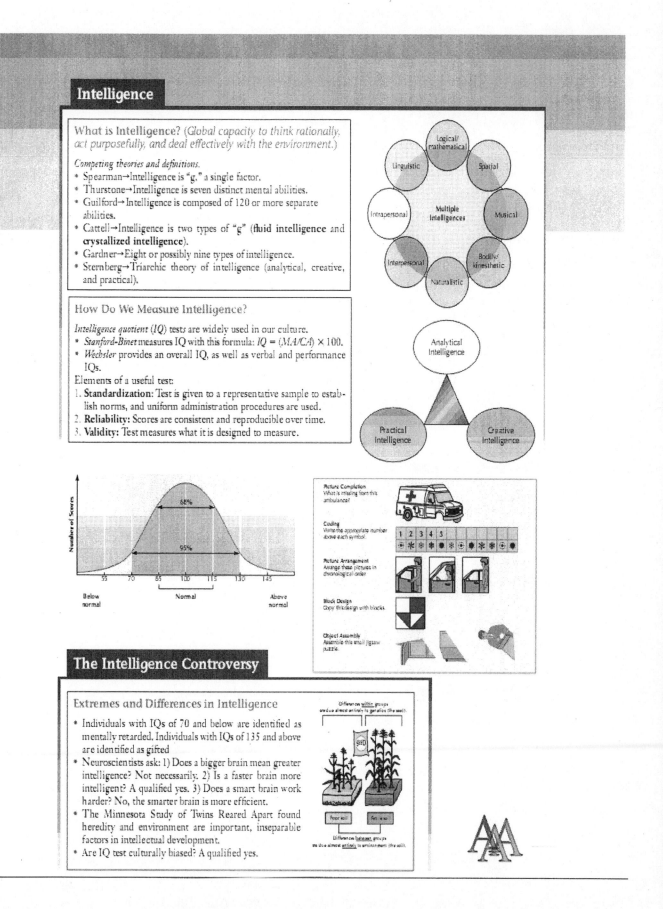

The Intelligence Controversy

Extremes and Differences in Intelligence

* Individuals with IQs of 70 and below are identified as mentally retarded. Individuals with IQs of 135 and above are identified as gifted
* Neuroscientists ask: 1) Does a bigger brain mean greater intelligence? Not necessarily. 2) Is a faster brain more intelligent? A qualified yes. 3) Does a smart brain work harder? No, the smarter brain is more efficient.
* The Minnesota Study of Twins Reared Apart found heredity and environment are important, inseparable factors in intellectual development.
* Are IQ test culturally biased? A qualified yes.

9
Life Span Development I

This outline section incorporates all six steps in the well-researched SQ4R method of learning. Begin by surveying the list of chapter topics in the left column. This "big picture" will help focus and guide your attention while you read. As you read through the chapter, briefly summarize each section in your own words in the space to the right. Also write down any *questions* that come to mind. Surveying, Questioning, Reading, Reciting, Reviewing, and wRiting are the foundation of the SQ4R method and an invaluable form of active learning. They also make your reading time more enjoyable and efficient! One thorough, focused SQ4R reading of a chapter is far better than several passive readings.

TOPIC   **NOTES**

I. STUDYING DEVELOPMENT

    A. Theoretical Issues

    B. Research Methods

       Gender and Cultural Diversity:
         Cultural Psychology's Guidelines
         For Developmental Research

II. PHYSICAL DEVELOPMENT

    A. Prenatal Period and Early Childhood

B. Adolescence and Adulthood

III. COGNITIVE DEVELOPMENT

A. Stages of Cognitive Development

B. Assessing Piaget's Theory

C. Information Processing

IV. SOCIAL-EMOTIONAL DEVELOPMENT

A. Attachment

B. Parenting Styles

Research Highlight:
   Romantic Love and Attachment

Critical Thinking/Active Learning:
   The Development of "Suicide Bombers"

LEARNING OBJECTIVES (Read, Recite, Review, & wRite)

In addition to the work you did in the Outline above, you can significantly improve your performance on exams by focusing on the following learning objectives. While reading the chapter or reviewing for exams, check your understanding by stopping periodically to *recite* (or repeat in your own words) and *writing* down your answers on a separate sheet. [Page numbers correspond to Chapter 9 in *Psychology in Action* (9e).]

9.1 Define developmental psychology. (p. 316)
9.2 Identify the three major issues in developmental psychology. (p. 317)
9.3 What are the two most common research methods in developmental psychology? (p. 318)
9.4 Describe cultural psychology's four guidelines for developmental research. (p. 319)
9.5 Identify the three major stages of prenatal development. (p. 321)
9.6 What are the major hazards to prenatal development? (p. 322)
9.7 Summarize early childhood physical development. (p. 324)
9.8 Describe the major physical changes associated with adolescence and adulthood. (p. 327)
9.9 Identify primary aging, and compare the programmed and damage theories of aging. (p. 330)
9.10 Describe Piaget's theory of cognitive development, and compare schema, assimilation, and accommodation. (p. 331)
9.11 Compare how children's development changes during Piaget's four stages. (p. 333)
9.12 Identify the major criticisms and contributions of Piaget's theories. (p. 336)
9.13 Describe the information-processing model of cognitive development. (p. 338)
9.14 Define attachment, and discuss its contributions across the life span. (p. 340)
9.15 Discuss the three key parenting styles. (p. 340)
9.16 Discuss how infant attachment may be related to romantic love. (p. 343)
9.17 What motivates suicide bombers? (p. 344)

KEY TERMS (Review & wRite)

Like other survey courses, introductory psychology is filled with a "wealth" of new and unfamiliar terminology. To do well on exams, you must master this new language! Writing a brief definition of each term in the space provided and carefully reviewing them before exams will significantly improve your course grade.

Accommodation: _____

_____

Ageism: _____

_____

Assimilation: _____

_____

Attachment: _____

_____

Concrete Operational Stage: _____

_____

Conservation: _____

_____

Critical Period: _____

_____

Cross-Sectional Method: _____

_____

Developmental Psychology: _____

_____

Egocentrism: _____

_____

Embryonic Period: _____

_____

Fetal Alcohol Syndrome (FAS): _____

_____

Fetal Period: _____

_____

Formal Operational Stage: _____

_____

Germinal Period: _____

_____

Imprinting: _____

_____

Longitudinal Method: _____

_____

Maturation: _____

_____

Object Permanence: _____

_____

Preoperational Stage: _____

_____

Puberty: _____

_____

Schema: _____

_____

Sensorimotor Stage: _____

_____

Teratogen: _____

_____

ACTIVE LEARNING EXERCISES

True mastery of information requires you to be an ACTIVE learner. Completing the following active learning exercises will improve your understanding of the chapter material and greatly improve your performance on exams. Answers to some exercises appear in Appendix A at the end of this study guide.

ACTIVE LEARNING EXERCISE I *Chapter 9 opens with a discussion of research issues related to developmental psychology. To test your understanding of this material, try the following exercise:*

Imagine yourself as a research psychologist who wants to answer the question, "Do feelings of attachment and marital happiness increase over time?" You conduct a longitudinal study of newly married couples, and then reexamine them after 5, 10, 15, and 20 years of marriage. You find that the longer couples are married the higher their levels of attachment and marital happiness. Before submitting your paper to professional journals for possible publication, what factor(s) should you consider that might explain or contaminate your findings?

_____

_____

_____

Possible answers appear in Appendix A at the end of this study guide.

ACTIVE LEARNING EXERCISE II *Evaluating Arguments: The Pro-Life/Pro-Choice Controversy*

Evaluation of arguments is important to active learning and critical thinking. Rather than carelessly agreeing or disagreeing, critical thinkers analyze the relative strengths and weaknesses of each position and are especially sensitive to arguments with which they personally disagree. They recognize a common tendency to ignore or oversimplify opposing information. After carefully evaluating all arguments, a critical thinker develops an independent position.

A contemporary, controversial issue related to material in Chapter 9 is that of abortion. Those who support the pro-life position on abortion believe that abortion is morally and religiously wrong and oppose it in almost all circumstances. On the other side, pro-choice advocates believe the right to an abortion should not be dictated by religion or government, and is a matter of choice for the pregnant woman. To help sharpen your critical thinking skills in this area, try the following:

1. Begin by listing three points and three counterpoints for each argument. When these points and counterpoints are not explicitly stated, you will need to make your best guess.

Point   Counterpoint

_____   _____

_____   _____

_____   _____

2. After clarifying the points and counterpoints, use the following analytical tools to critically evaluate each side of the issue:

   a. *Differentiating between fact and opinion.* The ability to recognize *statements of fact* versus *statements of opinion* is an important first step in successful analysis of arguments. After rereading the arguments you listed regarding the pro-life/pro-choice issue, see if you can state at least two facts and two opinions on each side.

   b. *Recognizing logical fallacies and faulty reasoning.* Several chapters in your text, and their corresponding critical thinking/active learning exercises, can help you recognize faulty logic. For example, the problem of incorrect assumption of cause/effect relationships is discussed in Chapter 1, and the problem of incorrect and distorted use of statistics is discussed in Appendix A.

c. *Exploring the implications of conclusions.* Questions can help expand your analysis of arguments (e.g., "What are the conclusions drawn by proponents of each side of the issue?" "Are there other logical alternative conclusions?").

d. *Recognizing and evaluating author bias and source credibility.* Ask yourself questions such as, "What does the author want me to think or do?" "What qualifications does the author have for writing on this subject?" "Is the author a reliable source of information?"

Although each of these steps requires additional time and energy, the payoff is substantial. You'll not only refine your critical thinking skills, but also improve your decision-making skills and make your opinions more educated and valuable.

CHAPTER OVERVIEW (Review)

The following chapter overview provides a narrative overview of the main topics covered in the chapter. Like the *Visual Summary* found at the end of each chapter in the text, this narrative summary provides a final opportunity to *review* chapter material.

I. STUDYING DEVELOPMENT
9.1 Define developmental psychology. (p. 316)
Developmental psychology studies age-related changes in behavior and mental processes from conception to death.

9.2 Identify the three major issues in developmental psychology. (p. 317)
Three important research issues are *nature versus nurture, continuity versus stages,* and *stability versus change.*

9.3 What are the two most common research methods in developmental psychology? (p. 318)
Researchers in developmental psychology generally use **cross-sectional** (different participants of various ages at one point in time) or **longitudinal** (same participants over an extended period) studies. Each method has its own advantages and disadvantages.

9.4 Describe cultural psychology's four guidelines for developmental research. (p. 319)
Cultural psychologists suggest that developmental researchers keep the following points in mind:
- Culture is the most important determinant of development,
- Human development cannot be studied outside its socio-cultural context,
- Each culture's ethnotheories are important determinants of behavior,
- Culture is largely invisible to its participants.

II. PHYSICAL DEVELOPMENT
9.5 Identify the three major stages of prenatal development. (p. 321)
The prenatal period of development consists of three major stages: the **germinal** (ovulation to implantation), **embryonic** (implantation to eight weeks), and **fetal** (eight weeks to birth).

9.6 What are the major hazards to prenatal development? (p. 322)
Development can be affected by environmental influences at any of the three major stages of prenatal development. Doctors advise pregnant women to avoid all unnecessary drugs,

especially nicotine and alcohol. Both legal and illegal drugs are potentially **teratogenic** (capable of producing birth defects).

9.7 Summarize early childhood physical development. (p. 324)
During the prenatal period and the first two years of life, the brain and nervous system grow faster than all other parts of the body. Early motor development (crawling, standing, and walking) is largely the result of maturation, not experience. Except for vision, the sensory and perceptual abilities of newborns are relatively well developed.

9.8 Describe the major physical changes associated with adolescence and adulthood. (p. 327)
At **puberty**, the adolescent becomes capable of reproduction and experiences a sharp increase in height, weight, and skeletal growth because of the *pubertal growth spurt*. Both men and women experience bodily changes in middle age.

9.9 Identify primary aging, and compare the programmed and damage theories of aging. (p. 330)
Although many of the changes associated with physical aging (such as decreases in cardiac output and visual acuity) are the result of *primary aging*, others are the result of disease, abuse, or neglect. Physical aging may be genetically built-in from the moment of conception (*programmed theory*), or it may result from the body's inability to repair damage (*damage theory*).

III. COGNITIVE DEVELOPMENT
9.10 Describe Piaget's theory of cognitive development, and compare schema, assimilation, and accommodation. (p. 331)
Piaget believed an infant's intellectual growth progresses in distinct stages, motivated by an innate need to know. He also proposed three major concepts: **schemas,** mental patterns or blueprints used to interpret the world; **assimilation**, absorbing new information "as is" into existing schemas; and **accommodation**, adjusting old schemas or developing new ones to fit with new information.

9.11 Compare how children's development changes during Piaget's four stages. (p. 333)
According to Piaget, cognitive development occurs in an invariant sequence of four stages: **sensorimotor** (birth to age 2), **preoperational** (ages 2 to 7), **concrete operational** (ages 7 to 11), and **formal operational** (ages 11 and up).

In the *sensorimotor stage,* children acquire **object permanence**. During the preoperational stage, children are better equipped to use symbols, but their thinking is limited by their lack of operations, **egocentrism**, and animism.

In the *concrete operational stage*, children learn to perform operations (to think about concrete things, while not actually doing them). They understand the principles of **conservation** and reversibility. During the *formal operational stage*, the adolescent is able to think abstractly and deal with hypothetical situations but is prone to a type of adolescent egocentrism.

9.12 Identify the major criticisms and contributions of Piaget's theories. (p. 336)
Although Piaget has been criticized for underestimating abilities and genetic and cultural influences, he remains one of the most respected psychologists in modern times.

9.13 Describe the information-processing model of cognitive development. (p. 338)
Psychologists who explain cognitive development in terms of the *information processing model* have found this model especially useful in explaining attention and memory changes across the life span. In contrast to pessimistic early studies, recent research is much more encouraging about age-

related changes in information processing.

IV. SOCIAL-EMOTIONAL DEVELOPMENT

9.14 Define attachment, and discuss its contributions across the life span. (p. 340)
Attachment is a strong affectional bond with special others that endures over time. Nativists believe it is innate, whereas nurturists believe it is learned. The Harlow and Zimmerman experiments with monkeys raised by cloth or wire surrogate mothers found that *contact comfort* might be the most important factor in attachment. Infants who fail to form attachments may suffer serious effects. When attachments are formed, they may differ in level or degree.

9.15 Discuss the three key parenting styles. (p. 340)
Parenting styles fall into three major categories: *permissive, authoritarian, and authoritative.* Critics suggest that a child's unique temperament, his or her expectations of parents, and the degree of warmth versus rejection from parents may be the three most important variables in parenting styles.

9.16 Discuss how infant attachment may be related to romantic love. (p. 343)
Research that identified *securely attached, avoidant,* and *anxious/ambivalent* infants found that early attachment patterns often carry over into adult romantic relationships.

9.17 What motivates suicide bombers? (p. 344)
There are several reinforcers for suicide bombers, including martyrdom, hero status, and a "ticket to Paradise," as well as money and status for their families.

SELF-TESTS (<u>R</u>eview & w<u>R</u>ite)

Completing the following self-tests will provide immediate feedback on how well you have mastered the material. In the labeling exercises, *crossword puzzle,* and *fill-in exercises,* write the appropriate word or words in the blank spaces. The *matching exercise* requires you to match the terms in one column to their correct definitions in the other. For the *multiple-choice questions* in Practice Tests I and II, circle or underline the correct answer. If you are unsure of any answer, mark the item, and then go back to the text for further review. Correct answers are provided in Appendix A at the end of this study guide.

Crossword Puzzle for Chapter 9

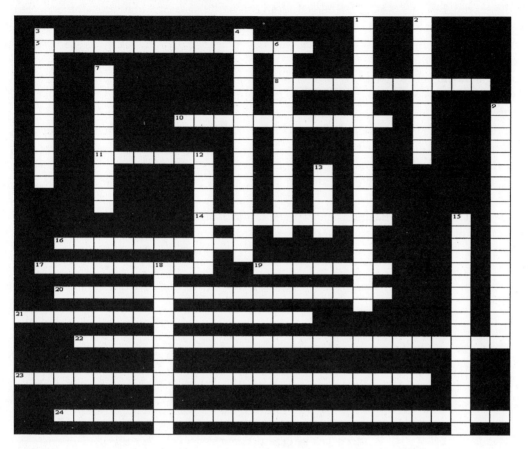

ACROSS

5 A period of special sensitivity to specific types of learning that shapes the capacity for future development.

8 The inability to consider another's point of view, which Piaget considered a hallmark of the preoperational stage.

10 The third, and final, stage of prenatal development (eight weeks to birth), characterized by rapid weight gain in the fetus and the fine detailing of body organs and systems.

11 Prejudice or discrimination against an individual based on physical age.

14 A strong affectional bond with special others that endures over time.

16 An innate form of learning within a critical period that involves attachment to the first, large moving object seen.

17 Environmental agent that causes damage during prenatal development; the term comes from the Greek word teras, meaning "malformation."

19 Biological changes during adolescence that lead to an adult-sized body and sexual maturity.

20 Piaget's first stage (birth to approximately age two years), in which schemas are developed through sensory and motor activities.

21 Second stage of prenatal development from uterine implantation through the eighth week.

22 Piaget's fourth stage (11 years and up) characterized by abstract and hypothetical thinking.

23 Measures individuals of various ages at one point in time and gives information about age differences.

24 Study of age-related changes in behavior and mental processes from conception to death.

DOWN

1 Piaget's third stage (roughly ages 7 to 11), when children can perform mental operations on concrete objects and understand reversibility and conservation.

2 Understanding that certain physical characteristics (such as volume) remain unchanged, even when their outward appearance changes.

3 In Piaget's theory, adjusting old schemas or developing new ones to better fit with new information.

4 Piaget's second stage (two to seven) characterized by the ability to employ significant language and to think symbolically.

6 Piagetian term for an infant's understanding that objects (or people) continue to exist even when they cannot directly be seen, heard, or touched directly.

7 In Piaget's theory, absorbing new information into existing schemas.

9 Combination of birth defects due to maternal alcohol abuse, which includes organ deformities and mental, motor, and/or growth retardation.

12 Development governed by automatic, genetically predetermined signals.

13 Cognitive structures or patterns that grow and differentiate with experience.

15 Measures a single individual or group of individuals over an extended period and gives information about age changes.

18 First stage of prenatal development beginning with conception and ending with uterine implantation.

FILL-IN EXERCISES

1. _____, _____, and _____ are the three major research issues in developmental psychology (p. 317).

2. The cross-sectional method examines individuals of various ages at _____ and gives information about _____. In contrast, the longitudinal method follows a single individual or group of individuals over _____ and gives information about _____ (p. 318).

3. _____ are environmental agents that can cause birth defects (p. 322).

4. _____ is the onset of menstruation in women; _____ is the first ejaculation in men (pp. 327-328).

5. Taking in new information that easily fits an existing schema is known as _____. _____ occurs when old schemas are changed to adapt to the new information (p. 332).

6. During the _____ stage of development, concepts are not yet operational and thinking is egocentric and animistic (pp. 333-335).

7. The ability to think abstractly and hypothetically occurs in Piaget's _____ stage (pp. 334-335).

8. During a critical period in development, baby geese will attach to, and then follow, the first, large moving object they see, which is known as _____ (pp. 340-341).

9. In studies of attachment that employed the "strange situation" procedures, infants who used the mother as a safe base for exploration were called _____ (p. 342).

10. According to Baumrind, parenting styles fall into three broad patterns: _____, _____, and _____ (pp. 340, 342).

MATCHING EXERCISES

Column A   Column B

a. Imprinting   1._____ Cognitive structures for organizing ideas.
b. Piaget   2._____ Egocentrism and animism.
c. Teratogen   3._____ Adolescent belief that their thoughts and feelings are unique.
d. Schemas   4._____ Adding new information to an existing schema.
e. Puberty   5._____ Children possess an innate need to know.
f. Personal Fable   6._____ Inability to consider another's point of view.
g. Assimilation   7._____ Contact comfort.
h. Egocentrism   8._____ Environmental agent that causes birth defects.
i. Harry Harlow   9._____ When sex organs become capable of reproduction.
j. Preoperational Stage   10._____ Attaching to first large moving object.

PRACTICE TEST I

1. _____ studies age-related changes in behavior and mental processes from conception to death.
    a. Thanatology
    b. Teratogenology
    c. Human development
    d. Developmental psychology

2. _____ is governed by automatic, genetically predetermined signals.
    a. Fetal development
    b. Primary Aging
    c. Thanatology
    d. Maturation

3. A _____ is the most appropriate research method for studying age-changes across the life span.
    a. case study
    b. natural observation
    c. longitudinal study
    d. cross-sectional study

4. In the area of child development, cultures have specific ideas and beliefs regarding how children should be trained. Such a set of ideas and beliefs is referred to as a(n) _____.
    a. egocentric bias
    b. cultural bias
    c. ethnotheory
    d. cohort effect

5. Conception occurs when a(n) _____.
    a. fertilized egg implants in the uterine lining
    b. ovum undergoes its first cell division
    c. ejaculation occurs
    d. sperm cell unites with an ovum

6. The _____ period begins with conception and ends with implantation in the uterus.
    a. fetal
    b. germinal
    c. embryonic
    d. conceptual

7. Ethan was born with facial abnormalities, motor and growth retardation, and low intelligence. These characteristics are most often related to _____.
    a. toxoplasmosis
    b. fetal alcohol syndrome (FAS)
    c. prenatal syndrome
    d. retardive dyskinesia (RD)

8. At birth, an infant cannot _____.
    a. see as well as an adult
    b. recognize the taste or odor of its own mother's milk
    c. feel pain
    d. turn its head without help

9. The period of life when an individual first becomes capable of reproduction is known as _____.
   a. the growth spurt
   b. adolescence
   c. puberty
   d. the latency period

10. Menarche is the _____.
    a. adolescent growth spurt
    b. end of a woman's reproductive capacity
    c. end of a man's reproductive capacity
    d. onset of the menstrual cycle

11. Menopause is _____.
    a. another name for the onset of the menstrual cycle
    b. a time of wild mood swings for all women due to fluctuations in hormones
    c. the cessation of the menstrual cycle
    d. none of these options

12. The physical and psychological changes associated with middle age in men are called the _____.
    a. testosterone crisis
    b. reproductive decline
    c. male climacteric
    d. male refractory period

13. According to Piaget, an infant acquires _____ when he or she understands that people and things continue to exist even when they cannot directly be seen, heard, or touched.
    a. conservation
    b. reversibility
    c. egocentrism
    d. object permanence

14. Piaget used the term *egocentrism* to describe the fact that _____.
    a. children are naturally selfish during the first few years of life
    b. children are unable to consider another's point of view
    c. the child's limited logic impedes his or her understanding of the need to share
    d. children are unable to conserve.

15. During Piaget's fourth stage of cognitive development, individuals first become capable of _____.
    a. egocentrism
    b. dealing effectively with transformations
    c. using language and other symbols
    d. hypothetical thinking

16. Roberta refuses to go to school today because she's afraid everyone will notice that she is having a really bad hair day. Her fears most clearly illustrate _____.
    a. formal operational thinking
    b. peer pressure
    c. adolescent egocentrism
    d. adolescent ethnocentrism

17. The _____ approach to cognitive development draws an analogy between the mind and the computer.
    a. human-machine system
    b. information processing
    c. mind-matter
    d. bio-mechanical

18. Which of the following is correctly matched?
    a. Lorenz, ageism
    b. Piaget, permissive parenting
    c. Harlow, contact comfort
    d. Baumrind, accommodation

19. Ainsworth's research suggests that a _____ infant is more likely to be have inconsistent caregivers.
    a. securely attached
    b. avoidant

c. anxious/ambivalent
d. Demanding

20. _____ parents generally set and enforce firm limits, while also being highly involved, tender, and emotionally supportive.
a. Securely attached
b. Authoritarian
c. Permissive
d. none of these options

PRACTICE TEST II

1. Age at crawling, walking, and toilet training is primarily dependent on the _____.
a. educational level of the parents
b. specific training techniques of the child's caretakers
c. maturational readiness of the child
d. genetic influences inherited from both the mother and father

2. A _____ is a time of special sensitivity to specific types of learning that shapes the capacity for future development.
a. preoperational stage
b. critical period
c. maturational adjustment
d. none of these options

3. The _____ method of research may confuse genuine age differences with cohort effects, differences that result from specific histories of the age group studied.
a. cross-cultural
b. longitudinal
c. cross-sectional
d. all of the above

4. According to Greenfield, the best predictor of future behavior in a child is _____.
a. the parenting style of his or her parents
b. his or her intellectual capacity

c. the sociocultural context for that child
d. his or her health status

5. Pregnant women should avoid all drugs because they are potential _____.
a. carcinogens
b. DNA disrupters
c. chromosomogens
d. teratogens

6. A child's brain reaches nine-tenths its full adult weight by _____ of age.
a. 16 months
b. 6 years
c. 10 years
d. 16 years

7. The psychological period of development that occurs between childhood and adulthood is called _____.
a. adolescence
b. puberty
c. the phallic stage
d. the identity stage

8. The clearest and most dramatic physical sign of puberty is the _____.
a. menarche
b. spermarche
c. growth spurt
d. none of the above

9. Prejudice or discrimination against an individual based on physical age is known as _____.
a. stereotypes
b. agecentrism
c. ageism
d. ethnocentrism

10. In the programmed theory of aging, it is believed that cells are genetically programmed to no longer divide once they reach the _____ limit.
a. outer
b. Hayword
c. Harlow
d. Hayflick

11. Schemas are cognitive structures that contain organized ideas about the world and _____.
    a. grow and differentiate with experience
    b. may assimilate new information
    c. may accommodate new information
    d. all of these options

12. According to Piaget, accommodation means that a schema has _____.
    a. been changed to fit new information
    b. been used to understand new information
    c. reversed itself
    d. conserved itself

13. Piaget's four stages of cognitive development start with the sensorimotor and preoperational stages, and end with the _____ stages.
    a. assimilation and accommodation
    b. operation and abstraction
    c. concrete and formal operational
    d. concept testing and deductive reasoning

14. Egocentrism is present in which of Piaget's stages of cognitive development?
    a. preoperational and formal operational
    b. preoperational only
    c. sensorimotor and preoperational
    d. sensorimotor only

15. A child who believes the sun follows him or her around and that trees have feelings is probably in the _____ stage of development.
    a. sensorimotor
    b. animistic
    c. preoperational
    d. concrete operational

16. The child who believes that everyone is watching him or her and that no one else can understand and sympathize with him or her is probably in the beginning stages of the _____ stage of development.
    a. "terrible twos"
    b. "terrible teens"
    c. concrete operational
    d. formal operational

17. Harlow's research with infant monkeys and artificial surrogate mothers indicates that _____.
    a. the most important factor in infant development is a loving environment
    b. attachment is not essential to normal development
    c. there is no significant difference in the choice of wire or terrycloth mothers
    d. the most important variable in attachment may be contact comfort

18. Studies of an infant's attachment to a parent and an adult's love for a romantic partner have found that _____.
    a. insecurely attached infants become ambivalently attached adults
    b. infant attachment is closely correlated with later patterns of romantic love in adulthood
    c. securely attached infants tend to be less attached as adolescents
    d. avoidant infants tend to be obsessed with their romantic partners as adults

19. Which of the following is incorrectly matched?
    a. Lorenz = imprinting
    b. Ainsworth = parenting styles
    c. Harlow = contact comfort
    d. Piaget = cognitive development

20. _____ parents are rigid and punitive, while also being low on warmth and responsiveness.
    a. Authoritative
    b. Authoritarian
    c. Anxious/ambivalent
    d. none of these options

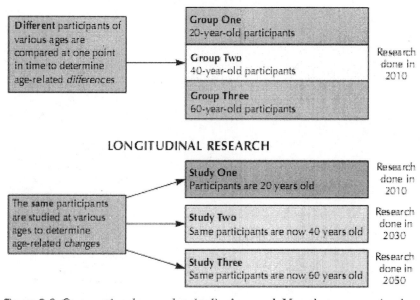

CROSS-SECTIONAL RESEARCH

Different participants of various ages are compared at one point in time to determine age-related *differences*

Group One
20-year-old participants

Group Two
40-year-old participants

Group Three
60-year-old participants

Research done in 2010

LONGITUDINAL RESEARCH

The same participants are studied at various ages to determine age-related *changes*

Study One
Participants are 20 years old

Research done in 2010

Study Two
Same participants are now 40 years old

Research done in 2030

Study Three
Same participants are now 60 years old

Research done in 2050

Figure 9.2 *Cross-sectional versus longitudinal research* Note that cross-sectional research uses different participants and is interested in age-related differences, whereas longitudinal research studies the same participants over time to find age-related changes.

TABLE 9.2 ADVANTAGES AND DISADVANTAGES OF CROSS-SECTIONAL AND
LONGITUDINAL RESEARCH DESIGNS

	Cross-Sectional	Longitudinal
Advantages	Gives information about age differences Quick Less expensive Typically larger sample	Gives information about age changes Increased reliability More in-depth information per participant
Disadvantages	Cohort effects are difficult to separate Restricted generalizability (measures behaviors at only one point in time)	More expensive Time consuming Restricted generalizability (typically smaller sample and dropouts over time)

Process Diagram 9.1
Prenatal Development

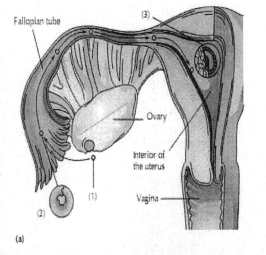

Fallopian tube

(3)

Ovary

Interior of
the uterus

(1)

Vagina

(2)

(a)

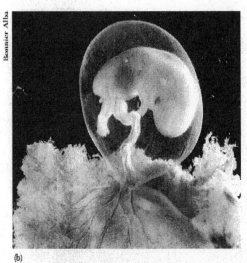

Bonnier Alba

(b)

(a) Germinal period: From ovulation to implantation. After discharge from either the left or right ovary (1), the ovum travels to the opening of the fallopian tube.

If fertilization occurs (2), it normally takes place in the first third of the fallopian tube. The fertilized ovum is referred to as a zygote.

When the zygote reaches the uterus, it implants itself in the wall of the uterus (3) and begins to grow tendril-like structures that intertwine with the rich supply of blood vessels located there. After implantation, the organism is known as an embryo.

(b) Embryonic period. This stage lasts from implantation to eight weeks. At eight weeks, the major organ systems have become well differentiated. Note that at this stage, the head grows at a faster rate than other parts of the body.

(c) Fetal period. This is the period from the end of the second month to birth. At four months, all the actual body parts and organs are established. The fetal stage is primarily a time for increased growth and "fine detailing."

Germinal Period *First stage of prenatal development, which begins with conception and ends with implantation in the uterus (the first two weeks).*

Embryonic Period *Second stage of prenatal development, which begins after uterine implantation and lasts through the eighth week.*

Fetal Period *Third, and final, stage of prenatal development (eight weeks to birth), which is characterized by rapid weight gain in the fetus and the fine detailing of bodily organs and systems.*

Petit Format/Nestle/Photo Researchers, Inc.

(c)

Process Diagram

Process Diagram

Process Diagram 9.2
Piaget's Four Stages of Cognitive Development

Birth to 2

Sensorimotor
Abilities: Uses senses and motor skills to explore and develop cognitively.
Limits: Beginning of stage lacks *object permanence* (understanding things continue to exist even when not seen, heard, or felt).

Doug Goodman/PhotoResearchers, Inc.

What's happening in these photos? *The child in these two photos seems to believe the toy no longer exists once it is blocked from sight. Can you explain why?*

Answer: According to Piaget, young infants lack object permanence—an understanding that objects continue to exist even when they cannot be seen, heard, or touched.

Age 2–7

Preoperational
Abilities: Has significant language and thinks symbolically.
Limits:
• Cannot perform "operations."
• *Egocentric* thinking (inability to consider another's point of view).
• *Animistic* thinking (believing all things are living).

Age 7–11

Concrete Operational
Abilities:
• Can perform "operations" on concrete objects.
• Understands *conservation* (realizing changes in shape or appearance can be reversed).
Limits: Cannot think abstractly and hypothetically.

Ellen B. Senisi/The Image Works

Test for conservation. *(a) In the classic conservation of liquids test, the child is first shown two identical glasses with liquid at the same level. (b) The liquid is poured from one of the short, wide glasses into the tall, thin one. (c) When asked whether the two glasses have the same amount or if one has more, the preoperational child replies that the tall, thin glass has more. This demonstrates a failure to conserve volume.*

Age 11 and up

Formal Operational
Abilities: Can think abstractly and hypothetically.
Limits: *Adolescent egocentrism* at the beginning of this stage, with related problems of the *personal fable* and *imaginary audience.*

Roy Melnychuk/Taxi/Getty Images

Self-consciousness. *What developmental phenomenon might explain why adolescents sometimes display what seem like extreme forms of self-consciousness and concern for physical appearance?*

Chapter 9 Visual Summary

Studying Development

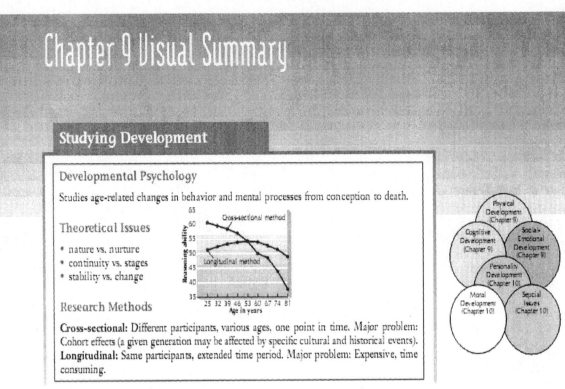

Developmental Psychology

Studies age-related changes in behavior and mental processes from conception to death.

Theoretical Issues

* nature vs. nurture
* continuity vs. stages
* stability vs. change

Research Methods

Cross-sectional: Different participants, various ages, one point in time. Major problem: Cohort effects (a given generation may be affected by specific cultural and historical events). **Longitudinal:** Same participants, extended time period. Major problem: Expensive, time consuming.

Physical Development

Prenatal and Early Childhood

* Three prenatal stages: **germinal, embryonic,** and **fetal.**
* **Teratogens:** Environmental agents capable of producing birth defects.
* Sensory and perceptual abilities are relatively well developed in newborns.
* Motor development primarily results from **maturation.**

Adolescence and Adulthood

* Adolescence: Psychological period between childhood and adulthood.
* **Puberty:** When sex organs become capable of reproduction.
* Menopause: Cessation of menstruation.
* Male climacteric: Physical and psychological changes in midlife.
* Primary aging: Inevitable, biological changes with age.
* Explanations of primary aging: *Programmed theory* (genetically built-in) and *damage theory* (body's inability to repair damage).

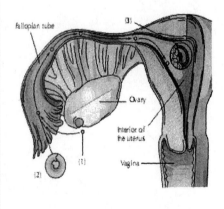

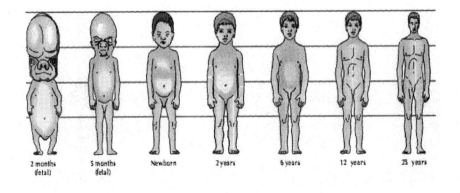

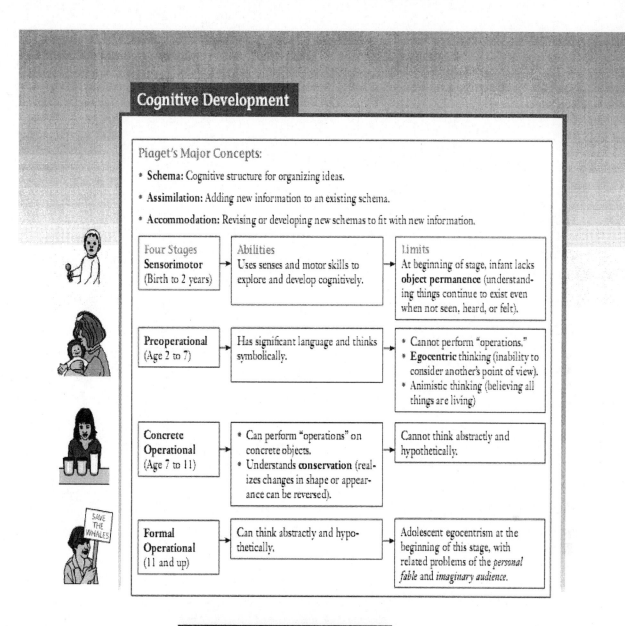

Cognitive Development

Piaget's Major Concepts:

* **Schema:** Cognitive structure for organizing ideas.

* **Assimilation:** Adding new information to an existing schema.

* **Accommodation:** Revising or developing new schemas to fit with new information.

Four Stages	Abilities	Limits
Sensorimotor (Birth to 2 years)	Uses senses and motor skills to explore and develop cognitively.	At beginning of stage, infant lacks **object permanence** (understanding things continue to exist even when not seen, heard, or felt).
Preoperational (Age 2 to 7)	Has significant language and thinks symbolically.	• Cannot perform "operations." • **Egocentric** thinking (inability to consider another's point of view). • Animistic thinking (believing all things are living)
Concrete Operational (Age 7 to 11)	• Can perform "operations" on concrete objects. • Understands **conservation** (realizes changes in shape or appearance can be reversed).	Cannot think abstractly and hypothetically.
Formal Operational (11 and up)	Can think abstractly and hypothetically.	Adolescent egocentrism at the beginning of this stage, with related problems of the *personal fable* and *imaginary audience*.

Social-Emotional Development

Attachment

* Infant attachment: **Imprinting:** Attaching to first moving object. Harlow's experiments found "contact comfort" very important to **attachment**. Infants who do not attach may suffer serious, lasting effects.

* Adult attachment: Patterns of infant attachment (secure, avoidant, and anxious/ambivalent) may carry over into adult romantic attachments.

Parenting Styles

There are three major categories (*permissive, authoritarian,* and *authoritative*), but critics suggest that a child's unique temperament, expectations of parents, and responsiveness degree of warmth and responsiveness from parents may be the most important determinants of parenting styles.

10
Life Span Development II

OUTLINE SQ4R (Survey, Question, Read, Recite, Review, & wRite)

This outline section incorporates all six steps in the well-researched SQ4R method of learning. Begin by surveying the list of chapter topics in the left column. This "big picture" will help focus and guide your attention while you read. As you read through the chapter, briefly summarize each section in your own words in the space to the right. Also write down any *questions* that come to mind. Surveying, Questioning, Reading, Reciting, Reviewing, and wRiting are the foundation of the SQ4R method and an invaluable form of active learning. They also make your reading time more enjoyable and efficient! One thorough, focused SQ4R reading of a chapter is far better than several passive readings.

TOPIC	NOTES

I. MORAL DEVELOPMENT

   A. Kohlberg's Research

   B. Assessing Kohlberg's Theory

   Critical Thinking/Active Learning:
     Morality and Academic Cheating

II. PERSONALITY DEVELOPMENT

   A. Thomas and Chess's Temperament Theory

   B. Erikson's Psychosocial Theory

III. MEETING THE CHALLENGES OF ADULTHOOD

A. Committed Relationships

Psychology at Work: Are Your Marital Expectations Unrealistic?

B. Families

Research Highlight: Children Who Survive Despite the Odds

Psychology at Work: Positive Careers and Rewarding Retirements

Gender & Cultural Diversity: Cultural Differences in Ageism

IV. Grief and Death

A. Grief

B. Attitudes Toward Death and Dying

C. The Death Experience

Psychology at Work: Dealing With
   Your Own Death Anxiety

LEARNING OBJECTIVES (Read, Recite, Review, & wRite)

In addition to the work you did in the Outline above, you can significantly improve your performance on exams by focusing on the following learning objectives. While reading the chapter or reviewing for exams, check your understanding by stopping periodically to *recite* (or repeat in your own words) and *writing* down your answers on a separate sheet. [Page numbers correspond to Chapter 10 in *Psychology in Action* (9e).]

10.1 What is the biological perspective on morality? (p. 350)
10.2 Describe Kohlberg's three levels and six stages of moral development. (p. 351)
10.3 What area the three major criticisms of Kohlberg's theory? (p. 351)
10.4 Describe Thomas and Chess's temperament theory. (p. 354)
10.5 Describe Erikson's eight psychosocial stages. (p. 355)
10.6 What are the major criticisms of Erikson's stages? (p. 355)
10.7 How do individualistic versus collectivistic cultures affect personality development? (p. 357)
10.8 Discuss the major problems with long-term relationships. (p. 359)
10.9 Describe how work and retirement affect development. (p. 364)
10.10 What are the three major theories of aging? (p. 364)
10.11 Discuss the major cultural differences in ageism. (p. 365)
10.12 Describe grief and list its four stages. (p. 367)
10.13 Discuss cultural and age variations in attitudes toward death and dying. (p. 368)
10.14 What are Kübler-Ross's five stages of death and dying, and what is thanatology? (p. 368)

KEY TERMS (Review & wRite)

Like other survey courses, introductory psychology is filled with a "wealth" of new and unfamiliar terminology. To do well on exams, you must master this new language! Writing a brief definition of each term in the space provided and carefully reviewing them before exams will significantly improve your course grade.

Activity Theory: _____

_____

Collectivistic Cultures: _____

_____

Conventional Level: _____

_____

Disengagement Theory: _____

_____

Individualistic Cultures: _____

_____

Postconventional Level: _____

_____

Preconventional Level: _____

_____

Psychosocial Stages: _____

_____

Resiliency: _____

_____

Socioemotional Selectivity Theory: _____

_____

Temperament: _____

_____

Thanatology: _____

_____

ACTIVE LEARNING EXERCISES

True mastery of information requires you to be an ACTIVE learner. Completing the following active learning exercises will improve your understanding of the chapter material and greatly improve your performance on exams. Answers to some exercises appear in Appendix A at the end of this study guide.

ACTIVE LEARNING EXERCISE I *Making Peace with Your Parents*
One characteristic of a critical thinker is the ability to think independently, which requires insight into one's own beliefs. When we feel at peace with people, we can consider their beliefs in an untroubled way and espouse them as our own or reject them freely. Many people consider independence to be merely financial. However, psychological independence is an

equally significant mark of adult development. Hopefully, exploring your relationship with your parents will help you become independent of them, as a critical thinker and as a person. Take a few moments to jot down your answers to the following:

1. Are you truly free of regrets and resentments from your childhood?
2. Are you relaxed and do you enjoy spending time with your parents? Or do you resent "having" to visit or interact with them?
3. Are you able to accept your parents, forgive them their mistakes, and give up trying to change them?
4. Do you feel loved and accepted by your parents?
5. Do you still compare yourself and compete with one of your brothers or sisters?
6. Are you still waiting to escape from your parents' rules, influence, or habits to become your own person?
7. Are you glad you had the parents you did?
8. If your parents are divorced, have you resolved your mixed feelings about this situation?
9. Do you have fears of being trapped or disappointed by a committed love relationship or marriage in your own life?
10. Have you completed your resentments and regrets toward your parent who may no longer be living? Can you accept the reality and inevitability of your own death?

Your answers are an important first step in actually recognizing and eventually working through these long-standing problems, and the questions were adapted from the paperback book Making Peace With Your Parents by Harold H. Bloomfield, M.D. and Leonard Felder, Ph.D. (New York: Ballantine Books, 1983). If you want more information on this topic, this book is a wonderful resource. If problems with your parents are longstanding and too overwhelming, you may want help from professional psychologists or counselors. Your psychology instructor may be willing to recommend someone in your area.

ACTIVE LEARNING EXERCISE II *Overcoming ageism*

One of the best ways to reduce ageism is through increased exposure to the elderly. Try visiting a local senior center, retirement home, and/or a convalescent hospital and talk with people of varying ages, abilities, and levels of activity. Try to really get to know them. Ask important questions about their political, spiritual, or personal beliefs about child rearing, divorce, or the value of a college education. Ask how they think things have changed since they were in their 20s, 30s, and so on. Once you've established a level of comfort, try asking about controversial topics like gun control, abortion, premarital sex, and so on. You might also try asking similar questions with elderly relatives. Younger people sometimes complain about "having to visit" their relatives, but their interest might increase if they asked interesting questions.

Stereotypes about aging and the elderly are generally based on lack of information. As you get to know a larger group of older people, you'll realize your previous stereotypes no longer fit. Just as African Americans or Latinos cannot be categorized under a few stereotypical traits or characteristics, the same is true for the elderly.

CHAPTER OVERVIEW (Review)

The following chapter overview provides a narrative overview of the main topics covered in the chapter. Like the *Visual Summary* found at the end of each chapter in the text, this narrative summary provides a final opportunity to *review* chapter material.

I. Moral Development

10.1 What is the biological perspective on morality? (p. 350)
From a biological perspective, morality may be prewired and evolutionarily based (e.g., adoption of a motherless chimp by other chimps promotes specie survival).

10.2 Describe Kohlberg's three levels and six stages of moral development. (p. 351)
According to Kohlberg, morality progresses through three levels. Each level consists of two stages. At the **preconventional level**, morality is self-centered. What is right is what one can get away with (Stage 1) or what is personally satisfying (Stage 2). **Conventional level** morality is based on a need for approval (Stage 3) and obedience to laws because they maintain the social order (Stage 4). **Postconventional** moral reasoning comes from adhering to the social contract (Stage 5), and the individual's own principles and universal values (Stage 6).

10.3 What area the three major criticisms of Kohlberg's theory? (p. 351)
Kohlberg's theory has been criticized for possibly measuring only moral reasoning and not moral behavior, and for possible culture and gender bias.

II. Personality Development

10.4 Describe Thomas and Chess's temperament theory. (p. 354)
Thomas and Chess emphasized the genetic components of certain traits (such as sociability) and the fact that babies often exhibit differences in **temperament** shortly after birth. They found three categories of temperament (*easy, difficult,* and *slow-to-warm-up children*) that appear to be consistent throughout the life span.

10.5 Describe Erikson's eight psychosocial stages. (p. 355)
Erikson proposed a theory of eight **psychosocial stages** covering the entire life span. The four stages that occur during childhood are *trust versus mistrust, autonomy versus shame and doubt, initiative versus guilt,* and *industry versus inferiority.* Erikson believes the major psychosocial crisis of adolescence is the search for *identity versus role confusion.* During young adulthood, the individual's task is to establish *intimacy over isolation,* and during middle adulthood, the person must deal with *generativity versus stagnation.* At the end of life, the older adult must establish *ego integrity,* or face overwhelming *despair* at the realization of lost opportunities.

10.6 What are the major criticisms of Erikson's stages? (p. 355)
Erikson's eight stages are difficult to test scientifically, and they may not apply cross-culturally.

10.7 How do individualistic versus collectivistic cultures affect personality development? (p. 357)
In **individualistic cultures**, the needs and goals of the individual are emphasized over the needs and goals of the group. The reverse is true in **collectivistic cultures**.

III. Meeting the Challenges of Adulthood

10.8 Discuss the major problems with long-term relationships. (p. 359)

A good marriage is one of the most important and difficult tasks of adulthood. Researchers have found six major traits and factors in happy marriages: established "love maps," shared power and mutual support, conflict management, similarity, supportive social environment, and a positive emphasis.

Family violence, teenage pregnancy, and divorce have significant effects on development. However, **resilient** children who survive an abusive and stress-filled childhood usually have good intellectual functioning, a relationship with a caring adult, and the ability to regulate their attention, emotions, and behavior.

10.9 Describe how work and retirement affect development. (p. 364)

The kind of work we do and the occupational choices we make can play a critical role in our lives. Before making a career decision, it is wise to research possible alternatives and take interest inventories. Life satisfaction after retirement appears to be most strongly related to good health, control over one's life, social support, and participation in community services and social activities.

10.10 What are the three major theories of aging? (p. 364)

One theory of successful aging, **activity theory**, says people should remain active and involved throughout the entire life span. Another major theory, **disengagement theory**, says the elderly naturally and gracefully withdraw from life because they welcome the relief from roles they can no longer fulfill. Although this disengagement theory is no longer in favor, the **socioemotional selectivity theory** does find that the elderly tend to decrease their social contacts as they become more selective with their time.

10.11 Discuss the major cultural differences in ageism. (p. 365)

There is considerable difference in the status and treatment of different elderly subgroups, and ethnic minority elderly, especially African Americans and Latinos, who face problems of both racism and ageism. Ageism is an important stressor for the elderly, but there are some cultures where aging is revered.

IV. Grief and Death

10.12 Describe grief and list its four stages. (p. 367)

Grief is a natural and painful reaction to a loss. For most people, grief consists of four major stages—*numbness, yearning, disorganization and despair,* and *resolution.*

10.13 Discuss cultural and age variations in attitudes toward death and dying. (p. 368)

Attitudes about death and dying vary greatly across cultures and among age groups. Some cultures regard death as a time for celebration, whereas others see it as a time for serious grief. Although adults understand the *permanence, universality,* and *nonfunctionality* of death, children often do not master these concepts until around age 7.

10.14 What are Kübler-Ross's five stages of death and dying, and what is thanatology? (p. 368)

Elisabeth Kübler-Ross's five-stage theory of dying (*denial, anger, bargaining, depression,* and *acceptance*) offers important insights into the last major crisis that we face in life. The study of death and dying, **thanatology,** has become an important topic in human development.

SELF-TESTS (Review & wRite)

Completing the following self-tests will provide immediate feedback on how well you have mastered the material. In the labeling exercises, *crossword puzzle*, and *fill-in exercises*, write the appropriate word or words in the blank spaces. The *matching exercise* requires you to match the terms in one column to their correct definitions in the other. For the *multiple-choice questions* in Practice Tests I and II, circle or underline the correct answer. If you are unsure of any answer, mark the item, and then go back to the text for further review. Correct answers are provided in Appendix A at the end of this study guide.

CROSSWORD PUZZLE FOR CHAPTER 10

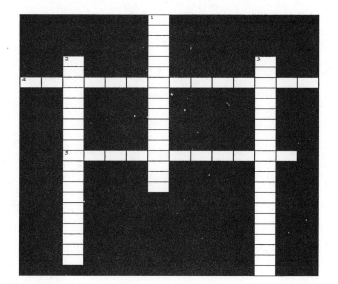

ACROSS

4 According to Erikson, a period of inner conflict during which an individual examines his or her life and values and makes decisions about life roles.

5 A basic, inborn disposition that appears shortly after birth and characterizes an individual's style of approaching people and situations.

DOWN

1 Kohlberg's second level of moral development, where moral judgments are based on compliance with the rules and values of society.

2 Kohlberg's first level of moral development, characterized by moral judgments based on fear of punishment or desire for pleasure.

3 Kohlberg's highest level of moral development, which occurs when individuals develop personal standards for right and wrong.

FILL-IN EXERCISES

1. Kohlberg proposed three broad levels in the evolution of moral reasoning: _____, _____, _____ (p. 352).

2. Individuals at the _____ level of Kohlberg's model make moral judgments based on rewards, fear of punishment, and exchange of favors (p. 352).

3. The _____ level of moral development occurs when moral judgments are based on compliance with the rules and values of society (p. 352).

4. An individual's innate behavioral style and characteristic emotional response is known as _____ (pp. 354-355).

5. Erikson's _____ theory suggests that all individuals pass through eight developmental stages and that each stage is marked by a unique crisis or conflict related to a specific developmental task (pp. 355-356).

6. In _____ cultures, the needs and goals of the group are emphasized over the needs and goals of the individual (p. 357).

7. Research shows that _____ is the most common reason for girls dropping out of high school (p. 362).

8. Some children survive and prosper even under the harshest environmental circumstances. They are known as _____ children (p. 363).

9. The _____ theory of aging suggests remaining active and involved as long as possible. In contrast, the _____ theory says older people should naturally and gracefully withdraw from life (p. 364).

10. Kübler-Ross's five stages of dying are _____, _____, _____, _____ and _____ (p. 369).

MATCHING EXERCISES

Column A   Column B

a. Thomas and Chess   1.____ Basic inborn disposition.
b. Gilligan   2.____ Psychosocial theory
c. Activity Theory   3.____ The study of death and dying
d. Grief   4.____ Good-child and law-and-order moral orientations
e. Erikson   5.____ Five stages of death
f. Postconventional Level   6.____ Criticized Kohlberg for possible gender bias
g. Yearning   7.____ Stage of grief
h. Conventional Level   8.____ Social contract and universal ethics moral orientations
i. Thanatology   9.____ Suggests older people should remain active
j. Kübler-Ross   10.____ A natural and painful reaction to a loss

PRACTICE TEST I

1. From a(n) _____ perspective, morality may be prewired and evolutionarily based.
   a. biopsychosocial
   b. biological
   c. both of these options
   d. none of these options

2. During Kohlberg's _____ level, right and wrong are judged on the basis of commonly accepted social rules because they ensure the social order.
   a. conventional
   b. amoral
   c. postconventional
   d. preconventional

3. When people have developed their own standards for right and wrong, they are judged by Kohlberg to be at the _____ level of morality.
   a. adolescent
   b. postconventional
   c. nonconventional
   d. conventional

4. Kohlberg's theory of moral development has been criticized for its _____.
   a. cultural bias toward Western ideas of morality
   b. political bias in favor of conservatives
   c. sexual bias in favor of women
   d. ethnic bias against Anglo-Saxons

5. _____ is an innate behavioral style and characteristic emotional response.
   a. Personality
   b. Trait theory
   c. Character
   d. Temperament

6. According to Thomas and Chess, a moody, easily frustrated, and overreactive child would be called _____.

   a. insecurely attached
   b. authoritative
   c. difficult
   d. normal

7. According to _____ theory, individuals pass through eight developmental stages.
   a. Freud's psychosexual
   b. Freud's psychoanalytic
   c. Maslow's hierarchical
   d. Erikson's psychosocial

8. Erikson proposed that the key challenge faced by infants in their first year is _____.
   a. weaning
   b. object permanence
   c. trust versus mistrust
   d. toilet training

9. According to Erikson, the need to develop a sense of identity is the principal task of _____.
   a. the phallic stage of psychosexual development
   b. adolescence
   c. middle adulthood
   d. the generativity versus stagnation stage of development

10. Erikson believes young adults need to form _____ connections with others, otherwise they face isolation and consequent self-absorption.
    a. mature
    b. political
    c. integrity
    d. intimate

11. In Erikson's final stage of psychosocial development, adults may _____.
    a. regret lost opportunities
    b. become despondent
    c. review their accomplishments
    d. any of these options

12. Kohlberg and Erikson's theories are largely rooted in the concept of _____, or how we define and understand ourselves.
    a. self-efficacy
    b. temperament
    c. stage theories
    d. the self

13. Research suggests that in _____ cultures the needs and goals of the individual are emphasized over the needs and goals of the group.
    a. collectivistic
    b. industrialized
    c. individualistic
    d. none of these options

14. Researchers suggest that during a(n) _____ divorce, ex-spouses must learn how to let go, develop new social ties, and redefine parental roles (when children are involved).
    a. midlife
    b. noncontested
    c. healthy
    d. all of these options

15. This is **NOT** a problem related to adolescent pregnancy.
    a. reduced educational achievement
    b. lower levels of depression
    c. more risks to maternal health
    d. more risks to the child's health

16. _____ children recover from trauma, display competence under stress, and prosper despite a high-risk status.
    a. Resilient
    b. Self-actualized
    c. Autonomous
    d. Attached

17. The _____ theory of aging says that one should remain active and involved in fulfilling activities as long as possible.
    a. engagement
    b. activity

    c. involvement
    d. life-enhancement

18. Helen has always looked forward to retirement as a time to "sit back and do nothing." She is therefore very surprised at recommendations to the contrary from her company's pre-retirement seminars. Her company apparently accepts the _____ theory of aging, whereas Helen apparently supports the _____ theory.
    a. vitality; relaxation
    b. involvement; retreat
    c. activity; disengagement
    d. incentive; drive-reduction

19. In the United States, _____ is one of the greater stresses experienced by the elderly.
    a. physical decline
    b. psychological decline
    c. fear of death
    d. ageism

20. During the _____ stage of grief, the mourner feels listless, apathetic, and submissive.
    a. yearning
    b. disorganization/despair
    c. resolution
    d. acceptance

PRACTICE TEST II

1. According to Kohlberg, moral judgment is self-centered and based on obtaining rewards and avoiding punishment during the _____ stage of moral development.
    a. trust versus mistrust
    b. industry versus inferiority
    c. conventional
    d. preconventional

2. During the _____ stage, an individual accepts, internalizes, and applies the rules of society in making moral decisions.
    a. formal conventional
    b. conventional
    c. informal operational
    d. social operational

3. Personal standards of right and wrong are found in Kohlberg's _____ level of moral development.
    a. lowest
    b. highest
    c. middle
    d. all of these options

4. Jeff is a private in a combat unit during a war. His commanding officer orders him to shoot two young adolescents whom they have taken prisoner. Jeff is LEAST likely to follow the orders if he is in Kohlberg's _____ stage.
    a. conventional
    b. preconventional
    c. postconventional
    d. none of the above

5. Thomas and Chess suggested that most children were born with one of these three temperament styles.
    a. easy, difficult, slow-to-warm-up
    b. attached, unattached, avoidant
    c. imprinted, attached, anxious
    d. introverted, extroverted, averted

6. You have a child who is a month old and seems to be shy, withdrawn, and needs time to adjust to new experiences. According to Thomas and Chess's temperament theory, your child might be classified as a(n) _____ child.
    a. extroverted
    b. slow-to-warm-up
    c. imprinted
    d. difficult

7. Trust, initiative, identity, and generativity are the odd-numbered stages in Erikson's psychosocial theory of development. The even-numbered stages include _____.
    a. autonomy, industry, intimacy, and ego integrity
    b. egocentrism, effort, caring, and retirement
    c. attachment, independence, genuineness, and self-actualization
    d. anal, phallic, latent, and genital

8. According to Erikson, industry is the result of the successful completion of this stage of development.
    a. infancy and toddlerhood
    b. ages 6 through 12
    c. young adulthood
    d. middle adulthood

9. During early childhood, children learn to exercise will, make choices, and control themselves. Erikson called this psychosocial stage _____.
    a. authoritarian discipline
    b. acceptance versus mistrust
    c. autonomy versus shame and doubt
    d. attachment versus autonomy

10. According to Erikson, resolution of the critical conflict of young adulthood leads to a sense of _____.
    a. parental rejection
    b. strong parental control
    c. intimacy
    d. none of these options

11. Which of the following is considered to be a collectivistic culture?
    a. Taiwan
    b. Hong Kong
    c. Columbia
    d. all of these options

12. According to Everett and Everett, when children are involved, ex-spouses must let go of the marital relationship, develop new social ties, and _____.
    a. gain joint-custody of the children
    b. spend equal time and money on the children to avoid "favorites"
    c. decide which parent will be the primary caretaker for the children
    d. none of these options

13. _____ refers to the ability to adapt effectively in the face of threat.
    a. Resiliency
    b. Socioemotional selectivity
    c. Activity theory
    d. Industry versus inferiority

14. Satisfaction during retirement is strongly related to good health, community and social activities, and _____.
    a. access to a willing sexual partner
    b. being closer to 65 than 75 years of age
    c. control over one's life
    d. all of these options

15. The _____ theory of aging suggests that a natural decline in social contacts occurs as older adults become more selective with their time.
    a. Kübler-Ross
    b. socioemotional selectivity
    c. developmental
    d. disengagement

16. What do Japan, China, Native-American, and African-American cultures/ethnic groups have in common? They each _____.
    a. support the disengagement theory of aging
    b. revere the elderly
    c. exploit the elderly for their wisdom
    d. have lower life-expectancies than other cultures and ethnic groups

17. Research on aging in the United States indicates that elderly men generally have more _____ than elderly women, but elderly women usually have more_____.
    a. income; sexual partners
    b. income; friends
    c. family relationships; money
    d. friends; sexual partners

18. Which of the following is NOT one of the four stages in the "normal" grieving process?
    a. numbness
    b. yearning
    c. bargaining
    d. resolution

19. Helpful tips for grieving include _____.
    a. recognizing the loss and allowing yourself to grieve
    b. setting up a daily activity schedule
    c. seeking help
    d. all of these options

20. As adults we understand death in terms of three general concepts: permanence, universality, and _____.
    a. spirituality
    b. painfulness
    c. nonfunctionality
    d. all of these options

Process Diagram 10.2

Erikson's Eight Stages of Psychosocial Development

Process Diagram

Stage 1
Trust versus mistrust
(birth–age 1)

Infants learn to trust that their needs will be met, especially by the mother; if not, mistrust develops.

Steve Raymer/NG Image Collection

Stage 2
Autonomy versus shame and doubt (ages 1–3)

Toddlers learn to exercise will, make choices, and control themselves. Caregivers' patience and encouragement help foster a sense of autonomy versus shame and doubt.

Prof. Karen Huffman

Stage 3
Initiative versus guilt (ages 3–6)

Preschoolers learn to initiate activities and enjoy their accomplishments. Supportive caregivers promote feelings of power and self-confidence versus guilt.

Dynamic Graphics, Inc./Creates

Stage 4
Industry versus inferiority (ages 6–12)

Elementary school-aged children develop a sense of industry and learn productive skills that their culture requires (such as reading, writing, and counting); if not, they feel inferior.

PhotoDisc/Getty Images, Inc.

Stage 5
Identity versus role confusion (adolescence)

During a period of serious soul-searching, adolescents develop a coherent sense of self and their role in society. Failure to resolve this identity crisis may lead to an unstable identity, delinquency, and difficulty in personal relationships in later life.

Randy Olson/NG Image Collection

Stage 6
Intimacy versus isolation (early adulthood)

After learning who they are and how to be independent, young adults form intimate connections with others; if not, they face isolation and consequent self-absorption.

Pablo Corral Vega/NG Image Collection

Stage 7
Generativity versus stagnation (middle adulthood)

Middle-aged adults develop concern for establishing and influencing the next generation. If this expansion and effort do not occur, an individual stagnates and is concerned solely with material possessions and personal well-being.

IT Stock

Stage 8
Ego integrity versus despair (late adulthood)

Older people enter a period of reflection; in which they feel a sense of accomplishment and satisfaction with the lives they've lived. If not, they experience regret and despair that their lives cannot be relived.

Richard Olsenius/NG Image Collection

Chapter 10 Visual Summary

Moral Development

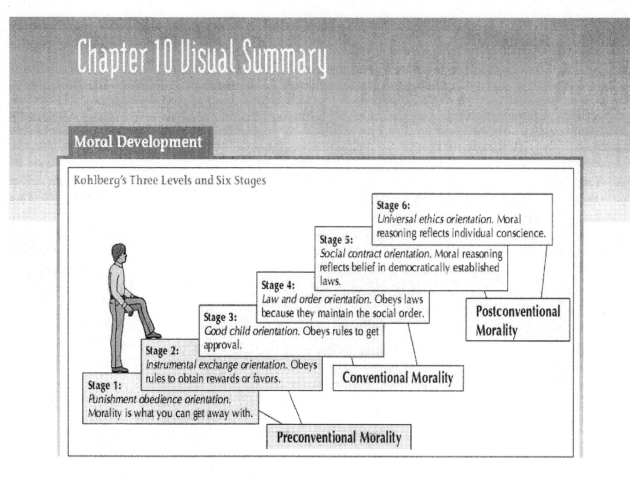

Kohlberg's Three Levels and Six Stages

Stage 6:
Universal ethics orientation. Moral reasoning reflects individual conscience.

Stage 5:
Social contract orientation. Moral reasoning reflects belief in democratically established laws.

Stage 4:
Law and order orientation. Obeys laws because they maintain the social order.

Stage 3:
Good child orientation. Obeys rules to get approval.

Stage 2:
Instrumental exchange orientation. Obeys rules to obtain rewards or favors.

Stage 1:
Punishment obedience orientation. Morality is what you can get away with.

Postconventional Morality

Conventional Morality

Preconventional Morality

Personality Development

Thomas & Chess's Temperament Theory

Temperament: Basic, inborn disposition. Three temperament styles: *easy, difficult,* and *slow-to-warm-up.* Styles seem consistent and enduring.

Erikson's Eight Psychosocial Stages

Stage	Approximate Age
1. Trust-vs-mistrust	Birth–1
2. Autonomy-vs-shame and doubt	1–3 years
3. Initiative-vs-guilt	3–6 years
4. Industry-vs-inferiority	6–12 years
5. Identity-vs-role confusion	Adolescence
6. Intimacy-vs-isolation	Early adulthood
7. Generativity-vs-stagnation	Middle adulthood
8. Ego integrity-vs-despair	Late adulthood

Ted Streshinsky/©Corbis

Meeting the Challenges of Adulthood

Families
* Family violence, teenage pregnancies, and divorce can influence development.
* **Resilience** helps some children survive an abusive or stress-filled childhood.

Occupational Choices

Occupational choice is critically important because most people channel their accomplishment needs into their work.

Aging

Three major theories of aging.

Activity Theory (should remain active)

Disengagement Theory (should gracefully withdraw)

Socioemotional Selectivity (elderly reduce social contacts because they're more selective)

Grief and Death

Grief

Grief: A natural and painful reaction to a loss, consists of four major stages:

1) numbness → 2) yearning → 3) disorganization and despair → 4) resolution

Attitudes

Attitudes toward death and dying vary greatly across cultures and among age groups. Children generally don't fully understand the *permanence, universality,* and *nonfunctionality* of death until around the age 7.

Death Experience

* Kübler-Ross proposes a five-stage psychological process when facing death (*denial, anger, bargaining, depression,* and *acceptance*).
* **Thanatology:** Study of death and dying.

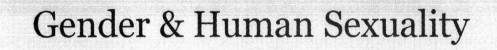

11
Gender & Human Sexuality

OUTLINE SQ4R (Survey, Question, Read, Recite, Review, & wRite)

This outline section incorporates all six steps in the well-researched SQ4R method of learning. Begin by surveying the list of chapter topics in the left column. This "big picture" will help focus and guide your attention while you read. As you read through the chapter, briefly summarize each section in your own words in the space to the right. Also write down any *questions* that come to mind. Surveying, Questioning, Reading, Reciting, Reviewing, and wRiting are the foundation of the SQ4R method and an invaluable form of active learning. They also make your reading time more enjoyable and efficient! One thorough, focused SQ4R reading of a chapter is far better than several passive readings.

TOPIC	**NOTES**

I. SEX AND GENDER

    A. What is "Maleness" and "Femaleness"?

    B. Gender Role Development

    C. Gender Identity Formation

    Case Study/Personal Story:
       The Tragic Tale of "John/Joan"

    D. Sex and Gender Differences

    Research Highlight: Video Games, Gender,
       And Spatial Skills

Critical Thinking/Active Learning:
   Gender Differences and Critical Thinking

II. THE STUDY OF HUMAN SEXUALITY

Gender & Cultural Diversity:
   A Cross-Cultural Look at Sexual Behaviors

III. SEXUAL BEHAVIOR

A. Sexual Arousal and Response

Gender & Cultural Diversity: Are There Evolutionary
   Advantages to Female Nonmonogamy?

B. Sexual Orientation

IV. SEXUAL PROBLEMS

A. Sexual Dysfunction

Research Highlight: Is Cybersex Harmful?

B. Sexually Transmitted Infections (STIs)

Psychology at Work: Protecting Yourself
   and Others Against STIs

Critical Thinking/Active Learning:
   Rape Myths and Rape Prevention

LEARNING OBJECTIVES (Read, Recite, Review, & wRite)

In addition to the work you did in the Outline above, you can significantly improve your performance on exams by focusing on the following learning objectives. While reading the chapter or reviewing for exams, check your understanding by stopping periodically to *recite* (or repeat in your own words) and *writing* down your answers on a separate sheet. [Page numbers correspond to Chapter 1 in *Psychology in Action* (9e).]

11.1 Compare and contrast sex and gender. (p. 376)
11.2 Define gender role, and describe the two major theories of gender role development. (p. 376)
11.3 Differentiate between gender identity, transsexualism, transvestism, and sexual orientation. (p. 378)
11.4 Describe the major sex and gender differences between men and women. (p. 381)
11.5 What is androgyny? (p. 383)
11.6 Describe early studies of sexuality and the contributions of Ellis, Kinsey, and Masters and Johnson. (p. 386)
11.7 Why are cross-cultural studies of sexuality important? (p. 387)
11.8 What are the four stages in Masters and Johnson's sexual response cycle? (p. 389)
11.9 Describe how the evolutionary perspective and the social role approach help explain male/female differences in sexual behavior. (p. 391)
11.10 Discuss the latest research on sexual orientation. (p. 391)
11.11 Describe how biological, psychological, and social forces contribute to sexual dysfunction. (p. 394)
11.12 Discuss how sex therapists treat sexual dysfunction, and list the four major principles of Masters and Johnson's approach. (p. 397)
11.13 What is cybersex, and is it harmful? (p. 399)
11.14 Discuss the major issues related to STIs and the special problem of AIDS. (p. 399)

KEY TERMS (Review & wRite)

Like other survey courses, introductory psychology is filled with a "wealth" of new and unfamiliar terminology. To do well on exams, you must master this new language! Writing a brief definition of each term in the space provided and carefully reviewing them before exams will significantly improve your course grade.

AIDS (Acquired Immunodeficiency Syndrome): _____

_____

Androgyny: _____

_____

Double Standard: _____

_____

Excitement Phase: _____

_____

Gender: _____

_____

Gender Identity: _____

_____

Gender Role: _____

_____

Gender Schema Theory: _____

_____

HIV positive: _____

_____

Orgasm Phase: _____

_____

Performance Anxiety: _____

_____

Plateau Phase: _____

_____

Refractory Period: _____

_____

Resolution Phase: _____

_____

Sex: _____

_____

Sexual Dysfunction: _____

_____

Sexual Orientation: _____

_____

Sexual Prejudice: _____

_____

Sexual Response Cycle: _____

_____

Sexual Scripts: _____

_____

Social Learning Theory of Gender Role Development: _____

_____

ACTIVE LEARNING EXERCISES

True mastery of information requires you to be an ACTIVE learner. Completing the following active learning exercises will improve your understanding of the chapter material and greatly improve your performance on exams. Answers to some exercises appear in Appendix A at the end of this study guide.

ACTIVE LEARNING EXERCISE I *The Role of Culture and Gender on Sexual Values*
A key ingredient of healthy sexuality is the ability to recognize and evaluate one's own *values* (ideals, mores, standards, and principles that guide behavior). Are the sexual values you hold a simple reflection of the values of your family or peer group? Or are they the result of careful, deliberate choice? Have you carefully examined opposing values and compared them to your own? How do your values reflect your culture and your gender role? Because sexual values have such a powerful influence on thinking, we offer the following exercise. Start by reading the four value statements on the left. Then, in the space to the right, simply check whether you agree or disagree.

	Agree	Disagree
1. Regardless of age or marital status, anyone who wants to prevent pregnancy should have easy access to reliable methods of contraception.	_____	_____
2. Gay and lesbian couples should be allowed the same legal protections (property inheritance, shared pension plans, shared medical benefits) as heterosexual married couples.	_____	_____
3. Abortion in the first four months of pregnancy should be a private decision between the woman and her doctor.	_____	_____

4. Sex education belongs in the home, not in public schools.   _____   _____

Each person's sexual values come from a host of sources, some internal and others external to the individual. Review your checked agree or disagree responses to the previous four statements. Indicate the degree to which each of the sources listed in the left-hand column has influenced your beliefs by placing a check mark in the appropriate column.

VS = Very Significant Influence
SS = Somewhat Significant Influence
NS = Not a Significant Influence

Sources	Contraception			Homosexuality			Abortion			Sex Education		
	VS	SS	NS	VS	SS	NS	VS	SS	NS	VS	SS	NS
Personal experience												
Family patterns												
Peer standards												
Historical events												
Religious views												
Research findings												

Now reexamine the checks you made for each of your four sexual values and their source of influence. Do you notice any patterns in your check marks? Which source has been most influential in the development of your sexual values? Do you think this source is the most appropriate and most justifiable? Why or why not? Which source has been least influential in the development of your sexual values? How do you explain this? Do you notice any inconsistencies in your choice of sources? In what cases has personal experience played a more significant role than family patterns, peer standards, and so on? To further clarify your sexual perspective, and sharpen your critical thinking skills, share your responses with a close friend, dating partner, or spouse.

ACTIVE LEARNING EXERCISE II *Exploring Your Own Gender Role Development*
To help you explore your values regarding "masculinity and femininity," we offer several critical thinking questions regarding your own gender role socialization. While reading through the questions, jot down your thoughts and try to think of specific examples from your personal history. After completing the exercise, we encourage you to share your responses with your significant other and close friends. You'll find this sharing generally leads to a fascinating discussion of "the proper roles for women and men."

1. During your early childhood, what gender messages did you receive from your favorite fairy tales, books, television shows? How were women and men portrayed? Are the roles of men and women different in the books and television programs you read and watch today?

2. Did anyone ever tell you that you were a "big boy now" or to "act like a lady?" What did they mean? How did you feel?

3. What were the power relationships like in your family? In what situations was your mother most powerful? Your father? Do you remember being treated differently from your opposite-sexed brother or sister? What is the division of labor in your family today (breadwinner, housekeeper, etc.)?

4. As a child, what did you want to be when you grew up? Did that change, and if so, when? Why? What career are you now pursuing? Why?

5. What were your favorite subjects in school? Your least favorite? Why?

6. Have you ever wished you were born as the opposite sex? If so, why?

7. Have you ever felt competitive with friends of your same sex? If so, over what?

8. In what ways do you express your emotions (crying, slamming doors, etc.), and how is your behavior related to your sex and gender?

9. What compliments and rewards do you receive related to your gender and sex (e.g., (attractiveness, strength, intelligence, business success, money earned, family status, etc.)? How does this relate to your gender role?

10. Have you ever strongly deviated from traditional expectations of you as a male or female? If so, what was your own and others' reaction to it? Have you ever felt restricted or pressured by social expectations of you as a man or woman? If so, in what way?

CHAPTER OVERVIEW (Review)

The following chapter overview provides a narrative overview of the main topics covered in the chapter. Like the *Visual Summary* found at the end of each chapter in the text, this narrative summary provides a final opportunity to *review* chapter material.

I. Sex and Gender

11.1 Compare and contrast sex and gender. (p. 376)
Sex refers to biological elements (such as having a penis or vagina) or physical activities (such as masturbation and intercourse). **Gender**, on the other hand, encompasses the psychological and sociocultural meanings and expectations added to biology (such as beliefs like "Men should be aggressive" and "Women should be nurturing.").

11.2 Define gender role, and describe the two major theories of gender role development. (p. 376)
The term **gender role** refers to the societal expectations for normal and "appropriate" female and male behavior. **Social learning theory of gender role development emphasizes** rewards, punishments, observation, and imitation. In contrast, **gender schema theory** combines social learning theory with active cognitive processing.

11.3 Differentiate between gender identity, transsexualism, transvestism, and sexual orientation. (p. 378)
Gender identity refers to an individual's self-identification as being either a man or a woman. *Transsexualism* is a problem with gender identity. *Transvestism* is cross-dressing for emotional

and sexual gratification. **Sexual orientation** (gay, lesbian, bisexual, or heterosexual) is unrelated to either transsexualism or transvestism.

11.4 Describe the major sex and gender differences between men and women. (p. 381)
Studies of male and female sex differences find several obvious physical differences, such as height, body build, and reproductive organs. There are also important functional and structural sex differences in the brains of human females and males. Studies find some gender differences (such as in aggression and verbal skills). But the cause of these differences (either nature or nurture) is still being debated.

11.5 What is androgyny? (p. 383)
Androgyny is a combination of traits generally considered male (assertive, athletic) with typically female characteristics (nurturing, yielding).

II. The Study of Human Sexuality
11.6 Describe early studies of sexuality and the contributions of Ellis, Kinsey, and Masters and Johnson. (p. 386)

Although sex has always been an important part of human interest, motivation, and behavior, it received little scientific attention before the twentieth century. Havelock Ellis was among the first to study human sexuality despite the repression and secrecy of nineteenth-century Victorian times.

Alfred Kinsey and his colleagues were the first to conduct large-scale, systematic surveys and interviews of the sexual practices and preferences of Americans during the 1940s and 1950s. In the 1960s, the research team of William Masters and Virginia Johnson pioneered the use of actual laboratory measurement and observation of human physiological response during sexual activity.

11.7 Why are cross-cultural studies of sexuality important? (p. 387)
Cultural studies provide important information on the similarities and variations in human sexuality. They also help counteract *ethnocentrism*—judging one's own culture as "normal" and preferable to others.

III. Sexual Behavior
11.8 What are the four stages in Masters and Johnson's sexual response cycle? (p. 389)
William Masters and Virginia Johnson identified a four-stage **sexual response cycle** during sexual activity---**excitement, plateau, orgasm,** and **resolution phases**.

11.9 Describe how the evolutionary perspective and the social role approach help explain male/female differences in sexual behavior. (p. 391)
Although there are numerous similarities and differences between the sexes, but differences are the focus of most research. According to the *evolutionary perspective*, males engage in more sexual behaviors with more sexual partners because it helps the species survive. The *social role approach* suggests this difference results from traditional cultural divisions of labor.

11.10 Discuss the latest research on sexual orientation. (p. 391)
Although researchers have identified several myths concerning the causes of homosexuality, the origins remain a puzzle. In recent studies, the genetic and biological explanation has gained the strongest support. Despite increased understanding, sexual orientation remains a divisive issue in the United States.

IV. Sexual Problems

11.11 Describe how biological, psychological, and social forces contribute to sexual dysfunction. (p. 394)
Biology plays a key role in both sexual arousal and response. Ejaculation and orgasm are partially reflexive, and the parasympathetic nervous system must be dominant during sexual arousal. The sympathetic nervous system must dominate for orgasm to occur. Psychological factors like negative early sexual experiences, fears of negative consequences from sex, and **performance anxiety** contribute to **sexual dysfunction**. Sexual arousal and response are also related to social forces, such as early *gender role training*, the **double standard**, and **sexual scripts,** which teach us what to consider the "best" sex.

11.12 Discuss how sex therapists treat sexual dysfunction, and list the four major principles of Masters and Johnson's approach. (p. 397)
Many sexual problems can be helped with sex therapy. Clinicians generally begin with tests and interviews to determine the cause(s) of sexual dysfunctions. Masters and Johnson emphasize the couple's relationship, combined physiological and psychosocial factors, cognitions, and specific behavioral techniques. Professional sex therapists offer important guidelines for everyone: Sex education should be early and positive, avoid a goal or performance orientation, and keep communication open.

11.13 What is cybersex, and is it harmful? (p. 399)
Cybersex includes a wide variety of online sex-oriented conversations and exchanges. Although some Internet connections can be healthy and satisfying, they also may contribute to serious personal and relationship problems.

11.14 Discuss the major issues related to STIs and the special problem of AIDS. (p. 399)
The dangers and rate of STIs are high, and higher for women than for men. Most STIs can be cured in their early stages. The most publicized STI is **AIDS (acquired immunodeficiency syndrome)**. Although AIDS is transmitted only through sexual contact or exposure to infected blood, many people have irrational fears of contagion. At the same time, an estimated one million North Americans are **HIV positive** and therefore carriers.

SELF-TESTS (<u>R</u>eview & w<u>R</u>ite)

Completing the following self-tests will provide immediate feedback on how
well you have mastered the material. In the labeling exercises, *crossword
puzzle*, and *fill-in exercises*, write the appropriate word or words in the
blank spaces. The *matching exercise* requires you to match the terms in one
column to their correct definitions in the other. For the *multiple-choice
questions* in Practice Tests I and II, circle or underline the correct answer. If
you are unsure of any answer, mark the item, and then go back to the text for
further review. Correct answers are provided in Appendix A at the end of
this study guide.

CROSSWORD PUZZLE FOR CHAPTER 11

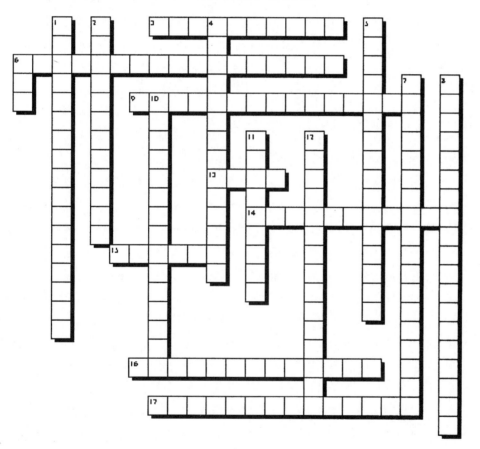

ACROSS

3 Societal expectations for normal and appropriate male and female behavior.

6 Impairment of the normal physiological processes of arousal and orgasm.

9 Final stage of the sexual response cycle when the body returns to its nonaroused state.

13 Human immunodeficiency viruses (HIV) destroy the immune system's ability to fight disease.

14 Third stage of the sexual response cycle when pleasurable sensations peak and orgasm occurs.

15 The psychological and sociocultural meanings added to biological maleness or femaleness.

16 Socially dictated descriptions of appropriate behaviors for sexual interactions.
17 Self-identification as either a man or a woman.

DOWN

1 Primary erotic attraction toward members of the same sex (homosexual or gay or lesbian), both sexes (bisexual), or other sex (heterosexual).

2 Second stage of the sexual response cycle, characterized by a leveling off of high arousal.

4 Beliefs, values, and norms that subtly encourage male sexuality and discourage female sexuality.

5 Phase following orgasm during which further orgasm is considered physiologically impossible.

6 Biological maleness and femaleness, including chromosomal sex. Also, activities related to sexual behaviors, such as masturbation and intercourse.

7 Fear of being judged in connection with sexual activity.

8 Masters and Johnson's description of the four stage bodily response to sexual arousal, which consists of excitement, plateau, orgasm, and resolution.

10 First stage of the sexual response cycle, characterized by increasing levels of arousal and increased engorgement of the genitals.

11 Combining characteristics considered typically male (assertive, athletic) with characteristics considered typically female (yielding, nurturant); from the Greek *andro,* meaning male, and *gyn,* meaning female.

12 Negative attitudes toward an individual because of her or his sexual orientation.

FILL-IN EXERCISES

1. _____ refers to biological maleness and femaleness (p. 376).

2. Societal expectations for appropriate female and male behavior are known as _____ (p. 376).

3. _____ refers to having a gender identity opposite that of the biological sex, whereas _____ refers to becoming sexually aroused by wearing the clothing of the other sex (pp. 378-379).

4. _____ refers to a sexual orientation toward the same sex. Being sexually attracted to both males and females is referred to as _____ (pp. 379-380).

5. _____ individuals combine some characteristics considered typically male with characteristics considered typically female (p. 383).

6. During the Victorian period, it was believed that _____ caused brain damage and death (p. 386).

7. During the resolution phase of the sexual response cycle, a male is likely to be in the _____ period (p. 390).

8. According to the _____, sexual differences (such as males having more sexual partners) evolved from an ancient set of mating patterns that helped the species survive (p. 391).

9. An irrational fear of homosexuality in others or oneself is known as _____ (p. 393).

10. Impairment of the normal physiological processes of arousal and orgasm is known as a _____ (p. 394).

MATCHING EXERCISES

Column A   Column B

a. Masters and Johnson   1.____ Self perception as either male or female.
b. Double Standard   2.____ Sexual orientation to both men and women.
c. Sex   3.____ Combination of both masculine and feminine.
d. Bisexual   4.____ Used direct measurement and observation of sex.
e. Havelock Ellis   5.____ Encourages male sexuality and discourages the female's.
f. Plateau Phase   6.____ Inability to respond to sexual arousal to point of orgasm.
g. Gender Identity   7.____ Leveling off of sexual arousal.
h. Orgasmic Dysfunction   8.____ Fearing won't meet self or partner's sexual expectations.
i. Performance Anxiety   9.____ Biological dimensions of maleness or femaleness.
j. Androgyny   10.____ Based his research on personal diaries.

PRACTICE TEST I

1. The term _____ refers to psychological and sociocultural meanings added to biological maleness or femaleness.
    a. gender role
    b. sex
    c. gender
    d. androgyny

2. The _____ theory states that children learn their gender roles through social learning and active cognitive processing.
    a. gender schema
    b. social-cognitive developmental
    c. information gathering
    d. mental schema

3. According to your text, _____ refers to the one's self-identification as either a man or a woman.
    a. sex role
    b. assigned sex
    c. gender dysphoria
    d. gender identity

4. A transsexual is a person who has a _____.

    a. mismatch between gender identity and his or her gonads, genitals, or internal accessory organs
    b. mismatch between gender role and his or her gonads, genitals, or internal accessory organs
    c. homosexual preference for sexual gratification
    d. need to wear clothing of the opposite sex for sexual gratification

5. A _____ individual is sexually attracted to the same sex.
    a. lesbian
    b. gay
    c. homosexual
    d. all of the above

6. _____ are two of the most researched gender differences.
    a. Structural and functional differences in the brain
    b. Brain size differences in the corpus callosum and hypothalamus
    c. Cognitive abilities and aggression
    d. all of these options

7. Studies on identical twins find that genetic factors account for about _____ percent of aggressive behavior.
   a. 50
   b. 75
   c. 92
   d. none of these options

8. Androgyny is another word for a(n) _____.
   a. homosexual, gay or lesbian
   b. combination of both male and female traits
   c. oversupply of androgens during prenatal development
   d. transvestite

9. _____ was a major pioneer in sex research who first used the case study method.
   a. B. F. Skinner
   b. Sigmund Freud
   c. Alfred Kinsey
   d. Havelock Ellis

10. One of the earliest and most extensive surveys of human sexual behavior in the United States was conducted by _____.
    a. Havelock Ellis
    b. William Masters and Virginia Johnson
    c. Emily and John Roper
    d. Alfred Kinsey

11. Limited exposure to the sexual practices of other cultures may lead to _____, the tendency to view our culture's sexual practices as normal.
    a. sexual prejudice
    b. ethnic typing
    c. ethnocentrism
    d. sexual predation

12. Orgasm refers to the _____.
    a. final phase of the sexual response cycle
    b. male refractory period
    c. experiencing a highly intense and pleasurable release of tension
    d. peak of the excitement phase

13. Research on the causes of homosexuality _____.
    a. has helped overcome many misconceptions and myths
    b. provides evidence of a biological foundation
    c. is inconclusive
    d. all of these options

14. _____ refers to negative attitudes toward an individual because of his or her sexual orientation.
    a. Homoeroticism
    b. Hate crimes
    c. Gay prejudice
    d. Sexual prejudice

15. The inability to obtain or maintain an erection sufficiently firm for intercourse is _____.
    a. primarily a problem with men in the United States
    b. sometimes associated with diabetes, hormonal deficiencies, stress, and anxiety
    c. experienced only by older males
    d. associated with long-term relationships

16. Painful intercourse in men or women is called _____.
    a. dyspareunia
    b. endorphin-deficient syndrome
    c. sexual aversion disorder
    d. priapism

17. The sexual double standard _____.
    a. encourages male sexuality
    b. discourages female sexuality
    c. makes women responsible for stopping male advances
    d. all of these options

18. _____ teach us "what to do, when, where, how, and with whom."
    a. Sex surrogates
    b. Sex therapists
    c. Sex manuals
    d. Sexual scripts

19. All of the following are principles of Masters and Johnson's approach to sex therapy except _____.
    a. setting goals to improve sexual performance
    b. examination of the relationship between the two people
    c. use of medical histories and physical examinations
    d. exploration of individual attitudes and sex education

20. Which of the following is a myth about rape?
    a. A man cannot be raped by a woman.
    b. All women secretly want to be raped.
    c. Women cannot be raped against their will.
    d. All of the above

PRACTICE TEST II

1. _____ is to biological as _____.
   a. Sex, gender is to psychosocial
   b. Androgyny, anatomy is to physiology
   c. Gender, intercourse is to making love
   d. Homosexuality, physiological is to psychological

2. Which of the following is **NOT** a gonad?
   a. ovary
   b. testicle
   c. uterus
   d. all of these are gonads

3. Rewards and punishment are most closely associated with _____.
   a. male gender roles
   b. identity dysphoria
   c. social learning theory
   d. schemas

4. Men are more likely to attribute their successes to internal abilities. In contrast, women are more likely to attribute their successes to _____.
   a. internal abilities
   b. external factors
   c. the men in their lives
   d. their mothers

5. Virtually all studies of human gender differences are _____, which makes it extremely difficult to separate the effects of biological, psychological, and social forces.
   a. limited to the western hemisphere
   b. correlational
   c. nonscientific
   d. all of these options

6. According to research, androgynous individuals _____.
   a. generally have higher self-esteem
   b. are more socially competent and motivated to achieve
   c. exhibit better overall mental health
   d. all of these options

7. The physiological aspects of human sexual responses were studied by _____.
   a. Havelock Ellis
   b. Freud
   c. Masters and Johnson
   d. Alfred Kinsey

8. Which of the following is NOT part of the sexual response cycle?
   a. resolution
   b. excitement
   c. orgasm
   d. performance anxiety

9. In your text's diving board analogy for the sexual response model, climbing up the ladder is analogous to the _____ phase
   a. excitement
   b. plateau
   c. orgasm
   d. resolution

10. The _____ first occurs during the excitement phase of the sexual response cycle.
    a. spermarche
    b. woman's refractory period
    c. man's refractory period
    d. sex flush

11. When a male cannot control how quickly he ejaculates in 50% or more of his sexual encounters, he is most likely experiencing a problem called _____.
    a. spermarche
    b. dyspareunia
    c. male orgasmic dysfunction
    d. premature ejaculation

12. Vaginismus is a sexual disorder that involves fear of _____.
    a. hormosexuality
    b. androgyn
    c. heterosexuality
    d. intercourse

13. Sexual arousal is dependent on the dominance of the _____ nervous system.
    a. parasympathetic
    b. autonomic
    c. somatic
    d. sympathetic

14. Based on your answer to the previous question, _____ can therefore interfere with sexual arousal.
    a. relaxation
    b. strong emotions
    c. foreplay
    d. none of these options

15. The _____ branch of the _____ nervous system is in dominance during orgasm and ejaculation.
    a. sympathetic; autonomic
    b. peripheral; somatic
    c. parasympathetic; autonomic
    d. somatic; parasympathetic

16. The fear of being judged in connection with sexual activity is known as _____.
    a. decreased sexual desire
    b. sexual dysfunctions

    c. inhibited orgasm
    d. performance anxiety

17. _____ refers to beliefs, values, and norms that subtly encourage male sexuality and discourage female sexuality.
    a. Gender dysphoria
    b. Gender identity disorder
    c. The double standard
    d. None of these options

18. Having AIDS generally refers to being infected with a virus that attacks the _____.
    a. central nervous system
    b. peripheral nervous system
    c. mucous membranes
    d. immune system

19. AIDS is the result of an infection by the _____ virus (HIV).
    a. human incapacitating
    b. herpes I
    c. human immunodeficiency
    d. none of these options

20. With regard to STIs, remaining abstinent, not using intravenous illicit drugs, and avoiding contact with blood, vaginal secretions, and semen are considered to be _____.
    a. a waste of time
    b. unusual sexual practices
    c. the only ways to prevent STI transmission
    d. methods of lessening your chance of contracting an STI

TABLE 11.1 DIMENSIONS OF SEX AND GENDER

		Male	Female
Sex Dimensions			
1.	Chromosomes	XY	XX
2.	Gonads	Testes	Ovaries
3.	Hormones	Predominantly androgens	Predominantly estrogens
4.	External genitals	Penis, scrotum	Labia majora, labia minora, clitoris, vaginal opening
5.	Internal accessory organs	Prostate gland, seminal vesicles, vas deferens, ejaculatory duct, Cowper's gland	Vagina, uterus, fallopian tubes, cervix
6.	Secondary sex characteristics	Beard, lower voice, wider shoulders, sperm emission	Breasts, wider hips, menstruation
7.	Sexual orientation	Heterosexual, gay, bisexual	Heterosexual, lesbian, bisexual
Gender Dimensions			
8.	Gender identity (self-definition)	Perceives self as male	Perceives self as female
9.	Gender role (societal expectations)	Masculine ("Boys like trucks and sports")	Feminine ("Girls like dolls and clothes")

Assessment

VISUAL QUIZ

Elizabeth Crews/ The Image Works

This type of "dressing up" is a good example of which dimension of gender?

Answer: Gender role

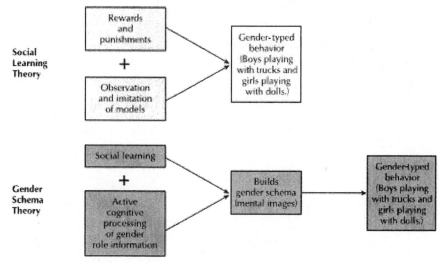

Figure 11.1 *Gender role development*

Process Diagram

Process Diagram 11.1

Masters and Johnson's Sexual Response Cycle

Note that this simplified description does not account for individual variation and should not be used to judge what's "normal."

2. During the **plateau phase**, biological and sexual arousal continue at heightened levels. In the man, the penis becomes more engorged and erect while the testes swell and pull up closer to the body. In the woman, the clitoris pulls up under the clitoral hood and the entrance to the vagina contracts while the uterus rises slightly. This movement of the uterus causes the upper two-thirds of the vagina to balloon, or expand. As arousal reaches its peak, both sexes may experience a feeling that orgasm is imminent and inevitable.

3. The **orgasm phase** involves a highly intense and pleasurable release of tension. In the woman, muscles around the vagina squeeze the vaginal walls in and out and the uterus pulsates. Muscles at the base of the penis contract in the man, causing ejaculation, the discharge of semen or seminal fluid.

1. The **excitement phase** can last for minutes or hours. Arousal is initiated through touching, fantasy, or erotic stimuli. Heart rate and respiration increase and increased blood flow to the pelvic region causes penile erection in men and clitoral erection, and vaginal lubrication in women. In both men and women, the nipples may become erect, and both may experience a sex flush (reddening of the upper torso and face).

4. Biological responses gradually return to normal during the **resolution phase**. After one orgasm, most men enter a **refractory period**, during which further excitement to orgasm is considered impossible. Many women (and some men), however, are capable of multiple orgasms in fairly rapid succession.

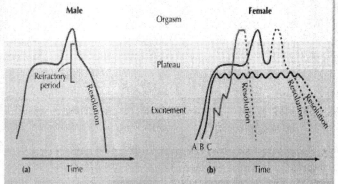

In the diagrams to the right, note in (a) that immediately after orgasm males generally enter a refractory period, which lasts from several minutes up to a day, in which they cannot have another orgasm. Note in (b) that female sexual responses follow one or more of three basic patterns: Pattern A resembles the male pattern, except it includes the possibility of multiple orgasm (the second peak in pattern A) without falling below the plateau level. Pattern B represents nonorgasmic arousal. Pattern C portrays a rapid rise to orgasm, no definitive plateau, and a quick resolution.

Excitement Phase *First stage of the sexual response cycle, characterized by increasing levels of arousal and increased engorgement of the genitals*

Plateau Phase *Second stage of the sexual response cycle, characterized by a leveling off in a state of high arousal*

Orgasm Phase *Third stage of the sexual response cycle, when pleasurable sensations peak and orgasm occurs*

Resolution Phase *Final stage of the sexual response cycle, when the body returns to its unaroused state*

Refractory Period *Phase following orgasm, during which further orgasm is considered physiologically impossible for men*

Chapter 11 Visual Summary

Sex and Gender

Definitions

Sex: Biological dimensions of maleness or femaleness, and physical activities (such as intercourse).
Gender: Psychological and sociocultural meanings of maleness and femaleness.

Gender Role Development

Gender role: Social expectations for appropriate male and female behavior.
Two major theories:
Social learning (reward, punishment, observation, and imitation)
Gender schema (social learning plus active cognitive processes)

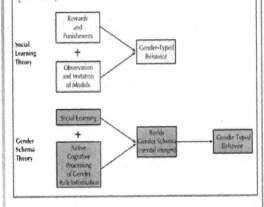

Sex and Gender Differences

Sex differences: Physical differences (like height) and brain differences (function and structure).
Gender differences: Females tend to score somewhat higher in verbal skills. Males score somewhat higher in math and are more physically aggressive.
Androgyny: Exhibiting both masculine and feminine traits.

Study of Human Sexuality

Havelock Ellis	Kinsey & Colleagues	Masters & Johnson	Cultural Studies
Based his research on personal diaries.	Popularized the use of surveys and interviews.	Used direct observation and measurement of human sexual response.	Provide insight into universalities and variations in sexual behavior across cultures.

Sexual Behavior

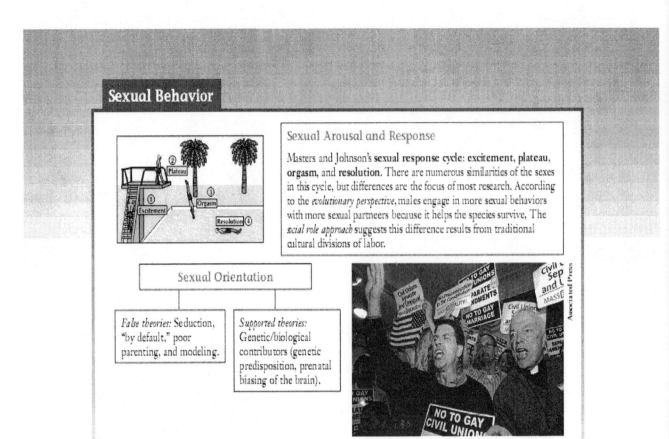

Sexual Arousal and Response

Masters and Johnson's **sexual response cycle: excitement, plateau, orgasm,** and **resolution.** There are numerous similarities of the sexes in this cycle, but differences are the focus of most research. According to the *evolutionary perspective*, males engage in more sexual behaviors with more sexual partneers because it helps the species survive. The *social role approach* suggests this difference results from traditional cultural divisions of labor.

Sexual Orientation

False theories: Seduction, "by default," poor parenting, and modeling.

Supported theories: Genetic/biological contributors (genetic predisposition, prenatal biasing of the brain).

Sexual Problems

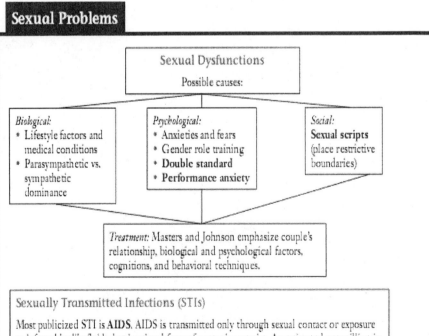

Sexual Dysfunctions

Possible causes:

Biological:
* Lifestyle factors and medical conditions
* Parasympathetic vs. sympathetic dominance

Psychological:
* Anxieties and fears
* Gender role training
* **Double standard**
* **Performance anxiety**

Social:
Sexual scripts (place restrictive boundaries)

Treatment: Masters and Johnson emphasize couple's relationship, biological and psychological factors, cognitions, and behavioral techniques.

Sexually Transmitted Infections (STIs)

Most publicized STI is **AIDS.** AIDS is transmitted only through sexual contact or exposure to infected bodily fluids, but irrational fears of contagion persist. An estimated one million in the United States are **HIV-positive** and therefore are carriers.

12
Motivation & Emotion

OUTLINE SQ4R (Survey, Question, Read, Recite, Review, & wRite)

This outline section incorporates all six steps in the well-researched SQ4R method of learning. Begin by surveying the list of chapter topics in the left column. This "big picture" will help focus and guide your attention while you read. As you read through the chapter, briefly summarize each section in your own words in the space to the right. Also write down any *questions* that come to mind. Surveying, Questioning, Reading, Reciting, Reviewing, and wRiting are the foundation of the SQ4R method and an invaluable form of active learning. They also make your reading time more enjoyable and efficient! One thorough, focused SQ4R reading of a chapter is far better than several passive readings.

TOPIC	**NOTES**

I. THEORIES AND CONCEPTS OF MOTIVATION

    A. Biological Theories

    Research Highlight: Sensation Seeking

    Psychology at Work: Overcoming Test Anxiety

    B. Psychosocial Theories

    C. Biopsychosocial Theory

II. MOTIVATION AND BEHAVIOR

A.   Hunger and Eating

Research Highlight: Fuel for Thought

B. Eating Disorders

Critical Thinking/Active Learning:
   Obesity—Weighing the Evidence

C. Achievement

III. THEORIES AND CONCEPTS OF EMOTION

A. Three Components of Emotion

Research Highlight: Mirror Neurons

B. Four Major Theories of Emotion

IV. CRITICAL THINKING ABOUT MOTIVATION AND EMOTION

A. Intrinsic Versus Extrinsic Motivation

B. The Polygraph as a Lie Detector

C. Emotional Intelligence (EI)

Case Study/Personal Story: The Emotional Intelligence
   of Abraham Lincoln

Gender & Cultural Diversity: Culture, Evolution,
*   and Emotion*

LEARNING OBJECTIVES (Read, Recite, Review, & wRite)

In addition to the work you did in the Outline above, you can significantly improve your performance on exams by focusing on the following learning objectives. While reading the chapter or reviewing for exams, check your understanding by stopping periodically to *recite* (or repeat in your own words) and *writing* down your answers on a separate sheet. [Page numbers correspond to Chapter 12 in *Psychology in Action* (9e).]

12.1 Define motivation and emotion, and explain why they're studied together. (p. 406)
12.2 Describe the six major theories of motivation. (p. 408)
12.3 Discuss the major biopsychosocial factors that influence hunger and eating. (p. 414)
12.4 How does expressing willpower affect later self-control? (p. 416)
12.5 Describe the three key eating disorders—obesity, anorexia, and bulimia. (p. 416)
12.6 Discuss the controversial study that found people live longer if they're slightly overweight. (p. 418)
12.7 Define achievement motivation, and list the characteristics of high achievers. (p. 419)
12.8 Describe the three key components of emotions. (p. 421)
12.9 Discuss how mirror neurons contribute to emotions and observational learning. (p. 423)
12.10 Compare and contrast the four major theories of emotion. (p. 425)
12.11 Define intrinsic and extrinsic motivation, and describe how they affect motivation. (p. 430)
12.12 Discuss polygraph testing and its effectiveness in lie detection. (p. 432)
12.13 What is emotional intelligence (EI), and why is it controversial? (p. 432)
12.14 List the five key traits of emotional intelligence (EI) shown by Abraham Lincoln. (p. 434)
12.15 Discuss culturally universal emotions and differing display rules. (p. 435)

KEY TERMS (Review & wRite)

Like other survey courses, introductory psychology is filled with a "wealth" of new and unfamiliar terminology. To do well on exams, you must master this new language! Writing a brief definition of each term in the space provided and carefully reviewing them before exams will significantly improve your course grade.

Achievement Motivation (nAch): _____

_____

Anorexia Nervosa: _____

_____

Bulimia Nervosa: _____

_____

Cannon-Bard Theory: _____

_____

Drive-Reduction Theory: _____

_____

Emotion: _____

_____

Emotional Intelligence (EI): _____

_____

Extrinsic Motivation: _____

_____

Facial-Feedback Hypothesis: _____

_____

Hierarchy of Needs: _____

_____

Homeostasis: _____

_____

Incentive Theory: _____

_____

Instinct: _____

_____

Instinct Theory: _____

_____

Intrinsic Motivation: _____

_____

James-Lange Theory: _____

_____

Mirror Neurons: _____

_____

Motivation: _____

_____

Polygraph: _____

_____

Schachter's Two-Factory Theory: _____

_____

ACTIVE LEARNING EXERCISES

True mastery of information requires you to be an ACTIVE learner. Completing the following active learning exercises will improve your understanding of the chapter material and greatly improve your performance on exams. Answers to some exercises appear in Appendix A at the end of this study guide.

ACTIVE LEARNING EXERCISE I *Charting Your Moods and Emotions: Self-understanding requires recognizing and analyzing your own emotions and the external factors that affect your emotions. This self-understanding will, hopefully, increase control of your own and others moods and needs, and improve your relationships.*

A good way to identify and understand your personal "mood swings" is to chart your emotions for at least one week. Each morning when you first wake up, or each night before retiring, complete your daily mood evaluation chart. Describe your primary mood at the time of your writing, how your body physiologically registers that emotion or mood, the thoughts, expectations, or beliefs surrounding that mood, and give a number or word to rank or evaluate the pleasure or intensity of that emotion.

	Primary Mood	Physiological Description	Cognitive Description	Behavioral Description	Subjective Evaluation
Day					
(1)					
(2)					
(3)					
(4)					
(5)					
(6)					
(7)					

ACTIVE LEARNING EXERCISE II *Subjective well being: Researchers in this area often ask participants to evaluate either their overall life satisfaction or their feelings of happiness (sometimes defined as a high ratio of positive to negative feelings).*

In the space provided, begin by estimating your current life satisfaction and happiness scores (using a scale from one to 100 with one as the lowest and 100 as the highest). Life Satisfaction score _____ Happiness score _____

Now circle true or false to the following items:

1. Among all age groups, America's senior citizens are the least happy and most dissatisfied with their life. True or False?
2. People who have complete quadriplegia (with both arms and both legs paralyzed) feel their lives are below average in happiness. True or False?
3. Having children is life's greatest joy; thus, parents report more overall happiness than those who do not have children. True or False?
4. Most people would be happier if they had more money. True or False?
5. People with a college education are happier and report more life satisfaction than people with only a high school diploma. True or False?

Check your answers to this exercise, which can be found in Appendix A at the end of this study guide—they may surprise you!

I. Theories and Concepts of Motivation

12.1 Define motivation and emotion, and explain why they're studied together. (p. 406)

Motivation refers to the set of factors that activate, direct, and maintain behavior, usually toward some goal. **Emotion**, on the other hand, refers to a subjective feeling that includes arousal (heart pounding), cognitions (thoughts, values, expectations), and expressive behaviors (smiles, frowns, running). In short, motivation is the "whys" of behavior, whereas emotions are the feelings. Because motivated behaviors are often closely related to emotions, these two topics are frequently studied together.

12.2 Describe the six major theories of motivation. (p. 408)

There are three general approaches to explaining motivation with two sub-approaches, which leads to six major theories: *biological theories* (including *instinct theory, drive-reduction theory, and arousal theory*), *psychosocial theories* (including *incentive* and *cognitive*), and *biopsychosocial* (*Maslow's hierarchy of needs*).

Instinct theories suggest there is some inborn, genetic component to motivation. **Drive-reduction theory** suggests that internal tensions (produced by the body's demand for **homeostasis**) "push" the organism toward satisfying basic needs. And **arousal theory** suggests organisms seek an optimal level of arousal that maximizes their performance. There are, however, individual differences in this need. According to Zuckerman, high sensation seekers are biologically "prewired" to need a higher level of stimulation, whereas the reverse is true for low sensation seekers.

Within the psychosocial theories, **incentive theory** emphasizes the "pull" of external environmental stimuli. *Cognitive theories* emphasize the importance of attributions and expectations.

One example of the biopsychosocial approach is Maslow's **hierarchy of needs** (or motives). This theory suggests that basic physiological and survival needs must be satisfied before a person can attempt to satisfy higher needs. Critics question the importance of sequentially working up through these steps.

II. Motivation and Behavior

12.3 Discuss the major biopsychosocial factors that influence hunger and eating. (p. 414)

Several biological, internal factors, including structures in the brain, numerous chemicals, and messages from the stomach and intestines, all seem to play important roles in hunger and eating. But psychosocial factors, such as stimulus cues, cultural conditioning, and willpower also play a role.

12.4 How does expressing willpower affect later self-control? (p. 416)
Research shows that a single act of willpower expends some of our body's fuel, which undermines our brain's ability to exert further self discipline.

12.5 Describe the three key eating disorders—obesity, anorexia, and bulimia. (p. 416)
A large number of people have eating disorders. Obesity (being 15 percent or more above the ideal for one's height and age) seems to result from biological factors, such as the individual's genetic inheritance, lifestyle factors, and numerous psychological factors. **Anorexia nervosa** (extreme weight loss due to self-imposed starvation) and **bulimia nervosa** (excessive consumption of food followed by purging) are both related to an intense fear of obesity.

12.6 Discuss the controversial study that found people live longer if they're slightly overweight. (p. 418)
One group of researchers looking at the effects of obesity suggested that it might be ok to be slightly overweight. But a different team supported by the conventional wisdom that obesity is a serious problem.

12.7 Define achievement motivation, and list the characteristics of high achievers. (p. 419)
Achievement motivation involves the desire to excel, especially in competition with others. People with high achievement needs prefer moderately difficult tasks and clear goals with competent feedback. They also tend to be more competitive, responsible, persistent, and accomplished.

III. Theories and Concepts of Emotion
12.8 Describe the three key components of emotions. (p. 421)
All emotions have three basic components: physiological arousal (e.g., heart pounding); cognitive (thoughts, values, and expectations); and behavioral expressions (e.g., smiles, frowns, running).

Studies of the *physiological component* of emotion find that most emotions involve a general, nonspecific arousal of the nervous system. This arousal involves the cerebral cortex, the limbic system, and the frontal lobes of the brain. The *cognitive component* explains how thoughts, values, and expectations help determine the type and intensity of emotional responses. The behavioral component refers to how we express our emotions, including facial expressions. The most obvious signs of physiological arousal (trembling, increased heart rate, sweating, and so on) result from activation of the sympathetic nervous system, a subdivision of the autonomic nervous system. The parasympathetic system restores the body to the "status quo."

12.9 Discuss how mirror neurons contribute to emotions and observational learning. (p. 423)
Mirror neurons fire both when performing actions and when simply observing the actions and emotions of others. This "mirroring" may explain our emotions, as well as imitation, language, and the emotional deficits of some mental disorders.

12.10 Compare and contrast the four major theories of emotion. (p. 425)
There are four major theories to explain what causes emotion. The **James-Lange theory** suggests emotions follow from physiological arousal and behavioral expressions, such as smiles, increased heart rate, and trembling. The **Cannon-Bard theory** suggests arousal and emotions occur simultaneously. According to the **facial-feedback hypothesis**, facial movements elicit and/or intensify specific emotions. **Schachter's two-factor theory** suggests that emotions depend on two factors---physical arousal and a cognitive labeling of the arousal. In other words, people notice what is going on around them, as well as their own bodily responses, and then label the emotion accordingly.

IV. Critical Thinking About Motivation and Emotion

12.11 Define intrinsic and extrinsic motivation, and describe how they affect motivation. (p. 430)

Intrinsic motivation comes from personal enjoyment of a task or activity. **Extrinsic motivation** stems from external rewards or threats and avoidance of punishment. Research with intrinsic versus extrinsic motivation shows that extrinsic rewards can lower interest and motivation if they are not based on competency.

12.12 Discuss polygraph testing and its effectiveness in lie detection. (p. 432)

A **polygraph** machine measures changes in sympathetic system arousal (increased heart rate, blood pressure, and so on). Although the polygraph is sometimes used in police work and for employment purposes, psychologists have found it a poor predictor of guilt or innocence or of truth or lies.

12.13 What is emotional intelligence (EI), and why is it controversial? (p. 432)

Emotional intelligence (EI) involves knowing and managing emotions, empathy, and maintaining satisfying relationships. Critics argue that the components of EI are difficult to identify and measure, and fear that a handy term like EI invites misuse.

12.14 List the five key traits of emotional intelligence (EI) shown by Abraham Lincoln. (p. 434)

As president, Lincoln demonstrated *empathy, magnanimity, generosity of spirit, self-control,* and *humor.*

12.15 Discuss culturally universal emotions and differing display rules. (p. 435)

Studies have identified 7 to 10 basic emotions that are universal ---experienced and expressed in similar ways across almost all cultures. Display rules differ across cultures and between men and women. Most psychologists believe that emotions result from a complex interplay between evolution and culture.

SELF-TESTS (Review & wRite)

Completing the following self-tests will provide immediate feedback on how well you have mastered the material. In the labeling exercises, *crossword puzzle*, and *fill-in exercises*, write the appropriate word or words in the blank spaces. The *matching exercise* requires you to match the terms in one column to their correct definitions in the other. For the *multiple-choice questions* in Practice Tests I and II, circle or underline the correct answer. If you are unsure of any answer, mark the item, and then go back to the text for further review. Correct answers are provided in Appendix A at the end of this study guide.

CROSSWORD PUZZLE FOR CHAPTER 12

ACROSS

3 Motivation results from environmental stimuli, which "pull" the organism in certain directions, rather than internal needs that drive or "push" the organism.

11 Behavioral patterns that are (1) unlearned, (2) always expressed in the same way, and (3) universal in a species.

12 A subjective feeling that includes arousal (heart pounding), cognitions (thoughts, values, and expectations), and expressions (frowns, smiles, and running).

13 Severe loss of weight resulting from an obsessive fear of obesity and self-imposed starvation.

14 Set of factors that activate, direct, and maintain behavior usually towards a goal.

16 Consuming large quantities of food (bingeing), followed by vomiting, extreme exercise, or laxative use (purging).

DOWN

1 Emotions result from physical arousal and cognitive labeling (or interpretation) of that arousal based on external cues.

2 Movements of the facial muscles produce or intensify emotional reactions.

4 Drive to excel, especially in competition with others.

5 Arousal, cognitions, and expression of emotions occur simultaneously.

6 A body's tendency to maintain a relatively stable state, such as a constant internal temperature.

7 Emotions result from physiological arousal and behavioral expression.

8 Motivation begins with a physiological need (a lack or deficiency) that elicits a psychological energy or drive directed toward behavior that will satisfy the original need. Once the need is met, a state of balance (homeostasis) is restored and motivation decreases.

9 Goleman's term for the ability to know and manage one's emotions, empathize with others, and maintain satisfying relationships.

10 Maslow's theory of motivation that some motives (such as physiological and safety needs) have to be satisfied before an individual can advance to higher needs (such as belonging and self-actualiztion).

11 Motivation resulting from personal enjoyment of a task or activity.

12 Motivation based on obvious external rewards or threats of punishment.

15 Instrument that measures heart rate, respiration rate, blood pressure, and skin conductivity to detect emotional arousal, which in turn supposedly reflects lying versus truthfulness.

FILL-IN EXERCISES

1. _____ refers to a set of factors that activate, maintain, and direct behavior toward a goal. In contrast, _____ refers to a subjective feeling that includes arousal, cognitions, and expressions (p. 406).

2. _____ theory says internal factors *push* us in certain directions, _____ theory says external stimuli *pull* us (pp. 409, 412).

3. The _____ motive causes us to look for a certain amount of stimulation and complexity from our environment (pp. 409-410).

4. Maslow's _____ suggests basic survival and security needs must be satisfied before moving on to higher needs such as self-actualization (pp. 409, 412-413).

5. If the _____ of a rat is destroyed, the rat will overeat to the point of extreme obesity (p. 415).

6. Consuming enormous quantities of food (binges) followed by purging with laxatives or vomiting is referred to as _____ (p. 417).

7. _____ refers to the desire to excel, especially in competition with others (p. 419).

8. There are three basic components of emotions: the _____, _____, and _____ (pp. 421-424).

9. Research on the _____ suggests that we feel happy because we smile (p. 425).

10. Research finds that people across a variety of cultures express emotions in strikingly similar ways. This supports _____ theories of emotion (pp. 435-436).

MATCHING EXERCISES

Column A   Column B

a. Maslow   1.____ A smile of real joy
b. Polygraph   2.____ Can sometimes lower interest and achievement
c. Extrinsic Motivation   3.____ Facial movements elicit specific emotions
d. Drive-Reduction Theory   4.____ Knowing and appropriately managing emotions
e. James-Lange Theory   5.____ Study of the "whys" of behavior
f. Emotional Intelligence   6.____ Cultural norms governing emotional expressions
g. Facial Feedback Hypothesis 7.____ Measures changes in emotional arousal
h. Display Rules   8.____ Subjective experience of emotion follows bodily arousal
i. Duchenne Smile   9.____ Internal tensions "push" organism toward basic needs
j. Motivation   10.____Hierarchy of needs

PRACTICE TEST I

1. Regarding motivation and emotion, which of the following is true?
   a. the terms "motivation" and "emotion" both come from the Latin word "movere"
   b. there is considerable overlap between motivation and emotion
   c. both a and b
   d. none of these options

2. Nest building is an example of _____.
   a. drive-reduction
   b. an incentive motive
   c. an instinct
   d. all of these options

3. Homeostasis is associated with which of the following theories of motivation?
   a. instinct
   b. incentive
   c. Maslow's hierarchy of needs
   d. drive-reduction

4. According to the drive-reduction theory, motivation begins with a _____.
   a. goal
   b. physiological need
   c. cognitive need
   d. motivational need

5. According to the _____theory, there is an ideal or optimal level of arousal that organisms are motivated to achieve and maintain.
   a. sensory arousal
   b. arousal
   c. sensation seeking
   d. achievement

6. This is **NOT** associated with the incentive theory of motivation.
   a. external stimuli
   b. an external "push"
   c. an internal "pull"
   d. none of these options

7. Cognitive theories of motivation focus on
   _____.
   a. attributions for the causes of
      behavior
   b. biological factors in thought
      processes
   c. previous learning experience
   d. the role of external stimuli

8. The psychologist associated with a
   hierarchy of needs is _____.
   a. Murray
   b. Darwin
   c. Maslow
   d. James-Lange

9. Belinda appears to be starving herself,
   and has obviously lost a lot of weight in
   just a few months. You suspect she
   might be suffering from _____.
   a. anorexia nervosa
   b. bulimia nervosa
   c. obesity phobia
   d. none of these options

10. What causes eating disorders?
    a. physical factors
    b. psychosocial factors
    c. cultural factors
    d. all of these options

11. Henry prefers moderately difficult tasks,
    wants a career that involves competition,
    and personal responsibility, and will
    persist until a task is done. He most
    likely has a _____.
    a. high need for arousal
    b. moderate need for sensation
       seeking
    c. high nAch
    d. none of the above

12. You suddenly see an oncoming car in
    your lane. You swerve to miss it, and
    your car finally comes to a bouncing halt
    in the ditch at the side of the road. At this
    point you notice your high level of fear.
    This reaction best supports the _____
    theory of emotions.
    a. Cannon-Bard
    b. James-Lange

c. two-factor
d. common sense

13. The _____ theory suggests that arousal
    and our subjective experience of emotion
    occur simultaneously.
    a. James-Lange
    b. Schachter's two-factor
    c. Cannon-Bard
    d. facial feedback

14. You grin broadly while your best friend
    tells you she was just accepted to
    Harvard Medical School. The facial-
    feedback hypothesis predicts that you
    will feel _____.
    a. happy
    b. envious
    c. angry
    d. all of these emotions

15. The _____ also supports Darwin's
    evolutionary theory that freely
    expressing an emotion intensifies it.
    a. James-Lange
    b. Schachter's two-factor
    c. Cannon-Bard
    d. facial feedback

16. You are kissing your dating partner good
    night and notice that you are
    physiologically aroused. You think about
    your feelings and decide that you are
    probably in love with this individual.
    This response best supports the _____
    theory of emotions.
    a. Cannon-Bard
    b. James-Lange
    c. Schachter's two-factor
    d. companionate love

17. _____ motivation comes from within
    the individual and results from personal
    enjoyment of a task or activity.
    a. Achievement
    b. Arousal
    c. Intrinsic
    d. all but one of these options

18. If you studied for this test solely to avoid a bad grade, it is most likely that you are

    _____.
    a. extrinsically motivated to study
    b. intrinsically motivated to study
    c. an above average student
    d. a typical student

19. The apparatus commonly used as a "lie detector" is called a(n) _____.
    a. electroencephalograph
    b. EEG
    c. polygraph
    d. galvanograph

20. Across cultures, people can reliably identify at least _____ basic emotions from a person's facial expression.
    a. 32
    b. 15
    c. 9
    d. 6

PRACTICE TEST II

1. _____ energizes and directs behavior; _____ represents the "feeling" response.
    a. Motivation; emotion
    b. Incentives; needs
    c. Motives; drives
    d. Motivation; compulsions

2. This is **NOT** characteristic of instincts.
    a. unlearned
    b. uniform
    c. fixed action patterns
    d. unique

3. The arousal motive _____.
    a. increases most people's need for achievement
    b. is correlated with high self-esteem
    c. leads us to seek novel and complex stimuli
    d. is related to sexual dysfunction

4. Advance preparation and hard work are the most important ways to combat

    _____.
    a. arousal overload
    b. low sensation seeking

    c. test anxiety
    d. all of these options

5. Maslow's theory of motivation suggests that, compared to physiological needs and needs for safety, needs for belonging and self-esteem _____.
    a. differentiate us from other species
    b. are satisfied first
    c. are stronger
    d. cannot be considered until the physiological and safety needs are met

6. Self-starvation and extreme weight loss are part of _____. In contrast, intense, recurring episodes of binge eating, followed by purging through vomiting or taking laxatives is known as _____.
    a. bulimia; anorexia
    b. anorexia; obesity
    c. anorexia nervosa; bulimia nervosa
    d. none of these options

7. The cortex, thalamus, and limbic system are all involved in _____.
    a. the experience of emotion
    b. motivation and desire
    c. reflexes and instincts
    d. sham rage experiments

8. During an "emergency," epinephrine and norepinephrine help maintain the activation of the _____ system.
    a. limbic
    b. sympathetic nervous
    c. parasympathetic nervous
    d. emotional motivation

9. You feel anxious because you are sweating and your heart is beating rapidly. This statement illustrates the _____ theory of emotion.
    a. James-Lange
    b. two-factor
    c. Cannon-Bard
    d. physiological feedback

10. Which of the following research findings supports the Cannon-Bard theory of emotion?

a. Animals who are surgically prevented from experiencing physiological arousal still demonstrate emotional behaviors.
b. Smiling improves self-ratings of positive mood-states.
c. Misinformed or uninformed research participants take on the emotional reactions of others around them.
d. There are distinct, though small, differences in the physiological response of several basic emotions.

11. A therapist who believes in the facial-feedback hypothesis regarding emotions might prescribe this if you were depressed.
a. Prozac
b. record your thoughts whenever you feel depressed
c. smile at least 3 times a day
d. get a PET scan to see if your thalamus is functioning properly

12. _____ suggested freely expressing an emotion intensifies it, whereas suppressing outward expression of emotions diminishes them.

a. Schachter
b. Cannon
c. James-Lange
d. Darwin

13. Schachter's two factor theory claims that we identify our emotions on the basis of _____.

a. physiological changes, specifically changes related to epinephrine
b. external, environmental cues
c. genetic predispositions
d. homeostatic counterbalance

14. Schacter's two factor theory emphasizes the _____ component of emotion.
a. stimulus-response
b. cognitive
c. behavioral-imitation
d. physiological

15. According to research on the four theories of emotion, which of the following is true?
a. facial feedback does seem to contribute to the intensity of emotions
b. some neural pathways involved in emotion bypass the cortex and go directly to the limbic system
c. victims of spinal cord still experience emotion
d. all of the above

16. A bill passed by the U.S. congress severely restricted the use of _____ in the courts, government, and private industry.
a. rational emotive therapy
b. polygraph tests
c. eyewitness testimony
d. none of these options

17. Which of the following is TRUE about the polygraph?
a. It does in fact measure sympathetic nervous system arousal
b. It cannot tell which emotion is being felt
c. Error rates range between 25 and 75 percent
d. all of these options

18. To improve motivation, researchers suggest we should _____.
a. limit extrinsic rewards
b. reward competency
c. emphasize intrinsic rewards
d. all of these options

19. Abraham Lincoln demonstrated many characteristics of emotional intelligence, including _____.
a. empathy
b. magnanimity
c. self-control
d. all of these options

20. Basic emotions, like fear and anger, seem to originate in _____.
a. higher cortical areas of the brain
b. subtle changes in facial expressions
c. the limbic system
d. the interpretation of environmental stimuli

TABLE 12.1 SIX MAJOR THEORIES OF MOTIVATION

Theory	View	
Biological Theories		
1. Instinct	Motivation results from behaviors that are unlearned and found in almost all members of a species.	Mattias Klum/NG Image Collection
2. Drive-Reduction	Motivation begins with a physiological need (a lack or deficiency) that elicits a *drive* toward behavior that will satisfy the original need and restore homeostasis.	
3. Arousal	Organisms are motivated to achieve and maintain an optimal level of arousal.	
Psychosocial Theories		*Name that theory Curiosity is an important aspect of the human experience. Which of the six theories of motivation best explains this behavior?*
4. Incentive	Motivation results from external stimuli that "pull" the organism in certain directions.	
5. Cognitive	Motivation is affected by expectations and attributions, or how we interpret or think about our own or others' actions.	
Biopsychosocial Theory		
6. Maslow's Hierarchy of Needs	Lower motives (such as physiological and safety needs) must be satisfied before advancing to higher needs (such as belonging and self-actualization).	

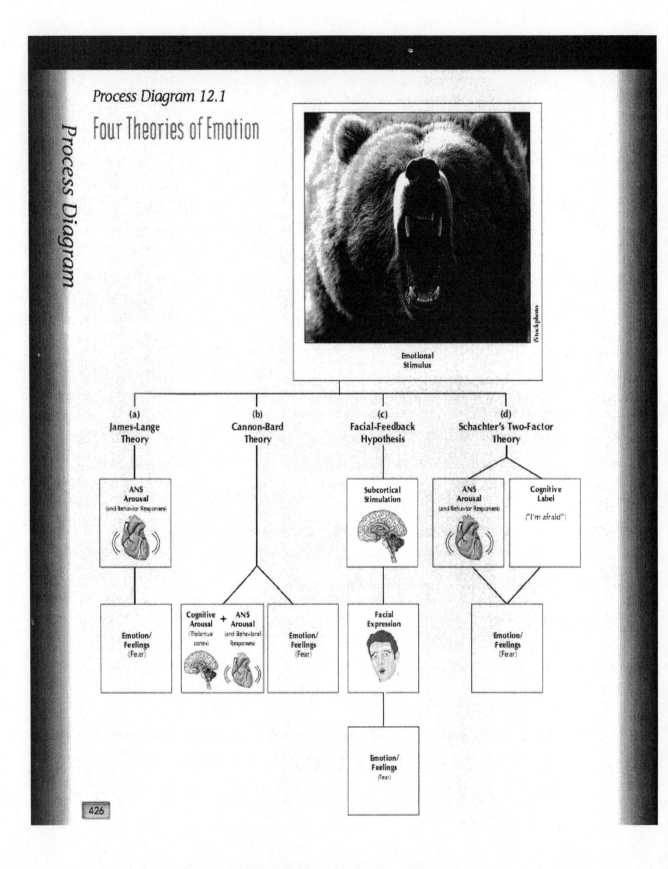

Process Diagram 12.1

Four Theories of Emotion

Process Diagram

Emotional Stimulus

(a) James-Lange Theory

(b) Cannon-Bard Theory

(c) Facial-Feedback Hypothesis

(d) Schachter's Two-Factor Theory

ANS Arousal (and Behavior Responses)

Subcortical Stimulation

ANS Arousal (and Behavior Responses)

Cognitive Label ("I'm afraid")

Emotion/ Feelings (Fear)

Cognitive Arousal (Thalamus/ cortex) **+ ANS Arousal** (and Behavioral Responses)

Emotion/ Feelings (Fear)

Facial Expression

Emotion/ Feelings (Fear)

Emotion/ Feelings (Fear)

426

Chapter 12 Visual Summary

Theories and Concepts of Motivation

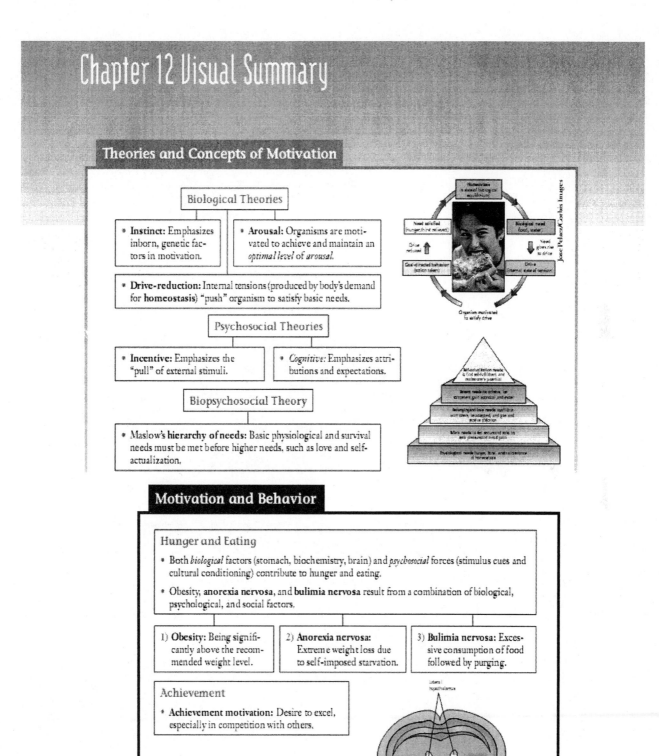

Biological Theories

* **Instinct:** Emphasizes inborn, genetic factors in motivation.

* **Arousal:** Organisms are motivated to achieve and maintain an *optimal level* of *arousal*.

* **Drive-reduction:** Internal tensions (produced by body's demand for **homeostasis**) "push" organism to satisfy basic needs.

Psychosocial Theories

* **Incentive:** Emphasizes the "pull" of external stimuli.

* *Cognitive:* Emphasizes attributions and expectations.

Biopsychosocial Theory

* **Maslow's hierarchy of needs:** Basic physiological and survival needs must be met before higher needs, such as love and self-actualization.

Motivation and Behavior

Hunger and Eating

* Both *biological* factors (stomach, biochemistry, brain) and *psychosocial* forces (stimulus cues and cultural conditioning) contribute to hunger and eating.

* Obesity, **anorexia nervosa**, and **bulimia nervosa** result from a combination of biological, psychological, and social factors.

1) **Obesity:** Being significantly above the recommended weight level.

2) **Anorexia nervosa:** Extreme weight loss due to self-imposed starvation.

3) **Bulimia nervosa:** Excessive consumption of food followed by purging.

Achievement

* **Achievement motivation:** Desire to excel, especially in competition with others.

How the brain affects eating.

Theories and Concepts of Emotion

Three Basic Components of Emotion

* Physiological (arousal): increased heart rate, respiration
* Cognitive (thinking): thoughts, values, expectations
* Behavioral (expressions): smiles, frowns, running

Four Major Theories of Emotion

James-Lange

Our subjective experience of emotion follows our bodily arousal.

Cannon-Bard

Arousal and our subjective experience of emotion occur simultaneously.

Facial-Feedback

Movement of facial muscles elicits and/or intensifies emotions.

Schachter's Two-Factor

Emotions depend on two factors—physical arousal and cognitive labeling of that arousal.

Karen Huffman

Critical Thinking about Motivation and Emotion

* **Intrinsic vs. extrinsic motivation:** Research shows extrinsic rewards can lower interest and achievement motivation.

* **Polygraph:** Measures changes in emotional arousal but is not valid for measuring guilt or innocence.

* **Emotional intelligence (EI):** Knowing and managing emotions, empathizing, and maintaining satisfying relationships.

* *Culture, Evolution, and Emotion:* Seven to ten basic, *universal* emotions suggest emotions may be innate; however, display rules differ across cultures.

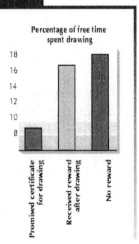

Percentage of free time spent drawing

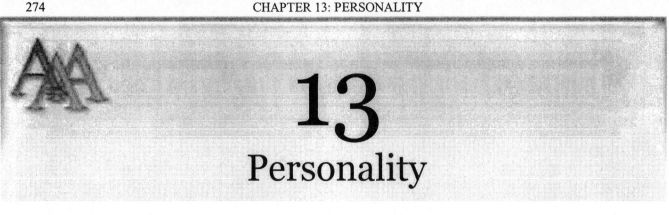

13
Personality

OUTLINE SQ4R (Survey, Question, Read, Recite, Review, & wRite)

This outline section incorporates all six steps in the well-researched SQ4R method of learning. Begin by surveying the list of chapter topics in the left column. This "big picture" will help focus and guide your attention while you read. As you read through the chapter, briefly summarize each section in your own words in the space to the right. Also write down any *questions* that come to mind. Surveying, Questioning, Reading, Reciting, Reviewing, and wRiting are the foundation of the SQ4R method and an invaluable form of active learning. They also make your reading time more enjoyable and efficient! One thorough, focused SQ4R reading of a chapter is far better than several passive readings.

TOPIC	**NOTES**

I. TRAIT THEORIES

   A. Early Trait Theorists

   B. The Five-Factor Model

   C. Evaluating Trait Theories

   *Psychology at Work: Personality and
      Your Career*

   *Research Highlight: Do Nonhuman
      Animals Have Personality?*

II. PSYCHOANALYTIC/PSYCHODYNAMIC THEORIES

A. Freud's Psychoanalytic Theory

B. Neo-Freudian/Psychodynamic Theories

C. Evaluating Psychoanalytic Theories

III. HUMANISTIC THEORIES

A. Rogers's Theory

B. Maslow's Theory

C. Evaluating Humanistic Theories

IV. SOCIAL-COGNITIVE THEORIES

A. Bandura's and Rotter's Approaches

B. Evaluating Social-Cognitive Theory

V. BIOLOGICAL THEORIES

A. Three Major Contributors

B. The Biopsychosocial Model

VI. PERSONALITY ASSESSMENT

A. How Do We Measure Personality?

B. Are Personality Measurements Accurate?

Critical Thinking/Active Learning: Why
Are Pseudo Personality Tests So Popular?

LEARNING OBJECTIVES (<u>R</u>ead, <u>R</u>ecite, <u>R</u>eview, & w<u>R</u>ite)

In addition to the work you did in the Outline above, you can significantly improve your performance on exams by focusing on the following learning objectives. While reading the chapter or reviewing for exams, check your understanding by stopping periodically to *recite* (or repeat in your own words) and *writing* down your answers on a separate sheet. [Page numbers correspond to Chapter 13 in *Psychology in Action* (9e).]

13.1 Differentiate between personality versus trait, and discuss early trait theories and the five-factor model. (p. 442)
13.2 What are the key research findings and criticisms of trait theories? (p. 444)
13.3 Discuss personality-job-fit theory. (p. 445)
13.4 Summarize the research on animal personality. (p. 446)
13.5 Describe Freud's psychoanalytic approach to personality. (p. 447)
13.6 Summarize Freud's five psychosexual stages. (p. 451)
13.7 Compare Freud's approach to personality versus that of the neo-Freudians. (p. 452)
13.8 Discuss the major criticisms of psychoanalytic theories of personality. (p. 453)
13.9 Discuss humanistic theories of personality, comparing the approaches of Rogers and Maslow. (p. 455)
13.10 What are the major criticisms of humanistic theories of personality? (p. 457)
13.11 Discuss the social-cognitive perspective on personality, comparing Bandura and Rotter's approaches. (p. 458)
13.12 What are the key strengths and weaknesses of the social-cognitive theories? (p. 460)
13.13 How does biology contribute to personality? (p. 460)
13.14 Describe how the biopsychosocial model blends various approaches to personality. (p. 462)
13.15 How do psychologists measure personality? (p. 463)
13.16 Describe the key advantages and disadvantages of personality measurement. (p. 466)
13.17 List the three major fallacies associated with pseudo-personality tests. (p. 468)

KEY TERMS (Review & wRite)

Like other survey courses, introductory psychology is filled with a "wealth" of new and unfamiliar terminology. To do well on exams, you must master this new language! Writing a brief definition of each term in the space provided and carefully reviewing them before exams will significantly improve your course grade.

Archetypes: _____

_____

Basic Anxiety: _____

_____

Collective Unconscious: _____

_____

Conscious: _____

_____

Defense Mechanism: _____

_____

Ego: _____

_____

Factor Analysis: _____

_____

Five-Factor Model: _____

_____

Id: _____

_____

Inferiority Complex: _____

_____

Minnesota Multiphasic Personality Inventory (MMPI-2): _____

_____

Morality Principle: _____

_____

Oedipus Complex: _____

_____

Personality: _____

_____

Pleasure Principle: _____

_____

Preconscious: _____

_____

Projective Tests: _____

_____

Psychosexual Stages: _____

_____

Reality Principle: _____

_____

Reciprocal Determinism: _____

_____

Reliability: _____

_____

Repression: _____

_____

Rorschach Inkblot Test: _____

_____

Self-Actualization: _____

_____

Self-Concept: _____

_____

Self-Efficacy: _____

_____

Superego: _____

_____

Thematic Apperception Test (TAT): _____

_____

Trait: _____

_____

Unconditional Positive Regard: _____

_____

Unconscious: _____

_____

Validity: _____

_____

ACTIVE LEARNING EXERCISES

True mastery of information requires you to be an ACTIVE learner. Completing the following active learning exercises will improve your understanding of the chapter material and greatly improve your performance on exams. Answers to some exercises appear in Appendix A at the end of this study guide.

ACTIVE LEARNING I *Answer "true" or "false" to the following:*

1. People get ahead in this world primarily by luck and connections rather than their own hard work and perseverance.
2. When someone does not like you, there is little you can do about it.
3. No matter how hard I study, I cannot get high grades in most classes.
4. I sometimes keep a rabbit's foot or other special objects as good-luck charms.
5. I sometimes refuse to vote because little can be done to control what politicians do in office.

Now, using these same five statements, ask 10 women and 10 men from your family and friends to complete this test. Be sure NOT to introduce it as an "internal versus external" scale, which could bias their responses. Once you collect their answers and analyze the data, you will probably find that female scores are slightly more *external* than males (i.e., they are more likely to answer true to each of the five statements). Can you explain this difference? Would there also be an age or ethnicity difference? Why or why not? If you would like to read more about this topic and see the original full-length version of Rotter's internal external scale, consult the following reference:

Rotter, J. B. (1966). Generalized expectancies for internal versus external control of reinforcement. Psychological Monographs, 80, 1-28.

ACTIVE LEARNING II *Employing Precise Terms: Defense Mechanisms*

By Freud's definition, defense mechanisms operate at the unconscious level; thus, we are not aware when we are using them. If, however, we practice observing their use by others, we may improve our self-insight, which also may help us replace inappropriate defense mechanisms with more appropriate thoughts, feelings, and behaviors.

Identify the following defense mechanisms. (Answers are provided in Appendix A at the end of this study guide.)

1. A woman who was assaulted and raped several years ago in a terrifying attack has forgotten the incident. _____

2. John told his fiancée Susan about his ongoing sexual involvement with other women, but Susan refuses to believe it even when she has seen him kissing other women.

_____

3. Leah has just read several articles describing danger signals for skin cancer. She carefully examines a dangerous looking mole on her own neck, and then with her doctor *she calmly and academically discusses the pros and cons of various treatment strategies and the fact that her mother died from skin cancer. _____*

4. Matt received notice that he is on academic probation. Because he will not be playing football while on probation, he decides to drop out of college "to do something worthwhile."
_____

5. The president of Parents Against Pornography was extremely active in campaigning against the "filth" our children are exposed to on the Internet. He was later arrested and convicted of 40 counts of soliciting minors on the Internet. _____.

CHAPTER OVERVIEW (Review)

The following chapter overview provides a narrative overview of the main topics covered in the chapter. Like the *Visual Summary* found at the end of each chapter in the text, this narrative summary provides a final opportunity to *review* chapter material.

I. TRAIT THEORIES

13.1 Differentiate between personality versus trait, and discuss early trait theories and the five-factor model. (p. 442)

Personality consists of unique and relatively stable patterns of thoughts, feelings, and actions. Gordon Allport described individuals by their trait hierarchy. Raymond Cattell and Hans Eysenck used **factor analysis** to identify the smallest possible number of **traits.** More recently, researchers identified a **five-factor model (FFM)**, which can be used to describe most individuals. The five traits are *openness, conscientiousness, extroversion, agreeableness,* and *neuroticism.*

13.2 What are the key research findings and criticisms of trait theories? (p. 444)

Evolutionary research and cross-cultural studies support the five-factor model. But trait theories are subject to three major criticisms: *lack of explanation* for why people develop certain traits or why traits sometimes change; *lack of specificity*--personality appears stable after age 30, but current theories do not identify which characteristics endure and which are transient; and *ignoring situational effects*--trait theories underestimate the influence of situational and environmental factors.

13.3 Discuss personality-job-fit theory. (p. 445)

According to John Holland, a match (or "good-fit") between personality and career choice is a major factor in job satisfaction.

13.4 Summarize the research on animal personality. (p. 446)

Studies report considerable overlap between animal and human personality on three of the five factors in the five-factor model (FFM)—extroversion, neuroticism, and agreeableness. One nonhuman dimension, dominance was important for describing animal personality. Researchers also found important cross-species sex differences.

II. PSYCHOANALYTIC/PSYCHODYNAMIC THEORIES

13.5 Describe Freud's psychoanalytic approach to personality. (p. 447)

Sigmund Freud founded the psychoanalytic approach to personality, which emphasizes the power of the unconscious. The mind (or psyche) reportedly functions on three levels (**conscious, preconscious,** and **unconscious**), and the personality has three distinct structures (**id, ego, and superego**). The ego struggles to meet the demands of the id and superego, and when these demands are in conflict, the ego may resort to **defense mechanisms** to relieve anxiety.

13.6 Summarize Freu d's five psychosexual stages. (p. 451)
According to Freud, all human beings pass through five **psychosexual stages:** oral, anal, phallic, latency, and genital. How specific conflicts at each of these stages are resolved is important to personality development.

13.7 Compare Freud's approach to personality versus that of the neo-Freudians. (p. 452)
Three influential followers of Freud who broke with him were Alfred Adler, Carl Jung, and Karen Horney. Known as neo-Freudians, they emphasized different issues. Adler emphasized the **inferiority complex** and the compensating will-to-power. Jung introduced the **collective unconscious** and **archetypes.** Horney stressed the importance of **basic anxiety** and refuted Freud's idea of penis envy, replacing it with power envy.

13.8 Discuss the major criticisms of psychoanalytic theories of personality. (p. 453)
Critics of the psychoanalytic approach, especially Freud's theories, argue that it is difficult to test, overemphasizes biology and unconscious forces, has inadequate empirical support, is sexist, and lacks cross-cultural support. Despite these criticisms, Freud remains a notable pioneer in psychology.

III. HUMANISTIC THEORIES
13.9 Discuss humanistic theories of personality, comparing the approaches of Rogers and Maslow. (p. 455)
Humanistic theories emphasize internal experiences, thoughts, and feelings that create the individual's **self-concept.** Carl Rogers emphasized the concepts of self-esteem and **unconditional positive regard.** Abraham Maslow emphasized the potential for **self-actualization.**

13.10 What are the major criticisms of humanistic theories of personality? (p. 457)
Critics of the humanistic approach argue that these theories are based on naive assumptions and are not scientifically testable or well supported by empirical evidence. In addition, their focus on description, rather than explanation, makes them narrow.

IV. SOCIAL-COGNITIVE THEORIES
13.11 Discuss the social-cognitive perspective on personality, comparing Bandura and Rotter's approaches. (p. 458)
Social-cognitive theorists emphasize the importance of external events and mental processes: how we interpret and respond to external events. Albert Bandura's social-cognitive approach focuses on **self-efficacy** and **reciprocal determinism,** whereas Julian Rotter emphasizes an *internal* or *external locus of control.*

13.12 What are the key strengths and weaknesses of the social-cognitive theories? (p. 460)
Social-cognitive theory is credited for its attention to environmental influences and its scientific standards. However, it has been criticized for its narrow focus and lack of attention to unconscious, environmental, and emotional aspects of personality.

V. BIOLOGICAL THEORIES

13.13 How does biology contribute to personality? (p. 460)

Biological theories emphasize brain structures, neurochemistry, and inherited genetic components of personality. Research on specific traits such as extroversion and sensation seeking support the biological approach.

13.14 Describe how the biopsychosocial model blends various approaches to personality. (p. 462)

The biopsychosocial/interactionist approach suggests that the major theories overlap, and each contributes to our understanding of personality.

VI. PERSONALITY ASSESSMENT

13.15 How do psychologists measure personality? (p. 463)

Psychologists use four basic methods to measure or assess personality: interviews, observations, objective tests, and projective techniques. Objective tests, such as the **Minnesota Multiphasic Personality Inventory (MMPI-2)**, use paper-and-pencil questionnaires or inventories. These tests provide objective standardized information about a large number of personality traits.

Projective tests, such as the **Rorschach Inkblot Test** or the **Thematic Apperception Test** (TAT), ask test takers to respond to ambiguous stimuli, which reportedly provide insight into unconscious elements of personality.

13.16 Describe the key advantages and disadvantages of personality measurement. (p. 466)

Both interviews and observations can provide valuable insights into personality, but they are time consuming and expensive, raters frequently disagree, and they often involve unnatural settings. Objective tests provide specific, objective information, but they are limited by respondents' deliberate deception and social desirability bias, diagnostic difficulties, and possible cultural bias. Projective tests are time consuming and have questionable reliability and validity. However, because they are unstructured, respondents may be more willing to talk honestly about sensitive topics, and projective tests are harder to fake.

13.17 List the three major fallacies associated with pseudo-personality tests. (p. 468)

The *Barnum effect, fallacy of positive instances,* and *self-serving bias* are the three most important fallacies of pseudo-personality tests.

SELF-TESTS (Review & wRite)

Completing the following self-tests will provide immediate feedback on how well you have mastered the material. In the labeling exercises, *crossword puzzle,* and *fill-in exercises,* write the appropriate word or words in the blank spaces. The *matching exercise* requires you to match the terms in one column to their correct definitions in the other. For the *multiple-choice questions* in Practice Tests I and II, circle or underline the correct answer. If you are unsure of any answer, mark the item, and then go back to the text for further review. Correct answers are provided in Appendix A at the end of this study guide.

CROSSWORD PUZZLE FOR CHAPTER 13

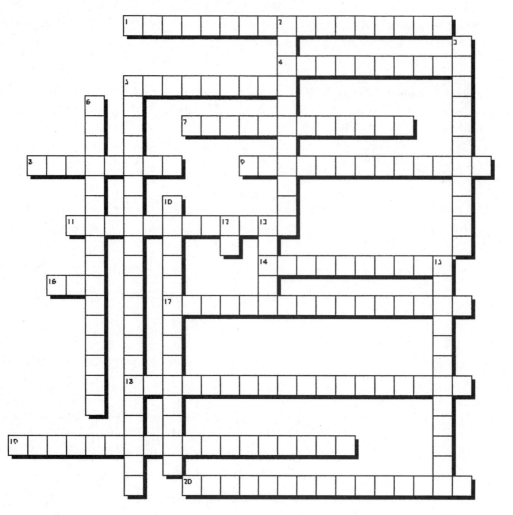

ACROSS

1 In Freud's theory, the principle on which the id operates---seeking immediate pleasure.
4 Freud's first and most basic defense mechanism, which blocks unacceptable impulses from coming into awareness.
5 In Freudian terms, thoughts or motives that a person is currently aware of or is remembering.
7 Freud's term for thoughts or motives that can be easily brought to mind.
8 In psychoanalytic theory, the part of the personality that incorporates parental and societal standards for morality.
9 According to Bandura, a person's learned beliefs that he or she is capable of producing desired results, such as mastering new skills and achieving personal goals.
11 According to Horney, the feelings of helplessness and insecurity that adults experience because as children they felt alone and isolated in a hostile environment.
14 According to Jung, the images and patterns of thoughts, feelings, and behavior that reside in the collective unconscious.
16 In Freud's theory, the rational part of the psyche that deals with reality and also tries satisfying the needs for social approval and self-esteem.
17 According to Freud, the principle on which the conscious ego operates as it tries to meet the demands of

the id and superego and the realities of the environment.

18 According to Maslow, an innate tendency toward growth that motivates all human behavior and results in the full realization of a person's highest potential.

19 Adler's idea that feelings of inferiority develop from early childhood experiences of helplessness and incompetence.

20 Psychological tests using ambiguous stimuli, such as inkblots or drawings, which reportedly allow the test-taker to project his or her true, unconscious conflicts and personality traits onto the test material.

DOWN

2 An individual's relatively stable and enduring pattern of thoughts, feelings, and actions.

3 Freud's term for thoughts, motives, impulses, or desires that lie beyond a person's normal awareness, but that can be made available through psychoanalysis.

5 Jung's concept of an inherited unconscious that all humans share.

6 A trait theory that explains personality in terms of openness, conscientiousness, extroversion, agreeableness, and neuroticism.

10 A statistical procedure used to determine the most basic units or factors in a large array of data.

12 According to Freud, the source of instinctual energy, which works on the pleasure principle and is concerned with immediate gratification.

13 A relatively stable and consistent characteristic that can be used to describe someone.

15 In Rogers' theory, all the information and beliefs individuals have about their own nature, qualities, and behavior.

FILL-IN EXERCISES

1. _____ is defined as an individual's unique and relatively stable pattern of thoughts, feelings, and actions. In contrast, a relatively stable and consistent characteristic that can be used to describe someone is known as a _____ (pp. 440-442).

2. Teresa is imaginative, curious, open to new ideas, and interested in cultural pursuits. On the Five-Factor model of personality, she would score high on _____ (p. 443).

3. _____ theories attempt to *explain* personality by examining unconscious forces. In contrast, _____ theories tend to *describe* personality as it currently exists (p. 447).

4. Freud believed thoughts or information we are currently aware of or are remembering are part of our _____, whereas the _____ contains thoughts or information we can become aware of easily, and the _____ contains our hidden thoughts, motives, impulses, and desires (p. 448).

5. The id is often described as operating on the _____, whereas the ego operates on the _____ (p. 449).

6. Rogers proposed that all the information and beliefs individuals have about their own nature, qualities, and behavior are known as their _____ (p. 455).

7. According to Bandura, an individual's cognitions, behaviors, and the learning environment interact to produce personality. This is known as _____ (p. 459).

8. The _____ is an objective, self-report test that was developed for the purpose of psychiatric diagnosis (pp. 464-465).

9. Two important criteria for evaluating the usefulness of tests used to assess personality are _____ and _____ (p. 467).

10. According to the _____, we tend to prefer information that maintains our positive self-image (p. 468).

MATCHING EXERCISES

Column A   Column B

a. Rogers   1.____ Self-concept and unconditional positive regard
b. Rorschach   2.____ Major personality theories overlap and contribute
c. Five-Factor Model   3.____ Focuses on self-actualization
d. Interactionism   4.____ Focuses on unconscious forces
e. Rotter   5.____ Carl Rogers
f. Maslow   6.____ OCEAN
g. Humanistic Theories   7.____ Cognitive expectancies and locus of control
h. Jung   8.____ Collective unconscious and archetypes
i. Psychoanalytic Theory   9.____ Self-efficacy and reciprocal determinism
j. Bandura   10._____ Projective "inkblot" test

PRACTICE TEST I

1. Which of the following is **NOT** associated with trait theories of personality?
    a. Cattell
    b. Allport
    c. Rorschach
    d. Eysenck

2. Eysenck believed personality is a relationship between all but one of these traits.
    a. extraversion-introversion
    b. neuroticism
    c. trustworthiness
    d. psychotism

3. This is **NOT** one of the Five-Factor personality traits.
    a. openness
    b. conscientiousness
    c. egoism
    d. agreeableness

4. Freud believed the _____ is the part of the psyche that provides instinctual motivation for behavior.

    a. id
    b. superego
    c. ego
    d. ego-ideal

5. _____ is the first and most basic defense mechanism, which keeps unacceptable impulses out of conscious awareness.
    a. Repression
    b. Denial
    c. Rationalization
    d. Displacement

6. During the _____, the Oedipus Complex is the major conflict in Freud's theory of psychosexual development.
    a. oral
    b. latent
    c. genital
    d. phallic

7. _____ developed the concept of the "inferiority complex."
    a. Freud
    b. Erikson
    c. Adler
    d. Jung

8. The collective unconscious contains
    _____.
    a. a personal unconscious
    b. your conscience
    c. the ego-ideal
    d. archetypes

9. Which of the following is NOT one of the
    criticisms of psychoanalytic theory?
    a. difficult to test
    b. inadequate evidence
    c. sexism
    d. overemphasis on social forces

10. Humanistic approaches to personality
    emphasize the importance of _____.
    a. intrapsychic conflicts
    b. archetypes
    c. observational learning
    d. the basic goodness in human
        nature

11. Rogers believed poor mental health
    developed from a mismatch between
    _____ and actual life experiences.
    a. self-efficacy
    b. ideal
    c. empathy
    d. self-concept

12. According to Rogers, it is important to
    receive _____ in order to develop our
    full potential.
    a. psychological help
    b. personal intervention
    c. empathy reduction
    d. unconditional positive regard

13. This term is most associated with
    Maslow.
    a. will to power
    b. basic anxiety
    c. self-actualization
    d. congruence

14. _____ is the inborn drive to develop all
    one's talents and capacities.
    a. Phenomenology
    b. Self-actualization
    c. The need for achievement
    d. The collective unconscious

15. The term _____ refers to Bandura's
    belief that cognitions, behaviors, and the
    environment interact to produce
    personality.
    a. self-efficacy
    b. reciprocal determinism
    c. biopsychosocial interaction
    d. none of these options

16. Rotter's concept of locus of control and
    Bandura's concept of self-efficacy share
    the belief that _____ influence(s)
    behavior.
    a. reciprocal determinism
    b. archetypes
    c. emotions
    d. expectancies

17. The MMPI is an example of a(n) _____.
    a. projective test
    b. structured interview
    c. objective personality test
    d. none of these options

18. The _____ is a widely used self-report
    test designed to detect disturbed
    personality characteristics.
    a. 16 PF
    b. MMPI
    c. Internal-External Locus of Control
        Test
    d. structured interview

19. The Rorschach tests a person's responses
    to _____.
    a. pictures
    b. movies
    c. sentences
    d. inkblots

20. Which of the following is a projective
    test?
    a. 16 PF
    b. MMPI
    c. TAT
    d. Internal-External Locus of Control
        Test

PRACTICE TEST II

1. Cheerful, honest, friendly, and optimistic are all _____.
   a. personality traits
   b. motives
   c. emotions
   d. all of these options

2. Which of the following acronyms can help you remember the Five-Factor personality traits?
   a. OCEAN
   b. BEACH
   c. SHORE
   d. WAVES

3. The main problem with all trait theories is that they _____.
   a. are unreliable
   b. do not explain personality
   c. are invalid descriptions of personality
   d. have not been standardized

4. The id, ego, and superego are _____.
   a. located in the unconscious
   b. three mental structures in the psyche
   c. present at birth
   d. the first three psychosexual stages of development

5. Perfection is a problem that is most associated with the _____.
   a. id
   b. ego
   c. superego
   d. none of these options

6. Violating the _____ results in feelings of guilt.
   a. pleasure principle
   b. reality principle
   c. morality principle
   d. self actualization principle

7. The defense mechanism of _____ is the most basic form of anxiety reduction.
   a. denial
   b. rationalization
   c. repression
   d. displacement

8. The genitals are the primary erogenous zones in which stage(s) of Freud's psychosexual theory of development?
   a. latency
   b. phallic
   c. phallic and genital
   d. latency, phallic, and genital

9. During the _____ stage, children do not have particular psychosexual conflicts.
   a. psychosexual
   b. oedipal
   c. latency
   d. latency, phallic, and genital

10. Basic anxiety is associated with which of the following Neo-Freudians?
    a. Horney
    b. Adler
    c. Jung
    d. Rogers

11. According to _____, there is an intimate connection among mental health, congruence, and self-esteem.
    a. Bandura
    b. Freud
    c. Horney
    d. Rogers

12. A major criticism of humanistic psychology is that most of its concepts and assumptions _____.
    a. are invalid
    b. are unreliable
    c. cannot be tested scientifically
    d. lack a theoretical foundation

13. Self-efficacy is associated with _____.
    a. Bandura
    b. Rogers
    c. Rotter
    d. Maslow

14. A criticism of the social-cognitive approach is that it overlooks or ignores the contribution of emotion and _____ in understanding personality.

a. scientific research
b. unconscious forces
c. motivation
d. expectancies

15. Dopamine is involved in the personality trait(s) of _____.
a. conscientiousness
b. extroversion and neuroticism
c. aggression and altruism
d. impulsivity and sensation-seeking

16. Based on inheritability studies, 40 to 50% of personality appears to be related to _____.
a. the environment
b. the family
c. family, friends, and the environment
d. genetic factors

17. A biopsychosocial approach might suggest that introversion is caused by _____.
a. high levels of cortical arousal
b. conditioning
c. cognitive processes
d. all of these options
e.

18. Projective tests reportedly measure your _____.
a. potential abilities
b. current knowledge and abilities
c. your interests and aptitudes
d. unconscious processes

19. Which of the following is a key measure of a good personality test?
a. reliability
b. validity
c. both of these options
d. none of these options

20. According to the _____, we tend to notice and remember events that confirm our expectations and ignore those that are nonconfirming.
a. self-serving bias
b. barnum effect
c. social perception bias
d. fallacy of positive instances

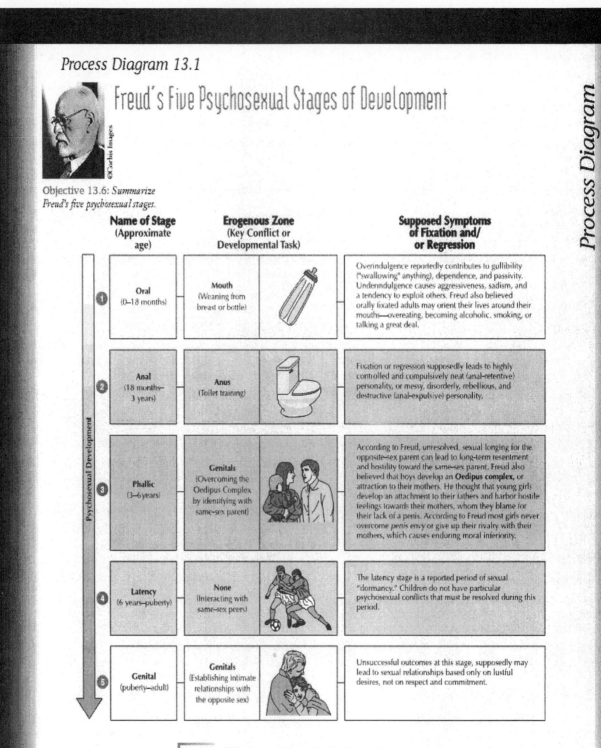

Process Diagram 13.1

Freud's Five Psychosexual Stages of Development

©Corbis Images

Objective 13.6: *Summarize Freud's five psychosexual stages.*

Name of Stage (Approximate age)	Erogenous Zone (Key Conflict or Developmental Task)		Supposed Symptoms of Fixation and/ or Regression
Oral (0–18 months)	**Mouth** (Weaning from breast or bottle)		Overindulgence reportedly contributes to gullibility ("swallowing" anything), dependence, and passivity. Underindulgence causes aggressiveness, sadism, and a tendency to exploit others. Freud also believed orally fixated adults may orient their lives around their mouths—overeating, becoming alcoholic, smoking, or talking a great deal.
Anal (18 months– 3 years)	**Anus** (Toilet training)		Fixation or regression supposedly leads to highly controlled and compulsively neat (anal-retentive) personality, or messy, disorderly, rebellious, and destructive (anal-expulsive) personality.
Phallic (3–6 years)	**Genitals** (Overcoming the Oedipus Complex by identifying with same-sex parent)		According to Freud, unresolved sexual longing for the opposite-sex parent can lead to long-term resentment and hostility toward the same-sex parent. Freud also believed that boys develop an **Oedipus complex,** or attraction to their mothers. He thought that young girls develop an attachment to their fathers and harbor hostile feelings towards their mothers, whom they blame for their lack of a penis. According to Freud most girls never overcome *penis envy* or give up their rivalry with their mothers, which causes enduring moral inferiority.
Latency (6 years–puberty)	**None** (Interacting with same-sex peers)		The latency stage is a reported period of sexual "dormancy." Children do not have particular psychosexual conflicts that must be resolved during this period.
Genital (puberty–adult)	**Genitals** (Establishing intimate relationships with the opposite sex)		Unsuccessful outcomes at this stage, supposedly may lead to sexual relationships based only on lustful desires, not on respect and commitment.

Psychosexual Development →

Oedipus [ED-uh-puss] Complex *Period of conflict during the phallic stage when children are supposedly attracted to the opposite-sex parent and hostile toward the same-sex parent*

Process Diagram

Chapter 13 Visual Summary

Major Personality Theories and Assessment Techniques

Theorists and Key Concepts

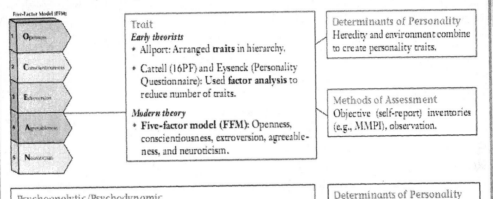

Five-Factor Model (FFM)

1 Openness
2 Conscientiousness
3 Extroversion
4 Agreeableness
5 Neuroticism

Trait

Early theorists

* Allport: Arranged **traits** in hierarchy.

* Cattell (16PF) and Eysenck (Personality Questionnaire): Used **factor analysis** to reduce number of traits.

Modern theory

* **Five-factor model (FFM):** Openness, conscientiousness, extroversion, agreeableness, and neuroticism.

Determinants of Personality
Heredity and environment combine to create personality traits.

Methods of Assessment
Objective (self-report) inventories (e.g., MMPI), observation.

Psychoanalytic/Psychodynamic

Freud

* **Levels of Consciousness**—**conscious, preconscious,** and **unconscious.**

* **Personality structure**—**id (pleasure principle), ego (reality principle), superego (morality principle).**

* **Defense Mechanisms**—**repression** and others.

* **Psychosexual Stages**—oral, anal, phallic, latency, and genital.

Neo-Freudians

* Adler—individual psychology, **inferiority complex,** and will-to-power.

* Jung—analytical psychology, **collective unconscious,** and **archetypes.**

* Horney—power envy vs. penis envy and **basic anxiety.**

Determinants of Personality
Unconscious conflicts between id, ego, and superego lead to defense mechanisms.

Methods of Assessment
Interviews and **projective tests:** Rorschach inkblot test, Thematic Apperception Test (TAT).

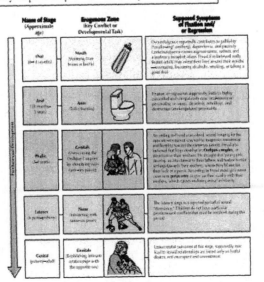

Major Personality Theories and Assessment Techniques (Continued)

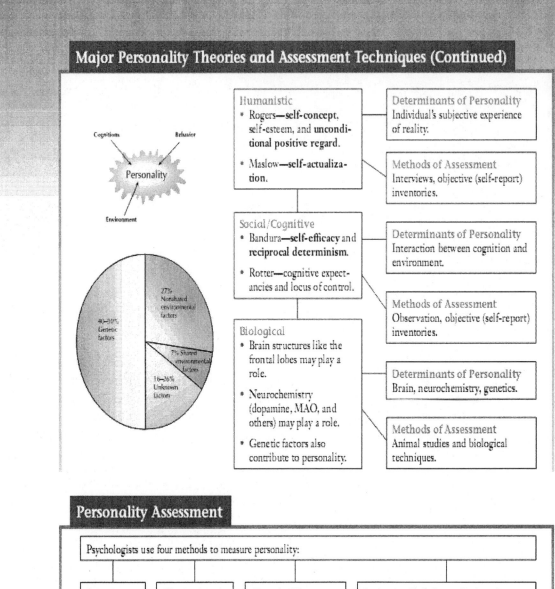

Humanistic
* Rogers—**self-concept, self-esteem,** and **unconditional positive regard.**
* Maslow—**self-actualization.**

Determinants of Personality
Individual's subjective experience of reality.

Methods of Assessment
Interviews, objective (self-report) inventories.

Social/Cognitive
* Bandura—**self-efficacy** and **reciprocal determinism.**
* Rotter—**cognitive expectancies** and **locus of control.**

Determinants of Personality
Interaction between cognition and environment.

Methods of Assessment
Observation, objective (self-report) inventories.

Biological
* Brain structures like the frontal lobes may play a role.
* Neurochemistry (dopamine, MAO, and others) may play a role.
* Genetic factors also contribute to personality.

Determinants of Personality
Brain, neurochemistry, genetics.

Methods of Assessment
Animal studies and biological techniques.

Personality Assessment

Psychologists use four methods to measure personality:

Interviews:
Can be either structured or unstructured.

Observations:
Involves direct observation with set of evaluation guidelines.

Objective Tests:
Self-report paper-and-pencil questionnaires, which provide objective standardized information about a large number of personality traits.

Projective Techniques [such as the **Rorschach "inkblot"** or **Thematic Apperception Test (TAT)**]:
Uses ambiguous stimuli to reportedly reveal unconscious elements of the personality.

Reliability and **validity** are the major criteria for evaluating the accuracy of personality tests.

Psychological Disorders

OUTLINE SQ4R (Survey, Question, Read, Recite, Review, & wRite)

This outline section incorporates all six steps in the well-researched SQ4R method of learning. Begin by surveying the list of chapter topics in the left column. This "big picture" will help focus and guide your attention while you read. As you read through the chapter, briefly summarize each section in your own words in the space to the right. Also write down any *questions* that come to mind. Surveying, Questioning, Reading, Reciting, Reviewing, and wRiting are the foundation of the SQ4R method and an invaluable form of active learning. They also make your reading time more enjoyable and efficient! One thorough, focused SQ4R reading of a chapter is far better than several passive readings.

TOPIC	NOTES

I. STUDYING PSYCHOLOGICAL DISORDERS

    A. Identifying Abnormal Behavior

    Gender & Cultural Diversity: Avoiding Ethnocentrism

    B. Explaining Abnormality

    C. Classifying Abnormal Behaviors

II. ANXIETY DISORDERS

    A. Five Major Anxiety Disorders

B. Explaining Anxiety Disorders

III. MOOD DISORDERS

A. Understanding Mood Disorders

*Gender & Cultural Diversity: How Gender and
    Culture Affect Depression*

B. Explaining Mood Disorders

Research Highlight: Suicide and Its Prevention

*Critical Thinking/Active Learning: How Your
    Thoughts Can Make You Depressed*

IV. SCHIZOPHRENIA

A. Symptoms of Schizophrenia

B. Types of Schizophrenia

C. Explaining Schizophrenia

Gender & Cultural Diversity: Schizophrenia
    Around the World

V. OTHER DISORDERS

A. Substance-Related Disorders

B. Dissociative Disorders

C. Personality Disorders

Psychology at Work: Testing Your
*   Knowledge of Abnormal Behavior*

LEARNING OBJECTIVES (Read, Recite, Review, & wRite)

In addition to the work you did in the Outline above, you can significantly improve your performance on exams by focusing on the following learning objectives. While reading the chapter or reviewing for exams, check your understanding by stopping periodically to *recite* (or repeat in your own words) and *writing* down your answers on a separate sheet. [Page numbers correspond to Chapter 14 in *Psychology in Action* (9e).]

14.1 Identify five common myths about mental illness. (p. 474)

14.2 Define abnormal behavior, and list four standards for identifying it. (p. 474)

14.3 Compare and contrast culture-general and culture-bound symptoms versus culture-general and culture-bound mental disorders. (p. 475)

14.4 Briefly describe the history of abnormal behavior. (p. 478)

14.5 Describe the purpose and criticisms of the DSM-IV-TR, and differentiate between neurosis, psychosis, and insanity. (p. 479)

14.6 Define anxiety disorders and the five major subtypes. (p. 483)

14.7 Identify the major contributors to anxiety disorders. (p. 486)

14.8 Compare and contrast the two major mood disorders. (p. 488)

14.9 What are the major similarities and differences in depression across cultures and between genders? (p. 489)

14.10 Describe the key biological and psychosocial forces that contribute to mood disorders. (p. 490)

14.11 What do we need to know about suicide and its prevention? (p. 491)

14.12 Briefly explain how faulty thinking may contribute to depression. (p. 492)

14.13 Define schizophrenia, and describe its five major symptoms. (p. 493)

14.14 Describe the key methods for classifying schizophrenia. (p. 496)

14.15 What are the major biological and psychosocial factors that influence schizophrenia? (p. 497)

14.16 What are the key similarities and differences in schizophrenia across cultures? (p. 498)

14.17 Identify substance-related disorders and comorbidity. (p. 500)

14.18 Describe dissociative disorders and dissociative identity disorder (DID). (p. 502)

14.19 Define personality disorders, and differentiate between antisocial and borderline personality disorders. (p. 503)

KEY TERMS (<u>R</u>eview & w<u>R</u>ite)

Like other survey courses, introductory psychology is filled with a "wealth" of new and unfamiliar terminology. To do well on exams, you must master this new language! Writing a brief definition of each term in the space provided and carefully reviewing them before exams will significantly improve your course grade.

Abnormal Behavior: _____

_____

Antisocial Personality: _____

_____

Anxiety Disorder: _____

_____

Bipolar Disorder: _____

_____

Borderline Personality Disorder: _____

_____

Comorbidity: _____

_____

Delusions: _____

_____

Diagnostic and Statistical Manual of Mental Disorders (DSM-IV-TR): _____

_____

Diathesis-Stress Model: _____

_____

Dissociative Disorder: _____

_____

Dissociative Identity Disorder (DID): _____

_____

Dopamine Hypothesis: _____

_____

Generalized Anxiety Disorder: _____

_____

Hallucinations: _____

_____

Insanity: _____

_____

Learned Helplessness: _____

_____

Major Depressive Disorder: _____

_____

Medical Model: _____

_____

Mood Disorder: _____

_____

Neurosis: _____

_____

Obsessive-Compulsive Disorder (OCD): _____

_____

Panic Disorder: _____

_____

Personality Disorders: _____

_____

Phobia: _____

_____

Psychiatry: _____

_____

Psychosis: _____

_____

Schizophrenia: _____

_____

Substance – Related Disorders: _____

_____

ACTIVE LEARNING EXERCISES

True mastery of information requires you to be an ACTIVE learner. Completing the following active learning exercises will improve your understanding of the chapter material and greatly improve your performance on exams. Answers to some exercises appear in Appendix A at the end of this study guide.

ACTIVE LEARNING EXERCISE I *Distinguishing Fact from Opinion*
To critically analyze controversial issues, we first need to distinguish between statements of *fact* and statements of *opinion*. A fact is a statement that can be proven true. An opinion is a statement that expresses how a person feels about an issue or what someone thinks is true. Although it is also important to determine whether the facts *are* true or false, in this exercise simply mark "O" for opinion and "F" for fact. After responding to each of the items, discuss your answers with friends and classmates who have not taken a course in general psychology. How do their answers compare to yours? Has your study of this chapter and the field of psychology affected your opinions about mental illness?

_____ 1. The mentally ill are more dangerous than the general population.
_____ 2. The insanity plea allows criminals back on the street too soon.
_____ 3. The term "split personality" is essentially the same as "schizophrenia."
_____ 4. People who talk to themselves are undoubtedly suffering from schizophrenia.
_____ 5. Everyone has a behavioral disorder of one type or another.
_____ 6. Delusions are the same as hallucinations.
_____ 7. Individuals with very clean and neat offices are probably obsessive-compulsive.
_____ 8. Everyone is occasionally depressed and will recover over time
_____ 9. Social phobias are labels created by psychologists and psychiatrists and probably do not really exist.
_____ 10. If not properly treated, neurosis can turn into psychosis.

CHAPTER OVERVIEW (Review)

The following chapter overview provides a narrative overview of the main topics covered in the chapter. Like the *Visual Summary* found at the end of each chapter in the text, this narrative summary provides a final opportunity to *review* chapter material.

I. STUDYING PSYCHOLOGICAL DISORDERS

14.1 Identify five common myths about mental illness. (p. 474)
The five common myths are: People with psychological disorders act in bizarre ways and are very different from "normal" people; mental disorders are a sign of personal weakness; mentally ill people are often dangerous and unpredictable; the mentally ill never fully recover; and most can only work at low-level jobs.

14.2 Define abnormal behavior, and list four standards for identifying it. (p. 474)
Abnormal behavior refers to patterns of emotion, thought, and action considered pathological for one or more of these reasons: statistical infrequency, disability or dysfunction, personal distress, or violation of norms.

14.3 Compare and contrast culture-general and culture-bound symptoms versus culture-general and culture-bound mental disorders. (p. 475)
Culture-general symptoms (nervousness or trouble-sleeping) are similarly expressed and identified in most cultures around the world, whereas *culture-bound* symptoms ("fullness in the head") are unique to certain cultures. Similarly, *culture-general* disorders (schizophrenia) are much the same across cultures, whereas *culture-bound* disorders ("Koro" or "running amok") are unique.

14.4 Briefly describe the history of abnormal behavior. (p. 478)
In ancient times, people commonly believed that demons were the cause of abnormal behavior. The **medical model,** which emphasizes disease, later replaced this *demonological model.*

14.5 Describe the purpose and criticisms of the DSM-IV-TR, and differentiate between neurosis, psychosis, and insanity. (p. 479)
The ***Diagnostic and Statistical Manual of Mental Disorders (DSM-IV-TR)*** classification provides detailed descriptions of symptoms, which in turn allow standardized diagnosis and improved communication among professionals, and between professionals and patients.

The DSM has been criticized for overreliance on the medical model, unfairly labeling people, possible cultural bias, and for not providing dimensions and degrees of disorders. enot paying sufficient attention to cultural factors, for relying too heavily on the medical model, and for labeling people.

Neurosis is an outmoded term for a disorder characterized by unrealistic anxiety and other associated problems, whereas **psychosis** is a current term for a disorder characterized by defective or lost contact with reality. **Insanity** is a legal term applied when people cannot be held responsible for their actions, or are judged incompetent to manage their own affairs due to mental illness.

II. ANXIETY DISORDERS
14.6 Define anxiety disorders and the five major subtypes. (p. 483)
People with **anxiety disorders** experience unreasonable, often paralyzing, fear and dread in facing everyday problems. In **generalized anxiety disorders (GAD),** there is a persistent free-floating anxiety. In **panic disorder,** anxiety is concentrated into brief or lengthy episodes of panic attacks. **Phobias** are intense, irrational fears and avoidance of specific objects or situations, such as agoraphobia, a fear of becoming trapped or helpless in open spaces. **Obsessive-compulsive disorder (OCD)** involves persistent anxiety-arousing thoughts (obsessions) which are relieved by ritualistic actions (compulsions) such as hand washing.

14.7 Identify the major contributors to anxiety disorders. (p. 486)
Anxiety disorders are influenced by psychological, biological, and sociocultural factors (the biopsychosocial model). Psychological theories focus on faulty thinking (hypervigilance) and maladaptive learning from conditioning and social learning. Biological approaches emphasize evolutionary and genetic predisposition, brain differences, and biochemistry. The sociocultural perspective focuses on environmental stressors that increase anxiety and cultural socialization that produces distinct culture-bound disorders such as taijin kyofusho (TKS).

III. MOOD DISORDERS
14.8 Compare and contrast the two major mood disorders. (p. 488)
Mood disorders are extreme disturbances of affect (emotion). In **major depressive disorder,** individuals experience a long-lasting depressed mood, feelings of worthlessness, and loss of interest in most activities. The feelings are without apparent cause, and the individual may lose contact with reality (psychosis). In **bipolar disorder,** episodes of mania and depression alternate with normal periods. During the manic episode, speech and thinking are rapid, and the person may experience delusions of grandeur and act impulsively.

14.9 What are the major similarities and differences in depression across cultures and between genders? (p. 489)
Some symptoms of depression, such as frequent and intense sad affect, seem to exist across all cultures, but other symptoms, like feelings of guilt, seem to be unique to certain cultures. Although both men and women suffer from depression, the rate for women in North America is two or three times the rate for men.

14.10 Describe the key biological and psychosocial forces that contribute to mood disorders. (p. 490)
Biological theories of mood disorders emphasize brain function abnormalities and disruptions in neurotransmitters (especially serotonin, norepinephrine, and dopamine). There is also evidence of a genetic predisposition for both major depression and bipolar disorder.

Psychosocial theories of mood disorders emphasize disturbed interpersonal relationships, faulty thinking, poor self-concept, and maladaptive learning. **Learned helplessness** theory suggests that depression results from repeatedly failing to escape from a source of stress.

14.11 What do we need to know about suicide and its prevention? (p. 491)
Suicide is a serious problem associated with depression. If you are having suicidal thoughts, seek help immediately. You also can help others who may be contemplating suicide by becoming involved and showing concern.

14.12 Briefly explain how faulty thinking may contribute to depression. (p. 492)
People with a depressive explanatory style tend to attribute bad events to internal factors and stable, global causes. In contrast, they explain good events as resulting from external factors

and unstable, specific causes. This pattern of negative thinking increases the chances for depression.

IV. SCHIZOPHRENIA

14.13 Define schizophrenia, and describe its five major symptoms. (p. 493)
Schizophrenia is a serious psychotic mental disorder that afflicts approximately 1 of every 100 people. The five major symptoms are disturbances in perception (impaired filtering and selection, **hallucinations**), language (word salad, neologisms), thought (impaired logic, **delusions**), emotion (either exaggerated or blunted emotions), and behavior (social withdrawal, bizarre mannerisms, catalepsy, waxy flexibility).

14.14 Describe the key methods for classifying schizophrenia. (p. 496)
There are five major subtypes of schizophrenia—*paranoid, catatonic, disorganized, undifferentiated,* and *residual.* Symptoms of schizophrenia alsocan be divided into a two-dimensioned classification system: Addition or exaggeration of normal thought processes and behaviors (e.g., delusions and hallucinations) is classified as positive symptoms, whereas loss or absence of normal thought processes and behaviors (e.g., toneless voice and flat emotions) is classified as negative symptoms.

14.15 What are the major biological and psychosocial factors that influence schizophrenia? (p. 497)
Biological theories of the causes of schizophrenia propose genetics (people inherit a predisposition), disruptions in neurotransmitters (the **dopamine hypothesis**), and abnormal brain structure and function (such as enlarged ventricles and lower levels of activity in the frontal and temporal lobes). Psychosocial theories of schizophrenia focus on the **diathesis-stress model** and disturbed communication.

4.16 What are the key similarities and differences in schizophrenia across cultures? (p. 498)
Researchers have found several *culture-bound* and *culture-general* symptoms and disorders that help us understand abnormal behavior. Schizophrenia is a good example. Many symptoms are *culturally general* (such as delusions), but significant differences also exist across cultures in *prevalence, form, onset,* and *prognosis.*

V. OTHER DISORDERS

14.17 Identify substance-related disorders and comorbidity. (p. 500)
Substance-related disorders involve abuse of, or dependence on, a mood- or behavior-altering drug. They are diagnosed when use of a drug interferes with social or occupational functioning, and drug tolerance or withdrawal symptoms occur. People with substance-related disorders also commonly suffer from other psychological disorders, a condition known as **comorbidity**.

14.18 Describe dissociative disorders and dissociative identity disorder (DID). (p. 502)
In **dissociative disorders,** critical elements of personality split apart. This split is manifested in a disassociation of significant aspects of experience from memory or consciousness. Developing completely separate personalities [**dissociative identity disorder (DID)**] is the most severe dissociative disorder. Environmental variables are the primary cause of dissociative disorders.

14.19 Define personality disorders, and differentiate between antisocial and borderline personality disorders. (p. 503)
Personality disorders involve inflexible, maladaptive personality traits. The best-known type is the **antisocial personality,** characterized by a profound disregard for, and violation of, the rights of others. Research suggests this disorder may be related to defects in brain activity, genetic inheritance, or disturbed family relationships. **Borderline personality disorder** (BPD) is the

most commonly diagnosed personality disorder. It is characterized by impulsivity and instability in mood, relationships, and self-image.

SELF-TESTS (Review & wRite)

Completing the following self-tests will provide immediate feedback on how well you have mastered the material. In the labeling exercises, *crossword puzzle*, and *fill-in exercises*, write the appropriate word or words in the blank spaces. The *matching exercise* requires you to match the terms in one column to their correct definitions in the other. For the *multiple-choice questions* in Practice Tests I and II, circle or underline the correct answer. If you are unsure of any answer, mark the item, and then go back to the text for further review. Correct answers are provided in Appendix A at the end of this study guide.

CROSSWORD PUZZLE FOR CHAPTER 14

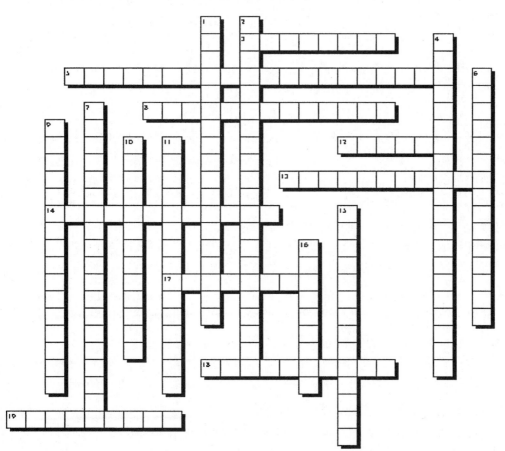

ACROSS

3 A large group of disorders characterized by unrealistic anxiety and other associated problems.

5 Stress-related disorder characterized by amnesia, fugue, or multiple personality.

8 Group of psychotic disorders involving major disturbances in perception, language, thought, emotion, and behavior.

12 Type of anxiety disorder characterized by intense, irrational fear and avoidance of a specific object or situation.

13 The co-occurrence of two or more disorders in the same person at the same time.

14 Perspective that assumes diseases have physical causes that can be diagnosed, treated, and possibly cured.

17 A legal term applied when people cannot be held responsible for their actions.

18 The specialized branch of medicine dealing with the diagnosis, treatment, and prevention of mental disorders.

19 Mistaken beliefs based on a misrepresentation of reality.

DOWN

1 A theory suggesting that schizophrenia is caused by an overactivity of dopamine neurons in a specific region of the brain.

2 Personality disorder characterized by egocentrism, lack of conscience, impulsive behavior, and manipulation of others.

4 Inflexible, maladaptive personality traits that cause significant impairment of social functions.

6 Type of abnormal behavior characterized by unrealistic, irrational fear.

7 In Seligman's theory, a state of helplessness or resignation in which people or animals learn that escape from something painful is impossible and depression results.

9 Patterns of emotion, thought, and action considered pathological (diseased or disordered) for one or more of these reasons: statistical infrequency, disability or dysfunction, personal distress, or violation of norms.

10 Type of anxiety disorder characterized by sudden and inexplicable attacks of intense fear.

11 Individuals who experience episodes of mania or of both mania and depression.

15 Sensory perceptions that occur without an external stimulus.

16 Serious mental disorders characterized by loss of contact with reality and extreme mental disruption.

FILL-IN

1. Abnormal behavior is defined in your text as patterns of emotion, thought, and action considered pathological for one or more of these reasons: _____, _____, _____, _____, or _____ (pp. 475-476).

2. In early treatment of abnormal behavior, trephining was used to _____. In contrast, exorcism was designed to _____ (p. 478).

3. _____ is a type of anxiety disorder characterized by intrusive, fearful thoughts and urges to perform repetitive, ritualistic behaviors (pp. 485-486).

4. The two main types of mood disorders are _____ and _____ (pp. 488-489).

5. According to Seligman, people who feel they are unable to control or escape from pain and sadness may develop _____ (pp. 490-491).

6. Schizophrenia is sometimes so severe that it is considered a form of _____, a term describing a general lack of contact with reality (p. 494).

7. Hearing voices, also known as _____, is a common symptom in _____ (p. 495).

8. _____ is the co-occurrence of two or more disorders in the same person at the same time (p. 501).

9. A mental disorder in which at least two separate and distinct personalities exist within the same person is known as _____ (p. 502).

10. The core features of _____ are impulsivity and instability in mood, relationships, and self image (pp. 503-504).

MATCHING EXERCISES

Column A

a. OCD
b. Neurosis
c. Schizophrenia
d. DSM-IV-TR
e. Phobias
f. Bipolar Disorder
g. Dopamine Hypothesis
h. Antisocial Personality
i. Insanity
j. Negative Symptoms

Column B

1.____ Exaggerated fear of specific objects or situations
2.____ Legal term implying a diminished responsibility
3.____ Mania and depression alternate with normal periods
4.____ Early term describing anxiety type disorders
5.____ Also known as psychopath or sociopath
6.____ Persistent thoughts are relieved by ritualistic actions
7.____ Categorizes mental disorders and their symptoms
8.____ Serious psychotic disorder affecting 1:100 people
9.____ Behavioral deficits in schizophrenia
10.____ Suspected contributor to schizophrenia

PRACTICE TEST I

1. Abnormal behavior is defined as patterns of _____ considered pathological for one of more of four reasons.
   a. emotions
   b. thoughts
   c. behaviors
   d. any of these options

2. Someone who drinks excessively and wishes to stop may be experiencing a type of abnormal behavior according to the _____ model.
   a. psychosocial
   b. sociocultural
   c. medical
   d. personal distress

3. Windigo psychosis, in which victims believe they are possessed by the spirit of a windigo that causes delusions and cannibalistic impulses, is a good example of a _____ disorder.
   a. psychotic
   b. culture-bound
   c. sociocultural
   d. none of these options

4. The DSM-IV-TR provides _____ for mental disorders.
   a. categorical descriptions
   b. treatment recommendations
   c. general prognosis
   d. all but one of these options

5. _____ is a common symptom of generalized anxiety disorder (GAD).
   a. Ritualistic action
   b. Free-floating anxiety
   c. Panic attack
   d. Irrational fear

6. Repetitive, ritualistic behaviors, such as hand washing, counting, or putting things in order, are called _____.
   a. obsessions
   b. compulsions
   c. ruminations
   d. phobias

7. In the Japanese social phobia called TKS, people fear that they will _____.
   a. evaluate others negatively
   b. embarrass themselves
   c. embarrass others
   d. be embarrassed by others

8. A key difference between major depressive and bipolar disorder is that only in bipolar disorders do people have _____.
   a. hallucinations or delusions
   b. depression
   c. a biochemical imbalance
   d. manic episodes

9. This is **NOT** a possible explanation for depression
   a. imbalances of serotonin or norepinephrine
   b. genetic predisposition
   c. lithium deficiency
   d. learned helplessness

10. Which of the following is a myth about suicide?
    a. People who talk about it are less likely to actually do it.
    b. Suicide usually occurs with little or no warning.
    c. Most people have never thought about suicide.
    d. all of these options

11. Hallucinations and delusions are symptoms of _____.
    a. mood disorders
    b. personality disorders
    c. anxiety disorders
    d. schizophrenia

12. Family studies have shown that when it comes to schizophrenia, children are more similar to their _____.
    a. biological parents than their adoptive parents
    b. adoptive parents than their biological parents
    c. friends than their families
    d. aunts/uncles than their brothers/sisters

13. Drugs that reduce _____ in the brain reduce or eliminate some symptoms of schizophrenia.
    a. dopamine activity
    b. serotonin synapses
    c. frontal lobe activity
    d. none of these options

14. Your coworker is seriously depressed and abusing alcohol and amphetamines. This is an example of _____.
    a. suicidal behavior
    b. comorbidity
    c. a death wish
    d. bipolar personality disorder

15. Amnesia, fugue, and dissociative identity disorder (DID) result from _____.
    a. a splitting apart of experience from memory or consciousness
    b. the presence of two or more distinct personality systems
    c. a split personality
    d. wandering away from home or work

16. Multiple personality disorder is now known as a _____.
    a. schizophrenia
    b. dissociative identity disorder (DID)
    c. amnesiatic personality disorder
    d. none of these options

17. Inflexible, maladaptive personality traits that disrupt occupational and social functioning are _____.
    a. characteristics of a personality disorder
    b. common in all of us
    c. found mostly in Western, individualistic cultures
    d. related to psychopathic deviation

18. Impulsive behavior, egocentrism, lack of a conscience, and _____ are all characteristic of an antisocial personality disorder.
    a. superficial charm
    b. lack of social skills
    c. sympathy for victims
    d. lack of intelligence

19. Impulsivity and instability in mood, relationships, and self-image are part of the _____ personality disorder.
    a. manic depressive
    b. bipolar
    c. borderline
    d. none of these options

20. People with _____ frequently have a childhood history of neglect and abuse, and as adults tend to see themselves and everyone else in absolutes.
    a. dissociative identity disorder
    b. schizophrenia
    c. generalized anxiety disorder
    d. borderline personality disorder

PRACTICE TEST II

1. Being unable to get along with others, hold a job, or eat properly might be classified as abnormal behavior according to the _____ standard.
   a. statistical infrequency
   b. personal distress
   c. disability or dysfunction
   d. none of the above

2. This was a Freudian term for the causes of anxiety.
   a. neurosis
   b. psychosis

   c. insanity
   d. hysteria

3. In the DSM-IV-TR, this category describes a person's psychosocial and environmental stressors.
   a. Axis I
   b. Axis II
   c. Axis IV
   d. Axis V

4. In the general population, _____ is the most frequently occurring category of mental disorders.
   a. schizophrenia
   b. personality disorder
   c. depressive disorder
   d. anxiety disorder

5. In _____ disorder, the individual suffers brief attacks of intense apprehension.
   a. phobic
   b. posttraumatic stress
   c. panic
   d. dissociative fugue

6. Distorted thinking that magnifies ordinary threats or failures is the _____ explanation for anxiety disorders.
   a. social learning
   b. faulty cognitions
   c. humanistic
   d. psychoanalytic

7. According to _____ theory, modeling and imitation may be the causes of some phobias.
   a. social learning
   b. psychobiological
   c. sociocultural
   d. cognitive-behavioral

8. Socialization towards activity, independence, and the suppression of emotions may explain why fewer men than women are diagnosed with _____.
   a. anxiety
   b. schizophrenia
   c. antisocial personality disorder
   d. depression

9. Mood disorders are sometimes treated by _____ drugs, which affect the amount or functioning of norepinephrine, dopamine, and serotonin in the brain.
   a.   antidepressant
   b.   antipsychotics
   c.   mood congruence
   d.   none of the above

10. If an identical twin suffers from a mood disorder, the other twin has about a _____ percent chance of developing the disorder as well.
   a.   25
   b.   10
   c.   75
   d.   50

11. Internal, stable, and global attributions for failure or unpleasant circumstances are associated with _____.
   a.   anxiety disorders
   b.   delusional disorders
   c.   depression
   d.   all of these options

12. Auditory hallucinations are most common in _____.
   a.   schizophrenia
   b.   posttraumatic stress disorder
   c.   bipolar disorder
   d.   dissociative identity disorder

13. Believing you are the Queen of England or Jesus Christ would be a symptom called _____.
   a.   hallucinations
   b.   mania
   c.   delusions
   d.   all of these options

14. Delusions, hallucinations, and disorganized speech are _____ symptoms of schizophrenia.
   a.   negative
   b.   positive
   c.   deficit
   d.   undifferentiated

15. The frontal and temporal lobes appear to be less active in some people with _____.
   a.   dissociative identity disorder
   b.   personality disorders
   c.   schizophrenia
   d.   all of these options

16. The co-occurrence of two or more disorders in the same person at the same time is called _____.
   a.   the synergistic effect
   b.   multiple personality disorder
   c.   comorbidity
   d.   borderline personality disorder

17. One of the most common comorbid disorders is _____.
   a.   dissociative identity disorder
   b.   schizophrenia
   c.   personality disorders
   d.   alcohol use disorder (AUD)

18. Emotional deprivation, harsh and inconsistent discipline, and inappropriate modeling are all highly correlated with _____.
   a.   dissociative identity disorder (DID)
   b.   antisocial personality disorder
   c.   schizophrenia
   d.   none of these options

19. Sociopath and psychopath are terms commonly used interchangeably with _____.
   a.   borderline personality disorder
   b.   antisocial personality disorder
   c.   mental illness
   d.   medical student's disease

20. One possible psychological cause of BPD is _____.
   a.   a childhood history of neglect
   b.   families with expressed emotionality
   c.   stressful situations
   d.   none of these options

Process Diagram 14.1

The Four Criteria and a Continuum of Abnormal Behavior

Rather than being fixed categories, both "abnormal" and "normal" behaviors exist along a continuum (Hansell & Damour, 2008).

Rare ——— Common

Statistical Infrequency
(e.g., believing others are plotting against you)

Normal — Abnormal

Low ——— High

Disability or Dysfunction
(e.g., being unable to go to work due to alcohol abuse)

Normal — Abnormal

Statistical Infrequency A behavior may be judged abnormal if it occurs infrequently in a given population. Statistical infrequency alone does not determine what is normal. For example, no one would classify Albert Einstein's great intelligence or Lance Armstrong's exceptional athletic ability as abnormal.

Disability or Dysfunction People who suffer from psychological disorders may be unable to get along with others, hold a job, eat properly, or clean themselves. Their ability to think clearly and make rational decisions also may be impaired.

Low ——— High

Personal Distress
(e.g., having thoughts of suicide)

Normal — Abnormal

Rare ——— Common

Violations of Norms
(e.g., shouting at strangers)

Normal — Abnormal

Personal Distress The personal distress criterion focuses on the individual's judgment of his or her level of functioning. Yet many people with psychological disorders deny they have a problem. Also, some serious psychological disorders (such as antisocial personality disorder) cause little or no personal emotional discomfort. The personal distress criterion by itself is not sufficient for identifying all forms of abnormal behavior.

Violation of Norms The fourth approach to identifying abnormal behavior is violation of social norms, or cultural rules that guide behavior in particular situations. A major problem with this criterion, however, is that cultural diversity can affect what people consider a violation of norms.

Chapter 14 Uisual Summary

Studying Psychological Disorders

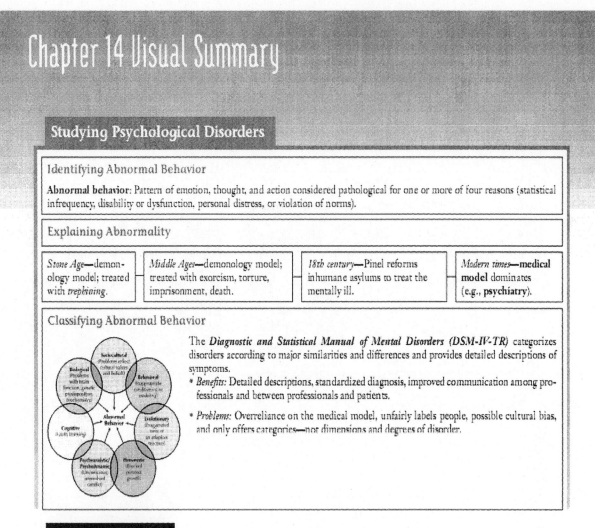

Identifying Abnormal Behavior

Abnormal behavior: Pattern of emotion, thought, and action considered pathological for one or more of four reasons (statistical infrequency, disability or dysfunction, personal distress, or violation of norms).

Explaining Abnormality

Stone Age—demonology model; treated with *trephining*.	*Middle Ages*—demonology model; treated with exorcism, torture, imprisonment, death.	*18th century*—Pinel reforms inhumane asylums to treat the mentally ill.	*Modern times*—**medical model** dominates (e.g., **psychiatry**).

Classifying Abnormal Behavior

The *Diagnostic and Statistical Manual of Mental Disorders (DSM-IV-TR)* categorizes disorders according to major similarities and differences and provides detailed descriptions of symptoms.

* *Benefits:* Detailed descriptions, standardized diagnosis, improved communication among professionals and between professionals and patients.

* *Problems:* Overreliance on the medical model, unfairly labels people, possible cultural bias, and only offers categories—not dimensions and degrees of disorder.

Anxiety Disorders

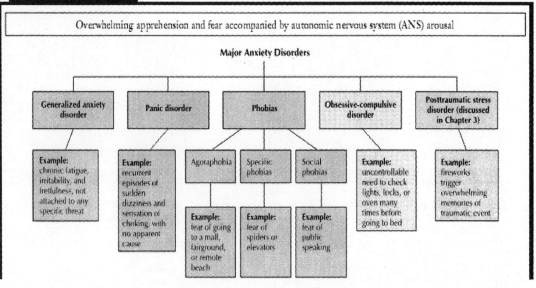

Overwhelming apprehension and fear accompanied by autonomic nervous system (ANS) arousal

Major Anxiety Disorders

Generalized anxiety disorder
Example: chronic fatigue, irritability, and fretfulness, not attached to any specific threat

Panic disorder
Example: recurrent episodes of sudden dizziness and sensation of choking, with no apparent cause

Phobias
Agoraphobia
Example: fear of going to a mall, fairground, or remote beach
Specific phobias
Example: fear of spiders or elevators
Social phobias
Example: fear of public speaking

Obsessive-compulsive disorder
Example: uncontrollable need to check lights, locks, or oven many times before going to bed

Posttraumatic stress disorder (discussed in Chapter 3)
Example: fireworks trigger overwhelming memories of traumatic event

Mood Disorders

Mood disorders are disturbances of affect (emotion) that may include psychotic distortions of reality. Two types:

- **Major depressive disorder:** Long-lasting depressed mood, feelings of worthlessness, and loss of interest in most activities. Feelings are without apparent cause and person may lose contact with reality.

- **Bipolar disorder:** Episodes of mania and depression alternate with normal periods. During manic episode, speech and thinking are rapid, and the person may experience delusions of grandeur and act impulsively.

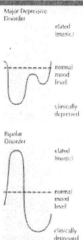

Schizophrenia

Schizophrenia: Serious psychotic mental disorder afflicting approximately one out of every 100 people.

Five major symptoms characterized by disturbances in:

1) Perception (impaired filtering and selection, **hallucinations**)

2) Language (word salad, neologisms)

3) Thought (impaired logic, **delusions**)

4) Emotion (either exaggerated or blunted emotions)

5) Behavior (social withdrawal, bizarre mannerisms, catalepsy, waxy flexibility)

Two-type Classification System:

Positive symptoms—distorted or excessive mental activity (e.g., delusions and hallucinations).	*Negative symptoms*—behavioral deficits (e.g., toneless voice, flattened emotions).

Other Disorders

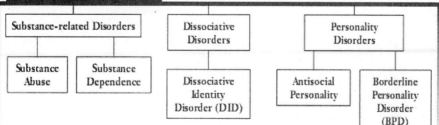

15
Therapy

OUTLINE SQ4R (S̲urvey, Q̲uestion, R̲ead, R̲ecite, R̲eview, & wR̲ite)

This outline section incorporates all six steps in the well-researched SQ4R method of learning. Begin by surveying the list of chapter topics in the left column. This "big picture" will help focus and guide your attention while you read. As you read through the chapter, briefly summarize each section in your own words in the space to the right. Also write down any *questions* that come to mind. Surveying, Questioning, Reading, Reciting, Reviewing, and wRiting are the foundation of the SQ4R method and an invaluable form of active learning. They also make your reading time more enjoyable and efficient! One thorough, focused SQ4R reading of a chapter is far better than several passive readings.

TOPIC	NOTES

I. INSIGHT THERAPIES

    A. Psychoanalysis/Psychodynamic Therapies

    B. Cognitive Therapies

    C. Humanistic Therapies

    D. Group, Family, and Marital Therapies

Critical Thinking/Active Learning: Hunting
for Good Therapy Films

II. BEHAVIOR THERAPIES

A. Classical Conditioning Techniques

B. Operant Conditioning Techniques

C. Observational Learning Techniques

D. Evaluating Behavior Therapies

III. BIOMEDICAL THERAPIES

A. Psychopharmacology

B. Electroconvulsive Therapy and Psychosurgery

C. Evaluating Biomedical Therapies

IV. THERAPY AND CRITICAL THINKING

A. Therapy Essentials

Psychology at Work: Careers in Mental Health

Research Highlight: Mental Health and the Family--PTSD

Gender & Cultural Diversity: Similarities and Differences

B. Institutionalization

C. Evaluating and Finding Therapy

Psychology at Work: Nonprofessional Therapy—
Talking to the Depressed

LEARNING OBJECTIVES (Read, Recite, Review, & wRite)

In addition to the work you did in the Outline above, you can significantly improve your performance on exams by focusing on the following learning objectives. While reading the chapter or reviewing for exams, check your understanding by stopping periodically to *recite* (or repeat in your own words) and *writing* down your answers on a separate sheet. [Page numbers correspond to Chapter 15 in *Psychology in Action* (9e).]

15.1 Discuss potential problems with media portrayals of therapy, four common myths about therapy, and its three general approaches. (p. 508)
15.2 Discuss psychotherapy and insight therapy. (p. 510)
15.3 Define psychoanalysis, and describe its five major methods. (p. 510)
15.4 What are the two major criticisms of psychoanalysis? (p. 512)
15.5 Differentiate between psychoanalysis and psychodynamic therapy. (p. 512)
15.6 Discuss cognitive therapy, self-talk, cognitive restructuring, and cognitive-behavior therapy. (p. 514)
15.7 What is the general goal of Ellis's rational-emotive behavior therapy (REBT)? (p. 514)
15.8 Describe Beck's cognitive therapy. (p. 515)
15.9 What are the chief successes and criticisms of cognitive therapy? (p. 518)
15.10 Define humanistic therapy, and describe Roger's client-centered therapy. (p. 518)
15.11 What are the key criticisms of humanistic therapy? (p. 519)
15.12 Discuss group, self-help, family, and marital therapies. (p. 521)
15.13 What is behavior therapy? (p. 524)
15.14 Describe how classical conditioning, operant conditioning, and observational learning are used in behavior therapy. (p. 524)
15.15 What are the key successes and criticisms of behavior therapy? (p. 527)
15.16 Define biomedical therapy. (p. 528)
15.17 Discuss psychopharmacology, electroconvulsive therapy (ECT), and psychosurgery. (p. 528)
15.18 What are the major contributions and criticisms of biomedical therapy? (p. 530)
15.19 Identify the five most common goals of therapy, and discuss the eclectic approach. (p. 532)
15.20 Identify the six key types of mental health professionals. (p. 533)
15.21 Briefly summarize the major effects of mental disorders, like PTSD, on the family. (p. 534)
15.22 Describe the major similarities and differences in therapy across cultures. (p. 535)
15.23 What are the unique concerns of women in therapy? (p. 536)
15.24 Discuss problems with involuntary commitment and deinstitutionalization. (p. 537)
15.25 Is therapy effective, and how can we find a good therapist? (p. 538)
15.26 Briefly summarize how to deal with someone who's seriously depressed. (p. 539)

KEY TERMS (Review & wRite)

Like other survey courses, introductory psychology is filled with a "wealth" of new and unfamiliar terminology. To do well on exams, you must master this new language! Writing a brief definition of each term in the space provided and carefully reviewing them before exams will significantly improve your course grade.

Active Listening: _____

_____

Antianxiety Drugs: _____

_____

Antidepressant Drugs: _____

_____

Antipsychotic Drugs: _____

_____

Aversion Therapy: _____

_____

Behavior Therapy: _____

_____

Biomedical Therapy: _____

_____

Client-Centered Therapy: _____

_____

Cognitive-Behavior Therapy: _____

_____

Cognitive Restructuring: _____

_____

Cognitive Therapy: _____

_____

Dream Analysis: _____

_____

Eclectic Approach: _____

_____

Electroconvulsive Therapy (ECT): _____

_____

Empathy: _____

_____

Free Association: _____

_____

Genuineness: _____

_____

Group Therapy: _____

_____

Humanistic Therapy: _____

_____

Interpretation: _____

_____

Lobotomy: _____

_____

Modeling Therapy: _____

_____

Mood Stabilizer Drugs: _____

_____

Psychoanalysis: _____

_____

Psychodynamic Therapy: _____

_____

Psychopharmacology: _____

_____

Psychosurgery: _____

_____

Psychotherapy: _____

_____

Rational-Emotive Behavior Therapy (REBT): _____

_____

Repetitive Transcranial Magnetic Stimulation (rTMS): _____

_____

Resistance: _____

_____

Self-help Group: _____

_____

Self-talk: _____

_____

Systematic Desensitization: _____

_____

Tardive Dyskinesia: _____

_____

Transference: _____

_____

Unconditional Positive Regard: _____

_____

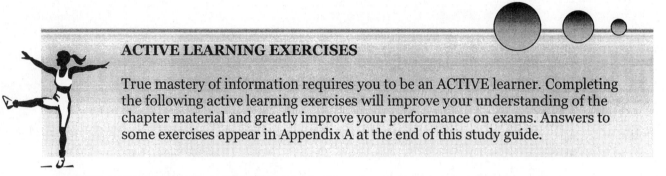

ACTIVE LEARNING EXERCISES

True mastery of information requires you to be an ACTIVE learner. Completing the following active learning exercises will improve your understanding of the chapter material and greatly improve your performance on exams. Answers to some exercises appear in Appendix A at the end of this study guide.

ACTIVE LEARNING EXERCISE I *Confronting Your Own Faulty Reasoning*

Albert Ellis believes that most human suffering results from illogical thinking. To improve *logical*, critical thinking skills, Part I discusses two basic tests for sound reasoning, and Part II provides practice applying these principles to your own irrational beliefs.

Part I Consider the following syllogism:
Premise 1:   *All dogs are animals.*
Premise 2:   *All animals are blue.*
Conclusion: *Therefore, all dogs are blue.*

Is this sound and logical reasoning? To determine whether an argument is sound and whether the conclusions should be accepted, critical thinkers ask two major questions: "Is the argument valid?" and "Are all premises true?" An argument is considered valid *if* the conclusion logically follows from the premises. The previous syllogism, for example, would be considered valid because *if* all dogs are animals, and all animals are blue, then *logically* all dogs *must* be blue. The second step in evaluating the soundness of arguments does require an examination of the content of argument. For an argument to be sound, each premise must also be true. This is where the previous syllogism falls apart. All dogs are obviously not blue.

The same faulty reasoning that underlies the blue-dog syllogism underlies the irrational beliefs that Ellis' form of cognitive therapy seeks to dispel. See if you can identify the problems with the following misconception.

Premise 1: I must have love or approval from everyone I find significant (in order to be happy).
Premise 2: I don't have approval from my mother, whom I consider significant.
Conclusion: Therefore, I am unhappy.

Is this argument valid? If not, why not? Are the premises of this argument true? If not, which ones are false and why?

Part II Consider your own irrational misconceptions (e.g., "I must make everyone happy," "Life must be fair," etc.). In the following spaces, analyze your "self-talk" about one of your misconceptions and try to put it in syllogism form--identify your two basic premises and your conclusion.

Premise 1: _____

Premise 2: _____
Conclusion: _____
Now answer the following questions: Is my argument valid? If not, why not?

_____

Are the premises of my argument true? If not, which one is false and why?

_____

For further practice (and self-insight), try using this same procedure on your other irrational misconceptions. By actively applying logical skills to your own thought processes, you will not only improve your basic critical thinking skills, but, according to Ellis, you will also be in a better position to change these self-destructive thought patterns and resultant behaviors.

ACTIVE LEARNING EXERCISE II *Expressing Empathy*

According to Dr. Thomas Gordon, people who wish to express empathy must avoid asking questions or giving advice. It is more appropriate to explore the other person's emotional state, and use "active listening," which uses open-ended statements that encourage the expression of feelings. Three basic active listening techniques are:
   a. *Repeating what was said as a statement—avoiding asking questions.*
   b. *Slightly rewording (or paraphrasing) the statement, which may be offered as a question.*
   c. *Stating the feeling you assumed was being expressed.*

To practice this technique, use an "a," "b," or "c" for each of the following statements:
Sample Statement = "I had the worst day of my life today at work."
Sample Active Listening Response =(b) "Do you mean that everything you did at work today seemed to go wrong?"

1. "I feel like a nobody. No one ever pays attention to me or seems to care about me."
_____

_____

2. "You always hurt my feelings."
_____

_____

CHAPTER OVERVIEW (Review)

The following chapter overview provides a narrative overview of the main topics covered in the chapter. Like the *Visual Summary* found at the end of each chapter in the text, this narrative summary provides a final opportunity to *review* chapter material.

I. PSYCHOANALYSIS/PSYCHODYNAMIC THERAPIES

15.1 Discuss potential problems with media portrayals of therapy, four common myths about therapy, and its three general approaches. (p. 508)
Films about mental illness and its treatment generally present unrealistic and negative stereotypes that bias the public. There are four common myths about therapy: There is one best therapy, therapists can read your mind, people who go to therapists are crazy or weak, and only the rich can afford therapy. There also are three general approaches to therapy—insight, behavior, and biomedical.

15.2 Discuss psychotherapy and insight therapy. (p. 510)
Professional **psychotherapy** refers to techniques employed to improve psychological functioning and promote adjustment to life. The general goal of **insight therapy** is to increase client/patient understanding and self-knowledge. Once people gain this "insight," they can control and improve their functioning.

15.3 Define psychoanalysis, and describe its five major methods. (p. 510)
Sigmund Freud developed the method of **psychoanalysis** to uncover unconscious conflicts and bring them into conscious awareness. The five major techniques are **free association, dream analysis,** analyzing **resistance,** analyzing **transference,** and **interpretation.**

15.4 What are the two major criticisms of psychoanalysis? (p. 512)
Like psychoanalytic theories of personality, psychoanalysis is the subject of great debate. It is primarily criticized for its limited availability (it is time-consuming, expensive, and suits only a small group of people) and its lack of scientific credibility.

15.5 Differentiate between psychoanalysis and psychodynamic therapy. (p. 512)
Compared to psychoanalysis, modern **psychodynamic therapies** are briefer, the patient is treated face-to-face (rather than reclining on a couch), the therapist takes a more directive approach (rather than waiting for unconscious memories and desires to slowly be uncovered), and the focus is on conscious processes and current problems (rather than unconscious problems of the past).

II. COGNITIVE AND HUMANISTIC THERAPIES

15.6 Discuss cognitive therapy, self-talk, cognitive restructuring, and cognitive-behavior therapy. (p. 514)
Cognitive therapy emphasizes the importance of faulty thought processes, beliefs, and negative **self-talk** in the creation of problem behaviors. Therapists use cognitive restructuring to challenge and change destructive thoughts or inappropriate behaviors. **Cognitive-behavior therapy** focuses on changing both self-destructive thoughts and self-defeating behaviors.

15.7 What is the general goal of Ellis's rational-emotive behavior therapy (REBT)? (p. 514)
Albert Ellis's **rational-emotive behavior therapy** (REBT) aims to replace a client's irrational beliefs with rational beliefs and accurate perceptions of the world.

15.8 Describe Beck's cognitive therapy. (p. 515)
Aaron Beck developed a form of cognitive therapy that is particularly effective with depression. He helps clients identify their distorted thinking patterns, followed by active testing of these thoughts and encouragement toward pleasurable activities.

15.9 What are the chief successes and criticisms of cognitive therapy? (p. 518)
Evaluations of cognitive therapies have shown success with a wide variety of disorders (e.g., Beck's success with depression). Both Beck and Ellis, however, are criticized for ignoring the importance of unconscious processes, overemphasizing rationality, and minimizing the client's past. Some critics also attribute any success with cognitive therapies to the use of behavioral techniques.

15.10 Define humanistic therapy, and describe Roger's client-centered therapy. (p. 518)
Humanistic therapies are based on the premise that problems result when an individual's normal growth potential is blocked. In Carl Rogers's **client-centered therapy,** the therapist offers **empathy, unconditional positive regard, genuineness,** and **active listening** as means of facilitating personal growth.

15.11 What are the key criticisms of humanistic therapy? (p. 519)
Humanistic therapies are difficult to evaluate scientifically, most outcome studies rely on self-reports, and research on specific therapeutic techniques has had mixed results.

III. GROUP, FAMILY, AND MARITAL THERAPIES
15.12 Discuss group, self-help, family, and marital therapies. (p. 521)
In **group therapy**, a number of people (usually 8 to 10) meet together to work toward therapeutic goals. A variation on group therapy is the **self-help group** (like Alcoholics Anonymous), which is not guided by a professional. Although group members do not have the same level of individual attention, group therapy has other advantages: It is less expensive, and it provides group support, insight and information, and opportunities for behavior rehearsal.

The primary aim of marital and family therapy is to change maladaptive family interaction patterns. Because a family is a system of interdependent parts, the problem of any one member unavoidably affects all the others.

IV. BEHAVIOR THERAPIES
15.13 What is behavior therapy? (p. 524)
Behavior therapies use learning principles to change maladaptive behaviors.

15.14 Describe how classical conditioning, operant conditioning, and observational learning are used in behavior therapy. (p. 524)
Classical conditioning principles are used to change faulty associations. In **systematic desensitization,** the client replaces anxiety with relaxation, and in **aversion therapy,** an aversive stimulus is paired with a maladaptive behavior. Shaping, reinforcement, and punishment are behavioral therapy techniques based on operant conditioning principles. Observational learning techniques often include **modeling therapy,** which is based on acquisition of skills or behaviors through observation.

15.15 What are the key successes and criticisms of behavior therapy? (p. 527)
Behavior therapies have been successful with a number of psychological disorders. But they are also criticized for possible lack of generalizability and the questionable ethics of attempting to control behavior.

V. BIOMEDICAL THERAPIES
15.16 Define biomedical therapy. (p. 528)
Biomedical therapies use biological techniques to relieve psychological disorders.

15.17 Discuss psychopharmacology, electroconvulsive therapy (ECT), and psychosurgery. (p. 528)
Psychopharmacology, or treatment with drugs, is the most common biomedical therapy. **Antianxiety drugs** (Valium, Ativan) are used to treat anxiety disorders, **antipsychotic drugs** (Thorazine, Haldol) treat the symptoms of schizophrenia, **antidepressants** (Prozac, Effexor) treat depression, and mood stabilizers (lithium) can stabilize patients with bipolar disorder. Although drug therapy has been responsible for major improvements in many disorders, there are also problems with dosage levels, side effects, and patient cooperation.

Electroconvulsive therapy (ECT) is used primarily to relieve serious depression when medication has not worked, but it is risky and considered a treatment of last resort. **Psychosurgeries,** such as a **lobotomy,** have been used in the past but are rarely used today.

15.18 What are the major contributions and criticisms of biomedical therapy? (p. 530)
Drug therapy is enormously beneficial, but it also has several problems. For example, it offers symptoms relief, but few "cures," patients often stop medications once symptoms are relieved, patients may become drug dependent, and little is known about drug interactions. In addition, there are the potentially dangerous side effects and possible over use. ECT and psychosurgery are both controversial and are generally used as a last resort.

VI. THERAPY AND CRITICAL THINKING
15.19 Identify the five most common goals of therapy, and discuss the eclectic approach. (p. 532)
There arc numerous forms of therapy, but they all focus treatment on five basic areas of disturbance — thoughts, emotions, behaviors, interpersonal and life situations, and biomedical problems. Many therapists take an **eclectic approach** and combine techniques from various theories.

15.20 Identify the six key types of mental health professionals. (p. 533)
Clinical psychologists, counseling psychologists, psychiatrists, psychiatric nurses, psychiatric social workers, and school psychologists are the six most common types of mental health professionals.

15.21 Briefly summarize the major effects of mental disorders, like PTSD, on the family. (p. 534)
Mental disorders, like PTSD, and their treatment have been studied extensively, but we often overlook the effects on the family who develop their own forms of pathology. The entire family also suffers from increased rates of divorce, substance abuse, unemployment, and other life problems. Support, education, and intervention should be provided for all family members.

15.22 Describe the major similarities and differences in therapy across cultures. (p. 535)
Therapies in all cultures share six culturally universal features: naming a problem, qualities of the therapist, establishing credibility, placing the problems in a familiar framework, applying techniques to bring relief, and a special time and place. Important cultural differences in therapies also exist. For example, therapies in individualistic cultures emphasize the self and control over one's life, whereas therapies in collectivist cultures emphasize interdependence. Japan's Naikan therapy is a good example of a collectivist culture's therapy.

15.23 What are the unique concerns of women in therapy? (p. 536)

Therapists must take five considerations into account when treating women clients: higher rate of diagnosis and treatment of mental disorders, stresses of poverty, stresses of multiple roles, stresses of aging, and violence against women.

15.24 Discuss problems with involuntary commitment and deinstitutionalization. (p. 537)
People believed to be mentally ill and dangerous to themselves or others can be involuntarily committed to mental hospitals for diagnosis and treatment. Abuses of involuntary commitments and other problems associated with state mental hospitals have led many states to practice *deinstitutionalization* — discharging as many patients as possible and discouraging admissions. Community services such as community mental health (CMH) centers try to cope with the problems of deinstitutionalization.

15.25 Is therapy effective, and how can we find a good therapist? (p. 538)
Research on the effectiveness of psychotherapy has found that 40 to 80 percent of those who receive treatment are better off than those who do not receive treatment. When searching for a good therapist, it's good to "shop around," and to consult your psychology instructor or college counselors for referrals. If you're in a crisis, get immediate help through hospital emergency rooms or telephone hotlines.

15.26 Briefly summarize how to deal with someone who's seriously depressed. (p. 539)
When talking to someone who's clinically depressed, you should not trivialize the disease, be a cheerleader/"fix-it," or equate it with normal down times. Instead, you should educate yourself, be Rogerian, and get help!

SELF-TESTS (Review & wRite)

Completing the following self-tests will provide immediate feedback on how well you have mastered the material. In the labeling exercises, *crossword puzzle*, and *fill-in exercises*, write the appropriate word or words in the blank spaces. The *matching exercise* requires you to match the terms in one column to their correct definitions in the other. For the *multiple-choice questions* in Practice Tests I and II, circle or underline the correct answer. If you are unsure of any answer, mark the item, and then go back to the text for further review. Correct answers are provided in Appendix A at the end of this study guide.

CROSSWORD PUZZLE FOR CHAPTER 15

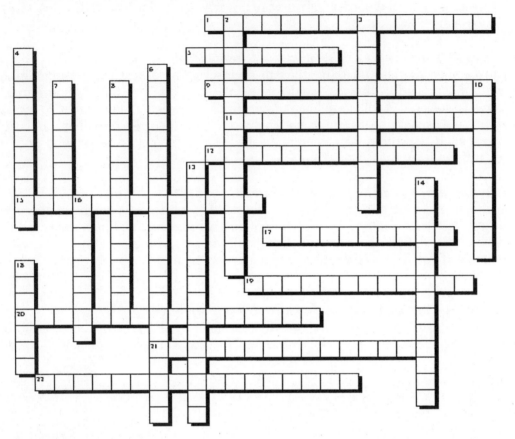

ACROSS

1 A group of techniques based on learning principles that are used to change maladaptive behaviors.

5 Internal dialogue; the things people say to themselves when they interpret events.

9 According to Rogers, the ability to listen with total attention to what another is saying. This involves reflecting, paraphrasing, and clarifying what the person says and means.

11 A psychoanalyst's explanation of a patient's free associations, dreams, resistance, and transference.

12 A psychological treatment that attempts to change maladaptive interaction patterns among members of a family.

15 Operative procedures on the brain designed to relieve severe mental symptoms that have not responded to other forms of treatment.

17 In psychoanalysis, the person's inability to discuss or reveal certain memories.

19 Treatment method in which multiple people meet together to work toward therapeutic goals.

20 Medications used to treat anxiety disorders.

21 Behavior therapy technique that pairs an aversive (unpleasant) stimulus with a maladaptive behavior.

22 Therapy involving physiological interventions to reduce symptoms associated with psychological disorders.

DOWN

2 An approach to therapy in which the therapist combines techniques from various theories to find the appropriate treatment for the client.

3 In psychoanalysis, the person may displace unconscious thoughts and feelings from past relationships onto new relationships.

4 A form of psychopharmacology, which involves using drugs to relieve or suppress the symptoms of psychological disturbances.

6 The policy of discharging as many people as possible from state hospitals and discouraging admissions.

7 A brain operation in which the nerve pathways between the frontal lobes and the thalamus and hypothalamus are cut in hopes of treating psychological disorders.

8 In psychoanalysis, reporting whatever comes to mind without monitoring its contents.

10 In Rogerian terms, authenticity or congruence; the awareness of one's true inner thoughts and feelings and being able to share them honestly with others.

13 Therapy that focuses on faulty thought processes and beliefs to treat problem behaviors.

14 Freudian therapy that seeks to bring unconscious conflicts into consciousness.

16 In psychoanalytic theory, the release of tension and anxiety through the reliving of a traumatic incident.

18 In Rogerian terms, an insightful awareness and ability to share another person's inner experience.

FILL-IN EXERCISES

1. _____ is defined as techniques employed to improve psychological functioning and promote adjustment to life (p. 510).

2. Freud's system of therapy that seeks to bring _____ conflicts into conscious awareness is known as _____ (p. 510).

3. The five major techniques of psychoanalysis are _____, _____, _____, _____, and _____ (p. 511).

4. In modern _____ therapy, treatment is briefer, face to face, and more directive (p. 512).

5. Ellis's _____ therapy works to eliminate emotional problems through rational examination of irrational beliefs (pp. 514-515).

6. Beck's _____ therapy has been successful in the treatment of depression and several other disorders (pp. 515-517).

7. _____ therapies assume problems develop from a blockage or disruption of normal growth potential (p. 518).

8. _____ is based on learning principles, which are used to change maladaptive behaviors (p. 524).

9. _____ is a gradual process of extinguishing a learned fear by associating a hierarchy of fear-evoking stimuli with deep relaxation (p. 524).

10. When other treatments have failed, ECT is occasionally used to treat severe _____ (p. 530).

MATCHING EXERCISES

Column A   Column B

a. Carl Rogers   1.____ Internal dialogue when interpreting events
b. Self-talk   2.____ Alcoholics Anonymous
c. Family Therapy   3.____ Reporting whatever comes to mind without censoring
d. Group Therapy   4.____ Clients watch and imitate positive role models
e. Self-Help Group   5.____ Relieve symptoms of schizophrenia
f. ECT   6.____ Client-centered therapy to facilitate personal growth
g. Aversion Therapy   7.____ Attempts to change maladaptive family interactions
h. Modeling Therapy   8.____ People meet together to work toward therapeutic goals
i. Free Association   9.____ Treatment for severe depression when medication fails
j. Antipsychotic Drugs   10.____ Aversive stimulus is paired with maladaptive behavior

PRACTICE TEST I

1. A collection of techniques designed to improve psychological functioning and promote adjustment to life is called _____. In contrast, _____ therapies use biological interventions to treat psychological disorders.
    a. Behavior therapy; drug
    b. Psychoanalysis; psychopharmacology
    c. Psychotherapy; biomedical
    d. None of these options

2. _____ is a psychoanalytic technique known as free association.
    a. Reporting whatever comes to mind without self-censorship
    b. Release of tensions and anxieties
    c. Attachment process that occurs between patient and therapist
    d. Therapist's educated explanations for a patient's behavior

3. In psychoanalytic dream interpretation, the symbolic meaning of dreams are known as the _____ content.
    a. manifest
    b. latent
    c. subconscious
    d. transference

4. Dream analysis and free association are psychoanalytic therapy techniques that are used to _____.
    a. uncover unconscious conflicts
    b. keep unconscious conflicts out of awareness
    c. restructure the self-concept
    d. countercondition behavior

5. In _____, mistaken beliefs or misconceptions are actively disputed.
    a. client-centered therapy
    b. psychoanalysis
    c. rational-emotive behavior therapy (REBT)
    d. systematic desensitization

6. According to rational-emotive behavior therapy (REBT), a consequence such as depression or anxiety occurs because of a(n) _____.
    a. activating experience
    b. stimulus event
    c. conditioning experience
    d. irrational belief

7. A _____ therapist emphasizes the importance of empathy, unconditional positive regard, genuineness, and active listening.
    a. psychodynamic
    b. phenomenological behavior
    c. cognitive-behavior
    d. client-centered

8. Sharing another person's inner experience is known as _____.
   a. unconditional positive regard
   b. genuineness
   c. empathy
   d. sympathy

9. Which of the following is **NOT** one of the usual benefits of group therapy?
   a. support from others with similar problems
   b. feedback and information
   c. opportunities for behavioral rehearsal
   d. group sympathy for patient complaints

10. A family therapist believes that the family's scapegoat _____.
    a. should be treated first
    b. is being blamed for deeper family issues
    c. requires hospitalization
    d. is the reason for the family's dysfunction

11. _____ pairs relaxation with a graduated hierarchy of anxiety-producing situations to extinguish the anxiety.
    a. Classical conditioning
    b. Shaping
    c. Systematic desensitization
    d. Maslow's pyramid training

12. Aversion therapy applies the principle of _____ by pairing an unpleasant stimulus with a maladaptive behavior to extinguish the behavior.
    a. classical conditioning
    b. operant conditioning
    c. positive reinforcement
    d. negative punishment

13. Therapists have successfully used _____ to help children with autism develop their language skills.
    a. shaping
    b. aversion therapy
    c. assertiveness training
    d. token economies

14. Asking clients with snake phobias to watch other (nonphobic) people handle snakes is an example of _____ therapy.
    a. time out
    b. aversion
    c. modeling
    d. unethical

15. _____ create feelings of tranquility and relaxation, while also decreasing over-arousal in the brain.
    a. ECT treatments
    b. Antianxiety drugs
    c. Trephining
    d. all of the above

16. How do traditional antipsychotic drugs work?
    a. They sedate the patient.
    b. They appear to decrease activity at the dopamine synapses.
    c. They lower the parasympathetic activity of the brain.
    d. All of these options

17. ECT is now used primarily in the treatment of _____.
    a. depression
    b. anxiety
    c. phobias
    d. schizophrenia

18. The original form of psychosurgery developed by Egaz Moniz disconnected the _____ lobes from the lower brain centers.
    a. occipital
    b. parietal
    c. temporal
    d. frontal

19. Tardive dyskinesia is thought to be a side effect of treatment with _____ medication.
    a. mood-altering
    b. psychoactive
    c. antianxiety
    d. antipsychotic

20. The policy of discharging as many people as possible from state hospitals and discouraging admissions is known as _____.
    a. transference
    b. repetitive transcranial magnetic stimulation (rTMS)
    c. deinstitutionalization
    d. none of these options

PRACTICE TEST II

1. A Freudian therapy designed to bring unconscious conflicts into consciousness is known as _____.
    a. electroconvulsive therapy
    b. psychoanalysis
    c. psychotherapy
    d. all of these options

2. Transference is the process of _____.
    a. changing therapists
    b. changing therapeutic techniques or strategies
    c. displacing associations from past relationships onto new relationships
    d. replacing maladaptive patterns with adaptive ones

3. According to some critics, traditional psychoanalysis is appropriate only for _____ clients.
    a. young and attractive
    b. verbal
    c. intelligent and successful
    d. YAVIS

4. If you are unhappy because you believe you must be perfect or must get straight A's, Ellis might point out the source of your unhappiness by saying, "You're _____."
    a. transferring earlier relationships
    b. an overachiever
    c. lacking unconditional positive regard
    d. none of these options

5. _____ believes selective perception and other distorted thinking patterns cause depression.
    a. Bandura
    b. Beck
    c. Rogers
    d. Perls

6. Cognitive therapy is effective for treating _____.
    a. depression
    b. anxiety
    c. eating and substance-related disorders
    d. all of these options

7. The client is responsible for discovering his or her own maladaptive patterns in _____ therapy.
    a. biomedical
    b. psychoanalytic
    c. client-centered
    d. all of these options

8. A client-centered therapist would not say, "You're right about that" because _____.
    a. it wouldn't be genuine
    b. the client is seldom right about his or her unconscious mind
    c. it implies that the therapist is judging the client
    d. it is not empathic

9. Reflecting back or paraphrasing what the client is saying is a part of _____.
    a. gestalt directness
    b. psychoanalytic transference
    c. cognitive restructuring
    d. active listening

10. A key difference between a self-help group and group therapy is that the former _____.
    a. does not deal with psychological problems
    b. provides more understanding and support
    c. does not have a professional leader
    d. all of these options

11. According to William Menninger, mental health problems do not affect three or four out of five persons, but _____.
    a. the vast majority of people
    b. also their families
    c. also the therapist
    d. one out of one

12. Maladaptive behaviors are most likely to be the focus in _____.
    a. cognitive therapy
    b. biomedical therapy
    c. psychoanalysis
    d. behavior therapy

13. Relaxation training is an important component in _____.
    a. systematic desensitization
    b. aversion conditioning
    c. time out training
    d. a token economy

14. People with phobias, delinquent behaviors, and eating disorders have been treated successfully with _____ therapy.
    a. electroconvulsive shock
    b. drug
    c. psychoanalytic
    d. behavior

15. To treat schizophrenia, therapists most commonly use _____ drugs.antidepressaant
    a. antipsychotic
    b. antianxiety
    c. none of the above

16. Someone with severe depression and suicidal ideation that has not been successfully managed with other treatment methods might require _____.
    a. a frontal lobotomy
    b. ECT
    c. combination drug and modeling therapy
    d. none of these options

17. When therapists combine techniques from various therapies, they are said to be using _____.
    a. psychosynthetic therapy
    b. biomedical therapy
    c. managed care
    d. an eclectic approach

18. Which of the following is **NOT** one of the five major concerns of women and psychotherapy?
    a. rates of diagnosis
    b. disturbed body image
    c. violence
    d. stresses of poverty

19. In emergency situations, a therapist can authorize temporary, involuntary commitment of a client for _____.
    a. 12 to 24 hours
    b. 24 to 72 hours
    c. as long as it takes for the client to improve
    d. none of these options

20. Which of the following is recommended for talking to someone who is seriously depressed
    a. Don't trivialize the disease.
    b. Don't be a cheerleader or a Mr. or Ms. Fix-it.
    c. Don't equate normal, everyday "down times" with clinical depression
    d. all of these options

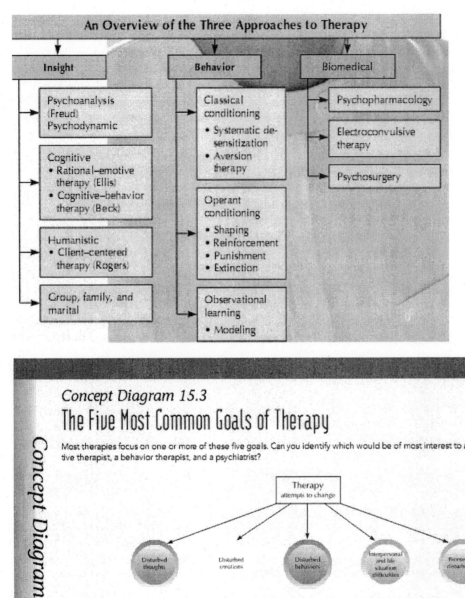

An Overview of the Three Approaches to Therapy

Insight	Behavior	Biomedical
Psychoanalysis (Freud) Psychodynamic	Classical conditioning • Systematic de-sensitization • Aversion therapy	Psychopharmacology
Cognitive • Rational–emotive therapy (Ellis) • Cognitive–behavior therapy (Beck)	Operant conditioning • Shaping • Reinforcement • Punishment • Extinction	Electroconvulsive therapy
Humanistic • Client-centered therapy (Rogers)		Psychosurgery
Group, family, and marital	Observational learning • Modeling	

Concept Diagram 15.3

The Five Most Common Goals of Therapy

Most therapies focus on one or more of these five goals. Can you identify which would be of most interest to a psychoanalyst, a cognitive therapist, a behavior therapist, and a psychiatrist?

Therapy attempts to change

Disturbed thoughts   Disturbed emotions   Disturbed behaviors   Interpersonal and life situation difficulties   Biomedical disturbances

Disturbed thoughts. Therapists work to change faulty or destructive thoughts, provide new ideas or information, and guide individuals toward finding solutions to problems.

Disturbed emotions. Therapists help clients understand and control their emotions and relieve their emotional discomfort.

Disturbed behaviors. Therapists help clients eliminate troublesome behaviors and guide them toward more effective lives.

Interpersonal and life situation difficulties. Therapists help clients improve their relationships with others and avoid or minimize sources of stress in their lives.

Biomedical disturbances. Therapists work to relieve biological disruptions that directly cause or contribute to psychological difficulties (for example, chemical imbalances that lead to depression).

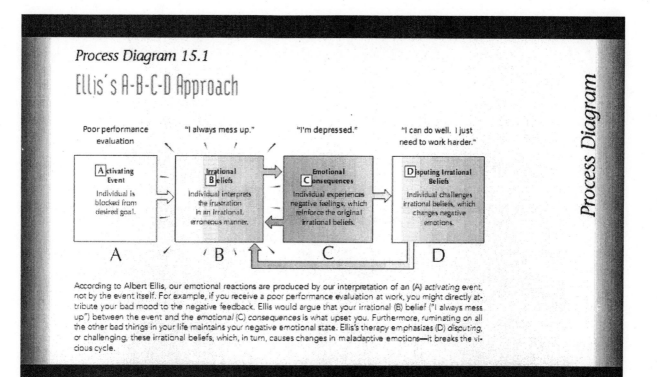

Process Diagram 15.1

Ellis's A-B-C-D Approach

Poor performance evaluation

"I always mess up."

"I'm depressed."

"I can do well. I just need to work harder."

Activating Event
Individual is blocked from desired goal.

Irrational **B**eliefs
Individual interprets the frustration in an irrational, erroneous manner.

Emotional **C**onsequences
Individual experiences negative feelings, which reinforce the original irrational beliefs.

Disputing Irrational Beliefs
Individual challenges irrational beliefs, which changes negative emotions.

A   B   C   D

Process Diagram

According to Albert Ellis, our emotional reactions are produced by our interpretation of an (A) *activating event*, not by the event itself. For example, if you receive a poor performance evaluation at work, you might directly attribute your bad mood to the negative feedback. Ellis would argue that your irrational (B) belief ("I always mess up") between the event and the *emotional* (C) *consequences* is what upset you. Furthermore, ruminating on all the other bad things in your life maintains your negative emotional state. Ellis's therapy emphasizes (D) *disputing*, or challenging, these irrational beliefs, which, in turn, causes changes in maladaptive emotions—it breaks the vicious cycle.

Process Diagram 15.2

Overcoming Maladaptive Behaviors — Phobias and Alcoholism

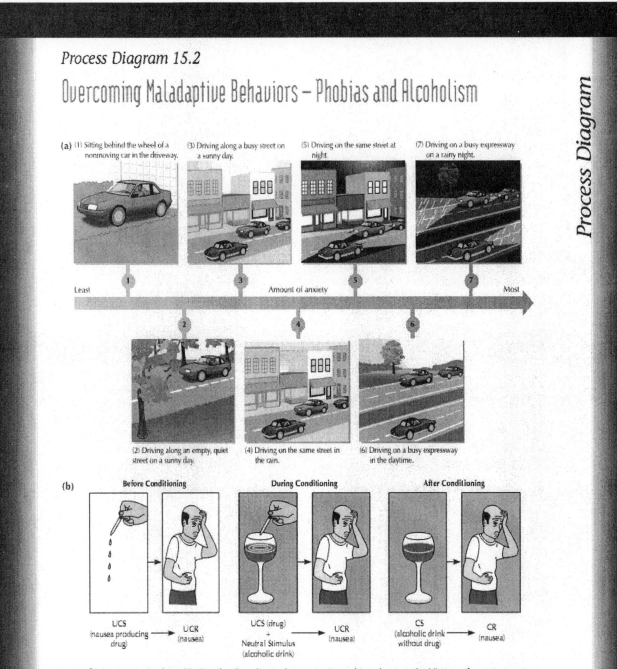

(a) (1) Sitting behind the wheel of a nonmoving car in the driveway.

(3) Driving along a busy street on a sunny day.

(5) Driving on the same street at night.

(7) Driving on a busy expressway on a rainy night.

Least   1   3   Amount of anxiety   5   7   Most

2   4   6

(2) Driving along an empty, quiet street on a sunny day.

(4) Driving on the same street in the rain.

(6) Driving on a busy expressway in the daytime.

(b)

Before Conditioning

UCS (nausea producing drug) → UCR (nausea)

During Conditioning

UCS (drug) + Neutral Stimulus (alcoholic drink) → UCR (nausea)

After Conditioning

CS (alcoholic drink without drug) → CR (nausea)

(a) *During systematic desensitization*, the client begins by constructing a hierarchy, or ranked listing, of anxiety-arousing images or situations starting with one that produces very little anxiety and escalating to those that arouse extreme anxiety. To extinguish a driving phobia, the patient begins with images of actually sitting behind the wheel of a nonmoving car and ends with driving on a busy expressway.

(b) *Aversion therapy for alcoholism* is based on classical conditioning. A nausea-producing drug (Antabuse) is paired with alcohol to create an aversion (dislike) for drinking.

Process Diagram

Concept Diagram 15.2

Drug Treatments for Psychological Disorders

Concept Diagram

Type of Drug (Chemical Group)	Psychological Disorder	Generic Name	Brand Name
Antianxiety drugs (Benzodiazepines)	Anxiety disorders	Alprazolam Diazepam Lorazepam	Xanax Valium Ativan
Antipsychotic drugs (Phenothiazines Butyrophenones Atypical antipsychotics)	Schizophrenia and bipolar disorders	Chlorpromazine Fluphenazine Thioridazine Haloperidol Clozapine Resperidone Quetiapine	Thorazine Prolixin Mellaril Haldol Clozaril Risperdal Seroquel
Mood stabilizer drugs (Antimanic)	Bipolar disorder	Lithium carbonate Carbamazepine	Eskalith CR Lithobid Tegretol
Antidepressant drugs (Tricyclic antidepressants Monoamine oxidase inhibitors (MAOIs) Selective serotonin reuptake inhibitors (SSRIs) Serotonin and norepinephrine reuptake inhibitors (SNRIs) Atypical antidepressants)	Depressive disorders	Imipramine Amitriptyline Phenelzine Paroxetine Fluoxetine Venlafaxine Duloxetine Bupropion	Tofranil Elavil Nardil Paxil Prozac Effexor Cymbalta Wellbutrin

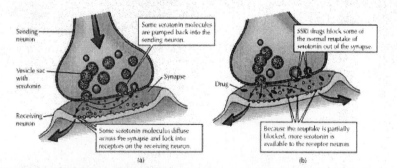

How Prozac and other SSRI antidepressants work (a) Under normal conditions, a nerve impulse (or action potential) travels down the axon to the terminal buttons of a sending neuron. If the vesicle sac of this particular neuron contains the neurotransmitter serotonin, the action potential will trigger its release. Some of the serotonin will travel across the synapse and lock into the receptors on the receiving neuron. Excess serotonin within the synapse will be pumped back up into the sending neuron for storage (the "serotonin reuptake"). (b) When selective serotonin reuptake inhibitors (SSRIs), like Prozac, are taken to treat depression and other disorders, they block the normal reuptake of excess serontonin that lingers in the synaptic gap after being released from the sending neuron. This leaves more serotonin molecules free to stimulate receptors on the receiving neuron, which enhances its mood lifting effects.

Chapter 15 Visual Summary

Insight Therapies

Description/Major Goals

- **Psychoanalysis/psychodynamic therapies:** Bring unconscious conflicts into conscious awareness.

- **Cognitive therapies:** Analyze faulty thought processes, beliefs, and negative **self-talk**, and change these destructive thoughts with **cognitive restructuring**. **Cognitive-behavior therapy:** Focuses on changing faulty thoughts and behaviors.

- **Humanistic therapies:** Work to facilitate personal growth.

- **Group, family, and marital therapies:** Several clients meet with one or more therapists to resolve personal problems.

Techniques/Methods

Five major techniques:
- **Free association**
- **Dream analysis**
- **Resistance**
- **Transference**
- **Interpretation**

Ellis's **rational-emotive behavior therapy (REBT)** replaces irrational beliefs with rational beliefs and accurate perceptions of the world.
Beck's **cognitive therapy** emphasizes change in both thought processes and behavior.

Rogers's **client-centered therapy** offers **empathy, unconditional positive regard, genuineness,** and **active listening** to facilitate personal growth.

Provide group support, feedback, information, and opportunities for behavior-rehearsal.
- **Self-help groups** (like Alcoholics Anonymous) are sometimes considered group therapy, but professional therapists do not conduct them.
- **Family therapies:** Work to change maladaptive family interaction patterns.

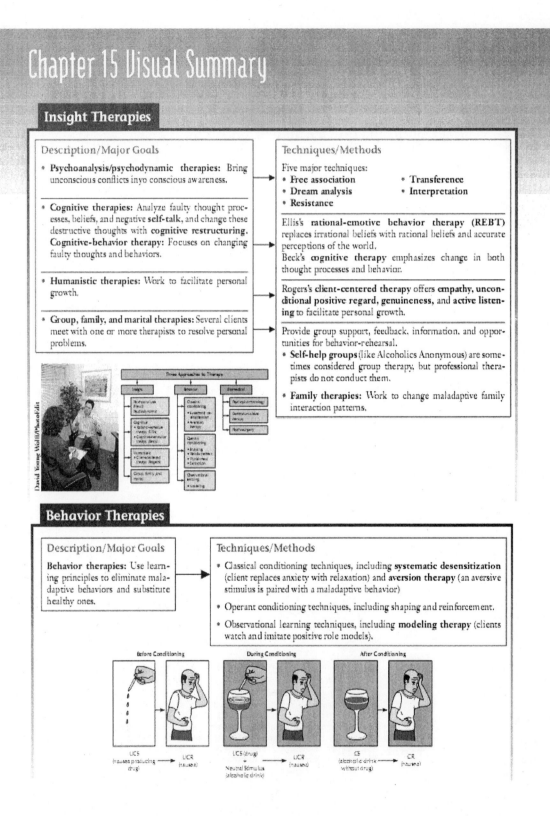

Behavior Therapies

Description/Major Goals

Behavior therapies: Use learning principles to eliminate maladaptive behaviors and substitute healthy ones.

Techniques/Methods

- Classical conditioning techniques, including **systematic desensitization** (client replaces anxiety with relaxation) and **aversion therapy** (an aversive stimulus is paired with a maladaptive behavior)

- Operant conditioning techniques, including shaping and reinforcement.

- Observational learning techniques, including **modeling therapy** (clients watch and imitate positive role models).

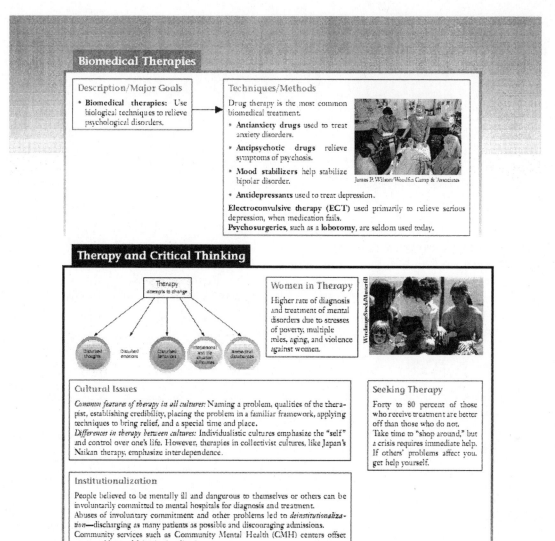

Biomedical Therapies

Description/Major Goals

* **Biomedical therapies:** Use biological techniques to relieve psychological disorders.

Techniques/Methods

Drug therapy is the most common biomedical treatment.

* **Antianxiety drugs** used to treat anxiety disorders.
* **Antipsychotic drugs** relieve symptoms of psychosis.
* **Mood stabilizers** help stabilize bipolar disorder.
* **Antidepressants** used to treat depression.

Electroconvulsive therapy (ECT) used primarily to relieve serious depression, when medication fails.
Psychosurgeries, such as a **lobotomy,** are seldom used today.

James P. Wilson/Woodfin Camp & Associates

Therapy and Critical Thinking

Therapy
attempts to change

Disturbed thoughts

Disturbed emotions

Disturbed behaviors

Interpersonal and life situation difficulties

Biomedical disturbances

Women in Therapy

Higher rate of diagnosis and treatment of mental disorders due to stresses of poverty, multiple roles, aging, and violence against women.

Wirelmage/Stock/Masterfil

Cultural Issues

Common features of therapy in all cultures: Naming a problem, qualities of the therapist, establishing credibility, placing the problem in a familiar framework, applying techniques to bring relief, and a special time and place.
Differences in therapy between cultures: Individualistic cultures emphasize the "self" and control over one's life. However, therapies in collectivist cultures, like Japan's Naikan therapy, emphasize interdependence.

Seeking Therapy

Forty to 80 percent of those who receive treatment are better off than those who do not.
Take time to "shop around," but a crisis requires immediate help. If others' problems affect you, get help yourself.

Institutionalization

People believed to be mentally ill and dangerous to themselves or others can be involuntarily committed to mental hospitals for diagnosis and treatment.
Abuses of involuntary commitment and other problems led to *deinstitutionalization*—discharging as many patients as possible and discouraging admissions.
Community services such as Community Mental Health (CMH) centers offset some problems of deinstitutionalization.

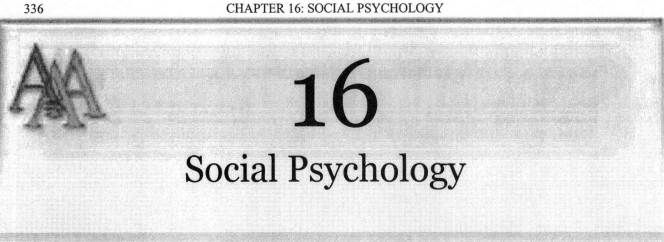

16
Social Psychology

OUTLINE SQ4R (Survey, Question, Read, Recite, Review, & wRite)

This outline section incorporates all six steps in the well-researched SQ4R method of learning. Begin by surveying the list of chapter topics in the left column. This "big picture" will help focus and guide your attention while you read. As you read through the chapter, briefly summarize each section in your own words in the space to the right. Also write down any *questions* that come to mind. Surveying, Questioning, Reading, Reciting, Reviewing, and wRiting are the foundation of the SQ4R method and an invaluable form of active learning. They also make your reading time more enjoyable and efficient! One thorough, focused SQ4R reading of a chapter is far better than several passive readings.

TOPIC	**NOTES**

I. OUR THOUGHTS ABOUT OTHERS

   A. Attribution

   B. Attitudes

II. OUR FEELINGS ABOUT OTHERS

   A. Prejudice and Discrimination

   B. Interpersonal Attraction

   Gender & Cultural Diversity: Is Beauty in the Eye of the Beholder?

   Psychology at Work: The Art and Science of Flirting

III. OUR ACTIONS TOWARD OTHERS

A. Social Influence

B. Group Processes

C. Aggression

D. Altruism

*Critical Thinking/Active Learning: When
    And Why Do We Help?*

IV. APPLYING SOCIAL PSYCHOLOGY TO SOCIAL PROBLEMS

A. Reducing Prejudice and Discrimination

*Research Highlight: Understanding
    Implicit Biases*

B. Overcoming Destructive Obedience

LEARNING OBJECTIVES (Read, Recite, Review, & wRite)

In addition to the work you did in the Outline above, you can significantly improve your performance on exams by focusing on the following learning objectives. While reading the chapter or reviewing for exams, check your understanding by stopping periodically to *recite* (or repeat in your own words) and *writing* down your answers on a separate sheet. [Page numbers correspond to Chapter 16 in *Psychology in Action* (9e).]

16.1 What is social psychology? (p. 544)

16.2 Describe the process of attribution and its two key errors. (p. 546)

16.3 Describe how culture affects attributional biases. (p. 548)

16.4 Define attitude and identify its three key components. (p. 548)

16.5 What is cognitive dissonance, how does it change attitudes, and how does culture affect it? (p. 548)

16.6 Define prejudice, identify its three key components, and differentiate between prejudice and discrimination. (p. 551)

16.7 Discuss the five major sources of prejudice and discrimination. (p. 551)

16.8 What are the three key factors in attraction? (p. 553)

16.9 Describe cultural and historical similarities and differences in judgments of attractiveness. (p. 554)

16.10 Discuss scientific research on flirting. (p. 555)

16.11 Differentiate between romantic and companionate love, and discuss problems with romantic love. (p. 557)

16.12 Define conformity, and explain the three factors that contribute to this behavior. (p. 560)

16.13 Define obedience and describe Milgram's classic study. (p. 561)

16.14 Identify the four key factors in obedience. (p. 562)

16.15 Discuss the importance of roles and deindividuation in Zimbardo's Stanford prison study. (p. 564)

16.16 How do group polarization and groupthink affect group decision making? (p. 566)

16.17 Define aggression, and identify the biological and psychosocial factors that contribute to its expression. (p. 568)

16.18 Describe three approaches to reducing aggression. (p. 569)

16.19 Define altruism, and describe the three models that attempt to explain it. (p. 570)

16.20 Describe Latane and Darley's decision-making model, and other factors that help explain why we don't help. (p. 570)

16.21 List four major approaches useful for reducing prejudice and discrimination. (p. 573)

16.22 Describe recent research on implicit biases. (p. 575)

16.23 Identify six ways to reduce destructive obedience. (p. 577)

KEY TERMS (Review & wRite)

Like other survey courses, introductory psychology is filled with a "wealth" of new and unfamiliar terminology. To do well on exams, you must master this new language! Writing a brief definition of each term in the space provided and carefully reviewing them before exams will significantly improve your course grade.

Aggression: _____

_____

Altruism: _____

_____

Attitude: _____

_____

Attribution: _____

_____

Cognitive Dissonance: _____

_____

Companionate Love: _____

_____

Conformity: _____

_____

Deindividuation: _____

_____

Diffusion of Responsibility: _____

_____

Discrimination: _____

_____

Egoistic Model: _____

_____

Empathy-Altruism Hypothesis: _____

_____

Foot-in-the-Door Technique: _____

_____

Frustration-Aggression Hypothesis: _____

_____

Fundamental Attribution Error: _____

_____

Group Polarization: _____

_____

Groupthink: _____

_____

Implicit Bias: _____

_____

Informational Social Influence: _____

_____

Ingroup Favoritism: _____

_____

Interpersonal Attraction: _____

_____

Just-World Phenomenon: _____

_____

Need Compatibility: _____

_____

Need Complementarity: _____

_____

Norm: _____

_____

Normative Social Influence: _____

_____

Obedience: _____

_____

Outgroup Homogeneity Effect: _____

_____

Prejudice: _____

_____

Proximity: _____

_____

Reference Groups: _____

_____

Romantic Love: _____

_____

Saliency Bias: _____

_____

Self-Serving Bias: _____

_____

Social Psychology: _____

_____

Stereotype: _____

_____

ACTIVE LEARNING EXERCISES

True mastery of information requires you to be an ACTIVE learner. Completing the following active learning exercises will improve your understanding of the chapter material and greatly improve your performance on exams. Answers to some exercises appear in Appendix A at the end of this study guide.

ACTIVE LEARNING EXERCISE I *Exploring Your Attitudes*

In the space next to each issue, place a number (1 to 5) in the first space that indicates your CURRENT attitude, and then enter a number (1 to 5) in the space to the right that indicates your PAST attitude (five to ten years ago). 1 = Strongly support, 2 = Mildly support, 3 = Neutral, 4 = Mildly oppose, 5 = Strongly oppose

	CURRENT	PAST
Drinking and driving	_____	_____
Gun control	_____	_____
Abortion	_____	_____

Smoking in public places   _____   _____

Divorce   _____   _____

1. Circle the top two issues you scored "highest" (either a 1 or 5). Briefly, state your attitudes toward each of these issues. How did these attitudes develop? Through direct experience, indirect observation, or what? Can you remember important experiences or significant individuals that influenced these attitudes? Try to identify the three components of each of your three attitudes (cognitive, affective, and behavioral).

_____

_____

_____

2. Now compare your CURRENT attitudes to those of your PAST. Which attitudes were the most subject to change? Why? On what issues were you most resistant to change? How would you explain this?

_____

_____

_____

3. Cognitive dissonance theory finds "changing behavior changes attitudes." Using this theory, how would you design a program to change an undesirable attitude (in yourself and others)?

_____

_____

_____

ACTIVE LEARNING EXERCISE II *Applying Knowledge to New Situations*

A critical thinker is able to take existing information and apply that knowledge to new or future situations. To increase your awareness of various forms of prejudice on your college campus, ask a member of the other sex to be your partner in the following exercise:

Visit one set of both male and female bathrooms in three separate buildings on your campus (e.g., the art department, business department, and psychology department). Record your observations below:

1. Did you notice any graffiti directed at certain minority groups?
2. Was there a difference between the male and female prejudices (as expressed by the graffiti)?
3. Did you notice a difference between the three buildings in their "graffiti prejudice?"
4. Did you gain new insights into the causes of and treatment of prejudice?

CHAPTER OVERVIEW (Review)

The following chapter overview provides a narrative overview of the main topics covered in the chapter. Like the *Visual Summary* found at the end of each chapter in the text, this narrative summary provides a final opportunity to *review* chapter material.

I. OUR THOUGHTS ABOUT OTHERS

16.1 What is social psychology? (p. 544)
Social psychology is the study of how others influence our thoughts, feelings, and actions.

16.2 Describe the process of attribution and its two key errors. (p. 546)
Attribution is the process of explaining the causes of behaviors or events. We do this by determining whether actions resulted from internal, dispositional factors (internal traits and motives) or external, situational factors (the situation). Attribution is subject to several forms of error and bias. The **fundamental attribution error (FAE)** is the tendency to overestimate internal, personality influences and underestimates external, situational factors when judging the behavior of others. When we explain our own behavior, however, we tend to attribute positive outcomes to internal factors and negative outcomes to external causes **(self-serving bias).**

16.3 Describe how culture affects attributional biases. (p. 548)
Collectivistic cultures, like China, are less likely to make the fundamental attribution error (FAE) and the self-serving bias because they focus on interdependence and collective responsibility. In contrast, individualistic cultures, like the United States, emphasize independence and personal responsibility.

16.4 Define attitude and identify its three key components. (p. 548)
Attitudes are learned predispositions to respond cognitively, affectively, and behaviorally toward a particular object. Three components of all attitudes are the *cognitive* responses (thoughts and beliefs), *affective* responses (feelings), and *behavioral* tendencies (predispositions to actions).

16.5 What is cognitive dissonance, how does it change attitudes, and how does culture affect it? (p. 548)
Cognitive dissonance is a feeling of discomfort caused by a discrepancy between an attitude and a behavior or between two competing attitudes. This mismatch and resulting tension motivate us to change our attitude or behavior to reduce the tension and restore balance (cognitive consonance). Individualistic cultures experience more cognitive dissonance than collectivistic cultures because our emphasis on independence and personal responsibility creates more tension when our attitudes are in conflict.

II. OUR FEELINGS ABOUT OTHERS

16.6 Define prejudice, identify its three key components, and differentiate between prejudice and discrimination. (p. 551)
Prejudice is a learned, generally negative attitude directed toward specific people solely because of their membership in a specific group. It contains all three components of attitudes --*cognitive, affective,* and *behavioral.* (The cognitive component is also known as **stereotypes** and the behavioral component is called **discrimination**.) Discrimination is not the same as prejudice. It

refers to the actual negative behavior directed at members of a group. People do not always act on their prejudices.

16.7 Discuss the five major sources of prejudice and discrimination. (p. 551)
The five major sources of prejudice are *learning* (classical and operant conditioning and social learning), *personal experience*, *mental shortcuts* (categorization), *economic and political competition*, and *displaced aggression* (scapegoating). While using mental shortcuts, people view members of their ingroup more positively than members of the outgroup (**ingroup favoritism**) and see more diversity in their ingroup (**outgroup homogeneity effect**).

16.8 What are the three key factors in attraction? (p. 553)
Physical attractiveness is very important to **interpersonal attraction.** Physically attractive people are often perceived as more intelligent, sociable, and interesting than less attractive people. Physical **proximity** also increases one's attractiveness. If you live near someone or work alongside someone, you are more likely to like that person. Although people commonly believe that "opposites attract" (**need complementarity**), research shows that similarity (**need compatibility**) is a more important factor in long-term attraction.

16.9 Describe cultural and historical similarities and differences in judgments of attractiveness. (p. 554)
Many cultures share similar standards of attractiveness (e.g., youthful appearance and facial and body symmetry are important for women, whereas maturity and financial resources are more important for men). Historically, what is judged as beautiful varies from era to era.

16.10 Discuss scientific research on flirting. (p. 555)
People use nonverbal flirting behaviors to increase their attractiveness and signal interest. In heterosexual couples, women are more likely to use flirting to initiate courtship.

16.11 Differentiate between romantic and companionate love, and discuss problems with romantic love. (p. 557)
Romantic love is intense, passionate, and highly valued in our society, but because it is based on mystery and fantasy, it is hard to sustain. **Companionate love** relies on mutual trust, respect, and friendship and seems to grow stronger with time.

III. SOCIAL INFLUENCE
16.12 Define conformity, and explain the three factors that contribute to this behavior. (p. 560)
The process of social influence teaches important cultural values and behaviors that are essential to successful social living. Two of the most important forms of social influence are *conformity* and *obedience*. **Conformity** refers to changes in behavior in response to real or imagined pressure from others. People conform for approval and acceptance **(normative social influence),** out of a need for more information **(informational social influence),** and to match the behavior of those they admire and feel similar to (their **reference group**).

16.13 Define obedience and describe Milgram's classic study. (p. 561)
Obedience refers to following commands from others, usually from an authority figure. Stanley Milgram's study showed that a surprisingly large number of people would obey orders even when another human being is physically threatened.

16.14 Identify the four key factors in obedience. (p. 562)
The four key factors include: legitimacy and closeness of the authority figure, remoteness of the victim, assignment of responsibility, and modeling or imitation of others.

IV. GROUP PROCESSES

16.15 Discuss the importance of roles and deindividuation in Zimbardo's Stanford prison study. (p. 564)
Groups differ from mere collections of people because group members share a mutually recognized relationship with one another. Group membership affects us through the roles we play. The importance of roles in determining and controlling behavior was dramatically demonstrated in Philip Zimbardo's Stanford Prison Study. Group membership can also lead to **deindividuation,** in which a person becomes so caught up in the group's identity that individual self-awareness and responsibility are temporarily suspended.

16.16 How do group polarization and groupthink affect group decision making? (p. 566)
Group polarization research shows that if most group members initially tend toward an extreme idea, the entire group will polarize in that direction. This is because the other, like-minded, members reinforce the dominant tendency. **Groupthink** is a dangerous type of thinking that occurs when a group's desire for agreement overrules its desire to critically evaluate information.

V. AGGRESSION AND ALTRUISM

16.17 Define aggression, and identify the biological and psychosocial factors that contribute to its expression. (p. 568)
Aggression is any behavior intended to harm someone. Some researchers believe it is caused by biological factors, such as instincts, genes, the brain and nervous system, substance abuse and other mental disorders, and hormones and neurotransmitters. Other researchers emphasize psychosocial factors, such as aversive stimuli, culture and learning, and violent media and video games.

16.18 Describe three approaches to reducing aggression. (p. 569)
Releasing aggressive feelings through violent acts or watching violence is not an effective way to reduce aggression. Introducing incompatible responses (such as humor) and teaching social and communication skills is more efficient.

16.19 Define altruism, and describe the three models that attempt to explain it. (p. 570)
Altruism refers to actions designed to help others with no obvious benefit to oneself. Evolutionary theorists believe altruism is innate and has survival value. Psychological explanations for altruism emphasize the **egoistic model,** which suggests that helping is motivated by anticipated gain, or the **empathy-altruism hypothesis,** which proposes that helping can also be activated when the helper feels empathy for the victim.

16.20 Describe Latane and Darley's decision-making model, and other factors that help explain why we don't help. (p. 570)
According to Latane and Darley, whether or not someone helps depends on a series of interconnected events, starting with noticing the problem and ending with a decision to help. Some people do not help because of the ambiguity of many emergencies or because of **diffusion of responsibility** (assuming someone else will respond). To increase the chances of altruism, we should reduce ambiguity, increase the rewards for helping, and decrease the costs.

VI. APPLYING SOCIAL PSYCHOLOGY TO SOCIAL PROBLEMS

16.21 List four major approaches useful for reducing prejudice and discrimination. (p. 573)
Research in social psychology can help reduce or eliminate social problems. *Cooperation and common goals, increased intergroup contact, cognitive retraining,* and *cognitive dissonance reduction* are four methods for reducing prejudice and discrimination.

16.22 Describe recent research on implicit biases. (p. 575)
Research shows that people have hidden biases that are activated by a mere encounter with an attitude object, and that these biases can be used as a quick guide to behaviors that they are not aware of and do not control. Although these biases were previously thought to be impervious to change, newer studies show that we can reshape them (or at least curb) their effects on our behavior.

16.23 Identify six ways to reduce destructive obedience. (p. 577)
To decrease dangerous forms of destructive obedience, we need to examine six important factors—*socialization*, the *power of the situation*, *groupthink*, the *foot-in-the-door technique*, *relaxed moral guard*, and *disobedient models*.

SELF-TESTS (Review & wRite)

Completing the following self-tests will provide immediate feedback on how well you have mastered the material. In the labeling exercises, *crossword puzzle*, and *fill-in exercises*, write the appropriate word or words in the blank spaces. The *matching exercise* requires you to match the terms in one column to their correct definitions in the other. For the *multiple-choice questions* in Practice Tests I and II, circle or underline the correct answer. If you are unsure of any answer, mark the item, and then go back to the text for further review. Correct answers are provided in Appendix A at the end of this study guide.

CROSSWORD PUZZLE FOR CHAPTER 16

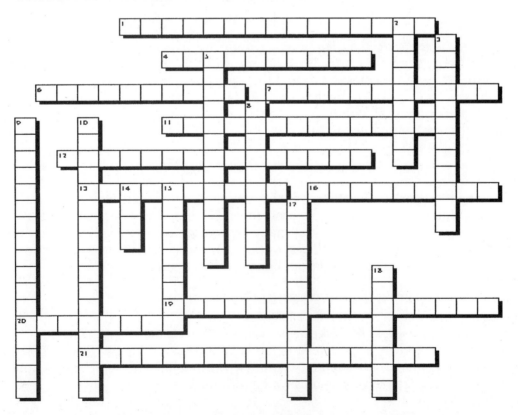

ACROSS

1 People to whom we conform because we like and admire them and want to be like them.
4 A set of beliefs about the characteristics of people in a group that is generalized to all group members.
6 Any behavior that is intended to harm someone.
7 Explanation for the cause of behaviors or events.
11 Negative behaviors directed at members of a group.
12 The increased arousal and reduced self-consciousness, inhibition, and personal responsibility that can occur when a person is part of a group, particularly when the members feel anonymous.
13 A type of social influence in which individuals change their behavior because of real or imagined group pressure.
16 A key factor in attraction involving geographic, residential, and other forms of physical closeness.
19 A strong feeling of attraction to another person characterized by trust, caring, tolerance, and friendship.
20 A learned predisposition to respond cognitively, affectively, and behaviorally to a particular object.
21 Viewing members of the ingroup more positively than members of an outgroup.

DOWN

2 A generally negative attitude directed toward others because of their membership in a specific group.
3 The tendency to focus on the most noticeable factors when explaining the causes of behavior.
5 The proposal that helping behavior is motivated by anticipated gain.
8 A condition that results when a highly cohesive group strives for agreement to the point of avoiding inconsistent information; the result is faulty decision-making.
9 A group's movement toward either riskier or more conservative behavior, depending upon the members' initial dominant tendency.
10 Attraction based on a sharing of similar needs.
14 Cultural rule of behavior that prescribes what is acceptable in a given situation.
15 A type of social influence in which an individual follows direct commands.
17 An intense feeling of attraction to another person, within an erotic context and with future expectations.
18 Actions designed to help others with no obvious benefit to the helper.

FILL-IN EXERCISES

1. _____ can be defined as the study of how others influence our thoughts, feelings, and actions (p. 544).

2. _____ is defined as the explanation for the cause of behaviors or events (p. 546).

3. As a result of the _____, when judging the causes of others' behavior, we tend to overestimate personality factors and underestimate social or situational factors. However, when judging our own behavior we take credit for successes and externalize failures, known as the _____ (pp. 546-547).

4. There are three major components to all attitudes: the _____, _____, and _____ (pp. 548-549).

5. According to the _____ theory, a perceived discrepancy between an attitude and a behavior or between two attitudes leads to tension, which then encourages attitude change (p. 549).

6. A learned, generally negative attitude directed toward members of a group is known as
    _____ (p. 551).

7. Stereotyping represents the _____ component of prejudice. In contrast, discrimination is
    the _____ component (p. 551).

8. The three key factors in attraction are _____, _____, and _____ (pp. 553-554,
    556).

9. A type of social influence where individuals change their behavior as a result of real or imagined
    group pressure is known as _____. In comparison, going along with a direct command,
    usually from someone in a position of authority, is known as _____ (pp. 560-561)

10. _____ refers to the tendency of groups to make decisions that are either riskier or more
    conservative than decisions made by individuals. In contrast, _____ refers to faulty
    decision making that occurs when a highly cohesive group strives for agreement and avoids
    inconsistent information (p. 566).

MATCHING EXERCISES

Column A

- a. Self-Serving Bias
- b. Need Compatibility
- c. Need Complementarity
- d. Normative Social Influence
- e. Egoistic Model
- f. Romantic Love
- g. Attitude
- h. Companionate Love
- i. Reference Group
- j. Proximity

Column B

1.___Based on mystery and fantasy.
2.___Increases attraction due to mere exposure effect
3.___Those we admire and feel similar to
4.___Attraction to others with opposite traits
5.___ Attraction to others based on similarity
6.____Taking credit for successes and externalizing failures
7.____Based on mutual trust, respect, and friendship
8.____ Helping is motivated by anticipated gain
9.____Learned predispositions toward an object
10.____Conforming out of a need for approval and
        acceptance

PRACTICE TEST I

1. Social psychologists study_____.
    a. how others influence an
        individual's thoughts
    b. how groups influence behavior
    c. how a person's feelings are affected
        by others
    d. all of these options

2. Attribution _____.
    a. explains how people use cognitive
        structures for exploring the world
        and explaining human behavior
    b. describes the principles we use in
        explaining what caused a behavior
        or event

    c. is usually unrelated to social
        perceptions
    d. describes our predisposition
        toward others or things

3. People engage in the fundamental
    attribution error (FAE) because _____.
    a. it is easier to blame people than
        "things"
    b. of the saliency bias
    c. we need to believe the world is just
        and fair
    d. all of these options

4. A learned predisposition to respond cognitively, affectively, and behaviorally to a particular object in a particular way is known as a(n)_____.
   a. attitude
   b. attribute
   c. cognition
   d. perceptual bias

5. Which statement does **NOT** illustrate a component of an attitude toward marijuana?
   a. the belief that marijuana is unsafe
   b. anxiety regarding the dangers of marijuana
   c. a predisposition to vote against the legalization of marijuana
   d. hallucinating while under the influence of marijuana

6. Cognitive dissonance may lead to a change in attitude due to _____.
   a. rational discourse between the id, ego, and superego
   b. rational discourse between people with opposite attitudes
   c. emotional thinking and reasoning
   d. psychological tension produced by personally discrepant attitudes

7. Cognitive dissonance is most prevalent in _____ cultures.
   a. Higher SES
   b. collectivist
   c. interdependent
   d. individualistic

8. Prejudice is a _____ directed toward others based on their group membership.
   a. negative behavior
   b. generally negative attitude
   c. stereotype
   d. all of these options

9. _____ is the cognitive component of prejudice.
   a. Harassment
   b. A stereotype
   c. Discrimination
   d. Ethnocentrism

10. Ingroup favoritism is defined as _____.
    a. any behavior intended to benefit your ethnic or religious group
    b. physical or verbal discrimination that favors your group
    c. viewing ingroup members more positively than members of an outgroup
    d. purposeful and accidental favoritism of any kind

11. Which of the following is an example of the outgroup homogeneity effect?
    a. "You don't belong here."
    b. "We are all alike."
    c. "You can't tell those people apart."
    d. all of these options

12. Research has consistently shown that physical attractiveness _____.
    a. has little or no effect on interpersonal attraction
    b. is one of the most important factors in liking
    c. is associated with socioeconomic status
    d. none of these options

13. An intense feeling of attraction to another within an erotic context and with future expectations defines _____.
    a. the arousal phase
    b. companionate love
    c. romantic love
    d. the sexual response cycle

14. Conforming to the typical behaviors of society out of a need for approval and acceptance is known as _____.
    a. normative social influence
    b. informational social influence
    c. obedience
    d. reference group adherence

15. Authority is most associated with which form of social influence?
    a. informational
    b. normative
    c. obedience
    d. reference group

16. In Zimbardo's prison experiment, the majority of participants with the role of prisoner became _____.
   a. combative
   b. defiant
   c. passive
   d. manic depressive

17. The tendency of a group to shift towards its initial dominant behavior or attitude is called _____.
   a. the risky shift
   b. the conservative movement
   c. groupthink
   d. group polarization

18. A group is strongly cohesive, and its members have a shared desire for agreement; the members should be alert to the dangers of this in their decision making.
   a. group polarization
   b. groupthink
   c. brainstorming
   d. the "bandwagon" effect

19. Altruism refers to actions designed to help others when _____.
   a. there is no obvious benefit to oneself
   b. there is a benefit to the altruistic person
   c. they have previously helped you
   d. they are in a position to help you in the future

20. Research shows that Kitty Genovese might have survived if she had been attacked _____.
   a. in the midwest instead of New York
   b. indoors instead of outdoors
   c. in the presence of only one neighbor who knew no one else was around
   d. during daylight hours instead of at night

PRACTICE TEST II

1. People often look back at the ground when they stumble or trip, which is their way of signaling others that there might be a(n) _____ for why they stumbled or tripped.
   a. situational attribution
   b. external disposition
   c. cognitive explanation
   d. internal attitude

2. Believing you do more than your share of the group work may be an example of _____.
   a. situational attribution
   b. saliency bias
   c. self-serving bias
   d. internal attribution

3. "All old people are slow drivers" is an example of _____.
   a. the generalization error
   b. prejudice
   c. ethnocentrism
   d. discrimination

4. After demeaning a member of another ethnic group, Walter experienced a brief rise in his own self-esteem. This is one way individuals learn _____.
   a. the self-serving bias
   b. prejudice
   c. ethnocentrism
   d. external attributions

5. According to _____ theorists, cross-cultural similarity in judgment of attractiveness reflects the fact that good looks generally indicate good health, sound genes, and high fertility.
   a. sociophysiological
   b. evolutionary
   c. biological
   d. none of the above

6. The reason _____ increases liking is that familiarity is less threatening than novelty.
   a. mere exposure
   b. physical attractiveness
   c. need complementarity
   d. need compatibility

7. Similarity is the most important factor in _____ relationships.
   a. forming
   b. appreciating
   c. ending
   d. long-term

8. According to _____, we are attracted to those with qualities we admire but personally lack.
   a. the similarity hypothesis
   b. need complementarity
   c. need compatibility
   d. reference group theory

9. Attraction based on sharing similar needs is known as _____.
   a. the fraternal-twin effect
   b. need compatibility
   c. both of these options
   d. none of these options

10. Illusions are one of the foundations of _____ love.
    a. companionate
    b. romantic
    c. fatuous
    d. empty

11. What did Benjamin Franklin have to say about vision and love?
    a. love lasts longest when your eyes are wide open
    b. look before you leap
    c. a glance is worth a thousand words
    d. wide-eyed at first, then half shut

12. Asch is best known for his study on _____.
    a. compliance
    b. obedience
    c. conformity
    d. persuasion

13. Normative social influence, informational social influence, and reference groups are explanations for _____.
    a. compliance
    b. the foot-in-the-door strategy
    c. obedience
    d. conformity

14. _____ percent of the people in Milgram's study followed orders to hurt a fellow participant.
    a. 15
    b. 25
    c. 65
    d. 95

15. Legitimate authority, distance between the teacher and learner, and _____ were several of the reasons participants in Milgram's study obeyed the researchers.
    a. letting others assume responsibility
    b. the saliency bias
    c. the self-serving bias
    d. lack of empathy

16. Roles are based on _____.
    a. social positions
    b. inborn dispositions
    c. acquired dispositions
    d. none of these options

17. The classic prison study that determined the power of roles in affecting people's behavior was conducted by _____.
    a. Milgram
    b. Zimbardo
    c. Bandura
    d. Asch

18. Appointing a devil's advocate in a cohesive group would _____.
    a. improve the group's decision making abilities
    b. hinder the group's decision making efforts
    c. have no effect on group decision making
    d. lead to chaos, resentment, and dissolution of the group

19. Evidence suggests that bystanders failed to intervene in the Kitty Genovese murder due to _____.
    a. a natural, apathy that occurs within large, depersonalized societies
    b. a diffusion of responsibility
    c. both of these options
    d. none of these options

20. If you were being mugged on a busy sidewalk, which of the following would be most likely to get you the help you need?
    a. fighting with the mugger
    b. yelling, "Help, help!"
    c. crying forlornly and looking helpless
    d. pointing to a specific person and asking them to call the police

Concept Diagram 16.1
What Influences Obedience?

Milgram conducted a series of studies to discover the specific conditions that either increased or decreased obedience to authority.

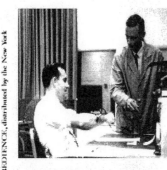

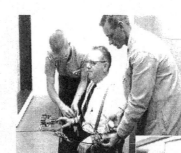

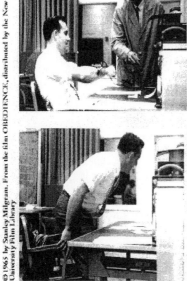

Milgram's Learner
Under orders from an experimenter, would you shock a man with a known heart condition who is screaming and begging to be released? Few people believe they would. But research shows otherwise.

Milgram's Shock Generator

Milgram's original study — A
Orders given by ordinary person or experimenter gives orders by phone — B
Learner 1½ away — C
Teacher holds learner's hand on shock plate — D
Teacher reads list of words while another delivers shock — E
Teacher chooses level of shock — F
Teacher watches two others disobey — G
Teacher watches two others obey — H

10 20 30 40 50 60 70 80 90 100
Percent of participants who gave 450-volt shocks

As you can see in the first bar on the graph (**A**), 65 percent of the participants in Milgram's original study gave the learner the full 450-volt level of shocks.

Four Factors in Obedience

1) Legitimacy and closeness of the authority figure

In the second bar (**B**), note that when orders came from an ordinary person, and when the experimenter left the room and gave orders by phone, the participants' obedience dropped to 20 percent.

2) Remoteness of the victim

Now look at the third and fourth bars (**C** and **D**), and note that the remoteness of the victim had an important impact. When the "learner" was only 1 1/2 feet away from the teacher, obedience dropped to 40 percent. And when the teacher had to actually hold the learner's hand on the shock plate, obedience was only 30 percent.

3) Assignment of responsibility

Looking at bars (**E**) and (**F**), note the dramatic importance of the teacher's degree of responsibility. When the teacher was responsible for choosing the level of shock, only 3 percent obeyed.

4) Modeling or imitating others

Finally, looking at bars (**G**) and (**H**), recognize the incredible power of modeling and imitation. When the teachers watched two others disobey, their own obedience was only 10 percent, but when they watched others follow orders, their obedience jumped to over 70 percent (Milgram, 1963, 1974).

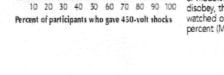

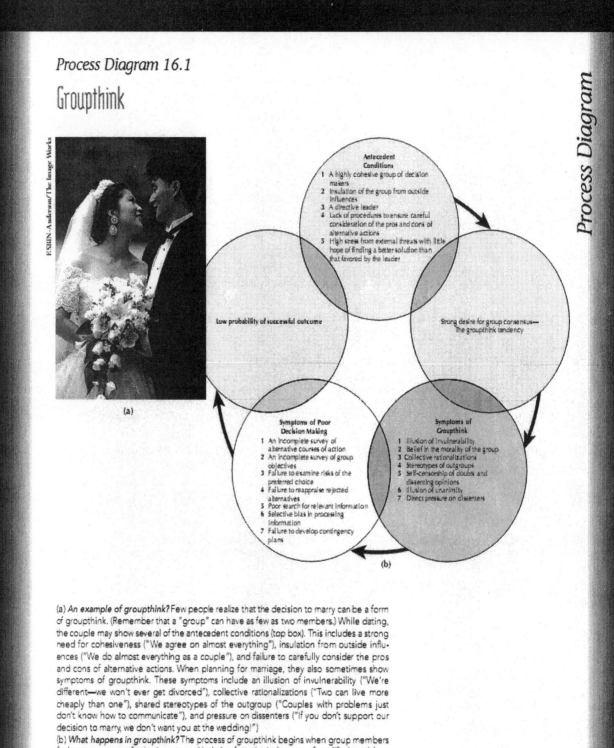

Process Diagram 16.1

Groupthink

Antecedent Conditions
1 A highly cohesive group of decision makers
2 Insulation of the group from outside influences
3 A directive leader
4 Lack of procedures to ensure careful consideration of the pros and cons of alternative actions
5 High stress from external threats with little hope of finding a better solution than that favored by the leader

Strong desire for group consensus— The groupthink tendency

Symptoms of Groupthink
1 Illusion of invulnerability
2 Belief in the morality of the group
3 Collective rationalizations
4 Stereotypes of outgroups
5 Self-censorship of doubts and dissenting opinions
6 Illusion of unanimity
7 Direct pressure on dissenters

Symptoms of Poor Decision Making
1 An incomplete survey of alternative courses of action
2 An incomplete survey of group objectives
3 Failure to examine risks of the preferred choice
4 Failure to reappraise rejected alternatives
5 Poor search for relevant information
6 Selective bias in processing information
7 Failure to develop contingency plans

Low probability of successful outcome

(a)

(b)

(a) *An example of groupthink?* Few people realize that the decision to marry can be a form of groupthink. (Remember that a "group" can have as few as two members.) While dating, the couple may show several of the antecedent conditions (top box). This includes a strong need for cohesiveness ("We agree on almost everything"), insulation from outside influences ("We do almost everything as a couple"), and failure to carefully consider the pros and cons of alternative actions. When planning for marriage, they also sometimes show symptoms of groupthink. These symptoms include an illusion of invulnerability ("We're different—we won't ever get divorced"), collective rationalizations ("Two can live more cheaply than one"), shared stereotypes of the outgroup ("Couples with problems just don't know how to communicate"), and pressure on dissenters ("If you don't support our decision to marry, we don't want you at the wedding!")

(b) *What happens in groupthink?* The process of groupthink begins when group members feel a strong sense of cohesiveness and isolation from the judgments of qualified outsiders. Add a directive leader and little chance for debate, and you have the recipe for a potentially dangerous decision.

Concept Diagram 16.2

Helping

(a) Three Models for Helping

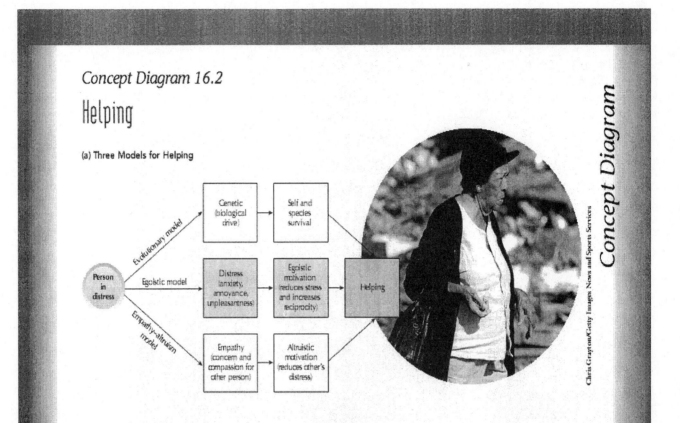

(b) When and Why Do We Help?

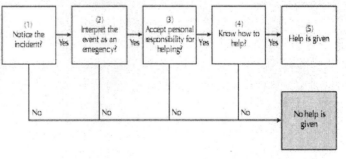

According to Latané and Darley's five-step decision process, if the answer at each step is yes, help is given. If the answer is no at any point, the helping process ends.

Chapter 16 Visual Summary

Our Thoughts About Others

Attribution

Attribution: Explaining others' behavior by deciding that their actions resulted from internal (dispositional) factors (their own traits and motives) or external (situational) factors. Problems: **fundamental attribution error** and **self-serving bias.**

Attitude

Attitude: Learned predisposition toward a particular object. Three components of all attitudes: cognitive, affective, and behavioral tendencies.

Cognitive Dissonance Theory

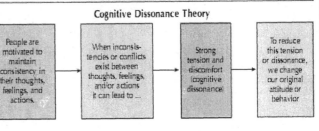

People are motivated to maintain consistency in their thoughts, feelings, and actions. → When inconsistencies or conflicts exist between thoughts, feelings, and/or actions it can lead to ... → Strong tension and discomfort (cognitive dissonance) → To reduce this tension or dissonance, we change our original attitude or behavior

Our Feelings About Others

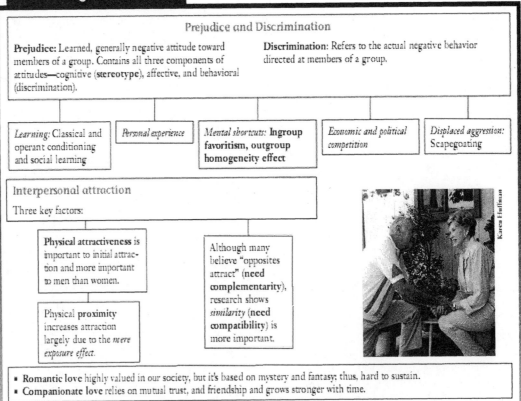

Prejudice and Discrimination

Prejudice: Learned, generally negative attitude toward members of a group. Contains all three components of attitudes—cognitive (**stereotype**), affective, and behavioral (**discrimination**).

Discrimination: Refers to the actual negative behavior directed at members of a group.

Learning: Classical and operant conditioning and social learning	*Personal experience*	*Mental shortcuts:* **Ingroup favoritism, outgroup homogeneity effect**	*Economic and political competition*	*Displaced aggression:* Scapegoating

Interpersonal attraction

Three key factors:

Physical attractiveness is important to initial attraction and more important to men than women.

Physical proximity increases attraction largely due to the *mere exposure effect.*

Although many believe "opposites attract" (**need complementarity**), research shows *similarity* (**need compatibility**) is more important.

- **Romantic love** highly valued in our society, but it's based on mystery and fantasy; thus, hard to sustain.
- **Companionate love** relies on mutual trust, and friendship and grows stronger with time.

Karen Huffman

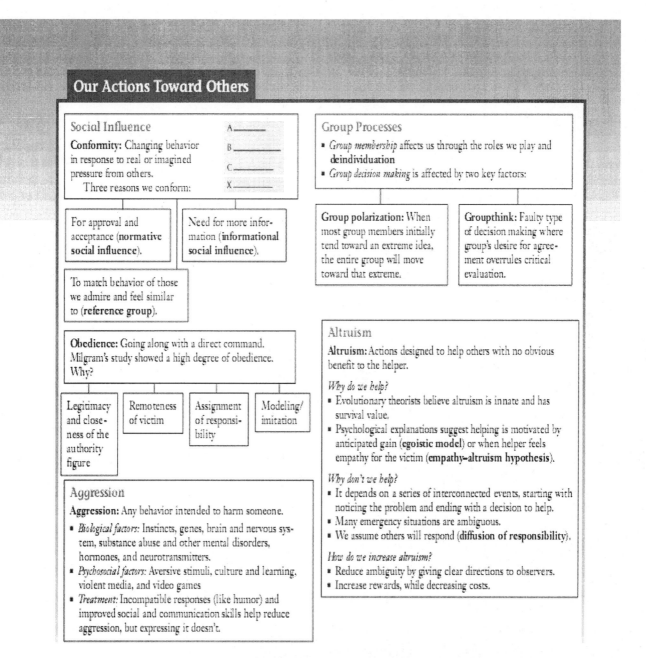

Our Actions Toward Others

Social Influence

Conformity: Changing behavior in response to real or imagined pressure from others.

Three reasons we conform:

A _____
B _____
C _____
X _____

For approval and acceptance (**normative social influence**).

Need for more information (**informational social influence**).

To match behavior of those we admire and feel similar to (**reference group**).

Obedience: Going along with a direct command. Milgram's study showed a high degree of obedience. Why?

- Legitimacy and closeness of the authority figure
- Remoteness of victim
- Assignment of responsibility
- Modeling/imitation

Aggression

Aggression: Any behavior intended to harm someone.

- *Biological factors:* Instincts, genes, brain and nervous system, substance abuse and other mental disorders, hormones, and neurotransmitters.
- *Psychosocial factors:* Aversive stimuli, culture and learning, violent media, and video games
- *Treatment:* Incompatible responses (like humor) and improved social and communication skills help reduce aggression, but expressing it doesn't.

Group Processes

- *Group membership* affects us through the roles we play and **deindividuation**
- *Group decision making* is affected by two key factors:

Group polarization: When most group members initially tend toward an extreme idea, the entire group will move toward that extreme.

Groupthink: Faulty type of decision making where group's desire for agreement overrules critical evaluation.

Altruism

Altruism: Actions designed to help others with no obvious benefit to the helper.

Why do we help?
- Evolutionary theorists believe altruism is innate and has survival value.
- Psychological explanations suggest helping is motivated by anticipated gain (**egoistic model**) or when helper feels empathy for the victim (**empathy-altruism hypothesis**).

Why don't we help?
- It depends on a series of interconnected events, starting with noticing the problem and ending with a decision to help.
- Many emergency situations are ambiguous.
- We assume others will respond (**diffusion of responsibility**).

How do we increase altruism?
- Reduce ambiguity by giving clear directions to observers.
- Increase rewards, while decreasing costs.

William Philpott/Reuters/Corbis Images

Applying Social Psychology to Social Problems

Social psychological research applied to social problems:

- Cooperation and common goals, intergroup contact, cognitive retraining, and reducing cognitive dissonance may help decrease prejudice and discrimination.
- Understanding socialization, the power of the situation, groupthink, the foot-in-the-door, a relaxed moral guard, and disobedient models may help reduce destructive obedience.

Appendix

APPENDIX A

ANSWERS

Answers to the *active learning exercises, crossword puzzles, fill-ins, matching exercises,* and *Practice Tests (I* and *II)* are provided in this following appendix.

Keep in mind that while these answers do offer immediate feedback on your mastery of the material, you should not try to simply memorize the answers. When you are unsure of your answer, or make an error, go back to your textbook and carefully review that section. This will greatly improve your scores on classroom exams and quizzes.

CHAPTER 1 ANSWERS

ACTIVE LEARNING EXERCISE I Study I correlational, positive; **Study II** experimental, IV = vitamin C vs. placebo, DV = number and severity of cold symptoms; **Study III** correlational, positive

ACTIVE LEARNING EXERCISE II Answers will vary

ACTIVE LEARNING EXERCISE III 1. SB; 2. CC; 3. CG; 4. EB.

CROSSWORD PUZZLE FOR CHAPTER 1

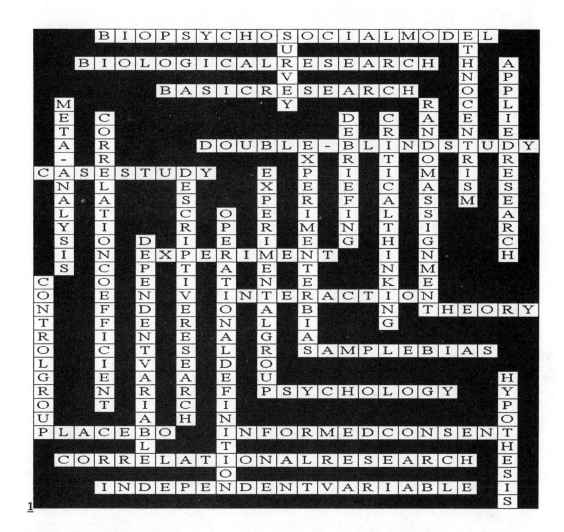

FILL-IN EXERCISES 1. 1879; 2. psychoanalytic; 3. humanistic; 4. advance scientific knowledge, solve practical problems; 5. debrief; 6. experimental; 7. independent variable; 8. case study; 9. Correlational; 10. survey, question, read, recite, review, and wRite.

MATCHING EXERCISES a. 4, b. 7, c. 8, d. 3, e. 1, f. 10, g. 6, h. 5, i. 2, j. 9

PRACTICE TEST I		PRACTICE TEST II	
1. d (p. 4)	11. b (p. 17)	1. b (p. 4)	11. b (p. 19)
2. c (pp. 4-5)	12. d (p. 21)	2. b (p. 6)	12. c (p. 19)
3. b (p. 6)	13. c (p. 21)	3. c (p. 6)	13. b (p. 21)
4. c (p. 9)	14. d (pp. 23-24)	4. b (p. 6)	14. a (pp. 21-23)
5. a (p. 10)	15. b (pp. 23-24)	5. c (p. 11)	15. b (pp. 23-24)
6. d (p. 11)	16. a (pp. 23-24)	6. c (p. 11)	16. d (pp. 23-24)
7. d (p. 14)	17. a (p. 22)	7. d (p. 12)	17. d (p. 25)
8. d (p. 16)	18. b (p. 25)	8. d (p. 13)	18. b (p. 29)
9. c (p. 16)	19. b (pp. 31-32)	9. c (p. 16)	19. b (p. 32)
10. c (pp. 16-17)	20. c (p. 35)	10. c (p. 17)	20. c (p. 35)

CHAPTER 2 ANSWERS

ACTIVE LEARNING EXERCISE I 1. right and left occipital lobes; 2. left parietal lobe; 3. left and right temporal lobes; 4. right frontal lobe; 5. vision = left and right occipital lobes, language processing = left temporal lobe.

ACTIVE LEARNING EXERCISE II *Neuron Drawing:* a. dendrite; b. cell body (soma); c. nucleus, d. myelin sheath; e. axon; f. terminal button of axon. *Brain Drawing:* 1. Broca's area; 2. frontal lobe; 3. temporal lobe; 4. cerebellum; 5. Wernicke's area, 6. occipital lobe; 7. visual cortex; 8. parietal lobe; 9. somatosensory cortex; 10. motor cortex.

ACTIVE LEARNING EXERCISE III Case 1: left hemisphere, in the frontal and temporal lobes, probably Broca's area. Case 2: frontal lobes and their interconnections with the limbic system. Case 3: having had her corpus callosum severed, her frontal, temporal, and occipital lobes are no longer integrating information from her left and right hemispheres. Case 4: left occipital lobe, corpus callosum.

CROSSWORD PUZZLE

FILL-IN EXERCISES 1. dendrites, cell body, and axon; 2. Myelin sheath; 3. hormones; 4. central nervous system (CNS), peripheral nervous system (PNS); 5. spinal cord; 6. parasympathetic, sympathetic; 7. cerebellum; 8. hypothalamus; 9. occipital; 10. split-brain research.

MATCHING EXERCISES a. 8, b. 10, c. 9, d. 5, e. 2, f. 6, g. 7, h. 4, i. 3, j. 1

PRACTICE TEST I		PRACTICE TEST II	
1. b (p. 50)	11. d (p. 60)	1. c (p. 53)	11. c (p. 69)
2. b (p. 52)	12. c (p. 60)	2. d (p. 53)	12. c (pp. 71-72)
3. c (p. 53)	13. c (p. 61)	3. c (p. 55)	13. a (p. 72)
4. b (p. 53)	14. b (p. 63)	4. c (p. 55)	14. c (p. 73)
5. d (p. 55)	15. b (pp. 67, 68)	5. c (p. 56)	15. a (p. 73)
6. b (p. 56)	16. d (pp. 67, 68)	6. b (p. 58)	16. d (p. 75)
7. c (p. 56)	17. b (p. 71)	7. d (p. 60)	17. c (p. 75)
8. b (p. 57)	18. c (pp. 71, 73)	8. c (pp. 61-62)	18. c (pp. 75-77)
9. d (p. 58)	19. d (p. 75)	9. b (p. 63)	19. d (p. 81)
10.c (p. 59)	20. d (p. 76)	10. c (p. 67)	20. c (p. 82)

CHAPTER 3 ANSWERS

CROSSWORD PUZZLE FOR CHAPTER 3

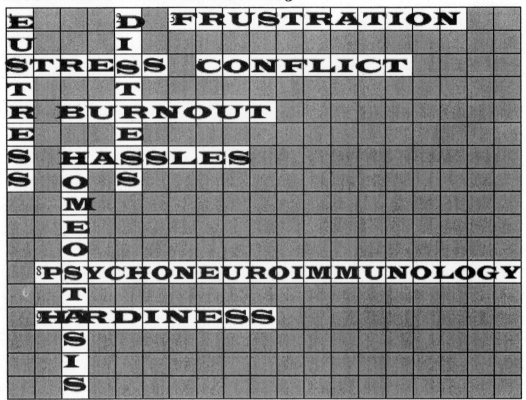

FILL-IN EXERCISES 1. distress; 2. Hassles; 3. avoidance-avoidance; 4. alarm reaction, resistance phase, exhaustion phase; 5. Type A, Type B; 6. health psychology; 7. binge drinking; 8. endorphins; 9. problem-focused; 10. internal locus of control.

MATCHING EXERCISES a. 6, b. 2, c. 1, d. 9, e. 3, f. 7, g. 10, h. 5, i. 8, j. 4.

PRACTICE TEST I		PRACTICE TEST II	
1. c (p. 92)	11. d (p. 111)	1. d (p. 95)	11. d (p. 112)
2. a (p. 93)	12. d (p. 112)	2. d (p. 95)	12. a (p. 115)
3. c (p. 93)	13. c (pp. 112-113)	3. c (p. 96)	13. d (p. 115)
4. c (p. 95)	14. c (p. 113)	4. d (pp. 100-101)	14. c (pp. 116-117)
5. d (p. 102)	15. b (p. 115)	5. c (pp. 102-103)	15. a (pp. 116-117)
6. b (pp. 105-106)	16. c (p. 115)	6. c (p. 102)	16. c (pp. 116-117)
7. b (p. 106)	17. c (pp. 116-117)	7. a (p. 106)	17. d (p. 118)
8. c (p. 106)	18. a (pp. 117-118)	8. d (pp. 106-107)	18. b (p. 120)
9. b (p. 108)	19. d (pp. 118-120)	9. b (p. 108)	19. d (p. 120)
10. b (p. 109)	20. b (p. 120)	10. a (p. 112)	20. b (p. 120)

CHAPTER 4 ANSWERS

ACTIVE LEARNING EXERCISE IV

1. **Recognizing personal biases.** After watching this reporter or reading this case, the ardent disbeliever (skeptic) might instantly reject it as nonsense. A true believer might focus exclusively on the psychic's apparent ability to provide hard "facts" about the case based on limited exposure and the reporter's statement from the Captain that Morrison provided even more private information that he referred on to the homicide unit. It is important to remain open-minded until a fair evaluation of all relevant evidence can be done. However, we must also remain skeptical about all claims of extrasensory perception (ESP) until they can be openly examined by nonbiased scientific tests.

2. **Analyzing data for value and content.** Good critical thinking requires careful analysis of the data or evidence and then looking for logical alternative explanations.

a) *Evidence.* After focusing her supposed psychic abilities on the running shoes, Morrison describes key aspects of an unsolved murder. She supposedly had no way of knowing the shoes were connected to the "Fairmount Park Rapist" case or what the rapist looked like.

Alternative explanation. Before the broadcast, Morrison could have researched "Fairmount Park Rapist" on the Internet and found dozens of related news stories. It was a prominent case and many reports mentioned "Rebecca Park was *raped* ("rape...woman...man") and *strangled* ("I feel pain...[grabs neck]...I can't breathe"). They also said that the victim was "clad only in *running shoes* and socks and almost all accounts included the same composite sketch of a man described as "Hispanic...with an olive complexion and about 6 feet tall..." ("He's 6, no, 5 (foot) 10, 5 (foot) 11...dark-skinned features..."). The victim was also described as a 5' 1" 100-pound college student ("A person grown up, yet a child...).

What about the additional information Morrison reportedly provided off camera? Because the Captain blocked our access to the street name and other information, we cannot validate the legitimacy or probability of her claims. Unfortunately, this is the type of "hard reporting" that leaves viewers with an overall impression of media support for the psychic's claims.

CROSSWORD PUZZLE FOR CHAPTER 4

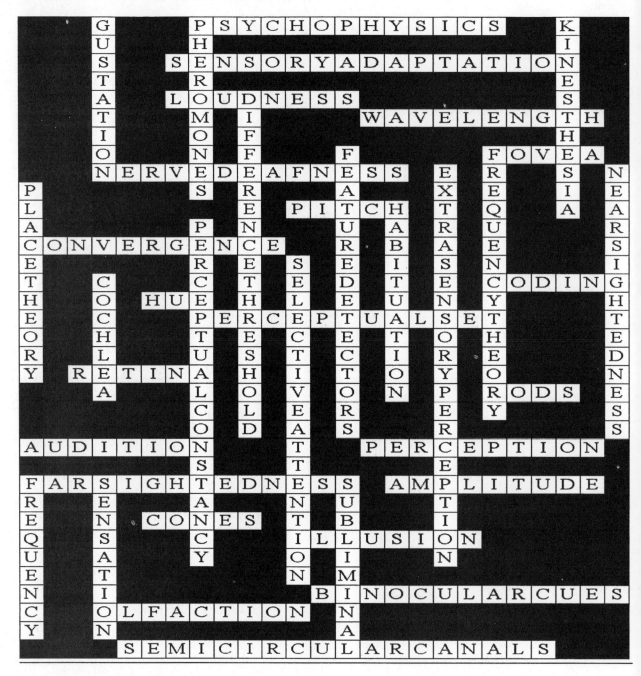

FILL-IN EXERCISES

1. Bottom-up processing, top-down processing 2. Psychophysics 3. hue or color, intensity or brightness; 4. cornea, pupil, lens, retina; 5. dark adaptation; 6. Nerve deafness; 7. illusions; 8. sensory adaptation, habituation; 9. Monocular cues, binocular cues; 10. telepathy.

MATCHING EXERCISES

a. 8, b. 10, c. 5, d. 6, e. 7, f. 4, g. 1, h. 3, i. 2, j. 9.

PRACTICE TEST I		PRACTICE TEST II	
1. b (p. 129)	11. b (pp. 150-151)	1. d (pp. 129-130)	11. d (p. 148)
2. c (p. 130)	12. d (pp. 153-155)	2. d (p. 132)	12. d (pp. 148-149)
3. b (p. 131)	13. a (pp. 156, 158)	3. c (p. 133)	13. c (p. 149)
4. a (p. 136)	14. c (p. 159)	4. a (pp. 136-138)	14. d (p. 151)
5. d (pp. 137-138)	15. d (p. 160)	5. a (p. 139)	15. d (p. 151)
6. c (pp. 138-139)	16. d (p. 161)	6. c (p. 140)	16. c (p. 156)
7. b (p. 142)	17. d (p. 161)	7. d (pp. 141-143)	17. b (p. 157)
8. c (p. 146)	18. c (p. 161)	8. c (pp. 143-144)	18. c (p. 158)
9. d (pp. 148-149)	19. d (pp. 161-162)	9. b (p. 146)	19. d (pp. 156-159)
10. d (p. 149)	20. c (pp. 161-162)	10. c (p. 146)	20. c (p. 160)

CHAPTER 5 ANSWERS

CROSSWORD PUZZLE FOR CHAPTER 5

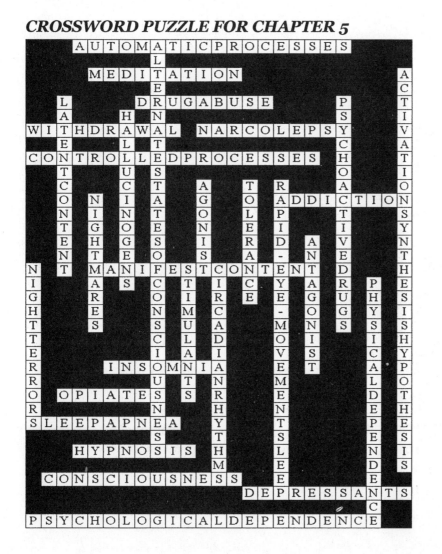

FILL-IN EXERCISES 1. Alternate states of consciousness (ASCs); 2. Controlled processes; 3. REM sleep; 4. repair/restoration, evolutionary/circadian; 5. latent content; 6. insomnia, sleep apnea, narcolepsy, nightmares, night terrors; 7. psychoactive; 8. Psychological dependence, physical dependence; 9. Stimulants, depressants; 10. Hypnosis.

MATCHING EXERCISES a. 4, b. 5, c. 6, d. 9, e. 1, f. 8, g. 2, h. 7, i. 3, j. 10.

PRACTICE TEST I		PRACTICE TEST II	
1. b (p. 166)	11. c (p. 186)	1. b (p. 171)	11. c (p. 187)
2. d (pp. 169-170)	12. b (p. 186)	2. c (p. 174)	12. a (pp. 189-190)
3. a (p. 171)	13. d (p. 189)	3. c (p. 174)	13. c (p. 192)
4. a (p. 174)	14. b (p. 189)	4. b (p. 175)	14. b (pp. 190, 192)
5. b (p. 177)	15. a (pp. 189-190)	5. d (p. 176)	15. d (pp. 192-193)
6. a (p. 178)	16. c (pp. 190, 192-193)	6. c (p. 180)	16. d (pp. 193-194)
7. b (p. 180)	17. b (pp. 190, 193)	7. c (p. 183)	17. d (p. 194)
8. c (p. 182)	18. c (p. 194)	8. b (p. 183)	18. d (p. 195)
9. c (p. 183)	19. b (p. 197)	9. b (p. 184)	19. d (p. 196)
10.b (p. 185)	20. d (p. 198)	10.c (p. 184)	20. b (p. 196)

CHAPTER 6 ANSWERS

ACTIVE LEARNING EXERCISE I
1. NS: saying "goodbye"
    UCS: loud noise from door slamming
    UCR: flinching
    CS: saying "goodbye"
    CR: flinching

2. NS: flash of light
    UCS: puff of air to the eye
    UCR: blinking
    CS: flash of light
    CR: blinking

ACTIVE LEARNING EXERCISE II 1. A. Operant, B. Negative Reinforcement; 2. A. Classical, B. NS = sight of mother, UCS = stroking, UCR = feelings of pleasure, CS = sight of mother, CR = feelings of pleasure; 3. A. Operant, B. Negative Punishment; 4. A. Classical, B. NS = sight of house, UCS = high temperature, UCR = perspiring, CS = sight of the house, CR = perspiring.

CROSSWORD PUZZLE FOR CHAPTER 6

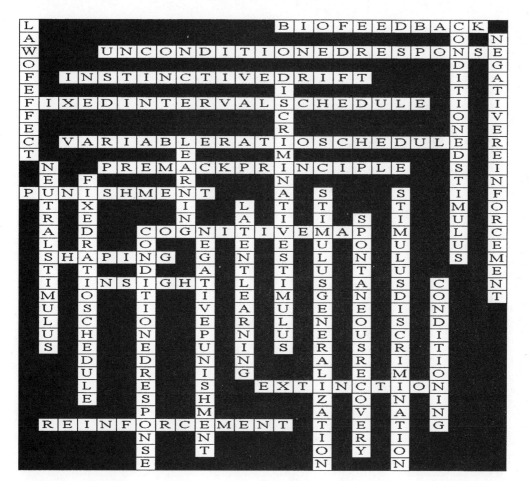

FILL-IN EXERCISES 1. learning, conditioning; 2. An unconditioned response (UCR); 3. extinction; 4. spontaneous recovery; 5. operant conditioning; 6. Reinforcement, punishment; 7. continuously, partially; 8. shaping; 9. biological preparedness; 10. superstitious behavior.

MATCHING EXERCISES a. 2, b. 7, c. 8, d. 9, e. 6, f. 10, g. 1, h. 4, i. 3, j. 5.

PRACTICE TEST I		PRACTICE TEST II	
1. d (pp. 205-206)	11. c (pp. 213-214)	1. b (p. 204)	11. a (p. 215)
2. b (pp. 205-206)	12. c (p. 214)	2. d (pp. 204-205)	12. d (p. 218)
3. c (pp. 205-206)	13. d (p. 214)	3. d (p. 205)	13. c (p. 224)
4. b (pp. 205-206)	14. c (p. 215)	4. d (p. 207)	14. a (p. 224)
5. a (p. 207)	15. d (pp. 215-216)	5. c (p. 207)	15. a (p. 225)
6. a (p. 209)	16. c (p. 222)	6. b (p. 207)	16. d (p. 225)
7. b (pp. 209-210)	17. a (p. 224)	7. c (p. 209)	17. b (p. 225)
8. b (pp. 210-211)	18. d (p. 225)	8. b (p. 210)	18. c (pp. 230-231)
9. b (p. 212)	19. d (p. 230)	9. b (pp. 210-211)	19. c (pp. 235-236)
10. c (p. 212)	20. d (pp. 232, 234-235, 237)	10. d (pp. 213-214)	20. b (p. 236)

CHAPTER 7 ANSWERS

Crossword Puzzle for Chapter 7

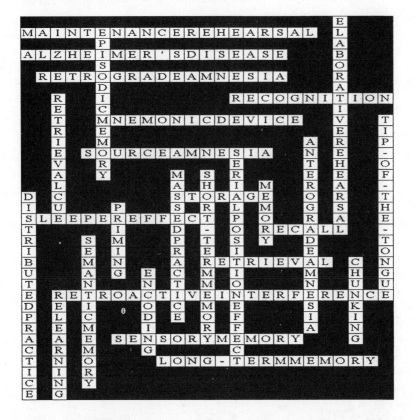

FILL-IN EXERCISES 1. information-processing model; 2. encoding, storage, retrieval; 3. maintenance rehearsal; 4. chunking; 5. semantic, episodic; 6. encoding, storage, retrieval; 7. recognition, recall; 8. biological decay over time; 9. mnemonics; 10. acronym.

MATCHING EXERCISES a. 6, b. 1, c. 10, d. 5, e. 8, f. 3, g. 4, h. 7, i. 2, j. 9.

PRACTICE TEST I		**PRACTICE TEST II**	
1. b (p. 244)	11. c (p. 260)	1. c (p. 244)	11. d (pp. 258-259)
2. d (pp. 244-246)	12. c (p. 260)	2. d (pp. 244-245)	12. d (pp. 258-259)
3. d (p. 248)	13. a (p. 263)	3. d (p. 248)	13. c (p. 260)
4. b (p. 248)	14. b (pp. 263-264)	4. c (pp. 249-250)	14. c (pp. 261-262)
5. d (pp. 249-250)	15. d (pp. 264-266)	5. c (p. 251)	15. b (pp. 263-264)
6. c (p. 251)	16. d (p. 266)	6. d (pp. 252-253)	16. c (p. 266)
7. b (pp. 254-255)	17. b (pp. 266-267)	7. c (p. 254)	17. c (p. 267)
8. b (p. 258)	18. b (p. 268)	8. d (p. 255)	18. a (p. 270)
9. b (pp. 258-259)	19. b (pp. 272-273)	9. d (p. 256)	19. d (pp. 272-273)
10. d (pp. 258-259)	20. a (p. 273)	10. b (p. 257)	20. c (pp. 272-273)

CHAPTER 8 ANSWERS

ACTIVE LEARNING EXERCISE I

Algorithm answer: 2 players = 1 match, 3 players = 2 matches, 4 players = 5 matches, and so on. The number of required matches is one less than the number of players, so it will take 1024 matches to select a winner.

Working backward—a heuristic answer: *The thief had one apple after sharing with the third security guard. After sharing with the second security guard, he had 6 apples (1/2 x 2 = 1, X =6). After sharing with the first security guard, he had 16 (1/2 x-2 = 16, X = 36). The thief stole 36 apples.*

CROSSWORD PUZZLE FOR CHAPTER 8

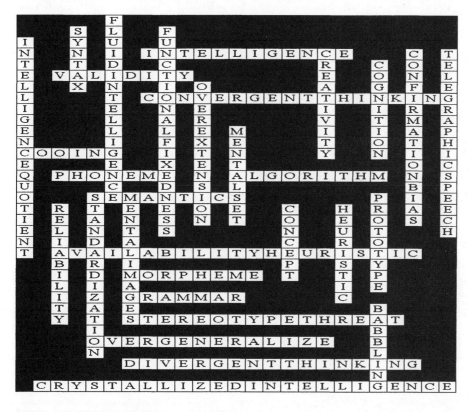

FILL-IN EXERCISES 1. Cognition; 2. prototype; 3. preparation, production, and evaluation; 4. mental sets, functional fixedness, confirmation bias, availability heuristic, and representativeness heuristic; 5. divergent, convergent; 6. morpheme; 7. cooing, babbling; 8. intelligence; 9. crystallized, fluid; 10. standardization, reliability, validity.

MATCHING EXERCISES a. 7, b. 2, c. 8, d. 9, e. 1, f. 4, g. 5, h. 6, i. 10, j. 3.

PRACTICE TEST I		PRACTICE TEST II	
1. c (pp. 280-281)	11. b (p. 291)	1. d (p. 281)	11. c (p. 292)
2. d (pp. 281-282)	12. a (pp. 298-299)	2. d (p. 282)	12. c (pp. 293-294)
3. b (pp. 283-284)	13. d (pp. 298-299)	3. c (pp. 283-284)	13. a (p. 293)
4. b (p. 284)	14. d (p. 298)	4. b (p. 284)	14. a (p. 298)
5. c (p. 284)	15. a (p. 300)	5. a (p. 284)	15. a (pp. 297-298)
6. b (p. 286)	16. c (pp. 300-301)	6. c (p. 286)	16. c (p. 298)
7. c (p. 286)	17. a (p. 302)	7. d (p. 287)	17. b (p. 300)
8. b (p. 288)	18. b (p. 302)	8. b (p. 287)	18. d (p. 302)
9. c (pp. 289-290)	19. b (pp. 303-304)	9. c (p. 288)	19. d (pp. 303-304)
10. c (pp. 291-292)	20. b (p. 306)	10. d (p. 292)	20. a (pp. 307-308)

CHAPTER 9 ANSWERS

ACTIVE LEARNING EXERCISE I
Attachment and Marital Happiness Research.
A major problem with longitudinal research is that people often drop out, and in this study the couples who were most likely to drop out were those who got divorced. After divorcing, they would not be available for your research after ten years of marriage, and they also were more likely to have been unhappy and less attached at the first measurement five years before. To account for this, you could omit those couples who were divorced after 10 years from the analysis of those who were married for 5 years. This would help control for the drop out and divorce factor.

CROSSWORD PUZZLE FOR CHAPTER 9

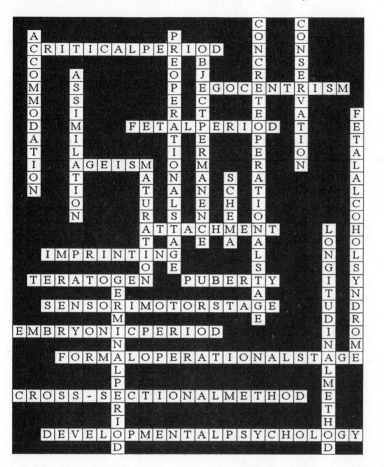

FILL-IN EXERCISES 1. Nature versus nurture, continuity versus stages, stability versus change; 2. one point in time, an extended period of time; 3. Teratogens; 4. menarche, spermarche; 5. assimilation, accommodation; 6. preoperational; 7. formal operational; 8. imprinting; 9. securely attached; 10. permissive, authoritarian, authoritative.

MATCHING EXERCISES a. 10, b. 5, c. 8, d. 1, e. 9, f. 3, g. 4, h. 6, i. 7, j. 2.

PRACTICE TEST I		PRACTICE TEST II	
1. d (p. 316)	11. c (p. 328)	1. c (p. 317)	11. d (p. 332)
2. d (p. 317)	12. c (p. 329)	2. b (p. 317)	12. a (p. 332)
3. c (p. 318)	13. d (pp. 333-334)	3. a (p. 318)	13. c (p. 334)
4. c (p. 320)	14. b (pp. 333-334)	4. c (p. 319)	14. a (pp. 334-336)
5. d (p. 322)	15. d (pp. 334-335)	5. d (p. 322)	15. c (pp. 333-334)
6. b (p. 323)	16. c (pp. 334-336)	6. b (p. 324)	16. d (pp. 334, 336)
7. b (p. 324)	17. b (p. 338)	7. a (pp. 327-328)	17. d (p. 341)
8. a (p. 326)	18. c (p. 341)	8. c (p. 328)	18. b (pp. 343-344)
9. c (p. 327)	19. c (p. 342)	9. c (p. 329)	19. b (p. 342)
10. d (p. 328)	20. d (pp. 340, 342)	10. d (p. 330)	20. b (p. 342)

CHAPTER 10 ANSWERS

CROSSWORD PUZZLE FOR CHAPTER 10

FILL-IN EXERCISES 1. preconventional, conventional, postconventional; 2. preconventional; 3. conventional; 4. temperament; 5. psychosocial; 6. collectivistic; 7. pregnancy; 8. resilient; 9. activity, disengagement; 10. denial, anger, bargaining, depression, acceptance.

MATCHING EXERCISES a. 1, b. 6, c. 9, d. 10, e. 2, f. 8, g. 7, h. 4, i. 3, j. 5.

PRACTICE TEST I		PRACTICE TEST II	
1. b (p. 350)	11. d (p. 356)	1. d (p. 352)	11. d (p. 357)
2. a (p. 352)	12. d (p. 357)	2. b (p. 352)	12. d (p. 359)
3. b (p. 352)	13. c (p. 357)	3. b (p. 352)	13. a (p. 363)
4. a (p. 351)	14. c (p. 359)	4. c (p. 352)	14. c (p. 364)
5. d (p. 354)	15. b (p. 362)	5. a (p. 355)	15. b (p. 364)
6. c (p. 355)	16. a (p. 363)	6. b (p. 355)	16. b (p. 365)
7. d (p. 355)	17. b (p. 364)	7. a (p. 356)	17. b (p. 365)
8. c (p. 356)	18. c (p. 364)	8. b (p. 356)	18. c (p. 367)
9. b (p. 356)	19. d (p. 365)	9. c (p. 356)	19. d (pp. 367-368)
10. d (p. 356)	20. b (p. 367)	10. c (p. 356)	20. c (p. 368)

CHAPTER 11 ANSWERS

CROSSWORD PUZZLE FOR CHAPTER 11

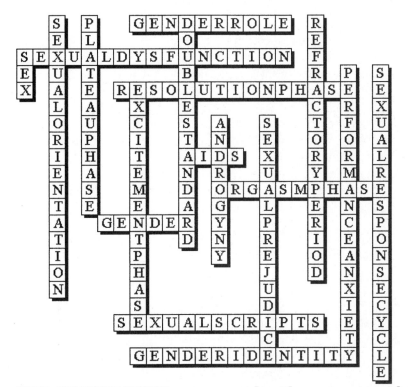

FILL-IN EXERCISES 1. sex; 2. gender roles; 3. transsexual, transvestite; 4. Homosexuality (or gay or lesbian), bisexuality; 4. gender roles; 5. Androgynous; 6. nocturnal emissions; 7. refractory; 8. evolutionary perspective; 9. sexual prejudice; 10. sexual dysfunction.

MATCHING EXERCISES a. 4, b. 5, c. 9, d. 2, e. 10, f. 7, g. 1, h. 6, i. 8, j. 3.

PRACTICE TEST I		PRACTICE TEST II	
1. c (p. 376)	11. c (p. 387)	1. a (p. 376)	11. d (p. 394)
2. a (p. 378)	12. c (p. 390)	2. c (p. 377)	12. d (p. 394)
3. d (p. 378)	13. d (pp. 391-393)	3. c (pp. 377-378)	13. a (p. 395)
4. a (p. 379)	14. d (p. 393)	4. b (p. 382)	14. b (p. 395)
5. d (p. 379)	15. b (p. 394)	5. b (p. 383)	15. a (p. 395)
6. c (pp. 381-383)	16. a (p. 394)	6. d (p. 383)	16. d (p. 395)
7. a (p. 383)	17. d (p. 396)	7. c (p. 387)	17. c (p. 396)
8. b (p. 383)	18. d (p. 396)	8. d (p. 390)	18. d (p. 400-401)
9. d (p. 386)	19. a (p. 398)	9. a (p. 390)	19. c (p. 400)
10. d (pp. 386-387)	20. d (p. 402)	10. d (p. 390)	20. d (pp. 401-402)

CHAPTER 12 ANSWERS

ACTIVE LEARNING EXERCISE II

Subjective well-being exercise
It may surprise you to learn that all five statements are false! This is a repeat of the questions and the research answers.
1. Among all age groups, America's senior citizens are the least happy and most dissatisfied with their life. True or False?
2. People who have complete quadriplegia (with both arms and both legs paralyzed) feel their lives are below average in happiness. True or False?
3. Having children is life's greatest joy; thus, parents report more overall happiness than those who do not have children. True or False?
4. Most people would be happier if they had more money. True or False?
5. People with a college education are happier and report more life satisfaction than those with only a high school diploma. True or False?

#'s 1, 3, and 5 Factors such as age, parenthood, and educational level (as well as race, gender, and physical attractiveness) do NOT play a measurable role in either overall life satisfaction or happiness.

#2 People who have serious physical disabilities are just as happy as others. For example, in one survey of 128 people who had suffered an injury causing quadriplegia, most acknowledged having considered suicide in the beginning. Yet, a year later only 10 percent rated their quality of life as poor (Whiteneck et al., 1985). In general, people seem to overestimate the long-term emotional consequences of tragic events.

#4 Does it surprise you that subjective well-being (life satisfaction and happiness) is NOT strongly correlated with income? Research shows that as long as people have enough money to buy essentials, extra money does not buy happiness (Myers and Diener, 1995, 1996). For example, in the past 40 years the average U.S. citizen's buying power has doubled. However, the reported happiness has remained almost unchanged (Niemi et al., 1989).

So what factors *are* correlated with subjective well being? Here the answers are less surprising:
• Having close friendships or a satisfying marriage
• Being optimistic and outgoing
• Having a challenging, satisfying job
• A meaningful religious faith
• Having high self-esteem
• Sleeping well and exercising

References:
Myers, D. G., & Diener, E. (1995). Who is happy? Psychological Science, 6, 10-19.

Myers, D. G., & Diener, E. (1996, May). The pursuit of happiness. Scientific American, pp. 70-72. Niemi, R. G., Mueller, J., & Smith, T. W. (1989). Trends in public opinion: A compendium of survey data. New York: Greenwood Press.

Whiteneck, G. G., et al. (1985). <u>A collaborative study of high quadriplegia</u>. Englewood, CO: Rocky Mountain Regional Spinal Cord Injury System for the National Institute of Handicapped Research.

CROSSWORD PUZZLE FOR CHAPTER 12

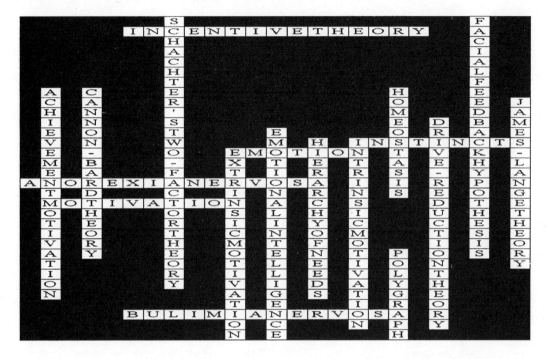

FILL-IN EXERCISES 1. Motivation, emotion; 2. Drive theory, incentive theory; 3. arousal; 4. hierarchy of needs; 5. ventromedial hypothalamus; 6. bulimia nervosa; 7. Achievement motivation; 8. physiological, cognitive,behavioral; 9. facial-feedback hypothesis; 10. evolutionary.

MATCHING EXERCISES a. 10, b. 7, c. 2, d. 9, e. 8, f. 4, g. 3, h. 6, i. 1, j. 5.

PRACTICE TEST I		PRACTICE TEST II	
1. c (pp. 406, 408)	11. c (pp. 419-420)	1. a (p. 406)	11. c (pp. 425-426)
2. c (pp. 408-409)	12. b (pp. 425-426)	2. d (pp. 408-409)	12. d (p. 427)
3. d (pp. 409-410)	13. c (pp. 425-426)	3. c (pp. 410-411)	13. b (pp. 426-428)
4. b (pp. 409-410)	14. a (pp. 425-426)	4. c (p. 411)	14. b (pp. 426-428)
5. b (pp. 410-411)	15. d (pp. 425-427)	5. d (pp. 412-413)	15. d (pp. 428-429)
6. b (p. 412)	16. c (pp. 426-428)	6. c (p. 417)	16. b (p. 433)
7. a (p. 412)	17. c (pp. 430-431)	7. a (p. 422)	17. d (p. 433)
8. c (p. 412)	18. a (pp. 430-431)	8. b (p. 423)	18. d (p. 432)
9. a (p. 417)	19. c (pp. 432-433)	9. a (pp. 425-426)	19. d (p. 434)
10. d (pp. 417-418)	20. d (p. 435)	10.a (pp. 425-426)	20. c (p. 436)

CHAPTER 13 ANSWERS

ACTIVE LEARNING EXERCISE II 1. repression; 2. denial; 3. intellectualization; 4. rationalization; 5. reaction formation.

CROSSWORD PUZZLE FOR CHAPTER 13

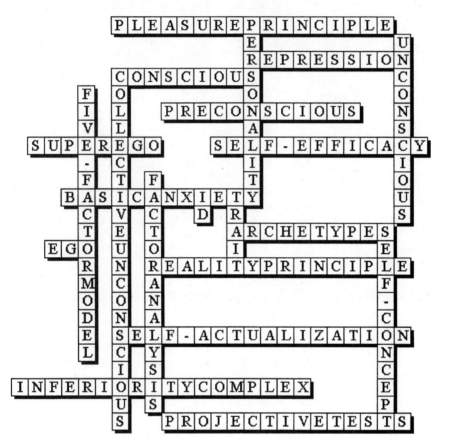

FILL-IN EXERCISES 1. Personality, trait; 2.openness; 3. Psychoanalytic, trait; 4. conscious, preconscious, unconscious; 5. pleasure principle, reality principle; 6. self-concept; 7. reciprocal determinism; 8. Minnesota Multiphasic Personality Inventory (MMPI); 9. reliability, validity; 10. self-serving bias.

MATCHING EXERCISES a. 1, b. 10, c. 6, d. 2, e. 7, f. 3, g. 5, h. 8, i. 4, j. 9.

PRACTICE TEST I		PRACTICE TEST II	
1. c (pp. 442-443)	11. d (pp. 455-456)	1. a (p. 442)	11. d (p. 456)
2. c (p. 443)	12. d (p. 456)	2. a (p. 443)	12. c (pp. 457-458)
3. c (p. 443)	13. c (p. 457)	3. b (p. 444)	13. a (p. 459)
4. a (p. 449)	14. b (p. 457)	4. b (p. 449)	14. b (p. 460)
5. a (p. 449-450)	15. b (p. 459)	5. c (p. 449)	15. d (p. 461)
6. d (p. 451)	16. d (p. 459)	6. c (p. 449)	16. d (pp. 461-462)
7. c (p. 452)	17. c (p. 464)	7. c (p. 450)	17. d (p. 462)
8. d (p. 452)	18. b (p. 464)	8. c (p. 451)	18. d (p. 465)
9. d (pp. 453-454)	19. d (pp. 465-466)	9. c (p. 451)	19. c (p. 467)
10. d (p. 455)	20. c (pp. 465-466)	10.a (p. 453)	20. d (p. 468)

CHAPTER 14 ANSWERS

CROSSWORD PUZZLE FOR CHAPTER 14

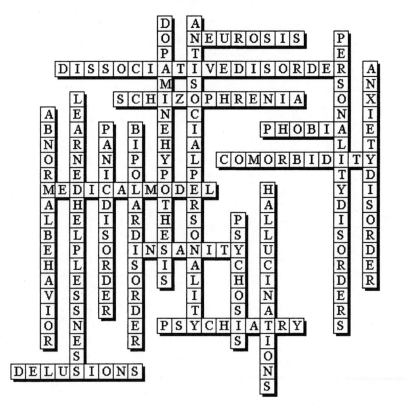

FILL-IN EXERCISES 1. statistical infrequency, disability or dysfunction, personal distress, or violation of norms; 2. allow evil spirits to escape, drive the devil out through prayer, fasting, etc.; 3. Obsessive-compulsive disorder (OCD); 4. major depressive disorder, bipolar disorder; 5. learned helplessness; 6. psychosis; 7. auditory hallucinations, schizophrenia; 8. Comorbidity; 9. dissociative identity disorder (DID); 10. borderline personality disorder (BPD).

MATCHING EXERCISES a. 6, b. 4, c. 8, d. 7, e. 1, f. 3, g. 10, h. 5, i. 2, j. 9

PRACTICE TEST I		PRACTICE TEST II	
1. d (p. 475)	11. d (pp. 495-496)	1. c (p. 476)	11. c (pp. 492-493)
2. d (p. 476)	12. a (p. 497)	2. a (p. 480)	12. a (p. 495)
3. b (p. 477)	13. a (pp. 497-498)	3. c (pp. 480-481)	13. c (p. 496)
4. a (p. 479)	14. b (p. 501)	4. d (pp. 483-484)	14. b (pp. 496-497)
5. b (p. 484)	15. a (p. 502)	5. c (pp. 484-485)	15. c (p. 498)
6. b (pp. 485-486)	16. b (p. 502)	6. b (p. 486)	16. c (p. 501)
7. c (p. 487)	17. a (p. 503)	7. a (pp. 486-487)	17. d (p. 501)
8. d (pp. 488-489)	18. a (p. 503)	8. d (pp. 489-490)	18. b (p. 503)
9. c (pp. 490-491)	19. c (pp. 503-504)	9. a (p. 490)	19. b (p. 503)
10. d (pp. 491-492)	20. d (p. 504)	10. d (p. 490)	20. a (p. 504)

CHAPTER 15 ANSWERS

CROSSWORD PUZZLE FOR CHAPTER 15

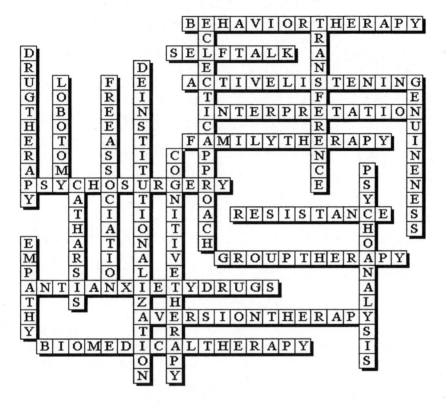

FILL-IN EXERCISES 1. Psychotherapy; 2. unconscious, psychoanalysis; 3. free association, dream analysis, analyzing resistance, analyzing transference, interpretation; 4. psychodynamic; 5. rational-emotive behavior; 6. cognitive-behavior; 7. Humanistic; 8. Behavior therapy; 9. Systematic desensitization; 10. depression.

MATCHING EXERCISES a. 6, b. 1, c. 7, d. 8, e. 2, f. 9, g. 10, h. 4, i. 3, j. 5

PRACTICE TEST I		PRACTICE TEST II	
1. c (pp. 510, 528)	11. c (pp. 524-525)	1. b (p. 510)	11. d (p. 522)
2. a (p. 511)	12. a (pp. 524-525)	2. c (p. 511)	12. d (p. 524)
3. b (p. 511)	13. a (p. 526)	3. d (p. 512)	13. a (p. 524)
4. a (p. 511)	14. c (p. 527)	4. d (pp. 514-515)	14. d (p. 527)
5. c (pp. 514-515)	15. b (p. 528)	5. b (pp. 515-516)	15. b (p. 528)
6. d (pp. 514-515)	16. b (p. 528)	6. d (p. 518)	16. b (p. 530)
7. d (pp. 518-519)	17. a (p. 530)	7. c (p. 518)	17. d (p. 533)
8. c (p. 518)	18. d (p. 530)	8. c (p. 519)	18. b (pp. 536-537)
9. d (pp. 521-522)	19. d (p. 530)	9. d (p. 519)	19. b (p. 537)
10. b (p. 522)	20. c (p. 538)	10. c (p. 521)	20. d (p. 539)

CHAPTER 16 ANSWERS

CROSSWORD PUZZLE FOR CHAPTER 16

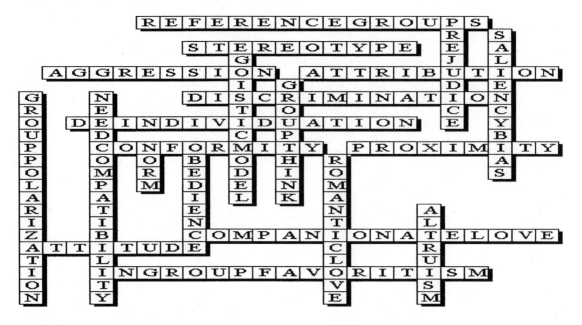

FILL-IN EXERCISES 1. Social psychology; 2. attribution; 3. fundamental attribution error, self-serving bias; 4. cognitive, affective, behavioral; 5. cognitive dissonance; 6. prejudice; 7. cognitive, behavioral; 8. physical attractiveness, proximity, similarity; 9. conformity, obedience; 10. group polarization, groupthink.

MATCHING EXERCISES a. 6, b. 5, c. 4, d. 10, e. 8, f. 1, g. 9, h. 7, i. 3, j. 2.

PRACTICE TEST I		PRACTICE TEST II	
1. d (p. 544)	11. c (p. 552)	1. a (p. 546)	11. d (p. 558)
2. b (p. 546)	12. b (pp. 553-554)	2. c (p. 547)	12. c (p. 560)
3. d (pp. 546-547)	13. c (p. 557)	3. b (p. 551)	13. d (p. 560)
4. a (p. 548)	14. a (p. 560)	4. b (p. 552)	14. c (pp. 561-563)
5. d (pp. 548-549)	15. c (p. 561)	5. b (pp. 554-555)	15. a (p. 563)
6. d (p. 549)	16. c (pp. 564-565)	6. a (p. 556)	16. a (p. 564)
7. d (p. 550)	17. d (p. 566)	7. d (p. 556)	17. b (pp. 564-565)
8. b (p. 551)	18. b (pp. 566-567)	8. b (p. 557)	18. a (p. 567)
9. b (p. 551)	19. a (p. 570)	9. b (p. 557)	19. b (p. 572)
10. c (p. 552)	20. c (pp. 570-572)	10. b (pp. 557-558)	20. d (p. 572)